VOICES OF THE REVOLUTION

VOICES OF
THE REVOLUTION

Edited by

Peter Vansittart

COLLINS
8 Grafton Street London W1
1989

William Collins Sons & Co. Ltd
London · Glasgow · Sydney · Auckland
Toronto · Johannesburg

BRITISH LIBRARY CATALOGUING IN PUBLICATION DATA

Voices of the Revolution
1. French Revolution, 1789–1799
I. Vansittart, Peter, 1920–
944.04

ISBN 0–00–215849 3

First published 1989
Introduction and compilation © Peter Vansittart 1989

Photoset in Itek Bembo by
Ace Filmsetting Ltd, Frome, Somerset
Printed and bound in Great Britain by
Mackays of Chatham plc, Letchworth

Dedicated to the memory of
J. M. THOMPSON,
historian of the Revolution

We desire to publish a Declaration for all mankind, for all time, for all countries, for an example to all the world.

The National Assembly. *The Declaration of the Rights of Man*, 1789

I swear it exists, that tender, impetuous and irresistible passion, torment and delight of magnanimous souls, that deep horror of tyranny, that compassionate zeal for the oppressed, that sacred love of one's country, that more sublime and sacred love of humanity without which a great revolution is merely one dazzling crime that destroys another; it exists, that generous ambition to establish on earth the first Republic in the World; that unselfishness of men still living which finds its celestial joy in the peace of a clear conscience and the joyful vision of the public good. You feel it burning in your soul at this very instant. I feel it in you.

MAXIMILIEN ROBESPIERRE, 26 July (8 Thermidor) 1794

His features were mean, his complexion pallid and his veins were greenish.

MADAME DE STAËL, on Robespierre

CONTENTS

AUTHOR'S NOTE

I have compiled this collection, a sampling of vast material, for those interested in history not as historians but as readers. The former will find it predictable and over-familiar, but the latter may gain some sensation of how the Revolution seemed to contemporaries and to much of the succeeding decades. I have no other motive. I think that we can learn from history, but that few seldom bother to: and that it neither improves nor worsens us. We may enjoy it for its own sake, or merely use it to reinforce our prejudices.

As a boy, thanks to Carlyle and indeed Orczy, and Hollywood, I was engrossed with the Revolution, and remain so; not because it supports my political ideology – rather meagre – but from its pull as a drama with ramifications deep in the modern world, enacted by those mostly devoid of genius, often with but average talent, though with tricks of personality by now more or less inscrutable. They were embraced by a convulsion over which they exercised disputable measures of control, enjoyed their hour, or moment, then were swept away, often uncomprehending, yet leaving a name: haunting, tragic or ludicrous. 'The greatest masters of statecraft,' A. J. P. Taylor wrote in 1963, 'are those who do not know what they are doing.'

I am not a professional historian, and much of the Introduction can be challenged, and unintended bias in my selections be exposed. 'History,' Tolstoy considered, 'would be altogether admirable – if only it were true.' The stimulus of history, like that of science, is precisely that it must be endlessly checked, extended and revised. Since 1934, my own opinion of Robespierre, for example, has had to be altered at least seven times, and doubtless will be again.

I have not attempted a comprehensive survey of the Revolution, though my entries are arranged in broad chronological order. Perhaps inevitably, Paris bulks large, at the expense of the provinces, the civil war in Brittany, the army and navy, the colonies, and scores of ordinary households, schools and monasteries. This is unfortunate, but drastic pruning was swiftly essential, and little that remained I would want removed. Here I must again thank my patient and ever-helpful editor, Ariane Goodman, her successor Jo Anne Robertson, and indeed Anthony Sheil, whose initiative originally prompted the book. I should also mention some useful help from Mr Theodore Wilden, and, most particularly, to Douglas Matthews for, as always, producing a splendid index.

I have included few living historians, whose views in this bicentenary year will be prominent elsewhere. Suffice to say that I owe much to my Oxford tutor, J. M. Thompson, and such successors as J. L. Talmon, George Rudé, Richard Cobb, Douglas Johnson, Alfred Cobban, M. J. Sydenham, Norman Hampson and such less specialised writers as Christopher Hibbert and Vincent Cronin, whom I rightly add to my Bibliography, though without quoting from them directly. From Stanley Loomis, Jean Robiquet and Friedrich Sieburg, among others, I include many details that I hope others will enjoy as much as myself.

For the Bibliography, translations and considerations of copyright I am entirely responsible. On this last, I have done my best to fulfil my obligations, but letters go astray, publishers change address or identity, and I fear that a few writers may be aggrieved or indignant. I ask them to forbear and, for redress, contact not the publishers but myself.

ACKNOWLEDGEMENTS

I am grateful to the following authors, executors, agents and publishers for permission to quote from their works:
Mrs H. D. Ziman, for an extract by her late husband; The Athlone Press, on behalf of M. J. Sydenham; Basil Blackwell, on behalf of the late J. M. Thompson; The Oxford University Press, on behalf of Dr Francis Scarfe; Professor Norman Cohn, for an extract; Reinhardt Books, on behalf of the late Sir John Elliot; Hamish Hamilton, on behalf of Antonia Vallentin; Peters, Fraser and Dunlop, on behalf of Hilaire Belloc and J. B. Morton, and of Marjorie Coryn; The Cambridge University Press, on behalf of Dr R. G. Darnton; David Higham Associates, on behalf of Sidney Hook; Mr Frederick Davies, for translations from *The Gods Will Have Blood* (*Les Dieux ont soif*); the poems by Robert Lowell are reprinted by permission of Faber & Faber; for extracts from Professor Norman Hampson, I am indebted to the continuous kindness of Colin Haycroft of Duckworth's. Certain sentences and references in my Introduction I have repeated from my article (January 22, 1989) in the *Sunday Telegraph*, and I must thank the editor, Peregrine Worsthorne.

INTRODUCTION

The bi-centenary of the French Revolution will revive old debates, stale legends, some ill-will. Doubtless a computer will establish it as a minor offshoot of an imbalanced trade cycle, or that it never actually happened. It has been seen as deicide, as a moral warning against power, as an appetite or a hypocrisy; as illustration of man as philosopher, man as a hunting animal; as retribution for aristocratic decadence; as a re-emergence of the Ego from traditional restraints; as a church with incorruptible pontiff, communion of saints, noble army of martyrs. Robespierre, so unimaginable in sabots and red cap, has been rated as the first modern dictator, Rousseau in action, a paranoiac and constipated eunuch, a morose Hamlet. To Hamel, he displayed democracy at its loftiest and noblest; for Acton he was the most hateful celebrity since Machiavelli and the Renaissance; for George Sand, 'the greatest man not only of the Revolution but of all known history'; for Victor Hugo, 'the algebra of the Revolution – the immense power of the straight line'. (Elsewhere, Hugo remarked that a straight line is unique in brutality.) Robespierre has been considered a suffering Messiah, speaking of enemies 'preparing me the hemlock'. Southey called him a ministering angel sent to kill thousands in order to save millions. Robespierre himself entrusted his reputation to 'the belated help of Time'. His own bi-centenary provoked fury in the French Assembly.

Attempts to interpret, overcome or fulfil the Revolution convulsed nineteenth-century France, producing three further kings, two republics, two emperors. Cobban saw it as victory for the conservative landowners, while Babeuf and his *enragés* denounced even the Jacobins for frustrating the 'real revolution', socialist and atheist, attempted in 1848 and 1871. Nietzsche condemned its Rousseauesque morality, 'enlisting all that is shallow and mediocre'. The 1789 Revolution can appear a sequence of desperate improvisations under stress, and what Burke termed 'mere ill-fortune'. Also, as the inevitable outcome of impersonal forces, the triumph of bourgeois liberalism over feudalism, necessary for economic and technological advance, as an opportunity for barely successful lawyers and failed

literary men; as vital motor for class warfare, blueprint for 'totalitar-
ian democracy', a Masonic conspiracy, a revolt of youth, the counter-
attack of freedom-loving Gauls against tyrannical Franks, the success
of Paris over reactionary provincial *parlements* and customs, as an
Orléanist plot, and as the death-wish of the over-sophisticated. Many
see it as a gigantic act of justice and retribution, 'a thunderclap for the
wicked' (Saint-Just), forerunning the Welfare State.

Few Revolutionary leaders began as professional troublemakers.
Never, wrote de Tocqueville, was any event so inevitable yet so
utterly unforeseen. Napoleon blamed Rousseau, others Richelieu,
others, George Washington; or bad harvests, steadily rising prices
and the dislocations of nascent industrialism, helped by royal inepti-
tude and aristocratic and clerical myopia.

The Revolution still raises questions about historical determinism, human motives, individual rights, questions never fully
answered, not always asked. Also about the acuteness of contemporary witness. The Queen thought the nobles caused the Revolution.
Talleyrand reflected: 'If historians strive to discover those to whom
they can give the honour or attribute the blame, for having caused,
organised or modified the French Revolution, they will be wasting
their time. It had no authors, leaders, guides. The seed was scattered
by writers who, in an era bold and enlightened, overthrew the principles of religion and of social life, and by incompetent ministers who
increased the embarrassment of the Treasury and the discontent of
the people.'

The Revolution has been applauded for attempting to restore a
wide European order and for replacing privilege by merit, enabling
an innkeeper's son to become, not indeed the first of equals, but King
of Naples. For Kant (1798), the Revolution 'discovered in the depths
of human nature the possibility of moral progress no statesman has
hitherto suspected'. It has been condemned for aggressive nationalism, for introducing manic Bonapartism and wars of 'liberation', now
so familiar, and for substituting superstition about the State for superstition of Throne and Altar.

Almost alone, though women were prominent in street riots,
clandestine intrigue and the public galleries of the Assembly, Femin-
ism cannot claim much of the Revolution. Trumpeting the Rights of
Man, the young enthusiasts lowered voices about those of women.
Women frequented cafés more often but, particularly after Charlotte
Corday's intervention, their claims were proscribed, the Jacobins

closed their clubs and brothels, and Fouché in 1798 forbade them wearing trousers without his permission. Olympe de Gouges, the most prominent feminist, was executed, feminist propaganda forbidden. No woman sat in ministry, committee, assembly; suffrage was confined to 'active citizens', tax-paying males. (Decades later, Lenin included only one woman in his first cabinet.) The Code Napoleon continued this: 'Woman belongs to man as the fruit tree to the gardener', actually reducing considerable legal rights, save those of inheritance, granted to, rather than won by, women in the Revolution. (Until 1907, married women had few rights over their own earnings; women had no vote until 1946.)

Children fared little better, despite more educational opportunities. Before Napoleon prepared them for docility and conscription, Robespierre had pronounced: 'Children belong to their mothers until five, afterwards to the Republic for life.' For Saint-Just, children should be neither beaten nor caressed and, until 16, be forbidden meat. Unconcerned with girls, he wished boys to be educated with stern discipline 'for love of silence'. To have imposed this on France would have constituted a revolution greater than what actually occurred.

European Jewry won rights from the Revolution, which briefly legislated against colonial slavery, though this largely persisted until 1848. When, excited by the Rights of Man, St Domingo blacks zestfully murdered their masters, the high-minded Assembly was not amused. Sodomy ceased to be criminal in 1791.

As always, what was intended to happen often did not. Kindly parents can produce monsters, benevolent laws promote anarchy. David's thrilling painting of Napoleon on the Alps is as misleading as the Emperor's memoirs. At the Brumaire crisis, his bleeding face aroused fervid sympathy from an apparent attempt on his life: actually, from nervousness, he had been scratching his pimples. Pitt promised fifteen years of peace immediately before a war lasting twenty. 'As long as I survive, France shall have peace,' Napoleon declared in 1800. Celebrated facts remain disputed. Some historians find rain dispersing Robespierre's last supporters, others deny it. Legends abound. 'Let them eat cake,' a canard suffering from poor translation, can be traced from Victoire, daughter of Louis XV, back to an ironic English archbishop. Heads on pikes were a traditional French indulgence. 'Expose his head on a lance, that will make his fiancée die' (Richelieu). Amongst some 40,000 victims of the Terror, fewer than 9 per cent were nobles, and of the 1500 September victims, about 25 were nobles. The guillotined, drowned and shot were mostly profiteers, forgers, hoarders, political losers, 'Pitt's spies', suspects, defeatists, unpopular neighbours, deserters, from the Third and Fourth Estates, with perhaps 6 per cent priests. The guillotine itself had long been used in Scotland, Yorkshire, Italy and Germany.

Literature, like music and film, has never forgotten the Revolution, since Coleridge and Southey collaborated on *The Fall of Robespierre*. For the Marxist Lukács, 1789 awoke in literature a sense of human greatness. In popular imagery, a Danton obliterates a Washington, Adams, Fox. Others still cast shadows. I was moved on learning from my tutor J. M. Thompson that, in 1940, only one French senator voted against the destruction of the Third Republic: 'the last defender of the Rights of Man – the great grandson of Lafayette'. The Hébertist *Père Duchesne* reappeared under the 1871 Commune; Committees of Public Safety re-formed in the crises of 1958 and 1968, the students adding a Jacobin Club.

The most sensational period between 1792 and 1794 remains haunting theatre, not all invented by Michelet and Lamartine. A huge phrase, soon an empty catchphrase, *the Sovereignty of the People*, invaded Europe. Saint-Just, arriving at Fleurus, cancelled the general's orders and led the charge, top hat on his stick; then Danton, at ebb tide, asking pardon of God and man for having instituted the Tribunal; Robespierre promising Danton eternal love and, a little later, in defeat, hearing 'the blood of Danton chokes you'; the assistant executioner working with a rose in his mouth; Robespierre's sudden cry, 'hideous to hear and see', as he lay shattered in his festival coat. The Princess of Monaco, before execution, cut off her hair for her family to preserve; they kept it in a glass case under a black veil, periodically uncovering it for ritual reverence.

A sinister glamour lit the era. Babies were rumoured to be born with red circles round their necks. At Victim Balls, relatives of the executed danced with necks shaved, red ribbons against faces starkly white. Figures emerged from nowhere into brilliance, then abruptly vanished. Marat, Brissot, Danton . . . .

Political dogmatism exaggerates class and factional homogeneity. Temperament and passionate circumstances outbid organisation. Peasant, bargee, St Antoine brewer, St Paul mason, silk spinner, printer's devil, gardener can all be catalogued as Fourth Estate, despite conflicting hopes and loyalties. (Similarly, in the 1960s, some 'workers' supported Enoch Powell, others did not.) The French court could be as divided as its enemies. Political groupings and alliances – Girondins, Jacobins, Royalists – were not disciplined, coherent parties: their structures, their personal relationships, frequently remained obscure, perverse or muddled. The Girondins drew electoral support from regions and communities wholly diverse. T. C. W. Blanning points to royalism often flourishing in areas economically advanced, republicanism sometimes strongest in the reverse. Perhaps two-thirds of 'the Church' supported the Revolution: the Oratorians enjoyed science, most bishops did not. From discontent, self-interest or good nature, many nobles supported reform, two founding the Jacobin Club. Parisian support shifted between Court, Commune, Church, Assemblies, sometimes through bribery, but seldom very predictably. 1788 Cahiers revealed anticlericalism sometimes strongest in 'reactionary' areas – as German anti-Semitism could flourish where no Jews lived. Robespierre and Danton were 'bourgeois', but so were Beaumarchais and the millionaire contractor Ouvrarde. Nobles could promote commerce, industry, inventions; many army officers, noble and parvenu, were disaffected. Loyalty, too, is wayward, tiresome to political philosophers. Badly treated by his seigneur, a Breton peasant might defend him until death; rewarded by his landlord, a Bordeaux farmer might denounce him. Status could outbid cash, which the Crown, in dealing with non-noble assistants, might forget. Rank could be purchased, prestige could not.

There remains difficulty in locating the erratic centres of power: Court, Ministries, Commune, Assemblies and their Cordeliers and Jacobins often, and unofficially, being more powerful than nominal ministers; then Committees, Representatives on Mission, urban Sections, all complicated by brief factional alliances. Commune and Assembly were usually rivals. Beliefs, tactics, continually altered amongst men totally inexperienced in government. Almost all political and military leaders, the King included, were under forty, harassed by sleeplessness and permanent crisis, not always of their own making. Cosy family men – Desmoulins, Fouché, Fouquier-Tinville – graduated to Terrorism. The young Saint-Just, like the young Himmler, trudged in all weathers to succour the poor, reiterating that the social contract should be maintained not by force but by virtue.

Robespierre, earlier favouring universal suffrage, supported plebiscites, until one was demanded for the King's fate. Denouncing censorship, he ended as censor supreme. Having denounced national schools as a threat to liberty, he favoured – horror to modernists – free, compulsory boarding schools. In 1789 most future Terrorists opposed the death penalty.

Witnessing the French triumph at Valmy, Goethe pronounced that a new age had begun. Yet there are no new ages, despite revolutionaries' constant claim to be establishing them, sometimes by restoring eras too remote to be disputed. Through Plutarch, through Corneille, the French zealots worshipped ancient Rome and Sparta. 'The world has been empty since the Romans,' cried Saint-Just, sometimes styling himself 'Brutus', a hero to whom Fouché and 'Anaxagoras' Chaumette dedicated a festival in 1793. To herself, if to few others, Madame Roland was 'Cato's Wife', and she wrote journalism as 'a Roman lady'. We remember 'Gracchus' Babeuf, the Revolution's genuine socialist; 'Anacharsis' Clootz, the Orator of Mankind. Robespierre was likened to Cato, Barère to Anacreon, Saint-Just to Lycurgus, Napoleon – with Charlotte Corday a devotee of Plutarch – to Scipio, Louis XVI to Tarquin. David's republican paintings and fêtes used classical sentiments and décor, the fasces, spears, lictors, to which the Revolution added plebiscite, senate, tribunate, consulate, empire. To remind citizens of the pristine Republic, Javogues would appear naked in public. Horace's Secular Hymn, once sung by Roman children in procession, was imitated in David's Festivals of Liberty. Robespierre, addicted to Tacitus, himself accused of being a triumvir, held that Stoicism had redeemed the honour of human nature. Socrates' belief that none knowingly does wrong, at which Frederick the Great would have chuckled, had impressed Rousseau, though the history of Greek city-states suggested otherwise. It was welcomed by the revolutionaries, happily pre-Freudian, who assumed that good laws swiftly restore natural goodness to those robbed of it by tyranny. The notion of man being born free, though contradicted by the nearest baby, was a potential toxicant.

Chanting the new, the Revolution continued much of the old: capital punishment, informers, political and masculine despotism. Decades after 1789, the passions aroused by Dreyfus revealed that, despite changes in land tenure, hierarchy and slogans, moral advance had been negligible. Revolutionary assumptions emphasised the benevolence of Nature and of primitives, the latter partly sanctioned by the great Captain Cook, before they killed him. Desmoulins, though scarcely ardent for colonial independence, dreamed of founding 'a new Tahiti'.

Mostly declassed or liberal noblemen and middle-class intellectuals, the revolutionaries would dogmatise about Nature from bastions of impressive ignorance, though a glance at a forest or a chat with de Sade and, perhaps, Malthus, would have suggested that a state of Nature is usually a state of chaos. Danton at least knew this. Others often resembled the gardener speaking to J. B. Priestley about Nature as if he were a member of the small committee that had appointed her. They were typical literary men. *Sublime*, a word favoured by Robespierre, is, like *eternal*, usually followed by something silly. In French aggression, street thuggery, Terror Red and White, Nature periodically issued reminders of her independence.

The *ancien régime*, of Encyclopaedia and Enlightenment, survived with some élitist, high-minded Girondins, and a few of their opponents, more lastingly with Talleyrand; 'Anything exaggerated is witless. . . . Above all, not too much zeal.' Talleyrand knew real human nature, and would have yawned at the threat of perfect happiness. Even the American Ambassador chuckled when Lafayette proclaimed that for a modern nation to be free, it is sufficient that it should wish to be free. Condorcet envisaged humanity 'freed from its chains, released from the rule of Fate and reactionaries, advancing with firm and certain steps along the path of truth, virtue and happiness'. He himself firmly advanced towards suicide when jailed by those with whom he had sought to abolish capital punishment and ensure liberty, free thought and equality.

Around 1710, Abbé de Saint-Pierre had announced the arrival, 'so to speak', of the Golden Age. The eighteenth-century Enlightenment dissected history, geo-politics, ecology, deism, atheism, moral and historical relativity, determinism, electricity, glandular secretions, even aeronautics, Montgolfier's balloon ascending in 1783 . . . if somewhat neglecting industrial technology. Suburb and factory would despoil Nature and *politesse*. The Revolutionary fêtes, with sheaves, poppies, garlands, trees of Liberty and artificial groves hankered after the bucolic. Saint-Just's utopia suggested rural simplicity. The Jacobins idealised small farmers. The Revolutionary Calendar emphasised wind, frost, harvest, sun.

From the Enlightenment, the Revolution regarded government as more than mere administration, certainly more than self-indulgence. It aimed beyond its predecessors. Government must promote virtue and 'compel people to be free'. Always a schoolmaster, Robespierre wished to substitute 'duties for elegance, magnanimity and power for amiability and frivolity, truth for wit, principles for habit'. He preferred good men to good company; his tragedy was that, unlike Mirabeau and Danton, he never understood that they could be identical. His associates largely accepted Enlightenment values, without cynicism but with an earnestness liable to bigotry.

Nature, Reason, Humanity. The early Revolution strove only to give them a push. Legislation, education, promised a shining world.

The *ancien régime* had been international. An Irishman, Wall, became a Spanish chief minister; the Scot, Law, stylishly mismanaged French finances; the Dutch Prince Nassau-Siegen served France and Russia as diplomat, and Russia as admiral, very badly, also claiming to have seduced the Queen of Tahiti; another Scot, John Paul Jones, paid by Louis XVI, sank a British battleship for America, and fought Turks for Catherine. Sir Charles Knowles reorganised the Russian Navy, Admiral Krussenstery served in the British. Even during the Napoleonic War, Humphrey Davey was invited to Paris to receive a scientific award; Napoleon, excited by Ossianic forgeries, founded an academy for Celtic studies. The Revolution at first continued this. Marat was Swiss-Sardinian, Pereira a Portuguese Jew, Clootz a Prussian; Tom Paine, though knowing no French, sat both in the Convention and the Luxembourg prison, and with Condorcet elaborated the 1792 Declaration of Rights. David Williams helped draft the 1793 Constitution. Clavière, Necker and Pache were Swiss, General Luckner a Bavarian, Carnot had refused service under Frederick the Great. The Duke of Brunswick, loser at Valmy, had been offered command of the French army and, calling himself 'General Marat', Prince Karl of Hesse commanded French troops at Orleans. A proposal was floated to transfer the French Crown to the Grand Old Duke of York. The American, Franklin, helped Lafayette draft the Rights of Man.

In 1790 the Assembly renounced the notion of conquest; however, in 1792, not for the last time, France declared war with a light heart, promising liberation. By 1793, Danton was demanding Geneva, Savoy and Belgium. Conquest, followed by plebiscite, secured the last, together with rape, pillage and theft of art treasures. Badly paid French soldiers brutally queried whether freedom should be given free. 'Live free or die' swiftly became 'plunder or starve'. Trees of Liberty and better street lighting were accompanied by rigged elections, extortions and executions. Occupying Rome in 1797, the French tactlessly abolished Sunday and lotteries, and decorated a bronze angel with a Cap of Liberty, renaming it 'the Genius of France'. The Archbishop of Imola, styling himself Citizen-Cardinal, prayed for Liberty and Equality though, as Pius VII, he ultimately consecrated Napoleon as Emperor. Revolution and Empire failed to transcend national greed.

Obvious defects impaired the *ancien régime*. Monarchy encouraged toadies. When a shower soaked a Polignac in the royal gardens, he obsequiously assured Louis XIV that the rain at Marly was never wet. Darker elements abounded. France, Richelieu complained, had two diseases – Heresy and Liberty. Also, 'In state affairs, justice does not require authentic proof.' French Christianity, claiming final and exclusive truth, obeyed the least attractive Gospel precepts: 'Compel them to come in.' 'He that is not with me is against me.' They foreran 'Liberty or Death', emerging with the fourth-century persecutor of 'heretics', St Martin of Tours. Fanaticism had recently languished in France, but had not vanished. Desmoulins praised the political clubs as 'inquisitorial tribunals of the people'. Rousseau, who so intoxicated the Jacobin youths, would not have dissented from Robespierre's 'There must be one will, and one will only'. He meant no personal tyranny but collective consent, but such language invites drastic opportunities for coarser spirits.

Louis XIV made war 'to liberate minorities', 'to incorporate racial comrades'. The Monarchy allowed arbitrary arrest, also torture until Louis XVI abolished it, though the Revolution retained branding. A man could be punished for marrying above his station. Some serfdom lingered on, though Louis freed his own serfs in 1789. Strikes were discountenanced, forbidden more energetically by the Revolution's le Chapelier Law, together with picketing and workers' assemblies, modified only by Napoleon III, who legalised certain strikes, and unions in 1864. A 'People's Army' famously suppressed a dock strike in Le Havre, and civilian dissent throughout France was similarly treated. Royal censorship was erratic; in 1788 Arthur Young was amazed at the Press licence. The Monarchy at least produced the Encyclopaedia, animated debate, spirited literature; Revolution – and Napoleon – allowed little literature and few ideas, executing its best poet, Chénier, and finest scientist, Lavoisier. 'The Revolution has no need of intellectuals and chemists' (Coffinhall). This, actually, was unfair to the Revolution, which promoted considerable scientific education. But Robespierre also mentioned, more significantly, that with the victory of the Revolution, any demand for Press freedom was counter-revolutionary. A lesson for Lenin and Hitler.

Arthur Young considered that, England excepted, France was the mildest governed Great Power. Yet the Monarchy was a machine potentially excellent but rusted, with vital parts missing and weak hands at the wheel. Thompson estimated that by 1789, 60 per cent of the State income never reached the Treasury. Furthermore, while Louis XVI had successfully armed and financed the American Revolution, the effort virtually bankrupted France and suggested the vulnerability of thrones. Antique rights obstructed law, supplies and distribution. Cobban considered food supplies and prices the clue to the turmoil of 1789–96. Three of Babeuf's children died of starvation. Lofty rhetoric balanced the high price of bread for which, after Thermidor, crowds were still shouting.

In 1789 the crisis might still have been overcome by strong leadership, intelligent self-interest and informed sensitivity. Formulating ideas and constitutions for all time, leaders, however, remained blind to many signs of the times. Voltaire and Montesquieu would have been astonished to find a Lafayette or Brissot in power, as Marx would have been by Hitler. Condorcet, writing confidently on the certainties of comets, mathematics and politics, was himself overtaken by the Terror.

Monarchical reform was indisputably essential. The Enlightenment had largely wished to strengthen the Crown against archaic feudal survivals. Republicanism was an abstract, classical ideal, at least until American victory. The Cahiers were pro-Monarchy and, if anti-clerical, scarcely anti-religion. Denmark, Sweden, Austria and Prussia showed that Monarchy could effect reform, and Louis XVI had aroused high hopes. Robespierre foretold that, as a progressive, he would surpass Charlemagne and Henri IV. Marat had called blessings on 'the best of kings'. Even after Varennes, Louis was allowed surprising powers. However, though tolerant and amiable, he had stubborn principles, particularly in religion, unpopular relatives, and a temperament guileless and sluggish. He had a sense of humour, coarse but apt. Irritated by the adulation of Benjamin Franklin in Paris, he had reproduced on a chamber pot a medallion praising the American's politics and electrical experiments – *He tore down the lightning from heaven and the sceptres from tyrants* – and sent it to one of the sage's female admirers. But despite stolid courage he was incapable of those spontaneous gestures that could dispel a crisis. He could placate, but not galvanise. His composure and forbearance proved inadequate, and provoked Mirabeau to gibe, with some truth, that the only man at court was the Queen. The Crown, furthermore, had long neglected its popular roots, knowing little of those it ruled. Its very reforms weakened it. French peasants already owned some third of the land, though hampered by feudal restrictions: they wanted more, and urban artisans demanded fuller employment, better conditions. Yet optimism in 1789 was boundless. Legislation would settle all, from the existence of God to the distribution of seaweed. The new men ignored a biblical injunction: 'Do not be over-righteous or over-wise. Why expose yourself to mockery?' Also, 'Do not be over-wicked, do not be a fool.' Mockery helped overthrow Robespierre, though not the Revolution. Thermidor returned it to the higher bourgeoisie, soon ready for an opportunist of some genius and oafish manners.

Though abused as novices stifled by theory, the young Jacobins showed astonishing practical ability. The Committee of Public Safety has been praised by Cobban as comprising 'perhaps the ablest and most determined men who have ever held power in France'. Allied armies had invaded, civil war involved half of France. Toulon and much of the Navy surrendered to the British, famine and unemployment were rampant. The monstrous Revolutionary Tribunal emerged under pressure from military reverses and prominent desertions. The Jacobins, often under pressure from the streets, responded with massive legislation. They attempted to control prices, wages, food, livestock, labour, with lip-service only to 'the liberty of one citizen ending where another's begins'. Theoretically pledged against State control, in crisis they requisitioned property of church, émigrés and 'traitors', imposed a super-tax, abolished the vestigial feudalism left over after the 1789 abolitions. Often lacking time to enforce them, the Convention issued nearly 12,000 decrees; raised 14 armies moving 120 paces a minute against the enemy's 70, and actually fought in winter, supplied by 6000 new workshops; they unified weights and measures, reorganised local government, promoted some primary and higher and much secondary education – though private education also flourished. They developed transport, established decimals, the semaphore telegraph, orphanages, hospitals, museums, art galleries, public works; nationalised the church and some bakeries, and at times conscripted and directed labour. The Great Committee was in a hurry and would have scorned Gandhi's precept that patient example best ensures reform. In the Convention, majority vote was apt to be ignored. From 1793, all houses were open to the police. France was centralised as never before. Napoleon's Civil Code, still underlying much Western law, incorporated Rome, the *ancien régime* and Revolution.

Little of this should gladden modern socialists. Girondins and Jacobins wanted workers to work, not fancy themselves a government. In the Convention there were only two working men, out of 749. The Monarchy attempted far more State control than the men of 1789, less than those of 1793. Equality meant equality before the law, not equality of goods, franchise and gender. They wanted free trade, save in emergency, not State control, and decreed death for anyone proposing an attack on property. Virtue was, however, considered more accessible to the needy and smallholding than to the 'grossly opulent'. The 'deserving poor' was a notion thoroughly Jacobin. The confiscatory laws of Ventôse are sometimes regarded as an attempt to transform a political revolution into an economic one, but appear more an expedient for renewed crisis of bread and prices.

Some anarcho-collectivism is discernible in the Commune, but Hébert and Chaumette were executed in 1794, as were Roux and Babeuf, with their *enragés* and 'Equals' by the Directory. Roux, unlike his modern equivalents, had at least been permitted to publish anti-government propaganda from prison. Babeuf had anticipated Proudhon's 'Property is theft', scarcely cherished by the war-profiteers, bankers and speculators, who underwrote the Directory. Napoleon was no egalitarian. Fouché's communism was a passing sop: Fouché believed only in Fouché.

Attempting to abolish the superstitious past – Christian, hierarchical, monarchical – the Revolution was audacious, if sometimes ludicrous. Condorcet, himself an author, believed that burning records would liberate the world. Titles were abolished, hand-clapping indicted as servile, Molière censored for using *valet de chambre*, Figaro banned in Marseilles. Chénier, the playwright and brother to the poet, wished to transform the theatre from 'a school of Flattery and Vice to one of Virtue and Liberty'. Bernard Shaw might have approved. The week was lengthened to ten days, excluding Sunday, the months were renamed and, superbly, 1792 became Year I – like Christianity introducing AD, as if human nature had changed. The Paris Commune lopped steeples, for Equality, then closed all churches before re-opening Notre Dame as the Temple of Reason. By majority vote, the Convention permitted a Supreme Being – as early Christian Councils admitted Jesus to godhead – though, established from above, the new cult was brief. Like Napoleon's coronation, its failure confirmed the resilience of the past.

By 1793 the Committees were omnipotent, their decrees sometimes registered as 'Popular Revolt'. Street gangs were periodically used to sway timid deputies, notably against the Girondins, who were illegally expelled from the Convention by a street invasion which, earlier, had invaded the Tuileries and toppled the Monarchy. Opposition parties, condemned by Saint-Just as organised crime, were outlawed, only Jacobin meetings allowed. And indeed, organised political parties were hitherto unknown in France: to distinguish between party and faction only later became a major political lesson, usually learnt very carelessly. By 1794, even minor query was downright treason. Had not Rousseau ordained expulsion for nonconformity? *Parlements*, guilds, corporations, labour unions, esoteric lodges, even begging were proscribed, leaving man facing the State alone. Scrawled on walls was *Supervision*, sometimes surmounted by an eye. The Law of Frimaire gave some 2000 Jacobin 'Supervision Committees' control of local government, reliable groups were paid to form juries, and attend Patriotic Rallies. 'The Sovereignty of the People!'

The Revolution, however, was mostly exaggerating established tendencies. Pious Habsburgs had despoiled monasteries; Catherine had imprisoned Russian dissidents as lunatics. Marat's murder is claimed to have instituted show trials, but Tudor and Stuart England knew these, also attainder, which pronounced guilt without trial. The Attorney General told Thomas More, 'Even though we should have no word or deed to charge upon you, yet we have your silence, and that is a sign of your evil intentions and a sure proof of malice.'

Red Terror is vividly remembered, White killings in 1794–5 and 1815, less so. Retribution was involved, however ignoble. Fox, Jefferson, Paine, Byron, Wordsworth, rejoicing at the Bastille's fall, shrugged off the breaking of the Governor's safe conduct. Bad faith dogs subsequent revolutions. *The Country is in Danger* and *Security* were blank cheques for the fanatic, the sadist, the mischievous. Tallien had a woman killed for mourning her executed husband. Treason! The Incorruptible tersely solved the 'ends-means' problem: 'To overcome Vice, all is permitted to Virtue.' He may not have known that *All is Permitted* was a motto of the twelfth-century

Assassins. Marat too raved about 'The Despotism of Liberty'. The great British concept of legal opposition, itself a revolution, was ignored or despised.

Could Law modify Nature? Apparently not, though the Terror was never a systematic criminal design. Saddled with a war they had not begun, with rebellions, with Lafayette and Dumouriez deserting, with inflation, panic and a siege-mentality, the Committee found pacific democracy ill-suited to crisis. A military order to charge was cancelled by majority vote! Anxious to change the world, the dedicated amateurs were more prone to excess, muddle and fear, than the world-weary professionals they had ejected. Their successes destroyed them. Repulsing external enemies, they succumbed to personal rivalries, paranoia, hypnotic abstractions – *Virtue, Republic, Nation*. Marat's murder increased the tempo. Words degenerated to slogans, detached from whatever they represented. Political debate was presented as the conflict between Virtue and Vice. In contrast, threats became hideously real. By 1794, administrative mishaps seemed axiomatic treachery. Appealing to the best instincts, the Committee, humourless to a man, was exploiting the worst. It had few political traditions to appeal to, save those of absolutism and conformity. Its subordinates were legalised mafia. The Law of Suspects encouraged concierge and neighbour to report suspected hoarders, saboteurs, grumblers and profiteers, like the servants in Rousseau's *La Nouvelle Héloïse*, praised for denouncing each other to their employer. A man was arrested, 'suspected of being suspect' (Olivier Blanc). Revolutionary algebra obstructed common sense. Perhaps, in all, some 40,000 were executed throughout France, thousands more perishing in civil war and rebellion. Though the rate of killing was subsiding in the provinces, nearly 2000 were executed in Paris in the six weeks before Thermidor. Against this must be placed the White Terror in Paris in 1871, with 17,000 officially shot without trial, recompense for the 500 victims of the Red Commune; and the gruesome unofficial deaths and tortures during the Liberation in 1944–5.

Eventually, denunciation was sufficient for arrest and, for handpicked juries, though acquittals could occur, mere arrest too often sufficed for guilt. On trial, Danton was silenced on orders from the Convention, accepting Saint-Just's lie about a 'conspiracy'. The Law of Prairial suspended defendants' rights; in practice, it allowed only acquittal or death. The trials of the Girondins and Dantonists were halted on orders from the Convention, when the judges began to fear acquittal, and summary condemnation passed.

Jacobins did not boast themselves above the law, but unscrupulously decreed new laws for purposes ever narrower. Couthon praised the removal of defence counsel as injuring wealthy privilege. The Committee was now the witch doctor, convincing tribesmen that they had lost their souls, which he alone could recover. Yet within the Convention, a majority wondered why, with invasion and rebellion overcome, the Terror, once the remedy for chaos, was prolonged. The zealots had the answer. Law must induce Virtue; France was not yet virtuous; failure did not invalidate the principle, therefore harsher laws for the general good. One last grand purge, and Virtue would surely descend. But 150 of the Convention were already killed or in hiding, prisons were packed, and protests were at last audible. Robespierre heard some of them. Mallet du Pan believed that he now clung to power less from ambition than from fear. But he could not change. He might have been wishing to halt the Terror, but his legend had become too big for him to handle. Tallien and Fouché, with more on their conscience and less self-confidence, fearful for their heads, realised that they must strike first. On 9 Thermidor, a night of see-saw crisis, the Convention outmanoeuvred the Jacobin Commune, and Robespierre, already outlawed, was disposed of without trial as a public nuisance, the sublime People mocking his last agony.

The Terror had hypnotic glamour, even for its victims. Hardly ever did one of these unfortunates try to resist his fate even at the last. This strange paralysis shows their awareness not only of the crushing power of the State but also of the primitive force of the Revolution. 'The measure of paralysis,' a contemporary remarked, 'was so strong that had you told a condemned man, "Go home now and await the tumbril that will arrive tomorrow to fetch you," he would have obeyed and next morning, at the right moment, have climbed onto the cart' (Sieburg). Read now the widow of Stalin's victim, Osip Mandelstam: 'We were all identical, either sheep advancing unprotesting to the slaughter, or respectful colleagues of the executioner. However we behaved, we were unnaturally servile, smothering all human instincts . . . it was not actually a question of fear but of something quite different, a paralysing sensation of personal impotence infecting us all, killed and killers.' She noted that, in all areas of life, 'conscience' was rejected, in favour of 'class-feeling' and 'for the good of the State'.*

At the Queen's condemnation, Herman rejoiced: 'Equality triumphs.' It did not. A few years later, France was sporting a House of Peers. Many great aristocratic estates survived the Revolution, flourishing under Empire and Restoration. 1789 has been called a national movement, 1848 a class movement. The former assailed privilege and inefficiency, both reappearing blatantly under the Directory which introduced the 1795 Constitution with a demand for the rights of the rich. Universal male suffrage, granted rather ineffectively in 1793, was abolished in 1797. Street disorders helped install Napoleon in 1799.

The Revolution had created political equality, and the equality of meritocracy: centralisation, conscription, some property redistribution with further peasant ownership and more emphatic State intervention in transport, education and agriculture. Juries became more influential, the bureaucracy larger, taxes more equitable, trousers more fashionable. Bonaparte, like de Gaulle, used plebiscites to bypass talkative Assemblies. He developed secular education, economic unity, allowed a limited male suffrage and still more limited political liberty, at the cost of several million lives. Lack of fraternity remained. The Revolution had abolished the sacramental quality of authority but successive regimes scarcely impaired Philip Guedalla's observation that France has generally regarded parliamentary institutions as a source of scandal rather than a form of government. The post-Napoleonic Press periodically regained freedoms. The old landowners regained considerable influence, the new rich, familiar through Balzac, Flaubert and Zola, made spectacular gains, through commerce, transport, building, colonies, all somewhat disappointing to the spirit of 1789. Urban workers received little until 1848 and the Second Empire. Moreover, having emptied Versailles, the Revolution had insisted that Paris controlled France. The question of who was to control Paris had not been finally settled a century later, though the 17,000 dead in 1871 showed a desperate attempt.

The Revolution quickened Irish and Polish nationalism and, through Napoleon, the questionable benefits of German and Italian. In 1815, some 300 German states were reduced to 39. Napoleonic

* Nadezhda Mandelstam: *Hope Abandoned*, London, 1974.

education fostered French chauvinism: Michelet enthused about 'One People, one Fatherland, one France'. For all its singular promises and personalities, the Revolution suggests that exciting government is usually bad government: that, save in crisis, gifted *ad hoc* committees are worse than the majority vote of parliamentary mediocrities who have inherited a tradition of horse-sense and restraint.

Barnave, sensibly investigating the relation of class to economics, was executed in 1793, retribution for his earlier applause of street murders. Regarding government not as art but method, the Revolution swiftly became sceptical of peaceful or organic reform, though this short-changed French genius. Reform could surely have been effected without the Terror and imperialism.

The Revolution's legacy, the either-or, Gordian Knot, short-cut solution – Liberty or Death – amounted to a belief in miracles. The sanctimonious public confessions and self-blame are remembered, with the purges, perjuries, accusations of conspiracy, censorship, the everlasting passing of the cruellest buck to an imaginary 'People'. For a year France was a police state, heyday of the informer, stool pigeon and bigot. All this was lapped up by the later extremes of the Left and Right – terms inherited from the Revolution – endangering society as Peel, Gladstone and Disraeli did not. The September Massacres anticipated twentieth-century 'People's Courts'. Like Rome, revolutionary France discovered that constant appeals to the streets were destructive, not least to the streets, and that military loyalties are too easily transferred from the State to particular generals. Also that, wise legislation notwithstanding, people remain susceptible to heroes, snobbery and crowns. Also, that to plunder a church does not eradicate religion; at Lyons, the scaffold was designated 'Altar of the Fatherland'; that idealism, venality, desire for glory are not peculiar to a particular class, and that a revolution relying on killings, secret police and censorship ceases to be a revolution. The real revolution, as Robespierre knew, transforms human nature. More human than he, Madame Roland, impeccably republican, avidly besought for her husband insignia of nobility to which he was not entitled.

The more significant legacy of 1789 was not economic or political, but surely moral contamination. Instead of breaking the inherited notion of the Elect, above all laws, sanctified by its own convictions, the Revolution reinforced it. It led to Napoleon remarking to Metternich in 1814 that a man like himself does not worry about a million deaths. Surveying piles of battle corpses, he was reassuring: 'Small change, small change. A night in Paris will repair all this,' like Hitler remarking, at someone's lament over Great War casualties, 'What else is youth made for?' Or Eichmann, dismissing five million victims as 'a statistic'. Marat, Carrier, Hébert and Collot lacked significant ideas but irrevocably contaminated politics. Fouché proudly used the word *holocaust* to describe his treatment of rebellious Lyons. The Incorruptible, arriving in Paris with six good shirts and three pairs of stockings, one almost new, dying barely solvent, was perhaps the most corruptible of all, surrendering to inflation of self and verbiage. Luxuriating in his millions, Talleyrand was the less deceiving. So was Danton.

Revolution and Napoleon precipitated a mass of imaginary selves, stalking through Romanticism; vast, dreaming, unscrupulous egos passionate for fulfilment and power. Yet when I consider the Revolution, it is not only to recall Danton defiant in '92, the guns at Valmy, September killers awash with blood and brandy, a haggard queen in a cart, even a dry, precise voice, 'He who trembles is guilty'. Not the facts but the myth of revolution. For myself, this is articulated by Thomas Mann: 'On the margins of great cities, where streets are ill-lit and policemen must walk in couples, are houses where you climb to the utmost summit, up, up, to garrets under the roof where pallid, youthful geniuses, criminals of the dream, brood with arms folded; up, into cheap studios decorated with symbolic signs, where, isolated, rebellious artists, inwardly gnawed, famished and proud, in their tobacco fumes strive with ideals appallingly final. Here is the end: ice, celibacy, barrenness. Here the air is so rarefied that life's mirages have disappeared. Here, the rule of defiance and adamant consistency, the ego stubborn in despair: here, freedom, madness, death, have total supremacy.'*

* Thomas Mann, 'At the Prophets' (1904) from: *Stories of Three Decades*, London, 1936.

THE ANTHOLOGY

THE PRELUDE

THE PROPHETS

The 1788th year after the Virgin's giving birth will see the astonishing of the world . . . the overthrow of empires.   JEAN MULLER, 1476

Very great and remarkable changes will happen in 1789 and last until 1814.   PIERRE TURREL of Autun, 1525

The Elected Capet will be captured at Varennes, fleeing by night through the forest and the outcome will be a slicing. . . .

In 1792, the scum of the revolutionary torrent will reach the surface. . . . Reds and Whites in the Republic will be equally misguided.

Against the Reds the Sections will unite. Peace will arrive and extinguish the fires, finish the water, iron, rope, to the end that those who contrived such matters will themselves perish, save One who will devastate the world.

An Emperor will be born near Italy who will prove expensive to the Empire; when people realise with whom he makes friends, they will find him less a prince than a butcher.

DR MICHEL DE NOSTRADAMUS, 1555

ANCIEN RÉGIME

I twist, turn, scheme, lie, prevaricate, manoeuvre, and hide it all in my red robe.   CARDINAL RICHELIEU

THE SUPPER

Egg soup with lemon juice and broth,
Cock's Comb,
Boiled Chicken,
Boiled Veal,
A Marrow Bone,
Chicken fried in breadcrumbs,
Jelly, Apricots,
Half a sugared Chestnut in Rose Water,
Preserved Cherries,
Bread,
Fennel Comfits.

A menu for the eleven-year-old Dauphin (later King Louis XIII)

THE DREAM

It is very fortunate that kings cannot err. Hence their contradictions never perplex us. In approving always, one is sure to be always right – which is pleasant. Louis XIV would not have liked to see at Versailles either an officer acting the cock, or a prince acting the turkey. That which raised the royal and imperial dignity in England and Russia would have seemed to Louis the Great incompatible with the crown of St Louis. We know what his displeasure was when Madame Henriette forgot herself so far as to see a hen in a dream – which was, indeed, a grave breach of good manners in a lady of the court. When one is of the court, one should not dream of the courtyard. Bossuet, it may be remembered, was nearly as scandalized as Louis XIV.

VICTOR HUGO. *The Laughing Man*, 1869

THE GREAT KING

Soon you will be King of a great realm. I urge you to never forget your dues to God; remember that you owe all to him. Try to remain at peace with your neighbours. I have loved war too much. Do not imitate me in this or in my extravagance. Consult others in all things, try to discover the best course and always follow it. Lighten your people's tasks as much as you can, and fulfil what I have unfortunately failed to do.

KING LOUIS XIV, on his deathbed, to his heir

When I have asked you for anecdotes about the age of Louis XIV, it is less about his person than about the arts which flourished in his time. I prefer details of Racine and Boileau, Quinault, Lulli, Molière, Le Brun, Bossuet, Poussin, Descartes . . . than of the battle of Steinkirk. Nothing but the name survives of the leaders of battalions and squadrons. Humanity gains nothing by these pitched battles. But the great men I refer to have prepared pure and lasting delights for posterity. A canal which joins two seas, a picture by Poussin, a fine tragedy, a truth discovered, are a thousand times more precious than all the archives of a Court, all the accounts of a campaign. You know that, for myself, the great men are in the vanguard, the heroes in the rear. I call great men those who excel in the useful or the agreeable: those who plunder provinces are mere heroes.

VOLTAIRE, to M. Thiriot

CATHERINE THE GREAT

Voltaire, my master, forbids foretelling the future because whoever does so likes to manufacture systems, and system-makers slip into the system only what fits and what does not, what tallies, what does not, and finally self-love becomes system-love, which itself creates obstinacy, intolerance and persecution – drugs against which this master of mine has warned me.

CATHERINE THE GREAT

Diderot's proposals would make fine books but bad politics. He only wrote on paper, which submits to everything and opposes no obstacle to the imagination, but I, poor Empress as I am, work on the human skin, which is irritable and ticklish to a very different degree.

CATHERINE THE GREAT

Incredulity is the first stage of philosophy.

DENIS DIDEROT

A SIGNIFICANT PERSON

You have been careful to make all Rome quail before you. Ruthlessly you commanded the most terrible government in all history. The Senate trembles before its pitiless champion. When someone demanded: 'Sulla, how much longer will you shed Roman blood?' your retort was to issue the proscriptions that decided which citizen was to live or die.

Sulla replied: 'It was precisely this bloodshed that enabled me to perform the greatest of all my deeds. If I had governed Rome with gentleness, it would probably have made me abdicate out of irritation, disgust, or mere caprice. But I renounced my dictatorship only when not one being in the world remained unconvinced that my only security lay in that dictatorship. I stood before the Roman people, a citizen amongst my fellow citizens, and I dared declare: "I am ready to answer for all the blood I have poured out on behalf of the Republic. I will render you an exact account to anyone who comes to plead for a father, a son, a brother." And all Rome was silent at my words.'

CHARLES DE SECONDAT MONTESQUIEU. *Dialogue entre Sulla et Eucrates*

The English Constitution has in fact reached the point of excellence, resulting in the restoration to all men of those natural rights of which, under almost all monarchies, they have been robbed. These rights are: total liberty of person and property; freedom of the press; the right of trial in all criminal cases, by an independent jury; the right of being tried only according to the strict letter of the law; and the right of all individuals to follow the religion of their choice.

VOLTAIRE. *Lettres Anglaises*

TRENDS

A philosophical wind is blowing towards us from England, a plea for free, anti-monarchical rule; it streams into people's heads and everyone realises how popular opinion conditions existence. Perhaps this new regime is already established in the general mind, to be put into practice at the very first opportunity, and the revolution might break out more peaceably than we imagine. All social orders share common discontent, a riot could become a revolt, and the revolt total revolution.

MARQUIS D'ARGENSON. *Journal*

D'Argenson had been a minister until 1747, when Louis XV dismissed him.

TWO WORDS

These two terms, *Nation* and *State*, were never uttered under Louis XIV; even the idea of them was lacking. We have never been so conscious as we are at present of the rights of the nation and of liberty.

MARQUIS D'ARGENSON. *Journal*
(See T. C. W. Blanning, 1987)

MID-CENTURY FRANCE

Thus the government no longer possessed any dignity, the finances any order, policy any consistency. France lost her European position. England was undisputed in sea-power and conquered France unopposed. The Northern Powers partitioned Poland for themselves. The Balance of Power, established by the Peace of Westphalia (1648) was shattered. The French monarchy was no longer a Great Power.

LOUIS-PHILIPPE, Comte de Ségur. *Mémoires ou Souvenirs et Anecdotes*, 1824–6
(For a concise study on this and subsequent developments, widely documented, see

T. C. W. Blanning, 1987.)

JEAN-JACQUES ROUSSEAU

Even the best of Kings wish to be able to exercise tyranny freely, if that is their caprice. There is one necessary and assured evil natural to monarchies, which must always make them inferior to Republics: it is this – while, where the people have power, men of talent and experience, whose talents honour whoever chooses them, are chosen by the people for the highest posts; those appointed at a nod from a King alone are, only too often, a disgrace to their position.

Whatever I feel is right is right, whatever I feel is wrong is wrong; conscience is the best of restraints.

It is vital for the state that every citizen should possess a religion, to make him love his duties. It is the obligation of authority to define the articles of civic belief, not exactly as religious dogmas but as social goals; no one is to be compelled to believe them, but whoever does not must be banished.

Rousseau's words were echoed with approval by Louis Antoine de Saint-Just, 1794.

SPECIAL ISSUES

We are abandoning our villages for the towns, the towns for the cities, the cities for the capital and this is what an entire nation is apt to do if the government does not trouble to reverse this drift.

Whoever lives his life merely receiving interest on capital is a lazy-bones at play, and the cause of most social evils.

VICTOR RIQUETI, Marquis de Mirabeau,
father of the Comte de Mirabeau. *L'Ami des Hommes*

INEQUALITY

God awarded us Reason, and the result is almost universal slavery. The true evil, nevertheless, is not inequality but dependence. It is inevitable for humanity to be divided into two classes, the oppressors and the oppressed, with numerous sub-divisions. Fortunately, use, custom, lack of leisure stops the majority of the oppressed from truly understanding their situation. When they come to recognise it, civil war follows, to end only in their enslavement, for a society is dominated by money. Equality is unreachable, because men are endowed with a disposition to bully, together with a distaste for hard work. Mankind can continue only through a boundless tribe of practical fellows who actually own nothing. Nevertheless, inequality should be kept moderate, not pushed to its limit.

VOLTAIRE. *Dictionnaire Philosophique*

FREEMASONS

No time need be wasted on the claim that the French Revolution was produced by a conspiracy reaching back to the fourteenth century. As for the obscure German group known as the Illuminati, they were not Freemasons at all but rivals of the Freemasons and had in any case been dissolved in 1786. Further, the role of the Freemasons was also fantastically over-simplified and exaggerated. It is true that the Freemasons shared that concern for humanitarian reform which is commonly associated with the Enlightenment – for instance, they contributed to the abolition of judicial torture and of witchcraft trials, and to the improvement of schools. On the other hand, at the time of the revolution most Freemasons were Catholic and monarchist – indeed King Louis XVI and his brothers were all Freemasons; while during the Terror Freemasons were guillotined by the hundred and their organisation, the Grand Orient, was suppressed.

NORMAN COHN, 1967

Freemasons included, with whatever historical effect or none, Washington, Jefferson, John Paul Jones, Philippe Egalité Duc d'Orléans, Paul Revere, Tom Paine, Joseph Bonaparte, Nelson, Benedict Arnold, Goethe, Kościuszko, Mozart, Mirabeau, Danton, Marat, Lafayette, Robespierre and the Grand Duke Paul (later Tsar Paul I).

A CHILDHOOD

As for the singular disappearance of Robespierre's father, it remains unsolved. It is said that, losing his wife, crazed with grief, bewildered, desperate, he abandoned his four children, the eldest, future member of the Convention, being only seven, travelled in turn through England and the German states, eventually dying in Munich, an explanation worth nothing at all. This paterfamilias in the prime of life, deserting four children, leaving them nothing, seeking abroad consolation for grief, might testify a loving husband, scarcely the ideal father. . . . That desertion fatally affected Robespierre's childhood. He became serious before his time; at ten, he seemed to realise that he could depend only on himself, and, nominally but a child, began pondering life's sadness and to see himself as sole captain of his fate. Thenceforward the future tribune is perceptible; he enters the college, carries off all the prizes, is an addict of all the classical orators and, thoughtful, melancholy, walks alone. At twelve he is sent to the Collège Louis-le-Grand, Paris. There he makes one friend – Camille Desmoulins. These two youths, avoiding all student games, were always seen together, pacing the cloisters, almost preternaturally serious, dreaming of the future. They were to play, a little later, another game, a terrible one, matched against each other, staking their heads.

When Louis XVI visited the venerable institution bearing his ancestor's name, the masters selected their star pupil, Robespierre, to utter the address of welcome, and many of those who witnessed the small rhetorician nervously bowing before the young King, with his Latin verses and obeisance, lived to consider that first meeting, remembering it on the day when their fellow-student, virtually ruler of France, sent the dethroned monarch to the scaffold.

G. Lenôtre, 1894

MARIE ANTOINETTE

Antonia was to be married!

Only the summer before she had been scampering breathlessly about with her brothers and the little princesses of Hesse through the shrubberies of Schoenbrunn's Tyrolean garden. And it was not so very long since Maria Theresa, passing through the long gallery where the little Archduchess was 'playing at marriage' with Mozart, had heard the young prodigy ask:

'I shall be your husband, shan't I?'

'Oh yes, no one but you.'

André Castelot, 1957

I never saw anyone so shy. She walked very swiftly, and so as to recognise others she went by without looking at them, since she had formed the habit of glancing sideways, like a hare. MADAME CAMPAN

PRINCE STAHREMBERG: 'What is your opinion of the Archduchess Antonia?'
AMBASSADOR MARQUIS DE DURFORT: 'Very attractive.'
STAHREMBERG: 'She will be a charming wife for the Dauphin.'
DURFORT: 'The morsel is dainty and will be in good hands, *if that really is the case.*'

Remain a good German.
                                    EMPRESS MARIA THERESA, to her daughter Marie Antoinette,
                                               on her departure to marry the Dauphin

She is like the perfume of Spring.   EDMUND BURKE, on Marie Antoinette

THE BOSOM

KING LOUIS XV: 'What did you think of the Dauphine? Has she any bosom?'
M. BOURET: 'She has a charming face and very beautiful eyes.'
LOUIS XV: 'That was not my question. I asked you if she had any bosom.'
M. BOURET: 'Sire, I did not take the liberty of extending my gaze so far.'
LOUIS XV: 'You are a fool! It's the first thing we look at in a woman.'

WEDDING NIGHT

KING LOUIS XV: 'Don't overload your stomach tonight.'
THE DAUPHIN: 'Why not? I always sleep better after a good supper.'

POLITICAL PHILOSOPHY

According to the principles of our latest philosophers, the throne no longer possesses divine sanction; they have decided that it derived from violence, and what force had the right to establish, force has the right to topple and destroy; that the People can never wholly surrender authority but can only lend it; that they are always entitled to recover it for the only governing principle, their personal interest. . . .

Nevertheless, if this principle of personal interest – the caprice of human passions – were to be generally accepted, and to such a degree that it made divine principle forgotten, then all idea of right and wrong, virtue and vice, moral good and evil, would be erased and destroyed in men's hearts, thrones would lose security, subjects become discontented and disobedient, and masters would lose their paternal benevolence. Kingdoms would thus be in eternal rebellion or suppression.   DAUPHIN LOUIS, father of King Louis XVI

My son, God is preparing for you the most splendid crown in the world. Providence has made you born so that eventually you shall govern a realm as certain of the true principles as it is devoted to its rulers. What a glittering prospect! But what duties it entails! And what great knowledge is demanded! . . .

Respect yourself and you will be respected.

Nothing is so dangerous as weakness. . . .

Never permit yourself to be ruled.

DAUPHINE MARIE-JOSÈPHE, mother of King Louis XVI

THE CHURCH

I am not sure whether, despite the glaring faults of certain of its members, there was ever a clergy more remarkable than the French at the moment of being engulfed in the Revolution – more enlightened, more national, less limited in the performance of private virtue, or better imbued with public morality and religious faith.

ALEXIS DE TOCQUEVILLE, 1855

We have had enough religion to hate and persecute; not enough to help and succour.   VOLTAIRE

PIE CRUST

Madame Victoire [a daughter of Louis XV], plump and pious, retained some faint traces of beauty. Her kindness made one forget her stupidity. It was she, according to Mme de Boigne, who said, with tears in her eyes, during a period of scarcity, when someone was talking of the sufferings of the unfortunate people who lacked bread: 'But if only they could resign themselves to eating pie crust!' It is only fair to explain that pie crust lay very heavy on her own stomach.

ANDRÉ CASTELOT, 1957

WOMEN'S RIGHTS

Either none of mankind possesses genuine rights, or everyone shares them equally; whoever votes against another's rights, whatever his religion, colour or sex, forswears his own.

ANTOINE-NICOLAS DE CONDORCET.
Sur l'admission des Femmes au Droit de Cité, Paris

YOUTH

Without nostalgia, without premonition, we younger nobles cheerfully bestrode the carpet of flowers which covered an abyss. We grinned derisively at ancient customs, our ancestors' feudal pride and solemn decorum; anything old we found tedious and ridiculous. The solemnity of antiquated beliefs over-oppressed us. The cheerful philosophy of Voltaire appealed to us because it was so entertaining.

Voltaire seduced our intellects, Rousseau moved our emotions.

We mocked the solemn fears of the old Court and Church, who stormed against this desire for novelty. We applauded republican plays, the philosophy debates at the Academy, the daring books of our authors. The concept of Liberty, however it was expressed, attracted us by its audacity, spirit of equality, overall convenience. Men are happy to lower themselves from their customary rank, as long as they feel they can easily resume it at will, and because we closed our eyes to the future, we could simultaneously exploit the gifts of aristocracy and the luxury of plebeianism.

LOUIS-PHILIPPE, Comte de Ségur. *Mémoires ou Souvenirs et Anecdotes*, 1824–6

SOCIETY

Poverty and pretension: such, for the most part, was the condition of the French aristocracy of the *ancien régime*, whom the writers of historical fiction have pictured in silk stockings, minuetting across the polished floors of Versailles. A short visit to Lignerie, in Normandy, or the countless households like it would have stilled a few of these fluent pens. In many of these houses the countess would breed her children beneath a roof shared by the rutting hogs and cattle of her husband's barnyard. The proximity of the manure pile, which added its own moist leachings to the muck and mire dropped by geese and pigs, lent to the scene a rustic character of a kind that has not been conveyed to us by the novels of Rousseau or the canvases of Fragonard. In the descriptions of the *ancien régime* which have come down to us from that period no mention is made of flies; the imagination must add these to the picture, swarming in profusion about the *fumier* and the hogpen. On more than one such *seigneurie* the count or marquis wore wooden shoes like his peasants and dressed little better than they. An intricate system of law and tradition prohibited these gentlemen entering the world of trade or negotiation. Even had convention permitted, it is unlikely that many of them would have chosen that particular path to prosperity. For the contempt these pedigreed peasants felt for the rising and wealthy class of men who traded in goods and money was matched only by the resentment the burgess class felt for the tattered and arrogant provincial nobility. The banker's wife wore jewels and scent, the countess's clothes were patched and often she smelled of the barnyard but there was no question in the mind of either as to who was to the manor born. The French nobility, though often poverty-stricken, then occupied a legal position attached to which were certain symbolic prerogatives, such as having frogs silenced during childbirth, and certain concrete privileges, such as immunity from taxation.   STANLEY LOOMIS, 1965

Tax immunity, though monstrous, was not total: the nobility were liable to the Vingtième *and the* Capitations.

    Ancien régime *France was not a homogeneous society, and conditions varied greatly from province to province, district to district. Similarly, patterns varied within each class. Those – some 400,000 – claiming noble birth had many conflicting aspirations, prejudices and traditions. By no means all held aloof from the allure and profits of industry, science, scholarship, literature and local government.*

SEXUAL SENSATIONALISM

The devout wife of a certain Maréchal de France (who suffers from an imaginary lung disease), finding a husband of that species too delicate, considers it her religious duty to spare him and so condemns herself to the crude caresses of her butler, who would still be a lackey if he hadn't proved himself so robust.

The public is warned that an epidemic disease is raging among the girls of the opera, that it has begun to reach the ladies of the court, and that it has even been communicated to their lackeys. This disease elongates the face, destroys the complexion, reduces the weight and causes horrible ravages where it becomes situated. There are ladies without teeth, others without eyebrows, and some completely paralysed.   CHARLES THEVENAU DE MORANDE. *Le Gazetier Cuirasse*

Robert Darnton comments:
This sexual sensationalism conveyed a social message: the aristocracy had degenerated to the point of being unable to reproduce itself; the great nobles were either impotent or deviant; their wives were forced to seek satisfaction from their servants, representatives of the more virile lower classes, and everywhere among *les grands* incest and venereal disease had extinguished the last sparks of humanity. . . .

Morande's chronicle of cuckoldry, buggery, incest and impotence in high places therefore reads as an indictment of the social order. And Morande did not merely leave the reader with a general impression of corruption. He associated the aristocracy's decadence with its inability to fulfil its functions in the army, the church, and the state.   *Literary Low Life in Pre-revolutionary France*, 1976

(See Douglas Johnson)

NEEDS

I must admit to you that I really desire some means for supplying my daily needs. Without the three shirts I have mentioned, a dressing gown and top coat, I will not survive the winter.

ANTOINE FOUQUIER-TINVILLE, future Public Prosecutor, to his mother

SO LITTLE EFFORT

How lucky it is for those in our position to gain the friendship of an entire kingdom with so little effort – yet this is the most precious of all; I became absolutely conscious of this, never to be forgotten. Something else which gave immense satisfaction during this splendid occasion was the manner of the Dauphin. To all the speeches he answered magnificently; he observed all services rendered him, and, particularly, he saw the enthusiasm and joy of the crowds, to whom he displayed plenty of benevolence.

> MARIE ANTOINETTE, to her mother Empress Maria Theresa,
> after her first visit as Dauphine, to Paris from Versailles

LOUIS XV DIES

Oh God, protect us, we are too young to reign.

> LOUIS XVI and MARIE ANTOINETTE

A VISIT TO VERSAILLES

I am happy that we will soon be departing. One more day like this and my hatred of these gentry would be so fierce that I would not know where to put it. . . .

They make me aware of injustice and force me to witness their ludicrous ways all day.

> MANON PHILIPON (later, Madame Roland), to her mother

ACCESSION

Advance, on all our hearts impose your yoke:
We twenty million subjects long to hear
The glorious speech that you may utter soon,
'I am no more than twenty, yet I make them all
Happy, happy, delighting in my rule.'

> *An Ode to King Louis XVI*

There is nothing more reassuring at this sad time when the country is mourning its late ruler, than the way in which his grandson has con-

ducted himself since his passing, the way in which he, partnered by
his adorable princess now enthroned with him, busies himself with
the responsibilities of his great position. All news arriving every minute swells the country's love for them. How can France conceivably
avoid magnifying such love of their rulers to the point of idolatry?

Nouvelles à la Main

HEADS AT VERSAILLES

The day after Louis XV's death elegant women wore a cypress and a
horn of plenty in their hair – mourning for the King and hope for the
new reign, or a rising sun symbolising Louis XVI (they did not know
him very well) and an olive tree, emblem of peace and plenty. More
simply one saw fields of corn being harvested by Hope. One morning
the Queen bore lightly on her head a whole English garden, with its
lawns, hills and silver streams.

The Duchesse de Lauzun, who was not afraid of headaches,
arrived one day at Mme du Deffand's house with a built-up *pouf* representing a whole countryside in relief. One could see a hunter aiming at the ducks flapping at the edge of a lake ruffled by the wind. On
the heights was a mill with the miller's wife being courted by a
sprightly curate, while the miller, who knew how to behave, went off
with his donkey in the direction of the Duchesse's ear.

Mlle Bertin was once nearly dethroned by a certain Beaulard,
who invented mechanical coiffures. One pressed a spring and a rose
flowered. There was also a real piece of machinery, called 'The good
miller's wife', which with the aid of a winch hidden in the chignon
could be lowered or raised when an old lady with retrograde ideas
entered or left the room. Mlle Bertin went pale with jealousy. But
Marie Antoinette remained faithful to Rose, who in collaboration
with Léonard invented for the Queen coiffures *au Lever de la Reine, à
la Puce* – naturally!, *à l'Iphigénie, à l'Eurydice* – to please Gluck, *à
la Modestie* and *à la Frivolité*. But above all Marie Antoinette liked
feathers. The coiffure *à la Minerve* had as many as ten, which were so
tall that one day she found it impossible to enter her coach to go to a
ball given by the Duchesse de Chartres. At the beginning of February
1775 Maria Theresa sharply criticised her daughter's 'plumage' and
when the Queen sent her a portrait of herself with her head covered
in feathers the Empress sent it back, feigning to imagine that there

had been a mistake in the destination of the present. 'I did not see the portrait of a Queen of France but that of an actress.'

ANDRÉ CASTELOT, 1957

COURT SONGS

Little queen, have a care;
If you behave with such an air
You'll be sent back over there.

The queen imprudently let out
To Besenval, her friend, one day:
'My husband is a sorry lout.'
The other answered, winking,
'Tis what all think, but do not say,
You say it without thinking.'

SCANDAL

Maurepas was impotent;
The King restored his power anew.
The grateful minister then went
To see the King and told him: Sire,
The only thing left I desire,
Would be to do the same for you. ANON

THE TIMES

It was the best of times, it was the worst of times, it was the age of wisdom, it was the age of foolishness, it was the epoch of belief, it was the epoch of incredulity, it was the season of Light, it was the season of Darkness, it was the spring of hope, it was the winter of despair, we had everything before us, we had nothing before us, we were all going direct to Heaven, we were all going direct the other way – in short, the period was so far like the present period, that some of its noisiest authorities insisted on its being received, for good or for evil, in the superlative degree of comparison only.

There were a king with a large jaw and a queen with a plain face, on the throne of England; there were a king with a large jaw and a queen with a fair face, on the throne of France. In both countries it was clearer than crystal to the lords of the State preserves of loaves and fishes, that things in general were settled for ever.

France, less favoured on the whole as to matters spiritual than her sister of the shield and trident, rolled with exceeding smoothness down hill, making paper money and spending it. Under the guidance of her Christian pastors, she entertained herself, besides, with such humane achievements as sentencing a youth to have his hands cut off, his tongue torn out with pincers, and his body burned alive, because he had not kneeled down in the rain to do honour to a dirty procession of monks which passed within his view, at a distance of some fifty or sixty yards. It is likely enough that, rooted in the woods of France and Norway, there were growing trees, when that sufferer was put to death, already marked by the Woodman, Fate, to come down and be sawn into boards, to make a certain movable framework with a sack and knife in it, terrible in history. It is likely enough that in the rough outhouses of some tillers of the heavy lands adjacent to Paris, there were sheltered from the weather that very day, rude carts, bespattered with rustic mire, snuffed about by pigs, and roosted in by poultry, which the Farmer, Death, had already set apart to be his tumbrils of the Revolution. But that Woodman and that Farmer, though they work unceasingly, work silently, and no-one heard them as they went about with muffled tread: the rather, forasmuch as to entertain any suspicion that they were awake, was to be atheistical and traitorous.   CHARLES DICKENS. *A Tale of Two Cities*, 1859

A monument of political wisdom, if compared to any others.
JEAN-PAUL MARAT, on the British Constitution. *Chains of Slavery*, 1777

TWO COUNTRIES

James I. Regulation.

'Anyone wandering about and begging is designated rogue and vagabond. J.P.s in petty session are ordered to have them whipped in public and, for a first offence, to send them to prison for six months, for a second, for two years. In prison they can be whipped as much and as often as the J.P.s deem fit.

The incorrigible and dangerous are to be branded on the left shoulder with R. for rogue, and set to Hard Labour and, if found beg-

ging yet again, are to be hanged without mercy.' These statutes, with
full force of law until around 1710, were repealed only by 12 Ann. c.23.

Similar laws existed in France where by the mid-17th Century, a
kingdom of vagrants had been formed within Paris itself. Even at the
start of Louis XVI's reign, by an Ordinance of July 13, 1777, every
able-bodied man from 16 to 60, if lacking any means of subsistence or
not engaged in a trade, was liable to the galleys.

KARL MARX. Das Kapital, 1867

FROM PHILADELPHIA

But hear, O ye swains ('tis a tale most profane),
   How all the tyrannical powers,
Kings, Commons, and Lords, are uniting again
   To cut down this guardian of ours.
From the east to the west blows the trumpet to arms,
   Thro' the land let the sound of it flee,
Let the far and the near – all unite with a cheer,
   In defense of our *Liberty tree.*

TOM PAINE. Pennsylvania Magazine
(See A. J. Ayer)

KING LOUIS XVI

From 1775 to 1791, I went out on 2,636 occasions.   *Diary*

The fellow's never jealous, he's indifferent: best able
at stuffing himself – like a swine,
swilling wine,
Elbows on table.   Popular song

ADVICE

You meddle in a great many matters which first of all do not concern
you, which you know nothing about and in regard to which the cabals
and associates who flatter you and know how to arouse your *amour
propre* or desire to shine or even foster a certain hatred or rancour,
cause you to take one step after another calculated to spoil the happiness of your life and certain to bring *extreme unpleasantness* upon you

sooner or later, and, by diminishing the King's friendship and esteem, to lose you the good opinion of the public and all the consideration which, with the aid of that opinion, you might acquire, and have acquired, astonishingly enough, until now. Why do you think it your business, my dear sister, to transfer Ministers, to send one to his estates, to have a particular office given to this man or that, to help another to win his lawsuit, to create a new and expensive post at your court, and finally, to talk about public affairs and even to use expressions by no means suited to your position? Have you ever asked yourself by what right you interfere in the affairs of the government and the French kingdom? What studies have you ever made? What knowledge have you acquired that you dare to imagine that your advice or opinion can be of any use, particularly in affairs which require wide knowledge? You are a pleasant young woman who all day thinks of nothing but frivolity, your appearance and your amusements. You never spend more than a quarter of an hour a month in reading or hearing anything intelligent. I am sure you never ponder or think out anything or reflect on the consequences of what you do or say. You act only from the impulse of the moment, and the words and arguments of the people you are protecting and in whom you trust are your only guides. Could anything more rash, unreasonable and improper be written than what you observed to the Comte de Rosemberg concerning the way in which you arranged a conversation at Rheims with the Duc de Choiseul? If such a letter ever went astray, if, as I have no doubt, you let slip similar words and observations to your intimate friends, I can only *foretell great unhappiness for you*, and I confess that on account of my attachment for you this distresses me very much.   EMPEROR JOSEPH II, to his sister Marie Antoinette

She received the letter, finally somewhat modified, with great anger.

PARIS

If [Emperor] Julian could now revisit the capital of France, he might converse with men of science and genius, capable of understanding and of instructing a disciple of the Greeks; he might excuse the lively and graceful follies of a nation whose martial spirit has never been enervated by the indulgence of luxury; and he must applaud the perfection of that inestimable art which softens and refines and embellishes the intercourse of social life.

EDWARD GIBBON. *The Decline and Fall of the Roman Empire*

STENCH

When Marie Antoinette opened the windows of her little apartments a terrible stench rose from the courtyard of the *Oeil de Boeuf*, for the Château was a veritable sink. 'The passages, the courtyards, the wings and the corridors,' reports a contemporary witness, 'were full of urine and faecal matter. The park, the gardens and the château made one retch with their bad smell.' Viollet-le-Duc tells how in 1830 he visited the Château with an old Marquise who had lived at the Court of Marie Antoinette. She seemed bewildered and could not find her way in the unfurnished rooms. Suddenly the two visitors found themselves at a place where 'a waste plug, which had burst owing to frost, had covered the floor with filth'. The smell drove them back. The old Marquise cried out with joy: 'Ah! I know where I am now! That was Versailles in my day. . . . It was like that everywhere.'

ANDRÉ CASTELOT, 1957

EXHORTATION

O ye that love mankind! Ye that dare oppose, not only the tyranny, but the tyrant, stand forth! Every spot of the old world is over-run with oppression. Freedom hath been hunted round the globe. Asia, and Africa, have long expelled her – Europe regards her like a stranger, and England hath given her warning to depart. O! receive the fugitive, and prepare in time an asylum for Mankind.

TOM PAINE. *Common Sense*

DECLARATION OF AMERICAN INDEPENDENCE

I felt that the American Revolution marked the start of a new political era; that this revolution would necessarily precipitate an important advance in general civilisation, and that it would soon effect great changes in the European social order.

CLAUDE HENRI DE ROUVROY, COMTE DE SAINT-SIMON.
Collected Works, Vol. 1, 1865

When we consider the mistaken ideas of government and philanthropy which these young men won in America and spread in France so enthusiastically and with such deplorable success – for this lunacy of imitation powerfully helped the French Revolution, though was not its sole cause – we have to admit that it would have been better for them and us if these youthful, red-headed philosophers had remained at home.   MATHIEU DUMAS. *Memoirs*, 1839

REPUBLICANS

These are the times that try men's souls. The summer soldier and the summer patriot will, in this crisis, shrink from the service of their country; but he that stands it *now*, deserves the love and thanks of Man and Woman. Tyranny, like hell, is not easily conquered; yet we have this consolation with us, that the harder the conflict the more glorious the triumph. What we obtain too cheap, we esteem too lightly; 'tis dearness only that gives everything its value. Heaven knows how to put a proper price upon its goods; and it would be strange indeed, if so celestial an article as *Freedom* should not be highly rated.   TOM PAINE. *The American Crisis*

The republican is the only form of government which is not eternally at open or secret war with the rights of Mankind.

THOMAS JEFFERSON, to William Hunter

ROUSSEAU AND ROBESPIERRE

What was Rousseau, the author of the *Contrat Social* but a believer without a church; and what was Robespierre but the only man who tried to put the *Contrat Social* into practice? Just as the eccentric Genevan could only understand the 'general will' when in a spiritual state so greatly akin to heavenly grace as to be mistaken for it, so the incorruptible achieved the contemplation of his god, 'the people', not through the laborious but valuable experiences of one who lives amongst the people, but by means of a sort of Revelation. He never liked the masses and was never intimate with them. But he idealized 'the people' as his fixed principle, and acted strictly according to that principle during the whole five years of his political life. What he wanted in reality was a theocracy, with the place of God taken by 'the people' – as he understood that image. That his doctrine should,

indeed must, unite illegalities, even crimes, with formidable martyr-
doms, was the outcome of this democratic mysticism, the deification
of 'the people's will', which he was certain was understood by himself alone. . . .

His shame is simultaneously glory; he acted not from material
appetites or selfishness, but as high priest of his new god, he was ruthless.

Though 'state' is rare in Robespierre's speeches, all his actions
can nevertheless be related to 'reasons of state'.

The complete denial of all individual demands for happiness, which
he required for the proclamation and fruition of Rousseau's 'general
will', the foundation for the ideal government of society, swiftly
transformed the Republic into a gloomy prison heavy with the sighs
of virtuous citizens and the jeering grins of scoundrels. The French
Revolution was successful while it concerned itself with human
needs, but failed when 'the People' came into the picture.

FRIEDRICH SIEBURG, 1936

*As a youth, Robespierre once visited the elderly Rousseau at Ermenonville but
no record exists of their talk. The exchange is imagined in a novel by Lion
Feuchtwanger.*

Robespierre's tireless study of Rousseau, beginning at school, never
achieved critical mastery of that confused sage's contradictory
notions, but remained forever a superficial experience which developed in him an outlook much akin to that of his hero.

FRIEDRICH SIEBURG, 1936

Virtue is only the concentration of the general will.

JEAN-JACQUES ROUSSEAU

The Republic is government guided by the general will, which itself
is law.   MAXIMILIEN ROBESPIERRE

Divinity! You it was who taught me how to know my own being.
In my youth, you it was who enabled me to understand the true stature of my soul, and to meditate on the great principles determining
society.   MAXIMILIEN ROBESPIERRE, on the dead Rousseau

That man will go far, for he really believes his own words.

COMTE DE MIRABEAU, on Maximilien Robespierre

A flea that will vanish in the winter.

ANTOINE-NICOLAS DE CONDORCET, on Maximilien Robespierre

BRUTAL JOYS

How many times have you left the marriage bed and the caresses of your husband to abandon yourself to Bacchantes or satyrs and to join yourself with them through their brutal joys?

ANON, a reprimand to the Queen

I should be neither grieved nor very annoyed if the King were to develop a passing and temporary attachment as he might thereby acquire more vitality and energy.   QUEEN MARIE ANTOINETTE

> Friend of Wisdom and of clear-eyed truth,
> Lover of pure Virtue, sycophancy's foe,
> Struggle forward, each mortal day that passes
> Is one stage nearer Immortality.

To King Louis XVI, on a popular print

A PROPHECY

A man is going to arise, perhaps hitherto lost in the obscurity of the crowd, who has made no reputation in speech or writing, who has meditated silently: a man, in fact, who has perhaps overlooked his own gifts, and has only been aware of his power while actually using it. He is going to grasp opinions, circumstances, chance, and will declare to the chief theoreticians what the professional architect said to the orator:

'All that my rival tells you, I will actually do.'

COMTE J. A. GUIBERT

GRUB STREET

The established writers enjoyed an 'estate'; they derived honour and wealth from the established cultural institutions. But the literary proletariat had no social location. Its ragged pamphleteers could not call themselves 'men of letters'; they were just *canaille*, condemned to gutters and garrets, working in isolation, poverty and degradation, and therefore easy prey to the psychology of failure – a vicious combination of hatred of the system and hatred of the self.

The Grub Street mentality made itself heard with exceptional vehemence during the last years of the Old Regime. It spoke through the *libelle*, the hack writers' staff of life, their meat; their favourite genre, and a genre that deserves to be rescued from the neglect of historians, because it communicates the Grub Street view of the world, a spectacle of knaves and fools buying and selling one another and forever falling victim to *les grands*. The *grand monde* was the real target of the *libelles*: they slandered the court, the church, the aristocracy, the academies, the salons, everything elevated and respectable including the monarchy itself with a scurrility that is difficult to imagine today, although it has had a long career in underground literature. For pamphleteers had lived by libel since the time of Aretino. They had exploited all the great crises in French history – in the propaganda produced by the Catholic League during the religious wars, for example, and in the *Mazarinades* of the Fronde. But the ultimate crisis of the Old Regime gave them an unusual opportunity, and they rose to the occasion with what seems to have been their greatest barrage of anti-social smut. ROBERT DARNTON, 1976

(See Douglas Johnson)

PHILOSOPHICAL BOOKS

Digging downward in intellectual history calls for new methods and new materials, for grubbing in archives instead of contemplating philosophical treatises. As an example of the dirt that such digging can turn up, consider the following titles taken from a manuscript catalogue that circulated secretly in France around 1780 and that were offered for sale under the heading 'philosophical books'. *Venus in the Cloister or the Nun in a Nightgown, The Woman of Pleasure, The Pastime of Antoinette* (a reference to the queen), *Authentic Memoirs of Mme La Comtesse Du Barry, Monastic News or the Diverting Adventures of*

Brother Maurice, Medley by a Citizen of Geneva and Republican Advice Dedicated to the Americans, Works of La Mattire, System of Nature. Here is a definition of the 'philosophical' by a publisher who made it his business to know what eighteenth-century Frenchmen wanted to read. If one measures it against the view of the philosophic movement that has been passed on piously from textbook to textbook, one cannot avoid feeling uncomfortable: most of those titles are completely unfamiliar, and they suggest that a lot of trash somehow got mixed up in the eighteenth-century idea of 'philosophy'. Perhaps the Enlightenment was a more down-to-earth affair than the rarified climate of opinion described by textbook writers, and we should question the overly highbrow, overly metaphysical view of intellectual life in the eighteenth century.   ROBERT DARNTON, 1976

(See Douglas Johnson)

In 1780 there could no longer be any chatter about French decline; quite the reverse, apparently her progress was to be boundless. Now it was that notions of human perfectability and unimpeded advance became fashionable. Two score years before the future appeared hopeless; in 1780, none had the slightest worry. Dazed by the promise of unprecedented happiness already within reach, people were literally unaware of the practical, prosaic improvements around them, and were urgent to give history a push.   ALEXIS DE TOCQUEVILLE, 1855

The Queen was anxious to learn the reasons for her unpopularity. This court song, in which 'Thémire' represents herself, was written at her suggestion:

> 'Phyllis asks for her portrait'
> Are you concerned to hear
> What's said about Thémire?
> At moments, it is said,
> You'd think she'd lost her head.
> Is that really so?
> Yes, but you must know
> She can so fashion it
> That her strange lack of wit
> Would even captivate
> A mind of Cato's weight.
>
> Too much good sense, 'tis said,
> Has never plagued her head,

But incense, so they say,
Enchants her all the day.
Is that really so?
Yes, but you must know
So full of skill is she
That every deity
Would come down to adore her
And burn incense before her.

If she has promised you
A private rendezvous
Or business talk, they say,
She soon forgets the day.
Is that really so?
Yes, but you must know
That when you meet once more
Her faults fly through the door,
And time itself will fly
Only too quickly by.

Self-centredness supreme –
That is her guiding theme,
She loves herself, they say,
As dearly as she may.
Is that really so?
Yes, but you must know
She must be left her creed.
Can she be blamed, indeed,
For loving as she does
What everybody loves?   DE BOUFFLERS

POLICE DOSSIERS

Mercier: lawyer, a fierce, bizarre man; he neither pleads in court nor consults. He hasn't been admitted to the bar, but he takes the title of lawyer. He has written *Le Tableau de Paris*, in four volumes, and other works. Fearing the Bastille, he left the country; then returned and wants to become attached to the police.

Marat: bold charlatan. M. Vicq d'Azur asks, in the name of the Société

Royale de Médecine, that he be run out of Paris. Many sick persons have died in his hands but he has a doctor's degree, which was bought for him.

Chénier: insolent and violent poet. He lives with Beaumenil of the Opera, who, in the decline of her charms, fell in love with him. He mistreats her and beats her – so much that her neighbours report that he would have killed her had they not come to her rescue. She accuses him of having taken her jewels; she describes him as a man capable of any crime and doesn't hide her regrets at having let herself be bewitched by him.

Fréron: who has neither the wit nor the pen of his father, is generally despised. It is not he who writes the *Année Littéraire*, although he has its privilege. He hires young unemployed lawyers. He's an insolent coward, who has received his share of beatings – and doesn't boast about it – most recently from the hand of the actor Desessarts, whom he had called a 'ventriloquist' in one of his issues. He is connected with Mouvel, who was expelled from the Comédie for pederasty.

Panis: young Lawyer of the Palais, protected by M. le Président d'Ormesson because of Panis's parents who are his (d'Ormesson's) fermiers; is employed by Fréron on the *Année Littéraire*. Panis has a mistress branded by the hand of the executioner.

Fabre d'Églantine: a trivial poet, who drags about in shame and destitution; he is despised everywhere; among men of letters he is considered an execrable subject.   Quoted by ROBERT DARNTON, 1976

(See Douglas Johnson)

GREATNESS

Do not try and copy the so-called greatness of Louis XIV. Doubtless Louis XIV was great, but Caesar was greater, and what honest fellow does not loathe Caesar? Louis XIV was great, but all the glittering plagues of the world were great, and they merit no more than the curses of humanity. Louis XIV was great, but with the greatness that spreads desolation and dishonours the human race. Woe to any minister, ignorant or perverse, who should offer such a model to our young Louis XVI, who still treats his conscience as a judge, witness, friend! Woe to whoever offers the King false conceptions of glory.

COMTE DE MIRABEAU, to Charles Gravier, Comte de Vergennes, Minister of Foreign Affairs

PREGNANCY

O sheltering Heaven protect
The life of Antoinette.

COLLOT D'HERBOIS, future Terrorist. *Ode to the Queen*

AT ARRAS

Sometimes my aunts and I would scold him for being so apparently
self-absorbed when we were all together in the evening. When the
rest of us sat at cards or discussing some petty, everyday matters, he
would leave us for some corner, where, on the sofa, he would relapse
into his own meditations quite as if he were alone.

CHARLOTTE ROBESPIERRE, on her brother Maximilien

LOUIS XVI

Father of his people, sagacious, strong,
Striving for their welfare, righting wrong,
Reproaching evil, setting countries free,
Restoring order, peace and liberty,
Posterity will exhibit him to sight
As Louis of France, ally of truth and right.

GIRARD DE LOURMARIN

The fragile tower will not survive my rhyme,
But Louis' Virtue in this evil time
Has raised a monument that takes its source
From gratitude: bronze itself has lesser force.
Your sword has now set the New World free;
And England's pride must bow its head to thee;
But on your Name a fiercer light is shed
When by your hand Poverty is warmed and fed.

Inscribed on a Paris snowman

FROM AMERICA

Soon the American representatives, Silas Deane and Arthur Lee arrived in Paris, and then, very soon, the celebrated Benjamin Franklin. I find it hard to convey the enthusiasm and excitement of their reception in France, within an ancient kingdom, these delegates of those rebelling against their own king. There was no more emphatic contrast between our luxuriant capital, our elegant fashions, the magnificence of Versailles, the urbane but disdainful hauteur of our aristocracy – in all, all the extant symptoms of the loyal pride of Louis XIV – with the most rural attire, the simple but dignified bearing, the candid, unadorned speeches, the unpowdered hair and, to conclude, that flavour of the classical world that suddenly introduced to our apartments, into the soft and flunkeyish culture left over from the 17th century, these wise associates of Plato, or of the republicans of the age of Cato or Fabius Maximus.

LOUIS-PHILIPPE, COMTE DE SÉGUR. *Mémoires ou Souvenirs et Anecdotes*, 1824–6

In his suburban house at Passy, the wise man of the New World received all Paris like a king. His judgments, ever balanced, his sayings, filled with robust good sense, were fresh air sweeping into the scented atmosphere of the salons. His imperturbable optimism infected everyone; two little words which he had so frequently employed in talk with French friends in America in the blackest moment of his country's struggle, 'so it goes', '*ça ira*', became fashionable in Paris. Very quickly those two words became the chorus of a Revolutionary song.

Young aristocrats were among Benjamin Franklin's most faithful followers. The youthful Duc de la Rochefoucauld regarded him as prophet of a new religion; he offered himself as Franklin's secretary, and translated into his own tongue those gospels of freedom, the constitutions of the American states. Other adherents of this new faith were the powerful family of Noailles. The grand old man's fierce hatred of any kind of aristocracy did not disturb these followers. They were prepared to overlook his singular calculations, destroying the very foundation of pride in lineage, that after a few generations the ancestral blood completely disappears.

Franklin's attention was attracted to the Comte de Mirabeau. In the Passy villa following the forming of the Order of Cincinnatus in America, Franklin discussed with Mirabeau his dislike of this anti-republican tendency in the newly-established Republic, and Franklin gave him his own writings on this with all necessary references. When Mirabeau began working on this, he felt that here indeed were his own ideas.

ANTONINA VALLENTIN. *Mirabeau: Voice of the Revolution*, 1948

'The times that tried men's souls' are over – and the greatest and completest revolution the world ever knew, gloriously and happily accomplished.   TOM PAINE. *The Crisis*

I was dragged into the unhappy affair of America; advantage was taken of my youth.   KING LOUIS XVI

> So it goes, it goes, it goes!
> Aristocrats, string 'em up!
> So it goes. . . .
> Aristocrats, they'll hang.
> Freedom, ours for ever,
> Spite of tyrants, so it goes.   Popular song

NOBLES

The castles which abound in our provinces and engorge large estates, misuse many rights of punting, fishing, woodcutting, and within them still lurk those proud seigneurs who so expertly detach themselves from common humanity, who pile their own taxes onto those of the King, and who all too easily oppress the impoverished and unhappy peasants, despite being no longer privileged to kill them, at the cost of a handful of silver strewn onto the grave.

The remainder of the nobility cluster round the throne, hands endlessly grasping for pensions and offices. They demand all for themselves – titles, jobs, exclusive preferments, forbidding ordinary folk promotion or reward, whatever their talents or public usefulness; they prevent them serving by land or sea, and for those of their own kind who shrink from actual work, they require bishoprics, abbacies and lucrative benefices.

LOUIS-SÉBASTIEN MERCIER. *Nouveau Tableau de Paris*

MONSEIGNEUR

Not many people had talked with him at the reception; he had stood in a little space apart, and Monseigneur might have been warmer in his manner. It appeared, under the circumstances, rather agreeable to him to see the common people dispersed before his horses, and often barely escaping from being run down. His man drove as if he were charging an enemy and the furious recklessness of the man brought no check into the face, or to the lips of the master. The complaint had sometimes made itself audible, even in that deaf city and dumb age, that, in the narrow streets without doorways, the fierce patrician custom of hard driving endangered and maimed the mere vulgar in a barbarous manner. But, few cared enough for that to think of it a second time, and, in this matter, as in all others, the common wretches were left to get out of their difficulties as they could.

With a wild rattle and clatter, and an inhuman abandonment of consideration not easy to be understood in these days, the carriage dashed through streets and swept round corners, with women screaming before it, and men clutching each other and clutching children out of its way. At last, swooping at a street corner by a fountain, one of its wheels came to a sickening little jolt, and there was a loud cry from a number of voices, and the horses reared and plunged.

But for the latter inconvenience, the carriage probably would not have stopped; carriages were often known to drive on, and leave their wounded behind, and why not? But the frightened valet had got down in a hurry, and there were twenty hands at the horses' bridles.

'What has gone wrong?' said Monsieur, calmly looking out. A tall man in a nightcap had caught up a bundle from among the feet of the horses, and had laid it on the basement of the fountain, and was down in the mud and wet, howling over it like a wild animal.

'Pardon, Monsieur the Marquis,' said a ragged and submissive man, 'it is a child.'

'Why does he make that abominable noise? Is it his child?'

'Excuse me, Monsieur the Marquis – it is a pity – yes.' The fountain was a little removed; for the street opened, where it was, for a space some ten or twelve yards square. As the tall man suddenly got up from the ground, and came running at the carriage, Monsieur the Marquis clapped his hand for an instant on his sword-hilt.

'Killed!' shrieked the man, in wild desperation, extending both arms at their length above his head, and staring at him. 'Dead!'

The people closed around, and looked at Monsieur the Marquis. There was nothing revealed by the many eyes that looked at him but watchfulness and eagerness; there was no visible menacing or anger. Neither did the people say anything; after the first cry, they had been silent, and they remained so. The voice of the submissive man who had spoken, was flat and tame in its extreme submission. Monsieur the Marquis ran his eyes over them all, as if they had been mere rats come out of their holes.

He took out his purse.

'It is extraordinary to me,' said he, 'that you people cannot take care of yourselves and your children. One or the other of you is for ever in the way. How do I know what injury you have done my horses?'   CHARLES DICKENS. *A Tale of Two Cities*, 1859

A MANIA AT VERSAILLES

We are in a tumult of feasts, delights and all manner of entertainments. We are always busy, always hurrying. We never have time to do all arranged for us. This giddy existence suits the Count de Haga very well. It does not suit myself nearly so well and I am left worn-out. We have already had a grand opera at Versailles and a State Ball, not to mention very many dinners and suppers. Tomorrow there is a feast in the queen's large garden at Trianon. This will be the last, but there remain many suppers and sights in Paris. We miss none of them, and would prefer to go without drink, food and sleep than to ignore any spectacle from the start to the very end. It is a mania!

COUNT AXEL VON FERSEN, the Queen's intimate friend, to his father

APPLAUSE

Glance at Beaumarchais' *Mariage de Figaro*; which now, after difficulty enough, has issued on the stage; and 'runs its hundred nights', to the admiration of all men. By what virtue or internal vigour it so ran, the reader of our day will rather wonder: – and indeed will know so much the better that it flattered some pruriency of the time; that it spoke what all were feeling, and longing to speak. Small substance in that *Figaro*: thin wiredrawn intrigues, thin wiredrawn sentiments and sarcasms; a thing lean, barren; yet which winds and whisks itself, as through a wholly mad universe, adroitly, with a high-sniffing air: wherein each, as was hinted, which is the grand secret, may see some image of himself, and of his own state and ways. So it runs its hundred nights, and all France runs with it; laughing applause. If the soliloquising Barber ask: 'What has your lordship done to earn all this?' and can only answer: 'You took the trouble to be born', all men must laugh: and a gay horse-racing Anglomaniac Noblesse loudest of all.   THOMAS CARLYLE, 1837

MADNESS

There is only one thing more crazy than my play, and that is its success.

PIERRE-AUGUSTIN CARON DE BEAUMARCHAIS, on *The Marriage of Figaro*

The 'revolutionary' message of *Le Mariage de Figaro*, if it exists, went unnoticed in pre-revolutionary France. Is not the play's refrain a formula for political quietism: 'Everything finishes with a song'? Beaumarchais was a wealthy, ennobled man-on-the-make like Voltaire, and he devoted much of his fortune to re-editing Voltaire's works.   ROBERT DARNTON, 1976

Much of Beaumarchais' fortune was made from supplying arms and general equipment to America during the revolutionary war with England.

SCHOOL REPORT

Reserved and diligent, he prefers study to any kind of conversation, and nourishes his mind on good authors. He is taciturn, with a love of solitude; is moody, overbearing and extremely egotistical. Though he speaks little, his replies are decisive and to the point, and he excels in argument. Much self-love and boundless ambition.

The Paris Cadet School, on Napoleon Bonaparte

THE YOUTH

The instinctive weapon of the bourgeois, the reading and writing class, is the book. Whenever he is in a state of danger or hope he starts furiously to write. So Napoleon, the typical and perfect bourgeois hero, spent these excited years in a furious autodidacticism. He read and tried to memorize a mass of uncoordinated stuff outside his military studies (which suffered from the competition) about Plato, the history of England, of Tartary, of Persia, of Egypt, China, Peru, the Incas, the Popes, everything. There is extant a whole series of copybooks containing Napoleon's notes, penned in an almost illegible handwriting. The contents of these reprinted fill almost four hundred pages. Here we find a map of the Saxon Heptarchy with a list of the kings for three centuries; the varieties of foot-races in ancient Crete; lists of the Hellenic fortresses in Asia Minor; the dates of twenty-seven caliphs, with a note on the strengths of their cavalry and an account of the misconduct of their wives. His miscellany is so scattered that there is even a note on the situation and climate of St Helena.

In such a ragbag anyone can find pretty much what he wants to make coincidences. All we need trouble to see is the deep colouring in the two predominant tastes of the day; the attraction of two book worlds, Plutarch's Greece and Rome, where everyone lived in heroic anecdotings, and the East of the Arabian Nights. Both moulded his imagination. The rest was mostly waste of time.

WILLIAM BOLITHO, 1929

ALTERNATIVES

Be my brother, or I'll murder you!

NICHOLAS-SÉBASTIEN ROCH DE CHAMFORT, on reading a popular graffito: *Fraternity or Death*

Whoever was not alive in the years before 1789 does not realise what the delights of life really are.   CHARLES MAURICE DE TALLEYRAND

THE SOUL

He would swap his soul for a heap of dung – and he would be right to do so.   COMTE DE MIRABEAU, on Talleyrand, Bishop of Autun

AN ATTACK

Where a man's native land gives him nothing, he in return owes it nothing, for duties are reciprocal. A man of feeling will swiftly abandon a country which tolerates despotism. If he cannot depart, he will feel personal degradation. Justice, of course, recognises no such principle as treason, under despotism, because a slave can neither owe anything nor be owed anything. It is impossible to break laws and regulations under a government whose nature consists of not possessing either of these.

Duty, self-interest, honour, demand resistance to arbitrary authority, even the dethronement of its wielder: the abuse of power may destroy liberty if no other means emerges to rescue it.

COMTE DE MIRABEAU. L'Essai sur le despotisme

REPARTEE

QUEEN MARIE ANTOINETTE: Do you realise, Monsieur de Chamfort, you have given pleasure to everyone at Versailles, I will not say by your wit but in spite of it?

NICHOLAS-SÉBASTIEN ROCH DE CHAMFORT: That's an easy matter to answer. At Versailles I resign myself to learning much of what I already know from people quite ignorant of it.

THE DIAMOND NECKLACE

Madame,

We are filled with happiness and venture to think that the last arrangements proposed to us, which we have performed with zeal and respect, are a further proof of our submission and devotion to Your Majesty's order, and we have genuine satisfaction in thinking that the most beautiful set of diamonds now existing will belong to the greatest and best of queens.

BASSENGE, Court Jeweller, to Queen Marie Antoinette

By forgery and imposture, the Cardinal de Rohan was persuaded into believing that the Queen wished him to stand security for the 1,600,000 livres needed by her to purchase a necklace intended for Madame du Barry by the late Louis XV, then purchase it for her. The subsequent exposure, punishment and scandal roused sympathy for the Cardinal and more unpopularity for the guiltless Queen.

Fools, that expect your verdant Millennium, and nothing but Love and Abundance, brooks running wine, winds whispering music, –

with the whole ground and basis of your existence champed into a mud of Sensuality; which, daily growing deeper, will soon have no bottom but the Abyss! Or consider that unutterable business of the Diamond Necklace. Red-hatted Cardinal Louis de Rohan; Sicilian jail-bird Balsamo Cagliostro; Milliner Dame de Lamotte, 'with a face of "some piquancy" '; the highest Church Dignitaries waltzing, in Walpurgis Dance, with quack-prophets, pickpurses and public women; – a whole Satan's Invisible World displayed; working there continually under the daylight visible one; the smoke of its torment going up for ever! The Throne has been brought into scandalous collision with the Treadmill. Astonished Europe rings with the mystery for ten months; sees only lie unfold itself from lie; corruption among the lofty and the low, gulosity, credulity, imbecility, strength nowhere but in the hunger. Weep, fair queen, thy first tears of unmixed wickedness! Thy fair name has been tarnished by foul breath; irremediably while life lasts. No more shalt thou be loved and pitied by living hearts, till a new generation has been born, and thy own heart lies cold, cured of all its sorrows.   THOMAS CARLYLE, 1837

Now the carefree, happy days were over, they would never come back. Goodbye now to those quiet and informal vacations at her beloved Trianon; eternal goodbye to those sparkling fêtes and galas that exhibited a showcase of all the dazzling splendours, flashing witticisms, the exquisite *ton* of the French Court. More even than this: goodbye for ever to respect and reverence for monarchy itself.

MADAME CAMPAN. *Mémoires de Marie Antoinette*, 1823

THE BASTILLE

Then shame to manhood, and opprobrious more
To France than all her losses and defeats
Old or of later date, by sea or land
Which God avenged on Pharaoh – the Bastille.
Ye horrid towers, the abode of broken hearts,
Ye dungeons and ye cages of despair. . . .
There's not an English heart that would not leap
To hear that ye were fallen at last, to know
That even our enemies, so oft employed
In forging chains for us, themselves were free.

WILLIAM COWPER. *The Task*

HARE, HOUND, AND HUNTER

Caesar, well-known pointer dog,
Boasted feats beyond compare.
Once he caught in woodland lair
A hare – with fear agog.
'Give in' he called, voice a-thunder,
Ruffling far-off forest birds,
'My name fills all the world with wonder.'
At this command our Jacky Hare,
Commending soul to God's good care,
Begs a word of how he'll fare.
'Your Much Respected Doggie Beast,
If I submit, is it really best?'
'Death, of course.' 'Indeed' said childlike Hare,
'But if to flee I should suggest?'
'Death, I repeat.' Caesar was impressed.
'Then, will you amnesty me,
Your so-beloved Majesty?
But, if it's Death what'er I choose,
Why, I must run. Nothing left to lose.'
On this, the brushwood champion flies,
He's innocent, whatever stern Cato said.
A hunter spots an easy prize,
Aims, shoots – but who falls dead:
The dog! What moral now would Fontaine advise?
'The Lord helps him who helps himself.'
And I respect that myself.   NAPOLEON BONAPARTE

THE PRESS

The intercourse of the French with the Americans whose manners
and opinions could not but have influence, have brought them nearer
to the English that they had ever been before. The almost
unrestrained introduction of our daily publications (tolerated indeed
by the Government from the conviction of the impossibility of pre-
venting it) having attracted the attention of the people more towards
the freedom and advantages of our constitution, has also infused into

them a spirit of discussion of public matters which did not exist
before.   DANIEL HAILES, to Lord Carmarthen

THE KING AT VERSAILLES

Sunday being the best day in the week for seeing Versailles, Mr
Broussonet accompanied me thither. The road was crowded with all
kinds of carriages, and those carriages with Chevaliers de St Louis.
We saw the royal family go to chapel, with young maids of honour
painted of a rose colour, and the old ones crimson. We saw the crowd
adoring their grand monarque, little thinking how soon this adoration would cease. The King's countenance seemed agreeable and
benignant, by no means vacant; his ears, which his hair never covered, were remarkably large and ugly, and he walked ill. He had
some very fine diamonds in his hat.   SIR JAMES EDWARD SMITH. *Letters*

ROYAL APPETITE

His Majesty's physical make-up demands a lot of exercise. Endowed
with exceptional strength, he balances this with his relish for food.
Here is an average breakfast menu. At six, the King leaves his bed and
inquires about breakfast. 'Sire, there is a plump fowl and chops.'
   'It would be simple to poach eggs in meat juices as well.' The
King attends to the cooking, devours four chops, the plump chicken,
the six eggs in meat juice with a cut of ham and swallows a bottle and a
half of champagne; he dresses, departs for the hunt, comes back with
a hunger unbelievable.

M. F. A. DE LESCURE (ed.). *Correspondence secrète inédite sur Louis XVI, et
Marie Antoinette, La Cour et La Ville de 1777 à 1792*, 1866

AT MONTAUBAN

The poor people seem poor indeed; the children terribly ragged, if
possible worse clad than if with no clothes at all; as to shoes and stockings they are luxuries. A beautiful girl of six or seven years playing
with a stick, and smiling under such a bundle of rags as made my heart
ache to see her: they did not beg, and when I gave them anything
seemed more surprised than obliged. One-third of what I have seen
in this province seems uncultivated, and nearly all of it in misery.

ARTHUR YOUNG

AN ENGLISH VIEW

One opinion pervaded the whole company, that they are on the eve of some great revolution in the government; that everything points to it; the confusion in the finances great; with a *deficit* impossible to provide for without the States-General of the kingdom, yet no ideas formed of what would be the consequence of their meeting; no minister existing, or to be looked to in or out of power, with such decisive talents as to promise any other remedy than palliative ones; a prince on the throne with excellent dispositions, but without the resources of a mind that could govern in such a moment without ministers; a court buried in pleasure and dissipation, and adding to the distress, instead of endeavouring to be placed in a more independent situation; a great ferment amongst all ranks of men, who are eager for some change, without knowing what to look for, or to hope for; a strong leaven of liberty, increasing every hour since the American Revolution; altogether form a combination of circumstances that promise e'er long to ferment into motion, if some master hand, of very superior talents and inflexible courage, is not found, at the helm to guide events, instead of being driven by them.   ARTHUR YOUNG

IN THE PROVINCES

My ambition is only the hope that one day I may live, in the country, the ordinary country life, with a wife and children, with books for my spare time, and for the rest, time to spare for the poor among my neighbours.   LOUIS ANTOINE DE SAINT-JUST, to Augustin Lejeune, at Rheims

I believe that some extraordinary event is likely to occur.
                    ANTOINE JOSEPH BARNAVE, at Grenoble. *Diary*

WITHIN VERSAILLES

The ceremony of the king's dining in public is more odd than splendid. The queen sat by him with a cover before her, but ate nothing; conversing with the Duke of Orleans and the Duke of Liancourt, who stood behind her chair. To me it would have been a most uncomfortable meal, and were I sovereign I would sweep away three-fourths of those stupid forms; if kings do not dine like other people, they lose much of the pleasure of life; their station is very well calculated to deprive them of much, and they submit to non-sensical customs, the sole tendency of which is to lessen the remainder.

The whole palace, except the chapel, seems to be open to all the world; we pushed through an amazing crowd of all sorts of people to see the procession. Many of them not very well dressed, whence it appears that no questions are asked. But the officers at the door of the apartment in which the king dined made a distinction, and would not permit all to enter promiscuously.

Travellers speak much, even very late ones, of the remarkable interest the French take in all that personally concerns their king, showing by the eagerness of their attention not curiosity only, but love. Where, how, and in whom these gentlemen discovered this, I know not. It is either misrepresentation, or the people are changed in a few years more than is credible.   ARTHUR YOUNG

THE POET

Believe me, youthful, lovely Ophélie,
Say the World what it will of it
Despite thy mirror, keep always thy modesty,
Content with thy beauty, yet unaware of it,
Always fear the power of thy charms;
Being only more loved if thou fearest not to be so.

MAXIMILIEN ROBESPIERRE, to an unknown lady of Arras

LAMPOON ON LOUIS XVI

While he was only a fool,
'Forgive the fool,' we said,
But now he seeks tyrannical rule
Let's bash him on the head.

ECONOMICS

Gentlemen, you understand that the King's expenditure cannot be governed by his revenue; his revenue must be governed by his expenditure.

COMTE D'ARTOIS, brother of King Louis XVI (later King Charles X)

A PLACARD IN PARIS

Palace for Sale. Ministers to be Hanged. Crown to be Given Away.

A THREAT

When it becomes essential to assail despotism because of its treachery or tyranny, I shall strike with all my strength fortified by my past restraint and the advice I have vainly tendered.

COMTE DE MIRABEAU, to Duc de Lauzun

LOYALTY

The glory of achieving for us the treasures of prosperity, of adorning your reign with all the glitter and delight of luxury – this, which seems to vulgar politicians the most admirable masterpiece of human wisdom, is scarcely the most important part of the mission entrusted to you by Providence and by your own soul. To guide humanity to happiness by Virtue, and to Virtue by laws established on eternal principles of universal morality, is even greater. Witness, under the impressive show of luxury and sham, prosperity which dazzles civil servants devoid of Civic Virtue, the huge fortunes of a few rising from the ruin and misery of all others.

MAXIMILIEN ROBESPIERRE, a memorial for King Louis XVI

A LESSON

You read a lot, sire, and know more than is generally thought. But, unless coupled with reflexion, reading is useless. Recently I re-read the chapter on Charles I in David Hume's *History of England*. Read it again, and consider it. That ruler was gentle, virtuous, ardent believer in the Law, a stranger to cruelty and adventurousness; yet he perished on the scaffold. I believe the cause of it was this. He reached the throne when dispute had arisen between the rights of the Crown and those of the nation as a whole. Had he surrendered his own, he would have been thought contemptible by those who from traditional habit and from benefits which they brought to the aristocracy, regarded them as sacred. Nevertheless, he was also the weaker party during that conflict, when new concessions were extracted from him on all sides. Had he lived fifty years previously, his good qualities would have rendered him an ideal monarch, and, fifty years later, when the opposing rights had been finally settled, he would have accepted them, for a reign lengthy and happy. You are in the same position. The conflict is between the former traditions of government, and the new popular demands! . . . Our own ways of being are gentler, and will protect you against the excesses of our ancestors. But many of your own rights will be slowly filched from you. Your onus is, when in Council, to establish a thoroughly worked-out plan as to what you will surrender, for the common benefit, and what you will never surrender. For its success, your firmness alone may be the deciding factor. Without that, from yourself, all is totally unpredictable. I can guarantee that matters will scarcely reach the degree which they did under Charles I; but I cannot guarantee the lack of certain other excesses. You must concentrate on repulsing them.

M. DE MALESHERBES, Minister, to King Louis XVI

FINANCE

By succeeding in rendering America free, France has so exhausted herself that in her triumph, having sought to humiliate English pride, she has ruined herself and now sees her finances exhausted, her credit diminished, the Ministry divided and the whole Kingdom in faction.

J. F. H. OLDENCOP, Russian Consul in Amsterdam, 1788

FOOD

Requisitioning, compulsory sale of food, and the fixing of maximum prices – all these were used by the *ancien régime*, which gave the Revolution many of its practices; all the Revolution added to those was a cruelty entirely of its own character. ALEXIS DE TOCQUEVILLE, 1855

ON THE VIRGIN MARY

We cannot expect too much of her. She was, when all's said and done, no more than a Nazareth bourgeoise. It was through marriage that she became part of the dynasty of David.

Maréchal de Noailles, in old age

THE REVOLUTION

IMPORTANT DATES OF THE REVOLUTION

1789	April	Riots in Paris and throughout France, after the bad harvest and severe winter.
	May 5	Meeting of the Estates General, which, by June, was calling itself the National Constituent Assembly.
	July 14	The Bastille falls.
	August 4	The formal abolition of Feudalism.
	October 5	Paris women march on Versailles and bring the Royal Family to Paris.
1790	July 12	Civil Constitution of the Clergy nationalises the French church, abolishes Papal authority, makes priests paid State officials, 'non-jurors' liable to deprivation of civic rights, even to death.
1791	April 2	Death of Mirabeau.
	June 20	The Flight to Varennes.
	July 17	The Massacre of the Champ de Mars.
	September 14	Louis XVI signs the Constitution of '91.
	October 1	The Legislative Assembly. Girondins dominant. Girondin deputies, Guadet and Isnard, propose introduction of the death penalty for political crimes.
1792	April 20	France declares war on Austria.
	June 29	Lafayette's proposal to close the Jacobin Club.
	July 25	The Brunswick Manifesto.
	July 29	Prussia declares war on France.
	August 9	Paris Commune becomes wholly republican, dominated by Jacobins.
	August 10	Paris crowds invade the Tuileries. Louis XVI suspended.
	August 19	Lafayette flees abroad.
	September 2–6	Prison massacres in Paris.
	September 20	French victory at Valmy over Prussians and Austrians, Dumouriez in command. The Convention replaces the Legislative Assembly.

	September 21	The Republic proclaimed. Girondins prominent.
	November 6	French victory at Jemmapes secures Belgium.
	December 11	The King examined, for start of formal trial.
1793	January 21	Execution of Louis XVI.
	February 1	France declares war on England and Holland. Food riots.
	March 1	Belgian revolt against French occupation.
	March 7	France declares war on Spain.
	March 9	Representatives on Mission despatched from Paris to restore order in the provinces and watch generals in the field.
	March 10	The Revolutionary Tribunal.
	March 10	Rebellion in La Vendée.
	March 18	Dumouriez loses Neerwinden, in Holland.
	April 4	Dumouriez fails to rouse his troops against Paris and deserts to Austrians.
	April 6	The Committee of Public Safety.
	April 13	Marat impeached and acquitted.
	June 2	Fall of the Girondins.
	July 17	Last feudal rights abolished.
	October 31	Girondin leaders executed.
1794	March 24	Hébert, Commune leader, executed.
	April 6	Dantonists executed.
	July 27	Overthrow of Robespierre Thermidor).
	July 28	Robespierre, Saint-Just and Couthon executed.
1795	November 3	The Directory. Jacobin Club closed.
1796		Napoleon's Italian Campaign. The Babeuf Plot of 'The Equals'.
1799	November 9	Brumaire. Napoleon becomes First Consul.

It is very easy to draft on paper great changes or great innovations, for paper makes no resistance, and it is much easier to write books than to govern men.   MADAME DE SABRAN

HUNGER

It is as though the Destroying Angel has visited the entire kingdom. Every scourge has been unleashed. Wherever I go, men can be seen dead of cold and hunger, for lack of flour even where wheat is plentiful. All mills are frozen.

COMTE DE MIRABEAU, in Provence, to the Marquis de Mirabeau

If you do not contribute to taxes in proportion to your property, what is it that you do give to the State in return for what it gives you, the security and laws that safeguard you?

MAÎTRE PASCALIS. *Memorandum to the French Nobility and Clergy, the First and Second Estates*

Never in my life have I seen a nobility more ignorant, more greedy and more insolent.   COMTE DE MIRABEAU

A PROPHET

Remember, my friend, what I am about to tell you. Everything in France is indeed going to change. Before long, poor Languillette, whom the de Fosseux despise, will be able to take well-earned retirement. The Languillettes will indeed become mayors, and the mayors will become Languillettes.

MAXIMILIEN ROBESPIERRE, to Languillette, an Arras cobbler waiting at table

A nobleman, Ferdinand de Fosseux, joked that Languillette could now expect to become Mayor of Arras. This indeed somewhat happened, when the Jacobin Representative on Mission had the Mayor guillotined, appointed de Fosseux in his place, but gave the dead man's house to Languillette.

EXHILARATION

You really can have no idea of the variety of people who regularly collect at the Palais Royal. The sight is truly amazing. I witnessed the circus; visited five or six cafés, and a Molière comedy itself would have rendered scant justice to the extraordinary difference of scenes I encountered. Here a man drafts reform of the constitution, there a

man reads aloud his own pamphlet; at another table someone is casti-
gating a minister; everyone is busy talking, each with his own attentive audience. I was there almost ten hours. The streets swarm with
young men and girls. Bookshops are dense with people browsing
through books and pamphlets.   MARQUIS DE FERRIÈRES, private letter

AN AMERICAN

Your Nation is now in a most important crisis, and the great question,
shall we hereafter have a Constitution or shall Will continue to be
Law, employs every mind and agitates every Heart in France. Even
Voluptuousness itself rises from its Couch of Roses and looks anx-
iously abroad at the busy scene to which nothing can now be indifferent. Your Nobles, your Clergy, your People are all in motion for the
Elections. A Spirit which has lain dormant for generations starts up
and stares about, ignorant of the means of obtaining, but ardently
desirous to possess its object. Consequently active energetic, easily
led, but also easily, too easily misled. Such is the instinctive Love of
Freedom which now boils in the Bosom of your country. That respect
for his Sovereign which forms the distinctive Mark of a Frenchman,
stimulates and fortifies on the present Occasion those sentiments
which have hitherto been deemed most hostile to Monarchy: for
Louis the Sixteenth has himself proclaimed from the Throne a Wish
that every Barrier should be thrown down which Time or accident
may have opposed to the general felicity of his People.

GOUVERNEUR MORRIS, to Comte de Moustier,
French Minister to the United States

*Morris was to be American Minister to France, 1792–4, following Thomas
Jefferson and Benjamin Franklin. He was also an eccentric speller.*

He is an American, a gentlemanlike, sensible man of property and
estimation in America. He was concerned in the line of finance during the war. He has only one leg, having been obliged to undergo an
amputation in consequence of jumping from a window in an affair of
gallantry.   HENRY TEMPLE, second Viscount Palmerston

APPREHENSIONS

The Materials for a Revolution in this Country are very different. Every Body agrees that there is an utter Prostration of Morals but this general Position can never convey to an American Mind the Degree of Depravity. It is not by any Figure of Rhetoric or Force of Language that the Idea can be communicated. An hundred Anecdotes and an hundred thousand Examples are required to show the extreme Rottenness of every Member. There are Men and Women who are greatly and eminently Virtuous. I have the Pleasure to number Many in my own Acquaintance but they stand forword from a background deeply and darkly shaded. It is however from such Crumbling Matter that the great Edifice of Freedom is to be erected here. Perhaps like the Stratum of Rock which is spread under the whole Surface of their Country it May harden when exposed to the Air, but it seems quite as likely that it will fall and crush the Builders. I own to you that I am not without such apprehensions for their is one fatel Principle which pervades all Ranks. It is a perfect Indifference to the Violation of Engagements. Inconstancy is so mingled in the Blood, Marrow and every Essence of this People that when a Man of high Rank and Importance laughs to Day at what he seriously asserted Yesterday, it is considered as in the natural Order of Things.

GOUVERNEUR MORRIS, to George Washington

WRITERS

Where does so much mad agitation come from? From a crowd of minor clerks and lawyers, from unknown writers, starving scribblers who go about rabble-rousing in clubs and cafés. These are the hot-beds that have forged the weapons with which the masses are armed today.   P. J. B. GERBIER

(For a suggestive essay on this, see Robert Darnton, in French Society and the Revolution, ed. Douglas Johnson.)

In this world nothing can be said to be certain, except death and taxes.

BENJAMIN FRANKLIN, to Jean-Baptiste Le Roy

BEGGARS OF PARIS

I believe your Apprehensions as to the Suffering of People here from Cold are not unfounded. But they have in that Respect, an Advantage which you did not think of, viz that they are stowed so close and in such little Cabins that if they live thro the first Five minutes they have an Atmosphere of their own about them. In Effect none of the Beggars I have seen complain to me of Cold. They all ask me for the Means to get a Morsel of Bread, and shew by their Countenances that by the Word Bread they mean Wine. And if the Vintners were to interpret this last Word the poor devils would find that it means a very different Liquor. Among the numerous Objects which present themselves doubtless some are deserving of Charity but these are scarcely to be noticed in the Crowd of Pretenders. However, they get from me all my small Change and I must confess to my Shame that I give rather for Peace' Sake than from Benefolence. The Rascals have, I suppose, found out by studying human Nature, that each Man loves himself better than his Neighbour, and therefore make it his Interest to give. The Rich in Return, as Patrons of Industry are vastly inattentive to those Importunities, and by withholding their Alms try to make it the Interest of the others to work rather than to beg. The Effects of Habit on each are wonderful. Not long since I saw a Gentleman of my Acquaintance weep at an Air of an Opera who had heard a beggar clatter his Crutches in Pursuit of him for the length of a Street without turning round to look at him. 'Tis true there is a difference in the Music.   GOUVERNEUR MORRIS, to his brother

ONLY TWELVE PRINCIPLES

The more I reflect on social abuses and the suggested remedies, the more I am convinced that it requires no more than twelve principles expressed in twelve lines, firmly fixed in the head of the ruler or his minister, and enforced in detail, to set everything to rights and restore the age of Solomon.

A week's discussion will solve the problem of bankruptcy.

Keep silent. The silence of the People is the education of Kings.

To the Estates General, advising how the King should be greeted

Let us be careful especially of book learning. Let us ignore what they did in the past and seek only what we should do now.

What have I done that was so blameworthy? I wanted my own Order to be wise enough to give away today what will unquestionably be taken from it tomorrow. . . .

I am far more blameworthy than is generally realised, for I believe that when the people complain they are invariably right, that their unflagging patience endlessly waits for the very last twist of the oppressor's screw before deciding ro resist . . . they do not understand that to make themselves a power in the land they have only to refuse to lend their hands to anything. . . .

Woe to the privileged Orders, for privileges will come to an end but the people are endless.   COMTE DE MIRABEAU

THE ESTATES GENERAL CONVOKED

No doubt it was to hand over to the most heroic virtues a country worthy of them that Providence decreed the existence of republics; and perhaps it was to punish ambition that it allowed the formation of mighty empires, the existence of kings and lords.

What is the inviolate privilege of the third Estate? That of the majority over the minority, for in proportion to the Nobility and the Clergy it exists as a hundred thousand to one. That of productive toil on lands otherwise fruitless, for without industrious hands the earth would be but a wild planet, never an organised society. That of very antiquity, since the plough existed before the escutcheon, the shepherd's crook before the crozier, workshops before lawcourts, traders before bankers, simple farmers before tax-farmers, the unprivileged before all those who now flaunt privileges, through royal favour.

COMTE DE LAUNAY D'ANTRAIGUES. *Memorandum sur les Etats Généraux*

The day I have been eagerly anticipating has finally come, and I find myself in the midst of the representatives of the Nation which it is my glory to rule. . . .

A general restlessness and an exaggerated desire for change have captured men's minds and would end by leading public opinion utterly astray were they not to be given proper direction by your wisdom and moderation. . . .

I appeal to the sentiments of a generous people whose love for its kings has always been its most obvious characteristic.

KING LOUIS XVI, to the Estates General

THE GREAT FEAR

The summer of 1789 began with an attack of cosmic fear. Men lay sleepless in their homes, a great red star was seen over the house, the will-o'-the-wisp danced in the marsh, shadows glided across the stream, the thatch rustled, church bells sounded without hands, the organ without warning played by itself after dark, doors flew open and banged again, though no draught was felt. A horseman galloped through the village at midnight, aroused the Mayor and summoned him to awake and arm all peasants, because three thousand brigands were approaching on the high road. In Brittany, the Dordogne Valley, the Alps, along the Mediterranean – everywhere gangs of brigands were reported. People said they were armed, ready to murder all, fire the villages, the crops, the cattle. Who were these murderous brutes? Where did they come from, who had actually seen them? Tocsins clamoured, peasants grabbed scythes, cudgels, hunting-knives, and advanced under some sturdy leader against the marauders, only to return next morning without glimpsing the least sign of them. In Artois, everyone was preparing to flee, because fugitives from the coast brought news of English troops landing. In other places, scared people arrived in carriages with all their possessions, imagining themselves pursued by Imperial cavalry. Mostly, however, they were terrified of those bands of brigands, seen by none, known of by all. A chronicler stated, 'Such panic gripped people's minds that they abandoned their houses to depart at random without knowing where they were going. From Ruille a priest, between 4 pm to 9.30 this morning, was hearing confessions of those scared witless by expectation of imminent death.' On every road meandered peasant groups, wavering between courage and fear, with pikes, axes, other weapons, awaiting the enemy. Would he arrive from south or north? In one Périgord village they ordered a carpenter to make 200 spear shafts immediately. He complied, but no one came to take them. Elsewhere, unknown messengers exhorted people to go to gendarmeries and barracks and pick up arms, as the next door village had been sacked by brigands. Almost at once, all France was virtually in arms.   FRIEDRICH SIEBURG, 1936

WARNING

Sire, the people over whom you hold sway have given clear proofs of their patience. They are a people martyred, whose lives seem spared only for the sake of them suffering even more.

MGR DE LA FARE, Bishop of Nancy, preaching before King Louis XVI and Queen Marie Antoinette, following the death of their son the Dauphin

A MEETING OF THE ESTATES GENERAL

Go to Versailles and a little after eight get into the hall. Sit there in a cramped situation til after 12, during which time the different Members are brought in. . . . When M. Necker comes in he is loudly and repeatedly clapped and so is the Duke of Orleans, also a Bishop who has lived in his Diocese and practised there what his Profession enjoins. Another Bishop, who preached yesterday a Sermon which I did not hear, is applauded but those near me say that this Applause is unmerited. An old man who refused to dress in the Costume prescribed for the Tiers and who appears in his Farmer's Habit, receives a long and Loud Plaudit. M. de Mirabeau is hissed, tho not very loudly. The King at length arrives and takes his seat, the Queen on his left, two steps lower than him. He makes a short speech, very proper and well spoken, or rather read. The tone and manner have all the *fierté* which can be desired or expected from the Blood of the Bourbons. He is interrupted in the Reading by Acclamations so warm and of such lively Affection that the Tears start from my Eyes in Spite of myself. The Queen weeps or seems to weep but not one Voice is heard to wish her well. GOUVERNEUR MORRIS. *Diary*

It is my fate to bring misfortune.

QUEEN MARIE ANTOINETTE, to Count Mercy-Argenteau, Austrian ambassador

No National Assembly ever threatened to be so stormy as that which will decide the fate of the monarchy, and which is gathering such speed and with so much mutual distrust. COMTE DE MIRABEAU

A SPEECH IN THE ESTATES GENERAL

Since you are the representative of a religion founded on contempt for riches, why not follow in the steps of your divine Master? Why not abandon your display of luxury, which insults the poor? Your canonical laws allow you to sell your very altar vessels, but you need not go as far as that. But send packing your haughty lackeys, surrender your expensive carriages, strip yourselves of your ornate trappings and, in the manner of the early Christians, relieve poverty with the money thus obtained.

MAXIMILIEN ROBESPIERRE, to the Archbishop of Mainz

That young man [Robespierre] has insufficient experience; he does not know when to stop. But there is eloquence at the root of him. He won't remain just one of the herd.

M. REYBAZ, to Etienne Dumont, secretary to the Comte de Mirabeau

A ROYAL ORDER

Consider gentlemen, that none of your plans, none of your arrangements, have any legal validity without my seal of approval. To mistrust me would be grave injustice. It is I who, up to this moment, have been responsible for my people's well-being, and it is perhaps very unusual that a monarch's sole ambition should be to get his subjects to agree that they should finally agree to accept his gifts. . . . I now order you gentlemen, to separate immediately and go, each one of you, tomorrow morning, to the places assigned to your several Orders, to resume your sittings. I therefore command the Grand Master of Ceremonies to get ready the halls.

KING LOUIS XVI, to the Estates General

The Third Estate demanded equal rights and numbers with the Clergy and Nobility, to avoid being in a permanent minority and treated separately. Failing in this, they met alone in the Royal Tennis Court, ultimately declaring themselves the National Assembly, resolved to frame a Constitution.

Go and tell those who have sent you that we sit here by the will of the People, and that we shall not leave except by force of bayonets.

COMTE DE MIRABEAU, speaking for the Third Estate,
to Marquis de Dreux-Brézé, Master of Ceremonies

Only too frequently History records actions befitting those of wild beasts, among whom heroes are very rare: let us now hope that we are introducing the History of men.   COMTE DE MIRABEAU

MY CHILDREN

Really, when you come down to it, are not those of the Third Estate my children too? and there are more of them. And even when the nobles lose some of their privileges and the priests a bit of their income, will I be any less their King?

KING LOUIS XVI, to Queen Marie Antoinette

THE ESTATES GENERAL BECOMES
THE NATIONAL CONSTITUENT ASSEMBLY

It was necessary to rise early for a seat in the packed galleries. Deputies arrived eating, chattering, gesticulating, then, divided by their political views, grouping themselves in different parts of the hall. The day's order was announced, the motion chosen debated, or else an emergency motion. There was no feeble wrangle about legal niceties but almost always discussion about some plan to destroy something or other. Deputies rose for this side or that, all improvised according to their ability. Arguments became empassioned, the galleries adding applause, cheers, hoots and catcalls. The President jangled his bell while deputies yelled at each other from one bench to another. . . .

Once I was seated behind the royalist opposition; before us was a Dauphine nobleman, small, swarthy, who jumped up, wild with anger, declaiming to his associates: 'Let's settle with this *Canaille*, with our swords!' He pointed at the majority. Market ladies, knitting in the galleries, hearing him, rose, all shouting simultaneously, holding their stockings, actually foaming: 'Take them to the lanterns!'

The Vicomte de Mirabeau, Lautrec, and a few aristocratic youths suggested an attack on the galleries. This uproar, horror, was swiftly overwhelmed by another: petitioners, grasping pikes, were swarming to the bar.

'The People starve. We should now get to grips with this and hurl down the aristocrats.'

The President assured these citizens that he respected their views. 'We are watching all traitors, the Assembly will guarantee justice.' This renewed the uproar. . . .

Evening sessions outmatched the morning in violence and scandal: under candlelight people are more eloquent, more courageous. At night the Riding-hall really became a theatre for one of the world's most significant dramas. The chief performers were remnants of the *ancien régime*: their replacements, men of menace, concealed behind them, remained more or less mute. When one emerged debate concluded. I saw a deputy of vulgar appearance, grey, expressionless features, hair neatly dressed, respectably attired like a steward of a manor or a village notary attentive to his appearance. He read out a report, lengthy, tedious, to which nobody listened. I enquired who he was. Robespierre. Those with buckled shoes were ready to quit the salons. Now the clogs were kicking at the doors.

FRANÇOIS-RENÉ DE CHATEAUBRIAND. *Mémoires*, 1842

In the National Assembly, the debates continue to be carried on with increasing violence, and bid defiance to monarchy. M. de Mirabeau is the leader of the patriotic party. The few following expressions, which he made use of in the assembly of the States General, will tend to show the unlimited freedom of speech which prevails.

'No person on Earth,' says he, 'has the right to say in this assembly I WILL or I ORDER IT. The plenitude of legislative power rests here, and it would be folly for any member, or any individual whatever, to protest against the proceedings of a whole nation.'

The Times, London

ANOTHER WARNING

The danger, Sire, is urgent, it affects everything, it's beyond all calculations of human prudence. The danger is for those in the provinces. Once they are scared about our liberty, we do not know how best restrain them. Danger is also for the capital. How will the people, sunk in poverty and obsessed by the most cruel anxieties, regard the seizure of their last foodstocks by threatening troops of soldiers? The presence of the troops will cause unrest, riot, wholesale ferment, and the first occasion of violence on pretext of maintaining order may set in train dire evils.

The danger, Sire, threatens the hard work which is our prime responsibility and which can succeed fully and endurably only if the people recognise them as resolved in freedom. Moreover, passionate movements are contagious; we are but mortal, and do not regard ourselves as anything more; fear of appearing timid may allow us to exceed our brief, leaving us prey to violent and extreme exhortations, to obsessions: sweet reason and wise harmony deliver no oracles from tumult, disorder, rampant factionalism.

Some great revolutions of the past have had less spectacular origins; more than once a movement fatal to nations, fatal to kings, has been ushered in with outward signs less sinister and less powerful than that now showing itself.

The National Assembly, to King Louis XVI (probably from an original draft by the Comte de Mirabeau)

VERSAILLES

In the afternoon we walked in the parks, gardens and woods belonging to the Palace – a fine country but the grounds badly laid out. In these walks we saw many members of the Assembly, particularly of the Tiers-Etat in black gowns, conversing apparently with much earnestness. It reminded us of the Athenian groves filled with philosophers. Nor could we see the splendour of the Palace, nor witness the King and Queen going to Mass, gazed upon by such a mixed multitude, without adverting in thought to the peculiar situation of the country; nor could we behold the face of Marie Antoinette, and not see symptoms of no common anxiety marked on it. The dignity of countenance which, according to various descriptions, formed at an earlier period of her life a most interesting addition to those claims of natural beauty so profusely bestowed on her, might be said, indeed, to remain, but it had assumed more of the character of severity. The forehead was corrugated, the eyebrows thrown forward, and the eyes but little open, and, turning with seeming caution from side to side, discovered, instead of gaiety or even serenity, an expression of suspicion and care which necessarily abated much of that beauty for which she had once with truth been celebrated.

DR EDWARD RIGBY, of Norwich. *Letters from France*

A DEPUTY'S WARDROBE

A coat of black cloth, an embroidered coat of black velvet bought at a Paris old-clothes shop and re-dyed, a satin waistcoat, quite well-made, a faded waistcoat of Saint-Maur silk, a pair of black velvet breeches, a pair of black cloth breeches, a pair of serge breeches. All three pairs much the worse for wear. Two clothes-brushes, six shirts, six cravats, six handkerchiefs. Three pairs of silk stockings, one pair almost new. Two pairs of shoes, one pair new. A powder-bag with puff, a little hat, to carry under the arm, an advocate's gown, a box containing silk, thread, worsted, needles.

G. LENÔTRE, on Maximilien Robespierre

THE FUTURE LOUIS XVII

'My son is four years and four months old, less two days,' Marie Antoinette wrote to Mme de Tourzel. 'I will not speak of his build or appearance, for you have only to see him. His health has always been good, but even when he was in the cradle it was noticed that his nerves were very delicate and that the slightest unexpected noise affected him. He was late with his first teeth, but they came through without illness or accident. It was only with the last, and I think with the sixth, that he had a convulsion at Fontainebleau. He has had two since, one in the winter of '87 or '88 and the other after his inoculation, but the latter was very slight. As a result of his delicate nerves he is always frightened by any noise to which he is not accustomed, for example, he is frightened of dogs because he heard one bark near him. I have never forced him to see them because I think as he gains in reasoning power his fears will disappear. Like all strong, healthy children, he is very thoughtless, very frivolous and violent in his anger, but he is good-natured, gentle and even affectionate when he is not carried away by his thoughtlessness. He has an exaggerated sense of self-esteem which, by good guidance, might one day be turned to his advantage. Until he is at ease with anyone, he knows how to control himself and even conquer his impatience and anger so as to appear gentle and amiable. He keeps his word faithfully once he has given it, but he is very indiscreet and easily repeats what he has heard and often, without meaning to lie, he adds things suggested by his own imagination. This is his greatest fault and it must be firmly corrected.

Apart from that, I repeat, he is good-natured and by using kindness and firmness, but without being too severe, one can do what one likes with him, but severity would make him rebel, for he has a strong character for his age. For example, even when he was very small, the word "Pardon" always shocked him. He will do and say whatever one likes when he is in the wrong but he will pronounce the word "Pardon" only with great difficulty and many tears. My children have always been taught to have complete trust in me and when they have done wrong to tell me so themselves. By this means, when I scold them, I appear more hurt and sorry at what they have done than angry. I have accustomed them to accepting a yes or no from me as being irrevocable, but I always give them a reason suited to their age, so that they do not think it is merely a whim on my part. My son cannot read and has great difficulty in learning, but he is too scatter-brained to concentrate. He has no ideas of grandeur and I should wish that to continue. Our children learn only too quickly what they are.

'He is very fond of his sister and has a good heart. Every time something pleases him, like going somewhere, or if someone gives him something, his first impulse is to ask for the same thing for his sister. He was born gay. His health requires plenty of air and I think the best thing is to let him play and work outside on the terrace rather than take him farther. The exercise taken by little children as they run and play in the open air is much healthier for them than being made to take walks, which often tires their backs.'

MARIE ANTOINETTE, to Mme de Tourzel, on her appointment as Governess

DANGER

There was fear of a royal coup, by troops brought in from the provinces to subdue Paris.

Inform the King that the hordes of foreign soldiers filling our city were yesterday visited by the royal princes, princesses and favourites, were caressed and inflamed by them and given presents; inform him that all through the night these alien hangers-on, stuffed with gold and wine, foretold, in profane song, slavery for the French people, and brutally threatened to destroy the National Assembly itself. Inform him that in Versailles itself his courtiers pirouetted to that barbarian music, and this was an exact reminder of the prelude to the St Bartholomew Massacre.

COMTE DE MIRABEAU, to a deputation sent to King Louis XVI

DISPUTE IN THE NATIONAL ASSEMBLY

Of course, letters are sacrosanct, I am quite aware of that, I am convinced of that, but when an entire nation finds itself in peril, when conspiracies exist against Liberty, when respectable Citizens suffer persecution, then what in ordinary times is criminal becomes at another time praiseworthy.   MAXIMILIEN ROBESPIERRE

Let those vulgar politicians who set above common justice whatever in their narrow, scheming minds they term political security, let them at least inform us what we are likely to learn from shameful inquisition into other people's letters. Do they actually suppose that even political news of the slightest importance passes through that channel? There can be no possible use in violating family privacies, missives between people separated from each other, confidences exchanged between friends and our own confidence in each other. This last refuge of liberty has been shattered by the very people whom the nation delegated to preserve all its rights.

COMTE DE MIRABEAU

This debate followed the arrest of Baron de Castelnau, French Ambassador at Geneva, and the forced inspection of his mail. One letter was to the King's brother, Comte d'Artois. The Assembly sided with Mirabeau.

A COMING MAN

He was the first to sense the scope that the Revolution afforded for mass politics, to appreciate the nature of a political machine and the tactics by which a radical minority could impose itself on an indifferent or hostile electorate. To have grasped all this in 1789 implied a talent of a remarkable, if not perhaps a very elevated order. For better or worse, and on the whole for worse, the machine that Danton created was to play a large part in determining the shape of French politics during the Terror.

NORMAN HAMPSON, on Georges-Jacques Danton, 1978

A NAME, NOT AN EXISTENCE

The States General have now been a long Time in Session and have done Nothing. Hitherto they have been engaged in a Dispute whether they shall form one Body or three. The Commons (Tiers), who are represented by a Number equal to both the others and who besides have at least one half the Representatives of the Clergy, insist on forming a single House. They have succeeded, but the Nobles deeply feel their Situation. The King after siding with them was frightened into an Abandonment of them. He acts from Terror only. The soldiery in this City, particularly the French guards, declare they will not act against the People. They are now treated by the Nobility and parade about the Streets drunk, huzzaing for the *Tiers*. Some of them have in Consequence been confined, not by the Force but by the Adroitness of Authority. Last Night this Circumstance became known and immediately a Mob repaired to the prison. The Soldiers on Guard unfixed their Bayonets and joined the Assaillants. A Party of Dragoons, ordered on duty to disperse the Riot, thought it better to drink with the Rioters and return back to their quarters. The Soldiers, with others confined in the same Prison, were then paraded in Triumph to the palais Royal, which is now the Liberty Pole of this City, and there they celebrated as usual their Joy. Probably this Evening some other Prisons will be opened, for *Liberté* is now the general Cry and *Autorité* is a Name, not a real Existence.

The *Gardes du Corps* are as warm Adherents (in general) to the *Tiers* as any Body else, strange as that may seem, so that in Effect the Sword has slipped out of the Monarch's Hands without his perceiving a Tittle of the Matter.   GOUVERNEUR MORRIS, to John Jay

THE ARMY

The tumult occasioned by the Royal Sittings has produced a very great fermentation among the people. The French Guards at Paris, amounting to 4000 men, have refused to obey the King's orders, and declared themselves to be the SOLDIERS OF THE NATION. The DUC DE CHATELET, their Colonel, went to Versailles and assured the King, that he could not answer for his safety, if he continued to enforce the Royal Orders.   *The Times*, London

The defection of the Army was not one of the causes of the Revolution, it was the Revolution itself.

COMTE MIOT DE MELITO, quoted by T. C. W. Blanning, 1987

THE GOVERNOR

The Governor of this fortress, the Comte de Launay, had no great military knowledge, no experience, small courage. Once the disturbances began, he appealed to the army commanders and begged for garrison reinforcements, having only eight – four elderly men. This was refused, the high command sceptical about the revolt becoming very violent, and about any likely attempt on the Bastille. He made a second appeal. Finally I was despatched with thirty men to the Bastille, on July 7th. The next day I got to know the Governor, though his preparations for defence were all absolutely ludicrous: and it was plain to me, from his incessant nervousness and hesitation, that we would be helpless against attack. He was so scared that at night he imagined the shadows of trees and much else were enemies, thus forcing us to stand guard all night. Staff officers, the royal Lieutenant, the Adjutant and myself often reasoned with him, both to reassure him about the weakness of the garrison, about which he moaned everlastingly, and to get him to dismiss trivial matters and attend to essentials. He would listen, appear to accept our advice, then do the opposite, his entire behaviour showing his timidity.

LIEUTENANT DEFLUE, of the Sakis-Samade Swiss guards, to his brothers

BASTILLE DAY

I was halted by a citizen, who informed me of shot being issued at the Hôtel de Ville. So I hastened there and was handed a few buckshot pellets. I then proceeded to the Bastille, loading as I went. I was joined by a group also on its way to the Bastille. We found four infantry of the Watch, armed with guns, and I begged them to join us. They replied that they lacked powder and shot. So we joined in giving each enough for two shots. Thus armed, they were glad to accompany us. As we passed before the Hôtel de la Régie we observed that two cases of bullets had been smashed and the bullets were being freely dispersed. I filled one of my pockets to give some to anyone who was short.

JEAN BAPTISTE HUMBERT, watchmaker

THE FALL OF THE BASTILLE

And so it lashes and it roars. Cholat the wine-merchant has become an impromptu cannoneer. See Georget, of the Marine Service, fresh from Brest, ply the King of Siam's cannon. Singular (if we were not used to the like): Georget lay, last night, taking his ease at his inn; the King of Siam's cannon also lay, knowing nothing of *him*, for a hundred years. Yet now, at the right instant, they have got together and discourse eloquent music. For, hearing what was forward, Georget sprang from the Brest Diligence, and ran. Gardes Françaises also will be there, with real artillery: were not the walls so thick! – Upwards from the Esplanade, horizontally from all neighbouring roofs and windows, flashes one irregular deluge of musketry – without effect. The Invalides lie flat, firing comparatively at their ease from behind stone; hardly through portholes, show the tip of a nose. We fall, shot; and make no impression!

Let conflagration rage; of whatever is combustible! Guard rooms are burnt, Invalides mess-rooms. A distracted 'Perruke-maker with two fiery torches' is for burning 'the saltpetres of the Arsenal'; – had not a woman run screaming; had not a Patriot, with some tincture of Natural Philosophy, instantly struck the wind out of him (butt of musket on pit of stomach), overturned barrels, and stayed the devouring element. A young beautiful lady, seized escaping in those Outer Courts, and thought falsely to be de Launay's daughter, shall be burnt in de Launay's sight; she lies swooned on a paillasse: but again a Patriot, it is brave Aubin Bonnemère the old soldier, dashes in and rescues her. Straw is burnt; three cartloads of it, hauled thither, go up in white smoke: almost to the choking of Patriotism itself; so that Elie had, with singed brows, to drag back one cart; and Réole the 'gigantic haberdasher' another. Smoke as of Tophet; confusion as of Babel; noise as of the Crack of Doom.

Blood flows; the aliment of new madness. The wounded are carried into houses of the Rue Cerisaie; the dying leave their last mandate not to yield till the accursed stronghold fall. And yet, alas, how fall? The walls are so thick . . . What to do? The firemen are here, squirting with their fire-pumps on the Invalides' cannon, to wet the touchholes; they unfortunately cannot squirt so high; but produce only clouds of spray. Individuals of classical knowledge propose catapults. Santerre, the sonorous Brewer of the Suburb Saint-Antoine, advised rather that the place should be fired by a 'mixture of phosphorus and oil-of-turpentine spouted up through forcing-pumps': O Spinola-Santerre, hast thou the mixture *ready*? Every man his own engineer! And still the fire-deluge abates not; even women are firing, and Turks, at least one woman (with her sweetheart), and one Turk. Gardes Françaises have come: real cannon, real cannoneers. . . .

How the great Bastille Clock ticks (inaudible) in its Inner Court there, at its ease, hour after hour; as if nothing special, for it or the world, were passing! It tolled One when the firing began; and is now pointing towards Five, and still the firing slakes not. – Far down, in their vaults, the seven prisoners hear muffled din as if of earthquake; their turnkeys answer vaguely.   THOMAS CARLYLE, 1837

THE BASTILLE

The attack on the Bastille was partly to plunder it of its arms and gunpowder and capture its artillery. De Launay surrendered on promise of a safe conduct. The prisoners numbered seven: four forgers, an incestuous nobleman, and two lunatics, one of them 'God'.

The population of Paris has overwhelmed the Bastille and murdered the Governor, M. de Launay, in the most dreadful way. At the Invalides they captured 36,000 rifles. They hanged the provost of Merchants, M. de Flesselle. . . . The Comte d'Artois and his children, the Princes de Condé, Conti, Bourbon and many more, including Baron de Breteuil, have fled across the frontier, with false names. Nobody was permitted exit from Paris; turmoil, disorder, dismay on all sides.   COUNT AXEL VON FERSEN, to his father

We can form some idea of the social pattern of the gathering of 954 people who, June 1790, were given the title, Conqueror of the Bastille. The professions of 661 are established. Easily the majority were artisans; first, furniture-workers from Faubourg Saint-Antoine, 49 joiners, 48 cabinet-makers, 41 locksmiths, 9 specialists in ivory, and inlay, 11 engravers, 28 casual and unskilled jobbers, four of them confessing themselves from the unemployed. Next, 28 cobblers, 27 'carvers', 23 gauze workers, 14 vintners, 9 jewellers, 9 hatters, 9 nailsmiths, 9 monumental stone workers, 9 tailors, 9 dyers: all amounting to 332. But some bourgeois were also amongst them: 4 tradesmen, 3 factory owners, a brewer, the celebrated Santerre, 35 assorted merchants, 4 rentiers, financially independent; 80 soldiers, including officers; the remainder divided amongst professions of very different sorts. In age, the oldest was Cretaine, a Paris bourgeois, the youngest, Cavallée, a boy of 8, one of the first to ascend the towers. . . . We can say, perhaps, that if we add to the 332 artisans the 202 people from the varied professions, that five-sixths of the 'Conquerors', and doubtless of the mass surging beneath the Bastille walls, were artisans, masters of journeymen; the remaining sixth bourgeois. JACQUES GODECHOT, largely citing an article by George Rudé, 1965 (See also Rudé. *The Crowd in the French Revolution*)

FROM THE BRITISH EMBASSY

In the course of the same evening, the whole of the *Gardes Françoises* joined the Bourgeoisie with all their cannon, arms and ammunition: the Regiments that were encamped in the *Champ de Mars*, by an order from Government left the ground at 2 o'clock yesterday morning and fell back to Sêve, leaving all their camp equipage behind them; the magazines of powder and corn at the *École Militaire* were immediately taken possession of and a *Garde Bourgeoise* appointed to protect them. Nothing could exceed the regularity and good order with which all this extraordinary business has been conducted: of this I have myself been a witness upon several occasions during the last three days as I have passed through the streets, nor had I any reason to be alarmed for my personal safety. . . .

Earlier in this despatch, Lord Dorset had described the murder of de Launay and others 'with circumstances of barbarity too shocking to relate'.

The general wish now is that the King would come to Paris, and it was hoped yesterday that His Majesty would be induced to show Himself here on this day, but it is said that He is prevented coming by indisposition: it is thought difficult to foresee what measures the people will have recourse to: the general idea however is that an armed body of Citizens to the number of at least 50,000 will go to Versailles and forcibly bring the Sovereign to the Capital. The disposition of the people at this moment is so unfavourable to the Court that I should not be surprized if the States-General, by appearing to give too much credit to the King's professions, should lose the consideration in which they have hitherto been held by the Nation. . . .

Thus, My Lord, the greatest Revolution that we know anything of has been effected with, comparatively speaking, the loss of very few lives: from this moment we may consider France as a free country; the King a very limited Monarch, and the Nobility as reduced to a level with the rest of the Nation.

JOHN FREDERICK SACKVILLE, Duke of Dorset, Ambassador Extraordinary, 1783–9, to the Duke of Leeds

TEMPLE TO LIBERTY

Were it not that France is dishonoured by too many palaces, and that the Assembly needs no other memorial than the imperishable constitution which it has to propose to the Nation, I should beg that, on the place where the Bastille, until lately, insulted the rights of man, we should erect a building for the representatives of the Nation, inscribed with this alone:

Under Louis XVI, on the ruins of a State Prison, consecrated to the vengeance of Ministers, and destroyed by the People of Paris, the National Assembly of 1789 has raised this Temple to Liberty.

COMTE DE MIRABEAU. *Etats généraux*

THE AFTERMATH

What country before ever existed a century and a half without a rebellion? And what country can preserve its liberties if their rulers are not warned from time to time that their people preserve the spirit of resistance? Let them take arms. The remedy is to set them right as to facts, pardon and pacify them. What signify a few lives lost in a century or two? The tree of liberty must be refreshed from time to time with the blood of patriots and tyrants. It is its natural manure.

THOMAS JEFFERSON, American Minister in Paris

How much the greatest event it is that has ever happened, and how much the best! CHARLES JAMES FOX

I myself will be the French Washington.

MARQUIS DE LAFAYETTE, sending George Washington a key of the Bastille

Human nature is reborn. WILLIAM WORDSWORTH

Heard'st thou, yon universal cry,
   And dost thou linger still on Gallia's shore?
Go, Tyranny! beneath some barbarous sky
   Thy terrors lost and ruin'd power deplore!
   What tho' through many a groaning age
   Was felt thy keen suspicious rage,
   Yet Freedom rous'd by fierce Disdain
   Has wildly broke thy triple chain.
And like the storm which Earth's deep entrails hide,
At length has burst its way and spread the ruins wide.

S. T. COLERIDGE

LOUIS XVI, THE HUNTSMAN

Tuesday 7th: Stag hunt at Port Royal, killed two.
Wednesday 8th: Nothing.
Thursday 9th: Nothing. Deputation of the Estates.
Friday 10th: Nothing. Replied to the deputation of the Estates.
Saturday 11th: Nothing. Departure of M. Necker.
Sunday 12th: Vespers and *salut*. Departure of M. de Montmorin,
   Saint-Priest and La Luzerne.
Monday 13th: Nothing.
Tuesday 14th: Nothing.   *Diary*

This seems primarily a sporting diary, and too much should not be made of the entry for the 14th, the day the Bastille fell, an entry for which Louis has been mocked for two centuries (once, foolishly, by myself, 1960).

The Bastille emergency had a curious sporting by-product. By enforcing the cancellation of a cricket match arranged in Paris for that day, it prevented the introduction of the game into France almost to the present.

THE KING AND HIS PEOPLE

Louis XVI went to the Hôtel de Ville on July 17, received by a hundred thousand armed like the monkish adherents of the 16th Century League. He was lectured by M. M. Bailly, Moreau de Saint-Mery, and Lally-Tolendal, all weeping. . . . The King likewise surrendered to his emotions, adorning his hat with a huge tricolour cockade, and was immediately hailed as 'virtuous; Father of the French People,

King of a free people', a people which, by grace of its freedom, was preparing to slice off the head of that virtuous man, its father and king.

Several days after this reconciliation, I was with my sisters and some Bicton acquaintances at my Hotel windows when we heard yells, 'Bolt up, bolt all doors!' A gang of beggarly fellows emerged at the end of the street, in their midst two standards, indecipherable at this distance. As they approached we clearly distinguished two heads, tumbled, mutilated, which the heralds of Marat were bearing on pikes; the heads of the ministers, M. M. Foullon and Bertier. My companions all retreated, but I stayed fast. The killers drew up before me, singing, capering, leaping to bring the pallid heads nearer my own head. One eye in one head had been pushed from its socket and was dangling on the corpse's face, the pike sticking through the gaping mouth, the teeth clenched on the iron.

'Brigands!' I stormed, with an uncontainable fury, 'is this how you interpret Liberty?'   FRANÇOIS-RENÉ DE CHATEAUBRIAND. *Mémoires*, 1842

The King's weakness and indecision are incredible. Imagine ivory balls smeared with oil that you vainly strive to hold firm!
STANISLAUS XAVIER LOUIS, COMTE DE PROVENCE (later King Louis XVIII), brother of King Louis XVI

The next step that the new COMMONWEALTH of France, for it truly deserves that appellation, will probably take, is the establishment of TRIAL BY JURY, and, of course, a total abolition of priestcraft, Torture, and the Bastille.

There is very little doubt but the French King will, by degrees, attempt to regain that despotic sceptre which has been wrested from his hands, and that Germany will afford him every assistance. But, on the other hand, it is to be considered that the great body of the people are for the new systems – that every peasant in France is a soldier, and that the foreign troops would, in the end, meet with the fate of General Burgoyne at Saratoga in the year 1777, and of Lord Cornwallis at York Town in 1781.   *The Times*, London

PROVINCIAL TROUBLE

His Majesty understands that bands of brigands from all over the countryside are constantly tricking the people of various villages, convincing them that, while still conforming to the authority of His Majesty, they are entitled to attack the local château, rob the archives and commit other excesses against the homes and properties of their seigneurs, the Noblesse of the Realm. His Majesty finds Himself compelled to inform all that such violence excites his indignation.

He observes with profoundest sorrow the evils afflicting his Country, evils fermented some time ago by malicious people who state their wicked course by planting rumours utterly false around the countryside so as to provoke fear and incite ordinary people to seize arms. His Majesty suggests all loyal citizens should oppose in every way they can the continuance of an unrest which is becoming scandalous, a disgrace to the good name of France, being contrary, being completely at variance with the benevolence that informs the King and the delegates of the Nation in their Labours to promote the happiness and prosperity of the whole people.

Given by Our Hand at Versailles, August 9, 1789

Louis

Rumours of these brigands scared most of rural France that summer, though few of such rumours were grounded in any truth. There were, nevertheless, attacks on feudal lords' homes, and burning of title deeds.

SEDITION

The business going forward in the pamphlet shops of Paris is incredible. . . . Every hour produces something new. . . . This spirit of reading political tracts, they say, spreads into the provinces, so that all the presses of France are equally employed. Nineteen-twentieths of these productions are in favour of liberty, and commonly violently against the clergy and nobility. I have today bespoken many of this description that have reputation; but inquiring for such as had appeared on the other side of the question, to my astonishment, I find that there are but two or three that have merit enough to be known. Is it not wonderful, that while the press teems with the most levelling and seditious principles, that if put into execution would overturn the monarchy, nothing in reply appears, and not the least step is taken by the Court to restrain this extreme licentiousness of publication? It is easy to conceive the spirit that must be raised among the people. But the coffee-houses in the Palais-Royal present yet more singular and astonishing spectacles; they are not only crowded within, but other expectant crowds are at the doors and windows, listening *à gorge deployée* to certain orators, who from the chairs or table harangue each his little audience. The eagerness with which they are heard, and the thunder of applause they receive for every sentiment of more than common hardiness or violence against the present government, cannot easily be imagined. I am all amazement at the ministry permitting such nests and hotbeds of sedition and revolt which disseminate among the people, every hour, principles that by and by must be opposed with vigour, and therefore it seems little short of madness to allow the propagation at present.   ARTHUR YOUNG

They assaulted a Countess a few days ago in the Palais-Royal where she had been abusing M. Necker. All loud enough to be heard assemble there nightly. They climb a table, an audience gathers to listen to whatever is read. The speakers select the most forthright topical piece. The silence is broken only by applause from the most excitable. Patriots demand a repetition. Three days back, a child of four, precocious and well-trained, was carried round the garden, in full daylight, on the back of a porter, at least twenty times. The infant squalled, 'The French People have decided: Madame de Polignac to be banished a hundred leagues from Paris. Condé too. Conti too. D'Artois too. The queen . . .' but I dare not repeat this to you.

CAMILLE DESMOULINS, to his father

CONFUSION

There is no longer either executive power, laws, magistrates or police. A horrible anarchy covers all.   THE VENETIAN AMBASSADOR

When you undertake to manage a revolution, the difficulty is not in making it move; it is in controlling it.   COMTE DE MIRABEAU

PROSPECTS

The King's authority is non-existent, like that of Parlements and Magistratures; the Estates themselves are fearful of Paris, and this affects their decisions. There is neither law nor order, right nor discipline, nor religion here. . . .

The National Assembly fears Paris, and Paris shrinks before the forty or fifty thousand brigands taking root in Montmartre or the Palais Royal, resisting all efforts to control them, and still provoking unrest. Provincials are drunk with ideas for so long pronounced by literary philosophers, asserting universal equality. . . . Taxes cannot be imposed, the soldiers corrupted by expectations of liberty or hard cash. Soon the King will be helpless before his commitments, bankruptcy looms. The aristocracy is at an end, the clergy teeters on the edge of mindlessness, the Third Estate is wholly at odds with the situation. Only the victorious mob is happy, with nothing to lose, all to gain. Nobody steels himself to give orders, none consents to obey. . . . The Duc d'Orléans is himself suspected of inspiring it all. . . .

The Aristocracy, Clergy, and Parlements, who first initiated rebellion and disaffection, have suffered first. Chaos increases day by day and, above all, it seems endless. Hardship is visible everywhere: true coinage has vanished, their replacements, assignats, are virtually useless. . . . Traders no longer sell, factories are being ruined, food prices soar, poverty increases at terrifying speed. . . .

COUNT AXEL VON FERSEN, to his father

The Parlements *were not political assemblies but law courts, usually far more reactionary than the Crown, which they often opposed. For long dispersed under Louis XV, Louis XVI, perhaps unwisely, recalled them, in an effort of appeasement.*

Assignats *were paper money guaranteed by the royal treasury.*

AN IDEALIST

How often have I regretted being without your wise advice and comradely help. Now, while the previous organisation has been dismantled, a new political construction is being erected; I do not say it is absolutely perfect but it is sufficient to guarantee liberty. Thus established, the nation will be in a position to elect, in a couple of years, a National Convention that will remedy any defects of our

Constitution. The outcome, I trust, will be felicitous for my people and indeed for all mankind. The beginnings of Liberty are perceptible in the other European states: I support their growth in all ways that I can.   MARQUIS DE LAFAYETTE, to President George Washington

AUGUST, AFTER THE FIRST BASTILLE DAY

In these last few days things seem to have somewhat improved, but one can rely on nothing. Wicked men have great power and are able to frustrate or prevent the most just doings. . . .

But you can always be certain that adversity has not been able to diminish my strength and courage.

I am finding all sorts of truly and sincerely sympathetic people of whom I had never before been aware.

QUEEN MARIE ANTOINETTE, to Madame de Polignac

FROM THE DECLARATION OF THE RIGHTS OF MAN

Society is obliged to provide subsistence for all its members, either by providing them work or by assisting those unable to work. The provision of the basic essentials for those without them is a debt posed for those who have more than they need.

Social distinctions can only be founded on their public utility.

These rights are Liberty, Property, Security, Resistance to Oppression.

Property is inviolable and sacred.

The free communication of thought and opinion is one of the most precious rights of Man.

Men are born free and remain equal in rights. Social distinctions can be based only on individual usefulness for the general good.

Liberty means the power to do anything that does not harm others.

This optimistic faith in the power of ideas was reinforced by the influence of foreign examples, the English Magna Carta and the American Declaration of Independence. The enthusiasm aroused by the Virginian Declaration of Rights was still fresh in men's memory. The American Ambassador laughed at this faculty of enthusiasm in the French deputies. 'They all have that romantic outlook and all those romantic ideas of which, happily for America, we were cured before it was too late.'   ANTONINA VALLENTIN, 1948

It was an American idea, and scarcely anyone did not regard such a declaration as an absolutely essential preliminary. I recall that lengthy discussion, going on for weeks, as an interlude of deadly boredom.
                          ETIENNE DUMONT, Secretary to the Comte de Mirabeau

The general colour of the Declaration is that of middle-class individualism.   J. M. THOMPSON, 1943

A lot of window-dressing and hoo-ha.   RICHARD COBB, 1988

From one positive principle I shall never depart – that executive power must remain with the Monarch alone. I am not going to discuss your Declaration of the Rights of Man; it contains excellent pointers for your work, but principles which provoke differences in application and even in interpretation cannot be truly appreciated, and indeed need not be appreciated, until their correct meaning is established by the laws to which they are intended to be a premise.
                          KING LOUIS XVI, to the Constituent Assembly

The King's reply is destructive not only of any Constitution, but of the nation's right to possess a Constitution.
                          MAXIMILIEN ROBESPIERRE, to the Constituent Assembly

ANOTHER PROPHET

What are these people at court thinking of? Cannot they see the abysses opening at their feet?

All is lost, the King and Queen are going to perish, and you yourself will see it. The mob will trample their bodies underfoot . . . yes, yes indeed, they will trample their bodies underfoot.
                          COMTE DE MIRABEAU, to Comte Auguste de La Marck

We shall never, I think, experience the gracious chance of being reduced to the painful extremity of seeking help from Mirabeau.

QUEEN MARIE ANTOINETTE, to Comte Auguste de La Marck

FROM NEW YORK

The revolution which has been effected in France is of so wonderful a nature, that the mind can hardly realize the fact. If it ends as our last accounts to the first of August predict, that nation will be the most powerful and happy in Europe; but I fear, though it has gone triumphantly through the first paroxysm, it is not the last it has to encounter before matters are finally settled. In a word, the revolution is of too great a magnitude to be effected in so short a space, and with the loss of so little blood. The mortification of the King, the intrigues of the Queen, and the discontent of the princes and noblesse, will foment divisions, if possible, in the National Assembly, and they will unquestionably avail themselves of every *faux pas* in the formation of the Constitution, if they do not give a more open, active opposition. In addition to these, the licentiousness of the people on one hand, and sanguinary punishments on the other, will alarm the best disposed friends to the measure, and contribute not a little to the overthrow of their object. Great temperance, firmness, and foresight are necessary in the movements of that body. To forbear running from one extreme to another is no easy matter, and should this be the case, rocks and shoals not visible at present, may wreck the vessel, and give a higher toned despotism than the one which existed before.

GEORGE WASHINGTON, to Gouverneur Morris

SELF-SATISFACTION

Only by me can the populace be quietened. Forty thousand assemble, excitement gets to fever pitch, then I make my appearance and one word from me suffices to disperse them. Already I have saved six from the gallows in different parts of the capital, but the mob, angry, inflamed, can be deaf even to me. While I write this, eighty thousand have encircled the Hôtel de Ville, bawling about betrayal, that the loyal troops are being allowed to remain, that the King must come to Paris. They will consent to nothing unless they see my signature on everything. In my absence their minds go soft. Thus I am

Master of Paris, governing an angry people manipulated by dreadful conspirators; yet, admittedly, they have endured a thousand wrongs against which they have every right to protest.

MARQUIS DE LAFAYETTE, to Madame Simiane

The disturbances in Paris . . . became so general on Monday last, that all the districts of the capital were summoned and the MARQUIS DE LA FAYETTE was ordered to proceed immediately to Versailles, at the head of a large body of troops, and bring the KING under his guard to Paris. On receiving these orders, the MARQUIS DE LA FAYETTE remonstrated, saying, that he would just go thither attended by only a few of the Magistrates and some guards, and make his report of the necessity of a reinforcement.

This was soon got wind abroad, and the mob ever ready to catch at anything that could bear an unfavourable construction, insisted that the MARQUIS DE LA FAYETTE, and the Mayor, whom they likewise suspected, were going over to betray them. While this suspicion was circulated, another party erected two gallows in the *Place de Creves*, and threatened to hang them if the orders were not instantly complied with.

We must own that we have never been particularly struck, or convinced of those heroic feats of valour which the MARQUIS DE LA FAYETTE is said to have performed in America. In a former number of this paper, we gave the outlines of this Nobleman's public character, and we think the event has greatly confirmed our opinions. In the present instance, M. DE LA FAYETTE betrayed a pusillanimity of character unworthy of his high rank and military capacity. He was conscious that the orders he received were treacherous and unjust, by his first refusal to obey them; but the threat of the mob struck such terror into him, that he chose rather to obey their commands, and bring his KING in ignominy to Paris, than risk his own safety by refusing their commands.   *The Times*, London

VANITY

Go thence to the Hôtel de Ville and with much Difficulty find out the Marquis de La Fayette, who is exhausted by a Variety of Attentions. Tell him I will send his Letters to America, and he must give me a Passport to visit the (ruined) Bastile. Agree to dine with him on Condition that I may bring my own Wine. Return Home; write, and ab^t

four go to the Hôtel de La Fayette. Find there Madame, the Duc de Rochefoucault etc. Dine. He gives me my Passport. Suggest to him my Plan respecting the Gardes Françaises, which he likes. Advise him to have a compleat Plan for the Militia prepared and to submit it to the Committee. Ask him if he can think of any Steps which may be taken to induce the King to confer on him the Government of the Isle of France. He tells me that he would prefer that of Paris simply. That he has had the utmost Power his Heart could wish and is grown tired of it. That he has commanded absolutely an hundred thousand men, has marched his Sovereign about the Streets as he pleased, prescribed the Degree of Applause which he should receive, and could have detained him Prisoner had he thought proper. He wishes therefore as soon as possible to return to private Life. In this last Expression he deceives himself or wishes to deceive me; a little of both perhaps. But in Fact he is the lover of Freedom from Ambition, of which there are two Kinds, the one born of Pride, the other of Vanity and his partakes most of the latter.   GOUVERNEUR MORRIS. *Diary*

One part of the capital names me amongst the chief authors of the Revolution, others go so far as to call me its sole author.
                                       CAMILLE DESMOULINS, to his father

THE BAKER FROM VERSAILLES

October 5 arrived, but I saw none of the events, reports of which reached Paris early the next morning, when we were warned to expect a royal visitation. I was as courageous in public places as I was shy in drawing rooms, convinced that my destiny was for solitude or the forum. I went with all speed to the Champs-Elysées. First came guns, harpies, burglars, whores astride them, lewdly shouting and gesturing. Next, surrounded by a mob of all ages and sexes, the Royal Guards, who had swopped hats, swords, bandoliers with the National Guards, each bearing on their horses several fishwives, bacchantes, filthy, drunken, clothes all at sea. Next tramped the deputation from the National Assembly, followed by the royal carriages, rolling along in a dusty mêlée of pikes and bayonets. Tattered ragpickers, butchers hung with bloody aprons, naked blades at their waist, arms bare, gripped the carriage doors; other sinister guardians had climbed onto the roof; still others clung onto footboards or perched on the box, all shooting muskets and pistols, bawling:

'Here come the Baker, the Baker's Wife, and the Baker's Little Boy.'

Bailly, himself an astronomer, informed Louis XVI at the Hôtel de Ville that 'the humane, respectful and loyal people' had now 'conquered' its monarch, and he himself then replied that he was 'greatly moved and gratified', that he had freely decided to return to his capitol; all this was a discreditable untruth, the result of mob violence and fear which then dishonoured all men, all factions. It was not that the King lacked sincerity but that he was weak; weakness itself is not insincerity but its substitute; the respect which both the virtue and tragedy of the saintly King and Martyr must arouse makes any mortal verdict almost an act of sacrilege.

FRANÇOIS-RENÉ DE CHATEAUBRIAND. *Mémoires*, 1842

MY HEAD

I know they have come from Paris to demand my head, but I learned from my mother not to fear death, and I shall await it with firmness.

QUEEN MARIE ANTOINETTE

M. de La Fayette is enjoying a good sleep.   QUEEN MARIE ANTOINETTE

During the October invasion of Versailles by several threatening and hungry crowds from Paris, who forced the Royal Family to abandon the Château for the Tuileries Palace in Paris, in essence a prison.

The nobles will ruin us.   QUEEN MARIE ANTOINETTE

THE ROYAL FAMILY FORCED FROM VERSAILLES TO THE TUILERIES PALACE, PARIS

The Tuileries, abandoned by the Court since Louis XVI's minority, had been slowly invaded by an unruly populace, difficult to manage – royal pensioners, artists, powerful nobles, aristocratic ladies, disabled soldiers, theatrical troupes. Here was real Babel, crowded with the most incongruous examples of all social classes; an over-filled town on seven floors, made up of those who treated as conquered land the King's palace now surrendered to them.

As a home, the Palace was scarcely enviable. People lived on top of each other, often forced to pass through a neighbour's kitchen or dining room to return to their quarters. They were almost suffocated in summer, for the corridors lacked ventilation, and, offsetting this, froze in winter for lack of chimneys. The Comte de Polignac wrote, September 14, 1785: 'I have left the Tuileries; I was perishing from cold. Your workmen are worthy fellows, but their work is useless.' The Palace soon threatened to fall into ruin. Private personages indeed secured, by endless petitions, some urgent repairs for themselves, but the royal apartments – virtually belonging to no-one – were decayed almost to collapse. The Comte d'Angevilliers had already observed, January 8, 1776: 'The Grand Almoner has now warned me that the Tuileries chapel is in parlous state; a few days ago at Mass, the priest almost deserted his altar from his alarm.'

The details of the royal reoccupation of the Palace, October 1789, may seem childish. . . . Nevertheless, they force us to clearly understand what, by ignorance of new ideas, by failure to comprehend topical political currents, controlled the Court, down to its slightest activities, so they do possess some significance. Its procession of unnecessary and expensive flunkeys, this tortuous, intricate deployment of the most trivial services, these parasitical blemishes encrusting the royal authority, stifled and exhausted it. This is what killed it, but so little did royalty realise its own sickness that it imagined that its survival was actually maintained by it. This becomes even more emphatic when set against the new and practical element now governing the rival power, the National Assembly. The people of Paris, who, for almost a century, had never seen, had utterly forgotten court ways, were astounded to behold the arrival in the capital of this veritable army which the Royal Family trailed behind it. Those thousands of functionaries, whose obsolete titles sounded from comic opera, no longer had any popular glamour for people who believed that it had achieved a revolution. It was a clumsy performance, recalling a past now reckoned dead, to parade these worn-out feudal trappings.   G. LENÔTRE, 1894

My friends, I am going to dwell amongst you, with my wife and my children.   KING LOUIS XVI, facing armed crowds from Paris,
on a balcony of the palace of Versailles

Consummatum est: it is finished, the King is in the Louvre, the National Assembly is at the Tuileries, the channels of circulation are being

cleared, the market is choked with sacks of grain, the Treasury is filling up, the corn–mills are turning, traitors are in full flight, priests are
trampled, aristocrats are virtually extinct, patriots have triumphed.

CAMILLE DESMOULINS

*Actually, the King was at the Tuileries, and, following him from Versailles,
the Assembly was in the Salle du Manège, once a riding school, and which has
now totally vanished.*

The National Constituent Assembly holds in its hand the destiny of
France and the universe.   MAXIMILIEN ROBESPIERRE

POLITICAL SEE-SAW

The Baker's wife has golden crowns
For which she never toiled.

Popular rhyme against the Queen

Gentlemen, the time has come that I should associate myself more
intimately and in ways even more open and direct with the successful
performance of all you are scheming on behalf of France. . . .

You, with all your many resources to enlighten public opinion,
explain to our people about their real interests, the people I love so
dearly, and who are said by those who wish to console me in my distress to love me in their turn. KING LOUIS XVI, to the Legislative Assembly

Oh, what an admirable King! We must certainly erect for him a
throne of gold and diamonds.   DEPUTY BERTRAND BARÈRE DE VIEUZAC

When to the greatness of the throne
There shall succeed the greatness of the state,
And when the people, glorious again,
Shall banish every prejudice and lie,
And once again possess themselves of Natural Right,
Then shall live sepulchres, dread Bastilles,
Crumble to dust beneath their generous hands
Which teach the Prince his duty, the clown also,
And eternally fix the limits of their power.
Then shall our posterity, a prouder race,
Many a leader but never a master own,

Happy, beneath a justice-loving King
Who restores them all their Liberty and Laws!

MARIE-JOSEPH CHÉNIER, playwright and brother of the poet André Chénier.
Charles IX, or The School of Kings

MIRABEAU DEFEATED

An amendment was proposed that no member of the Assembly should henceforth join the Royal Ministry throughout the session.

Mirabeau advanced to the tribune to defend his own opposition, speaking with eloquent and biting irony, and ending with proposing an amendment to exclude him from the Ministry. But he had already known that the issue was decided . . . the eloquence and biting irony failed against the prejudices of the Assembly. The first amendment was voted. That day, November 7, saw the collapse of Mirabeau's political career. He remained true to his general policy, aimed at uniting King and people, but was unable any longer to openly work for such reconciliation. The decision of November 7 thrust him into shadowy intrigues and his powerful destiny suffered fatal deviation. He was no longer incarnation of pure Revolutionary flame. He was discouraged by the day's outcome. 'Don't tell me about these hatreds, either too stupid or too atrocious,' he wrote to his sister, 'and don't worry about us but about the welfare of the State and the Revolution, which these gentlemen understand not a jot.'

ANTONINA VALLENTIN, 1948

THEATRE

Mr Richard called this Morning before I was up. . . . He tells me that the Duke of Orleans offered Beaumarchais 20pc for a loan of 500,000 and that he has since applied to their House for a loan of 300,000, but in both cases without success. That their House are so pushed for Money they know not where to turn themselves. Go to dinner at Madame la Tour's. Arrive very late but luckily the Count D'Alfrey and the Bishop D'Autun (Talleyrand) arrive still later. We have a bad Dinner and more Company than can sit at the Table. Every Thing is *ennuyeux*.

Perhaps it arises in a great Measure from myself. Go with the

Count D'Alfrey to the Representation of *Charles neuf*, a Tragedy grounded on the Massacre of St Bartholomew. It is a very extraordinary Piece to be represented in a Catholic Country. A Cardinal who excites the King to violate his Oaths and murder his Subjects, then in a Meeting of Assassins consecreates their Daggers, absolves them from their Crimes and promises everlasting Felicity. All this with the Solemnities of the established Religion. A Murmur of Horror runs thro the Audience. There are several Observations calculated for the present Times and I think this Piece, if it runs thro the Provinces as it probably will, must give a fatal Blow to the Catholic Religion. My friend the Bishop D'Autun has gone a great Way towards its Destruction by attacking the Church Property. Surely there never was a Nation which verged faster towards Anarchy. No Law, no Morals, no Religion, no Principles.   GOUVERNEUR MORRIS. *Diary*

SUNSET

The elegant, tasteful aristocrat élite gathered at the Hôtel de La Rochefoucauld, at the soirées of Mmes de Poix, d'Henin, de Simiane, and de Vandreuil, or in the few salons of the *noblesse de robe* still continuing. At M. Necker's, at M. le Comte de Montmorin's, and various ministerial mansions, there collected, along with his daughter, Mme de Staël, the Duchesse d'Aiguillon, Mmes de Beaumont and de Seruilly . . . all the latest arrivals in French society with all the freedom of the new style. The cobbler knelt to measure your foot, ablaze in the outfit of the National Guard, the monk who last Friday trailed his black or white gown through the dust turned up on Saturday in round hat and layman's jacket; the clean-shaven Capuchin read the journals in a tavern bar, and a nun sat quietly surrounded by lightminded women – some sister or aunt expelled from her convent. The mob crowded into such religious houses now open to the public as tourists at Granada wandered through the empty spaces of the Alhambra or, at Tivoli, lingering under the columns of the Temple of the Sibyl.

As for the remainder, there would be many duels and love affairs, prison liaisons, political alliances, shrouded meetings, among ruins, beneath calm skies within all the peace and poetry of Nature; walks remote, silent, solitary, conflicting with deathless oaths and nameless affections, together with the dull roar of a world now being extinguished, the distant clamour of a crumbling régime which, toppling, menaced all delights beneath it. After a mere twenty four hours apart, people could never be sure of reunion. Some joined the revolutionary movement, others prepared for civil war; others emigrated to Ohio, sending on before them plans for châteaux amongst the savages, and others departed to join the émigré Princes. All this was done gaily, often in utmost poverty, Royalists proclaiming that the whole turmoil would be halted one morning by a decree of the Assembly: and the patriots, sympathetic to the new times, were equally joyous in their hopes, hailing the reign of peace, happiness and liberty.

FRANÇOIS-RENÉ DE CHATEAUBRIAND. *Mémoires*, 1842

THE PACE QUICKENS

A PROVINCIAL EPISODE

In another big town of the South, Montpellier, social life remained brilliant as always during the winter of 1789–90, if we are to believe Pierre-Louis Pascal Jullian, then a law student there. Two companies of amateur actors, one noble, the other bourgeois, were rivals in presenting plays. Many salons kept their doors open and gave customary hospitality, particularly that of the Comte de P, who continued to give excellent balls. But during one such ball an event occurred which many found highly disturbing. When the revels were at their most sparkling, the leader of the popular faction, not named by Jullian but very possibly Cambon, hustled in with the latest news and showing 'his customary insolence'.

'Do you realise, M. le Comte,' this fellow demanded, 'that your precious authority is a buggeration, and all that's now left for you is to bugger off?'

All guests showed their anger and wanted to throw the dirty-tongued gate-crasher out of the window, but the Count halted them. 'I myself shall depart when duty to my King no longer demands that I should remain here, and when he orders me to join him.'

This reply carried considerable address, nevertheless the episode provoked a sense of scandal and the ball ended in considerable unease. It was not long before the uproars in Paris reached most of the large urban areas, and perhaps on that evening fashionable Montpellier had danced its final Minuet.   JEAN ROBIQUET, 1938

IN PARIS

I have been waiting so long for happiness, but at last it has come, and this day sees me as happy as Mortal Man can be. Lucile, of whom I have so often written to you, and whom I have loved for eight years, has promised her hand, and her parents have finally approved. A moment ago her mother, weeping for joy, came to give me the wonderful tidings. She escorted me to her daughter's room and I went on my knees to Lucile. Hearing her laugh, I looked up, surprised. But, like me, she was shedding tears of happiness, and she wept as she laughed. I have never seen anything so lovely.

CAMILLE DESMOULINS, to his father

Witnesses of the marriage included Robespierre, Pétion and Brissot. Mirabeau was unavoidably absent.

LAFAYETTE AGAIN

I go thence to la Fayette's. Converse about Half an Hour. He asks my Opinion of his Situation. I give it *sans* ménagement and while I speak he turns pale. I tell him that the Time approaches when all good Men must cling to the Throne. That the present King is very valuable on Account of his Moderation and if he should possess too great Authority might be persuaded to grant a proper Constitution. That the Thing they call a Constitution which the Assemblée have framed is good for Nothing. That as to himself his personal Situation is very delicate. That he nominally but not really commands his Troops. That I really cannot tell how he is to establish Discipline among them but that unless he can accomplish that Object he must be ruined sooner or later. That the best line of Conduct perhaps would be to seize an Occasion of Disobedience and resign, by which means he would preserve a Reputation in France which would be precious and hereafter useful. He says that he is only raised by Circumstances and Events, so that when they cease he sinks, and the Difficulty now is how to excite them. I take Care not to express even by a Look my Contempt and Abhorrence but simply observe that Events will arise fast enough of themselves if he can but make a good Use of them, which I doubt because I do not place any Confidence in his Troops.

GOUVERNEUR MORRIS

To begin then with our friend Lafayette who has hitherto acted a splendid Part. Unfortunately both for himself and his Country he has not the Talents which his Situation requires. This important Truth known to the few from the very Beginning is now but too well understood by the People in general. His Authority depends on Incidents and sinks to nothing in a Moment of Calm, so that if his Enemies would let him alone his twinkling Light would expire. He would then perhaps raise Commotions in Order to quell them. This his Enemies have long charged him with, unjustly I believe, but I would not answer for the future. The King obeys but detests him. He obeys because he fears. Whoever possesses the royal Person may do what he pleases with the royal Character and Authority. Hence it happens that the Ministers are of Lafayette's Appointment. A short Description of their Use was given the other Day by Mirabeau. We make Ministers, says he, as we used formerly to send Servants to keep our Boxes at the Playhouse. . . . Lafayette thinks that these his Creatures will worship their Creator, but he is mightily mistaken. You know du Portail, the Minister of War. He is said to be violent in favor of the Revolution. . . .

There is not a Man among them fitted for the great Tasks in which they are engaged, and greater Tasks are perhaps impending. I have no proofs, but I have a well founded Opinion that the Leaders of one Party wish what those of the other fear and both expect, viz the Interference of foreign Powers. One previous Step would be to carry off, if possible, the King and Queen.

GOUVERNEUR MORRIS, to George Washington

I will rip out that damnable Lafayette's heart before all his army of flunkeys. JEAN-PAUL MARAT. *L'Ami du Peuple*

THE NATIONAL ASSEMBLY

The purpose of the National Assembly of France is to abolish every contrivance and fraud by which a single man, or a few may enjoy privilege, first to benefit, then to harm millions; to destroy the principle of all modern governments, that a part is greater than the whole, and instead of applying a mechanism called Monarchy, Aristocracy or Democracy, to govern the community for the good of individuals, orders, or professions, to organize the community itself; to compose it into a real unity; to spread a lively and poignant awareness over it; to connect all members with the central point of reflection and thought; and to introduce that general good feeling which always stops a finely-proportioned body from injuring any of its parts.

ANONYMOUS. *Lessons to a Young Prince from an Old Statesman*

A LONDON VOICE

I should suspend my congratulations on the new liberty of France, until I was informed how it had been combined with government; with public force; with the discipline and obedience of armies; with the collection of an effective and well-distributed revenue; with morality and religion; with the solidity of property; with peace and order; with civil and social manners. All these (in their way) are good things too; and, without them, liberty is not a benefit while it lasts, and is not likely to continue long.   EDMUND BURKE, 1790

Some popular general who understands the art of conciliating the soldiery, and who possesses the true spirit of command, shall draw the eyes of all men upon himself. Armies will obey him on his personal account. There is no other way of securing military obedience in this state of things. But the moment in which that event shall happen, the person who really commands the army is your master; the master (that is little) of your king, the master of your assembly, the master of your whole republic.   EDMUND BURKE, 1790

REBIRTH

When the third summer brought its liberty
A Fellow Student and myself, he, too,
A Mountaineer, together sallied forth
And, staff in hand, on foot pursu'd our way
Towards the distant Alps. An open slight
Of College cares and study was the scheme,
Nor entertain'd without concern for those
To whom my worldly interests were dear:
But Nature then was sovereign in my heart,
And mighty forms seizing a youthful Fancy
Had given a charter to irregular hopes.
In any age, without an impulse sent
From work of Nations, and their goings-on,
I should have been possessed by like desire:
But 'twas a time when Europe was rejoiced,
France standing on the top of golden hours,
And human nature seeming born again.

WILLIAM WORDSWORTH. *The Prelude*

This poem, begun about 1799, was published in full, 1850, after his death.

UNHAPPY LOUIS

The unhappy Louis XVI was a man of the best intentions that probably ever reigned. He was by no means deficient in talents. He had a most laudable desire to supply by general reading, and even by the acquisition of elemental knowledge, an education in all points originally defective; but nobody told him (and it was no wonder that he should not himself divine it) that the world of which he read, and the world in which he lived, were no longer the same. Desirous of doing everything for the best, fearful of cabal, distrusting his own judgment, he sought his ministers of all kinds upon public testimony. But as courts are the field for caballers, the public is the theatre for mountebanks and impostors. The cure for both these evils is in the discernment of the prince. But an accurate and penetrating discernment is what in a young prince could not be looked for.

His conduct in its principle was not unwise; but, like most of his other well-meant designs, it failed in his hands. It failed partly from mere ill-fortune, to which speculators are rarely pleased to assign that very large share to which she is justly entitled in human affairs. The failure, perhaps, in part was owing to his suffering his system to be vitiated and disturbed by those intrigues, which it is, humanly speaking, impossible wholly to prevent in courts, or indeed under any form of government.

However, with these aberrations, he gave himself over to a succession of the statesmen of public opinion. In other things he thought that he might be a king on the terms of his predecessors.

EDMUND BURKE, 1796

A PLEDGE

Devoted as I am both from duty and inclination to the cause of the people, I shall oppose with equal zeal aristocracy, tyranny, and factionalism. I recognise the faults of the National Assembly, but it seems to me very dangerous, nay, blameworthy, to discredit it. I hate personal predominance; but I am far more impressed than you are by the need to restore the executive power of the Crown. I believe that the sole way of avoiding civil war is to take advantage of the present situation, and work with and through partnership with the King and the Paris Assembly. MARQUIS DE LAFAYETTE, to Jean-Joseph Mounier

COMTE DE MIRABEAU

I declare, and shall maintain in the face of all earthly powers, that slaves are as much to blame as their tyrants, and I do not know whether Liberty should complain more of those insolent enough to injure her, or of the imbeciles who do not know how to defend her.

On reading his father's book, *L'Ami des Hommes*

The elder of my sons seems to me, at least up to now, to have the makings of no more than an incurable Madman, above all his vile characteristics. I perceive in him the nature of a beast, and I doubt any possibility of ever making anything worthwhile of him.

VICTOR RIQUETI, father of the Comte de Mirabeau

I have always believed and I shall always believe, that indifference to injustice is treason and cowardice. . . . Whether or not I myself am free, I shall proclaim until my death the rights of humanity. What can be a more natural occasion for struggling against despotism than when one is groaning in its chains?

To the Lieutenant of Police, while in the Vincennes prison.
Des Lettres de Cachet et des Prisons d'État, 1778

The Comte de Mirabeau was imprisoned, by the influence of his father, and held under a royal lettre de cachet: *imprisonment by royal whim without trial.*

Which of us, if he wished to consecrate here the live image of justice and adorn it with the charms of beauty, would not place before us the august effigy of our Queen?   On Queen Marie Antoinette, Aix, 1783

America can and will determine with absolute decision whether humanity is destined by Nature to liberty or to slavery.

Considérations sur l'ordre de Cincinnatus, 1785

Talk about English generosity is false. Habitually calculating everything, they calculate even talent and friendship; most of their writers have almost literally perished from starvation.

To Nicholas-Sébastien Roch de Chamfort, 1786

Among the worst social evils I rate unconcern towards the most deplorable conditions when before our very eyes they daily recur.

We live within wholesale oppression and wretchedness that scarcely affects our feelings at all; if we avert our gaze it is not from pity but to avoid offending our good taste.

In England, at least in regard to legal administration, I believe there are only matters which require improving, whereas what we need in France is an utterly new start. *Imité de l'Anglais*, 1787

There must be no repeating of pompous platitudes about the need for conciliation. Nothing is more easy for the unthinking, or even for good citizens more honest than knowledgeable, more zealous than far-seeing, to be trapped by such a quack cure as that; for anyone of honest intentions desires peace and harmony; but the percipient also understand that lasting harmony depends on justice alone.

To the National Assembly, 1789

Mirabeau was, perhaps, the only one in the Assembly who from the first recognised the Revolution in its true quality, that of total subversion. DEPUTY PIERRE MALOUET. *Mémoires*

The rollcall of our foes is very much exaggerated, many who differ from us are very far from meriting that hateful title. Fellow citizens who, like ourselves, seek only the public good though by another avenue, men fettered by prejudices deriving from education and training, are not strong enough to stem the tide; men who, observing us in a stance wholly new to them, have been scared of us making too great political demands and are nervous about their possessions and also that liberty may be no more than an excuse for anarchy; all these people deserve our consideration; some need pity, others more time to understand us; all need more knowledge and general avoidance of any poisoning of the differences of opinion, inevitable from the weakness of human nature, which could arouse quarrels involving self-esteem and factionalism. Our destiny is in our Wisdom. Violence might endanger or even destroy the liberty which human reason promises us. Draft of speech to the National Assembly, 1789

I have been more consistent than perhaps any other human being in attempting to perform, improve and extend a Revolution which will do more than any other to advance Humanity.

To Jakob Mauvillon, 1789

Mirabeau is the Shakespeare of eloquence. ANTOINE JOSEPH BARNAVE

A memorable year marked by great and immortal happenings. The throne is endangered more because of its failure to govern than because of any plots. If no pilot appears, the ship will probably run aground. If, on the other hand, circumstances force the summoning of an intelligent man and allow the courage to crush all false human values and the petty jealousy that always oppose it, you have no conception how easy the ship of state can be refloated. Our nation's resources, its very mobility, which is its chief vice, offer so many expedients and channels that in France you can never really tell.

To Jakob Mauvillon, 1789

I do not believe that men who are to fight public causes as true brothers-in-arms, behave well if they fight as base gladiators; to wage war with insinuation and intrigue instead of talent and wisdom; to look for guilty victory, transitory spoils which wound all, even glory itself – in the fields of mutual ruin and recrimination. But I declare to you all; among my own followers you will find all the moderates who deny that wisdom is the outcome of fanaticism, or that the courage to pull down must never yield to the courage to rebuild. Amongst us you will see those tribunes of the people whom, despite the squeals of envious mediocrities, the nation will for a long time yet, recognise as standing amongst the national saviours.

To the Constituent Assembly, 1790

DEFERENCE

You have often lectured to me about deferring to the King and Queen, but that is unnecessary because such behaviour is part of my make-up, now that sad times are upon them. All the same, believe me when I say that a rough man would do better both for them and the popular cause. They are only grown children, who do not swallow their beneficial medicine unless threatened by the Big Bad Man. Don't imagine that I am indulging in frivolity about authority: there is universal agreement about my own role in that.

MARQUIS DE LAFAYETTE, to Madame Simiane

RENDEZVOUS OF
WORST AND BEST

Through Paris lay my readiest path, and there
I sojournéd a few days, and visited
In haste each spot of old and recent fame
The latter chiefly, from the field of Mars
Down to the suburbs of St Anthony,
And from Mont Martyr southward, to the Dome
Of Geneviève. In both her clamorous Halls,
The National Synod and the Jacobins
I saw the revolutionary Power
Toss like a ship at anchor, rock'd by storms;
The Arcades I traversed in the Palace huge
Of Orleans, coasted round and round the line
Of Tavern, Brothel, Gaming-house, and Shop,
Great rendezvous of worst and best, the walk
Of all who had a purpose, or had not;
I star'd and listen'd with a stranger's ears
To Hawkers and Haranguers, hubbub wild!
And hissing Factionists with ardent eyes,
In knots, or pairs, or single, ant-like swarms
Of Builders and Subverters, every face
That hope or apprehension could put on,
Joy, anger, and vexation in the midst
Of gaiety and dissolute idleness.

WILLIAM WORDSWORTH. *The Prelude*

A LAST HOPE FOR
THE MONARCHY

It would disgust me to have any active concern during the present
conflict and turmoil were I not absolutely certain that the re-estab-
lishment of lawful royal authority is France's paramount need and
sole remedy. But I so plainly recognise that we are surrounded by
anarchy, into which we daily descend deeper; I am so angry at any
notion that I should have done no more than to assist in a giant
destruction, and the fear of seeing some other supreme authority than

the King is so intolerable to me, that I feel myself urgently recalled to public affairs, even during a period when I am partially determined to stay silent and have only retirement to hope for.

This, then, is the text of my beliefs, demanded by the King, and ..hich will always remain my manifesto or witness; I vow to put all my influence behind the royal course; and, so that this statement may not seem too imprecise, I declare my conviction that counter-revolution is dangerous and criminal, and I simultaneously hold equally wild-goose the hope or plan of any authority without a leader given all powers essential to bolster the enforcement of law with official force.

A quack will guarantee speedy cure, but will kill the patient. The true physician duly observes, acts, especially through trusted prescriptions, doses, measures, and he sometimes achieves a cure.

I promise the King my loyalty, zeal, activity, energy, and a courage of which others may know very little. In conclusion, I promise him all save success, for this never depends on one individual. It would be most rash, most blameworthy, to give any absolute guarantee, in face of the dire sickness that is undermining authority and threatening its chief.   COMTE DE MIRABEAU, secret memorandum

Where will the storm-tossed ship be borne? I know not, but if I do save myself from the wreckage, I shall always say, with pride, in my retirement: 'I risked destruction to save each one of them, but they refused to be saved.'   COMTE DE MIRABEAU

A LETTER FROM THE PROVINCES TO PARIS

You are not only the deputy of a province, you are the deputy of mankind and of the Republic.   LOUIS ANTOINE DE SAINT-JUST, to the Deputy for Arras, Maximilien Robespierre

THE ABOLITION OF TITLES
IN FRANCE

The National Assembly decrees that the hereditary nobility is abolished for all time; thus the titles of *prince, duc, comte, marquis, baron, messire, écuyer, noble* and all other such titles shall not be taken or given to any person.

That the distinction of ranks in France, has been carried to a ridiculous, an unnatural, and impolitic height, is readily acknowledged: – but, if to destroy any part of a system, because it has been abused, be a principle of their present Government, – they will lay the axe to the root of religion itself, – and when they annihilate coronets, and titles, they must on the same principle level their churches with the ground.

We have continually foretold, that the mad spirit of change now prevalent in France, will, in the end, destroy its own object, – and we are not afraid to repeat the prophecy. Reformation is certainly necessary; but to be effectual it must be slow in its progress and moderate in its exertions. Violence will defeat it, – and will operate like the spirit of Brother Jack, in the Tale of a Tub, – who, in the ardour of his zeal to separate the embroidery from the coat, *tore the cloth along with it*.
The Times, London

ENGLISH OBSERVERS

I am inclined to think that the application of theory in matters of government is a surprising imbecility in the human mind.
ARTHUR YOUNG

When the poor rise to destroy the rich, they act as wisely for their own purposes as when they burn mills and throw corn into the river, to make bread cheap.
EDMUND BURKE

THE OPTIMIST

We are immediately brought to the point of seeing government begin, as if we had lived at the beginning of time.
TOM PAINE. *The Rights of Man*

AN ATTACK ON THE NATIONAL CONSTITUENT ASSEMBLY

Frenchmen! Free and frivolous! Will you never realise the evils threatening you? Will you always go to sleep on the very edge of the abyss? Thanks to the myopia of your former rulers, to the laziness of the national enemies, and to a medley of unexpected events, you have shed your fetters, you have grasped your weapons. But instead of tirelessly seeking to punish the nation's enemies, you have surrendered to the rule of the feeble, the corrupt, who are struggling to snatch those enemies from your just vengeance and restore them. . . .

Throughout the realm the country is convulsed by wounds, you suffer misfortunes, your workshops are empty, production is abandoned, trade stagnant, finances ruined, troops disbanded. . . .

Reflect carefully. The political set-up never rights itself without violence – the air is never cleared without a storm. So let us assemble in the public squares and decide on how to save the State; but, alas, would we still be able to recognise the means? Our present misfortunes derive from too many committees, too little wisdom: government recruits do no more than ferment unrest on all sides. Our only salvation is in purging the committees of those with suspect or dangerous beliefs. . . .　　　JEAN-PAUL MARAT. *L'Ami du Peuple*

PASSING COMMENTS

We have a few Words on La Fayette's subject. He [William Short, Thomas Jefferson's secretary] expresses his Astonishment at this Man's Inaptitude and Imbecility. Poor La Fayette. He begins to suffer the Consequences which always attend too great Elevation.

GOUVERNEUR MORRIS. *Diary*

See France in Freedom's Mantle gay
Her former State disdains
Yet proud her fav'rite Bard T' obey,
The dead his Spirit reigns.

The Common Road to Pow'r he trod:
Cried pull all Tyrants down!
And Making of the Mob a God
Has gain'd from them a Crown.

GOUVERNEUR MORRIS, after a performance in Paris of Voltaire's *Brutus*

POPULAR PROTEST

All day upon the land
In the heat and cold I stand,
Though poor, to have enough in hand
To pay the rector:
Work I do the whole year round,
To win my harvest from the ground
Which may content when he comes around,
The tax-collector.   ANON

WARNING TO FRANCE

Deaf to my voice you sleep in the arms of your enemies and now that
they prepare to devour you, you are affrighted by menacing perils
and do naught to save yourselves. You have permitted the King's
aunts to escape and perhaps the Dauphin with them. The King's
brother is about to flee in his turn and eventually the King himself
and his wife will follow. My imagination quakes at the evils ahead:
scarcely will the King have crossed the frontier before the enemy
legions will swarm towards our homesteads, filling the rivers with
blood. None of you will be spared, men, women, children, and the
first victims will be your Deputies.   JEAN-PAUL MARAT. *L'Ami du Peuple*

FASHION

My little sweetheart, I am doing your pieces of shopping for you and
will forget nothing. I have bought you a truly pretty hat, the very
latest fashion, entitled, To Liberty. It is most enticing, the very last
word of fashion, and, dear heart, because the rain would detach the

ribbons, I've had an exceptionally pretty hatband added, completely golden, with fringes and many little details, the whole affair combining beauty and reliability.   THE MARQUIS DE MESMON, to a girl of Paris

ROYAL AUTHORITY

M. Bailly [Mayor of Paris] had informed the King earlier that his departure would provoke disorder and that the popular mood was against it. The King's response was that, having permitted freedom of mobility to everyone else, it would be eccentric to refuse it to himself alone. He descended, with the Queen, Madame Elizabeth, the children, Madame de Tourzel. . . .

All six entered the coach but when the horses reached the gates, the National Guards refused to unbar them and permit the King's egress. M. de Lafayette vainly attempted to convince them that this behaviour was thoroughly unconstitutional. Such restriction would reduce the King to a prisoner and was against all the edicts. The response was only insults; they were inflexible, the King could not proceed. They indulged in the foulest abuse: the King was a fucking aristocrat, an aristocratic bugger, a fat swine. He was incapable of government and should abdicate for the Duc d'Orléans; he was but a bureaucrat, monstrously overpaid at 25 million and should do what people demanded. The people unanimously agreed; he mixed only with aristocrats and stubborn clergy and should dismiss them. M. de Lafayette asked the Mayor to read the riot act and haul down the red flag; he refused. Lafayette was told he would become an object of ridicule and would be the first to suffer. He offered to resign, was asked to make haste. He addressed the crowd, unavailingly. Troops of grenadiers, turning up, swore that the King was not permitted to depart. Some displayed bullets, declaring that they would aim at the King at his slightest attempt to leave. His retainers approaching the coach were insulted; the Majordomo, M. de Gougenot, stepped to the Queen's door for instructions for dinner. He was pulled off, would have been at the gallows had not the grenadiers rescued him.

While feigning assault, they whispered that, despite appearances, he could inform the King that good and faithful people remained who could save those loyal to him. The Queen came forward, to tell them that he should remain, being in the royal service. They retorted that she had no standing to order them about, their officers alone could do that. Others cried: 'Who is this bitch who imagines she can tell us what to do?' M. de Lafayette sent to the Commune, demanding a state of emergency proclaimed, but, no reply. He asked the King whether he should use force to ensure the departure and respect for Law. The soldiers denied his authority, saying that they had removed their bayonets, to avoid using them against honest Citizens. The King rejected the use of force and explained: 'I desire no blood to be shed for me. . . .'   COUNT AXEL VON FERSEN, to Baron Evert Taube

Louis XVI is incapable of ruling because of his apathy, of the resignation he mistakes for courage, and his unconquerable rejection of any form of hard thinking, which makes him detach himself from any real talk and any disposition to reflect on the dangerous situation in which his good nature has deposited himself and his realm.

COMTE AUGUSTE DE LA MARCK, to Comte de Mercy-Argenteau,
Austrian Ambassador

SIGNS OF THE TIMES

The King has been forced to accept a nationalised, constitutional church, a change which has totally divided French Catholicism. Clergy who refuse to accept the changes, despite royal sympathy, are increasingly driven underground and proscribed. These are 'non-jurors'.

We have this Day very much of a Riot at the Tuileries. The King intends for St Cloud but is stopped, not meerly by the Populace but by the Milice nationale, who refuse to obey their General [Lafayette]. It seems that his Majesty, having sanctioned the Decree respecting the Clergy and afterwards applied to one of the non Jurors to perform the Ceremonies enjoined at this Season, has incurred the Charge of Duplicity. I am a long Time in Expectation of a Battle, but am at length told that the King submits.   GOUVERNEUR MORRIS. *Diary*

Sworn priest and patriotism being now synonyms, free-thinking Paris was rabidly determined that the King make his Easter communion and by means of a Constitutional priest. Consumed by remorse for his sanction of Clergy's Civil Constitution he wanted to attend Paschal Mass without communicating, wanted this to pass without comment, longed for privacy of Saint-Cloud, for ministrations of a

Man of God, old regime. Their Majesties' carriage is turned back in Place du Carrousel, Danton in command of organized riot in which well-known Orléanists move in disguise. A milestone in career of La Fayette when National Guard flout his order to clear passage for royal coach, which returns to Tuileries. His authority cut to pieces La Fayette reports to Commune, resigns his command, faints dead away in Hôtel de Ville, scene of his first revolutionary triumph.

Besieged in his house by hundreds of penitent imploring Guards, on fourth day he is once again their Commander-in-Chief. Baron de Staël says that he should have broken his sword the instant the Guard disobeyed. The sword seems intact – but not quite.

BEATRIX CARY DAVENPORT, 1939

Louis Philippe Joseph, Duc d'Orléans, and his home, the Palais Royal, became a centre of opposition to his cousin, Louis XVI, for whose death he voted. Increasingly extreme, the Duc renounced his title, becoming Citizen Philippe Egalité which did not prevent his execution during the Terror of 1793. His son, Louis-Philippe, was proclaimed King of the French by Lafayette, during the revolution of 1830, and reigned until the revolution of 1848, the Second Republic soon electing Louis Napoleon as President.

MIRABEAU

Mirabeau is throughout financed by the Court, whom he assists; nevertheless, he is now unable to work as publicly for a good cause as formerly he did for a bad cause, and to keep his influence is made to appear the democrat. His beliefs are still wrong-headed, but are the best, compared to the rest.

COUNT AXEL VON FERSEN, to King Gustav III of Sweden

FUNERAL OF MIRABEAU

Yesterday I went to visit M. de Mirabeau; the house was crowded and I visited with a degree of sadness even greater than that of the public grief. That sight of desolation filled me with the spirit of death, it was everywhere save in the soul of he who was in the closest danger. M. de Mirabeau even then remained a public figure and it is in this light that we should regard as precious fragments his last words wrested from the immense prey that Death was about to seize.

MAURICE DE TALLEYRAND, Bishop of Autun, to the Assembly

I am crushed by the realisation that the only thing I have accomplished is to help cause a dreadful destruction. COMTE DE MIRABEAU

The funeral of Mirabeau (attended it is said by more than 100,000 Persons in solemn Silence) has been an imposing Spectacle. It is a vast Tribute paid to superior Talents, but no great incitement to virtuous Deeds. Vices both degrading and detestable marked this extraordinary Creature. Compleatly prostitute, he sacrificed every Thing to the Whim of the Moment. *Cupidus alieni prodigus sui Venal.* Shameless and yet greatly virtuous when pushed by a prevailing Impulse, but never truly virtuous because never under the steady Control of Reason nor the firm Authority of Principle. I have seen this man, in the short space of two years, hissed, honored, hated, mourned. Enthusiasm has just now presented him gigantic. Time and Reflection will shrink that Stature. The busy Idleness of the Hour must find some other Object to execrate or to exalt. Such is Man, and particularly the french Man. GOUVERNEUR MORRIS. *Diary*

The last remaining reverence of Parisians was for brains. Shuffling through heavy dust of a spell of fine weather, following the titan burnt out by overwork and overdissipation, someone complained that the streets had not been watered, a woman said that the people would lay the dust with their tears. Mirabeau thought France needed a King, but also a Richelieu and that he, not La Fayette, was mentally equipped for the part; but this socialist-royalist, demagogue-aristocrat had played such a deep double game that no side could trust him; excessive in all things in size and glitter of buckles and buttons, in splendor of clothes and words, in enormities of his pleasures.

BEATRIX CARY DAVENPORT, 1939

Perhaps in every historical age there exist figures who may be reckoned as symbols of good and evil. Examples are Cicero and Catiline in Rome; Necker and Mirabeau in France. I admit that my father's enemy possessed the greatest mental energy and intellectual breadth. Mirabeau knew everything, he foresaw everything.

MADAME DE STAËL, daughter of Jacques Necker, twice Finance Minister to Louis XVI. *Du caractère de M. Necker. Considération sur les principaux événements de la Révolution française*, 1861 edition

Years later Madame de Staël met Napoleon: they talked together for some time, then separated, each convinced of having been unable to get a word in.

For more than a year, Mirabeau had very little left of the influence which his oratory should seem to have guaranteed him; the notoriety of his vices was greater than the renown of his talents, but he finally swayed the majority in the Assembly by a unique mingling of principles good and bad, often approaching the soundest political maxims, and, only slightly less often, relinquishing them to maintain himself in the popular faction. Self-interest, ambition, and the correctness of his opinions never allowed him to close his eyes to the abyss opening beneath us. His patriotism did not extend, as that of many others did, to absurdity; Liberty he loved. Liberty he desired, but, like myself, he was convinced that in pursuit of it we were leading ourselves astray.   PIERRE MALOUET. *Mémoires*

One day, when the President's Chair is relegated to the treasures of Saint-Denis, the Benedictine responsible for showing it to the curious visitor will never explain, 'This was the Presidential Chair of the National Assembly.' He will simply say, 'This was Mirabeau's Chair.'
                                                CAMILLE DESMOULINS

All is turning against us. There is no use fighting against such misfortune.   QUEEN MARIE ANTOINETTE, to Comte Auguste de La Marck

For the first time in France a man celebrated by his writings and his eloquence received honours formerly accorded to great noblemen and warriors.   MADAME DE STAËL, on Mirabeau's funeral

I carry away with me the last vestiges of the Monarchy.
                                                Dying, to Talleyrand

DR JEAN-PAUL MARAT, MD (St Andrew's)

I always sought truth and must flatter myself that I found it, to judge by the mean persecutions inflicted on me for more than ten years by the Royal Society of Science. These started when the Academy understood that my discoveries about the Nature of Light contradicted its own researches there, and that I had no interest whatsoever in enrolling in its ranks. Because the d'Alemberts, Condorcets, Moniers, Monges, Lavoisiers and all the rest of those quacks of that scientific institution wished to grab all the publicity for themselves, and because they monopolised the trumpet of Fame, it's easy to see why they sneered at my revelation, throughout the breadth of Europe, poisoned the hearts of learned men against me and had all academic journals denied me, so that to get publication at all I was forced to employ a pseudonym. For more than five years I submitted to this cowardly persecution. Then the Revolution proclaimed itself, with the Meeting of the Estates-General. Swiftly I saw the omens and at last began to breathe in the hope of seeing Mankind avenged and I myself enthroned in my rightful place.   *L'Ami du Peuple*

The digest of my experiments on Light were at last published throughout all Europe; all newspapers spoke of little else. I had people from Court and City in my house for half a year. Realising that it was unable to prevent my discoveries, the Academy attempted to pass them off as their own! Three different Academic institutions sent me delegations on the same day begging me to show up as a candidate! Several crowned heads sought me out, because of the celebrity of my works!   *L'Ami du Peuple*

Sensibly, perhaps, Marat does not name the crowned heads.

In order to ensure public tranquillity, two hundred thousand heads must go.
    Brand them! Split their tongues! Slice off their thumbs! Impale them.   On the Constitutional Moderates, notably
                    Lafayette, Mirabeau, Bailly and Condorcet

A WARNING AGAINST MARAT

Returning to this capital after so long an absence, my heart and mind are directed towards you, the Assembly. You would have found me kneeling in profound respect before your Majestic congress if my old age and infirmities had permitted me to address you on your noble deeds, and also on whatever else remains to be achieved so as to establish in our unhappy country the Peace, Liberty, and Happiness which you aim to build us.

Not such a long time ago I ventured to remind the kings of their duties. Allow me this day to speak to the People of its errors, and to you, its delegates, of the dangers that threaten us all. I do not hesitate to tell you that I am deeply grieved by the crimes that have made us a nation of Mourners. I am shocked to confess that I myself am numbered with those who, once struggling against despotism, may have encouraged not Liberty but licence. . . .

I am on the verge of death, about to depart from our great family, whose happiness has been the most urgent wish of my life, but what do my old eyes now see? Religious dissension, some people cringing with fear, others hot with bullying ambition, a government which is no more than a tool of the lowest reaches of the street and a den of refuge for those who wish to dictate or destroy the Law. I see armies without discipline, rulers without power, ministers lacking all support, certain political clubs dictating to the State, clubs where the corrupt and ignorant pose as political savants. . . .

This, and I am no liar, is what is really happening in France. I can dare say this not only because conscience impels me, but, being eighty years of age, I can be accused by none of you of pining for the *ancien régime* because, in denouncing to you those who have wilfully set our kingdom ablaze or who have perverted our people's thoughts by their writings, I cannot be condemned for disregarding the value of a free and honest press. My heart brimmed with joy and hope at the sight of you establishing popular happiness, abolishing feudal abuses, proclaiming the Rights of Man, uniting our separate provinces under uniform law and government. I weep to see certain licentious people corrupting this revolution with vilest intrigue; to see the honoured word 'Patriot' prostituted, to see anarchy victorious under flags of Liberty. . . .

In this city, once the city of light and of civilisation itself, I behold the populace ferociously applaud the most appalling manifestoes and grin at tales of assassination, boasting of crimes as if they were battles honourably won. People of this sort are unaware that the smallest misdeed can introduce unending disasters. Their frivolity as they laugh and dance above the abyss agitates me more than all else.   ABBÉ RAYNAL, letter read before the National Legislative Assembly

This, from a survivor from the eighteenth-century Enlightenment, the author of the widely read Histoire des Deux Indes, *seems to have had a decisive*

influence on Marat's assassin, Charlotte Corday, with results which the Abbé could not have foreseen. One wonders what he would have thought of her means of silencing the hated Terrorist.

FERSEN PREPARING THE ROYAL ESCAPE

The King sanctioned the route designed by you. Now we are considering the position of the bodyguards. I am going to despatch you *assignats* worth a million by tomorrow's or Wednesday's mail, addressed to M. de Contades and hidden in white taffeta; we have altogether four million, of which one is abroad. The King wishes the departure to be for the first week in June, for by then the Civil List will have supplied him with two million.

No precautions are necessary from here until Châlons; preferably, dispense with all. Everything rests on speed and secrecy; if you are uncertain of your troops, it would be best to keep them in barracks, or at least station them only beyond Varennes, so as not to be seen by the country folk. The King would merely drive straight through. The bodyguards here cannot be paraded, because of this secrecy matter.   COUNT AXEL VON FERSEN, to the Marquis de Bouillé, commander of the Metz garrison loyal to the King

The departure is now finally decided for June 20, midnight. A treacherous nurse of the Dauphin who could not be dismissed and who will not be leaving before Monday night, makes it necessary to postpone the journey until then; but you can be assured that it will take place. Horses will be changed at Chaintrix, the journey will merely continue with the mail. The King will be in red; if the Duke de Choiseul tells him that the disposition of the troops is favourable, he will make himself known. To escape suspicion and disorder at Châlons, the body of soldiery at the Sommevesle Bridge should delay reaching it before Wednesday noon, because the King could arrive there at 2.30.

COUNT AXEL VON FERSEN, to the Marquis de Bouillé

FLIGHT TO VARENNES

The event which has just happened confirms us more than ever in our plans. Our position is dreadful! We absolutely must flee from here next month. The King wishes this even more vehemently than myself.   QUEEN MARIE ANTOINETTE, to Comte de Mercy-Argenteau, former Austrian Ambassador, after the crowds had prevented the Royal Family leaving Paris for Saint-Cloud

Thursday 16. With the Queen at 9.30. Took the things myself; nothing suspected here or in town.

Friday 17. To Bondy and Bourget [outlying towns on the route to Montmédy].

Saturday 18. With the Queen from 2.30 to 6.

Sunday 19. Took 800 livres and the Seals. Remained in the Palace from 11 to midnight.

Monday 20 June. It's arrived.
    COUNT AXEL VON FERSEN, organiser of the royal flight from Paris to reach loyal troops at Montmédy. Diary

June 20.
Both their Majesties told me that at any price they must leave. We arranged the exact times. Should they be arrested I must go to Brussels and try to do what I can on their behalf. On leaving me, the King said: 'M. de Fersen, whatever the outcome, I shall never forget all your efforts for me.' The Queen shed many tears. I left her at 6, when she took the children on her usual walk, with no particular security arrangements. At 11.15 the children came, and were taken to the coach. Lafayette went by, then Madame Elizabeth [the King's sister], followed by the King, then the Queen.
    COUNT AXEL VON FERSEN. Journal

June 22.
My dear friend, the King and Queen, Madame Elizabeth, the Dauphin and Madame departed from Paris at Midnight. I was with them without any mishap, until Bondy, and am now journeying forward to meet them.   COUNT AXEL VON FERSEN, to Baron Evert Taube

June 23.
Fine but chilly. Reached Arlon at 11 pm. There found Bouillé; learnt that they have caught the King. I know no details. The King was wanting in firmness and resilience.   COUNT AXEL VON FERSEN. Journal

June 23.
My dear father, all is over and I am plunged into hopelessness. The
King was arrested at Varennes, sixteen miles from the frontier. M. de
Bouillé came here to announce it to me.

COUNT AXEL VON FERSEN, to his father

DROUET'S RIDE, 21 JUNE 1791

*Louis XVI and Marie Antoinette were intercepted just before they reached
safety by one Drouet, who galloped near midnight by a short cut from Sainte-
Menehould to the town of Varennes through the forest and roused the populace.*

Drouet was by nature a silent man; tall, and with a face like a hawk.
He had long, clean legs, suitable for riding on a horse; he had the roll
of the cavalry, for he had served in that arm. He went down to his
stables and saddled the two horses by lantern-light, and so went
riding out with his companion. The crowd gathered round him; as he
came to the limit of the town he got free of them, and immediately
broke into a gallop down the Clermont road. . . .

Over the crest of the hill and down into the steep and muddy
ravine where the mountain village of Islettes, dirty and clumped,
squats by the brookside, they galloped on . . . for the long flat rise
before them did not check their course. But just as they approached
its summit in a place where the great trees of Argonne line the road
upon the right, and upon the left are separated from it by nothing but
a narrow strip of mead (where today the railway runs), there mixed
with the noise of the hoof-beats beneath them the noise of a distant
hail. They drew rein, and very soon tall riding figures loomed up in
the night upon the skyline of the hill-top before them, and when they
hailed again Drouet recognised his own grooms. The groups mingled, and to the panting of the two strained beasts, the occasional
pawing of the tired post-horses of the others, the story of the coach
was rapidly told. It was on two miles ahead, rolling rapidly to
Neuville, and so to Varennes. It was bewildering news, for all Ste
Menehould had thought that the king's flight was to Metz. And in a
moment the active mind that lay behind the close-set eyes of Drouet
seized the tactics of that night upon which depended the fate of the
Capetian monarchy, and of all Europe too. The coach had doubled.
Its start upon him was too great to be caught up by following the
road; they would be at Varennes, and screened by a belt of soldiery

before he could ride them down. He must – it was his one opportunity – plunge across the base of that triangle and head the fugitives; but this short cut lay not even over fields or common, it lay through the immense forest of Argonne and the high tangled ridge of the hill. He had, across such country, not an hour before him, and more than eleven miles to cover. He leapt the ditch, he crossed the meadow, he took the thick of the trees on his left, and urged his mount by a direct threading of the undergrowth, until he came to the summit whence proceeds the long line of the hills. For that short mile only was the sound of the hoof-beats hushed and time lost in necessity of walking his horse. At the summit an alley opened before him; he struck spurs and galloped furiously down again.

He was so native to Champagne that he knew what none but the countryfolk knew, and what indeed no historian has discovered, that an old track lay along the summit of the hill, open through the dense growth of trees, dry from its situation on the ridge, with here and there a fallen trunk or a hummock of ground to imperil one, but still a road of a kind. It is of immense antiquity; the Gauls have used it, and the Romans, but the forest has grown up round its southern end; it comes up blindly against the undergrowth and leads nowhere. It had had no purpose in the history of the nation during all that thousand years in which the great edifice of the French monarchy had risen to the benefit of mankind; and now this deserted and haunted lane in the wood was the instrument by which that monarchy was destroyed.

Down it and down it, mile after mile, the horses thundered. The night wore on, and from the distant steeples of the villages in the plain beneath the half-hour struck; a couple of miles away down on the plain, and parallel to Drouet's riding, ran the straight high road, and on it, still rolling ahead, but gained on with every bound of the cavalryman's horses, went the berline and the destiny of the Bourbons.

The riders came to a place where years before murder had been done, and where a great white stone had been set by the peasantry, who dread the powers of evil that haunt such spots. This stone was Drouet's mark, for here there branches from the ridgeway a narrow and foul path which leads downwards on to the Varennes road, and strikes that road just as it issues from the forest and at the gate of the little town. By this way alone can a man on horseback get from the high ridgeway down to the plain, unless indeed he is to go all the way round and strike the main road through the pass which lies a mile or two ahead. This turning alone could accomplish Drouet's purpose, and even so the issue was very near. The hardest pace might fail to head the berline, and he might have ruined his mount and clattered into Varennes too late. They galloped and they galloped on, till the woods suddenly ceased upon either side. They heard beneath them the setts of the high road, and immediately saw before them such lights as still shone from the higher windows of Valmy. The clock was striking the hour. Drouet dismounted: wisely, for in the tortuous streets of the little place and with the business before him he was freer on foot than in the saddle.

The whole place was silent. One would have said that no one watched. The sluggish river slipping between the piles of the bridge was the only sound. He ran breathlessly up the High Street. Between him and the archway that crossed clean over it up the hill there was not a human being nor light, save at one door, from which light streamed, and in which a group of men were talking – politics of course, for it was a tavern; but of the coach, of soldiers, even of the horses for the change, not a sign. He thought for a moment that he had failed. He dashed into the tavern and asked if a berline had rolled by. The stolid people of these hills looked at him rather stupidly, wondering what he meant. But he was known, and they answered him. Nothing had been heard, nothing had been seen. Then Drouet for the first time in that night of thundering hoofs and riding saw the conclusion of his plan. He told them that in the coach was the king. Such time as it took, not to convince them, but to get the mere fact into their heads, was wasted: but soon they had understood or believed: they rose, they scattered, one man to raise the militia, another to find the mayor, a third to arm himself. As for Drouet, he went out into the air of the street, could see nothing at first for the glare of the light, waited a moment till his eyes should be accustomed to the darkness, then rapidly breasted the hill, keeping close upon the houses. And suddenly before he quite knew it, there was the berline right on him, a huge mass of leather and of packages and of humanity within and without, girding on its brakes and sliding down the stone of the street. His work was done, and the doom of the monarchy was accomplished.   HILAIRE BELLOC, 1908

AT VARENNES

CAPTAIN BAYON: 'Sire, you are aware . . . all the people of Paris are . . . Sire, you will proceed no further . . . interests of State. . .'
KING LOUIS XVI: 'Well, what is it you want?'
BAYON: 'Sire, a decree from the Assembly. . .'
LOUIS: 'Where is it?'
BAYON: 'My companion has it.'
LOUIS (taking it from Jean Louis Romeuf and reading it): 'There is no longer a King of France.'

One must have the soul of a monster to shed the blood of one's own subjects.   KING LOUIS XVI

Well, Madame, you are in a very unpleasant position, but my husband is not responsible. I don't want him to get into any trouble.

MADAME SAUCE, a grocer's wife, to Queen Marie Antoinette

VARENNES, THE DEPARTURE

At about half past seven, I saw the royal carriage approaching, surrounded by a squad of armed men. It passed very near me, and so slowly that I could observe the Queen returning my salute. The King made a gesture that showed his profound desolation and prostration. The Queen seemed even more distressed.

In all my life I have never felt such a sensation, and the poignant scene has never left my imagination.   A French Officer of Dragoons

We will eat her heart and liver.

From the crowds at Rheims, agitating against Marie Antoinette

AFTER VARENNES

Immediately we reached Varennes, we were sent back. Why, I do not understand. . . .

I have had a horrible dream; I was surrounded by wolves and tigers and wild animals eager to eat me.

LOUIS, THE DAUPHIN (later Louis XVII), aged six, back in Paris

You will have heard the various Channels of the King's Escape from the Tuileries. Bye the bye he was said to be in perfect Liberty there, but yet our friend La Fayette was very near being hanged because he got away, and his Justification tends to shew that his Majesty, besides his parole given, was so closely watched that he had but little chance of getting off unobserved. This Step was a very foolish one. Public Affairs were in such Situation that if he had been quiet he would have soon been Master because the Anarchy which prevails would have shown the Necessity of conferring more Authority, and because it is not possible to ballance a single Assembly against a Prince but that one must prove too heavy for the other or too light for the Business. The Assembly also, very strongly suspected of corrupt Practises, was falling fast in the Public Estimation. His Departure changed every Thing and now the general Wish seem to be for a Republic, which is quite in the natural Order of Things. Yesterday the Assembly decreed that the King being inviolable, he could not be involved in the Accusations to be made against those concerned in his Evasion. This has excited much Heart against them. The People are now assembling on the Occasion and the Militia (Many of them opposed to the King) are out. As I lodge near the Tuileries it is far from improbable that I shall have a Battle under my Windows. The Vanguard of the Populace is to be formed by two or three thousand Women. A good smart Action would I think be useful rather than pernicious, but the great Evil arises from a Cause not easily removed. It will I think be scarcely possible to confer Authority on, or in other Words to obtain Obedience for a Man who has entirely forfeited the public Opinion; and if they lay him aside, I do not see how they are to manage a Regency. His Brothers are abroad and so is the Prince of Condé. The Duke of Orleans is loaded with universal Contempt, and if they should name a Council of Regency they would be obliged to take either feeble or suspected Characters. Add to this the Struggle which must arise in a State where there is a King dethroned, and that for trivial causes. At the same Time the State of their Finances is detestable and growing worse every Day. . . .

(Four days later) My last was of the sixteenth. The Riot of that Day went off pretty easily but the next Morning two Men were lanterned and mangled in the parisian Taste. This occasioned some little Stir. There had been a pretty general Summons to the friends of Liberty, requesting them to meet in the Champ de Mars. The Object of this Meeting was to perswade the Assembly by the gentle Influence of the

Cord, to undo what they had done respecting the imprisoned Monarch. As the different Ministers and Municipal Officers had received it in Charge from the Assembly to Maintain Peace and see to the Execution of the Laws, they made Proclamation and displayed the red Flag. In coming from the british Embassadors about seven in the Evening, I met a Detachment of the Militia with the red Flag flying and some of the civil Officers. I went shortly after to a Heighth to see the Battle but it was over before I got to the Ground, for as the Militia would not as usual ground their Arms on receiving the Word of Command from the Mob, this last began according to Custom to pelt them with Stones. It was Hot Weather and it was a Sunday Afternoon for which Time, according to Usage immemorial, the Inhabitants of this Capital have generally some pleasurable Engagement. To be disappointed in their Amusement, to be paraded thro the Streets under a scorching Sun and then stand like Holiday Turkeys to be knocked down by Brick-Bats, was a little more than they had Patience to bear, so that without waiting for Orders they fired and killed a dozen or two of the ragged Regiment: the rest ran off like lusty fellows. If the Militia had Waited for Orders they might I fancy have been all knocked down before they received any. As it is, the Business went off pretty easily. Some of them have since been assassinated, but not above five or six, as far as I can learn. Lafayette was very near being killed in the Morning but the Pistol snapped at his Breast. The Assassin was immediately secured but he ordered him to be discharged. These are Things on which no Comment is necessary.

GOUVERNEUR MORRIS, to Mr Robert Morris of Philadelphia

The King's flight became known throughout the capital between 8 and 9, the tocsin sounded, guns were fired, the big drum was banged, people shouted, 'To arms, citizens!' I rushed to the Place de Grève, they arrested the Duc d'Aumont [commander of National guard responsible for restricting the King], bawling that he should be hanged. M. de Lafayette appeared, his long sheep's head white as this very paper. After he had admitted his responsibility for the King, all asked where he had hidden him and cried, 'Hang him from the lampposts.'

M. DEVEAUX, to Count Axel von Fersen

'Royal' has vanished from all shop fronts, anti-royalist tirades remain as hostile as ever, the moderate democrats are completely disarrayed, the Jacobins propose a Republic, without yet getting their way. . . .

Great excitement rages here. The King will probably be returned tonight. All legislation is now counter-rebellion, yesterday all theatres showed the tragedy *Brutus*, the Republic is openly demanded, the people stuffed with a mass of lies; I cannot write all the disgusting gossip about the King and Queen. The police are arresting dozens in the Palais Royal. Today's Freedom is dreadful tyranny. Almost all Paris is outside doors and ready to greet the King. The mob armed with pikes and scythes scare me. Oh, could we but have him secure in the Tuileries.

Finally he arrived, at seven a.m., escorted by thirty thousand. I could not bring myself to Witness his arrival but I gather that, save for three persons, no one shouted insults at him. Immediately he reached the Tuileries, utter silence is said to have descended. All kept their hats on and leaned on their arms. . . .

According to rumour, many of those arrested wished to murder the King.   M. DEVEAUX, to Count Axel von Fersen

I am alive.

Oh, the anxiety I have been feeling for you and the sorrow I feel for all you must have undergone in not hearing from us. God grant that this reaches you. Do not write to me, this would compromise all of us and above everything do not come back under any circumstances. Everyone knows that you helped us to escape and should you show yourself, all would be lost. We are guarded night and day, I do not care. Do not feel sad for me, nothing will be happening to me. The National Assembly will be forgiving. . . .

I am able to tell you, that I love you and have time only to do that. I am well. Suffer no pain for me. I should be glad to know you are not worrying. Write to me by post, in code, address it M. de Browne – with another envelope to M. de Gougens. Your servant should write the address. Let me know where I should send my letters so that I can write to you, for without them I cannot survive. Farewell, my most beloved and loving of men. I embrace you with all my heart.

QUEEN MARIE ANTOINETTE, to Count Axel von Fersen

We are in the same position as we were after the capture of the Bastille – free and with no more King. It remains to be seen whether it will help us to propose another of this breed. We beseech you, in the name of the nation, either to at once declare that France is a monarchy no longer and that we are a republic, or at least, to delay only until each of the Departments and all the primary Assemblies have pronounced their will, before for a second time thrusting the finest realm in the world into the whips and scorpions of kingship.

The Cordeliers' Club

AN AMERICAN IN PARIS

The Nation can never give back its confidence to a man who, false to his trust, perjured to his oath, conspires a clandestine flight, obtains a fraudulent passport, conceals a King of France under the disguise of a valet, directs his course towards a frontier covered with traitors and deserters, and evidently meditates a return to our country with a force capable of imposing his own despotic laws. . . .

In every sense in which the question can be considered, the reciprocal obligation which subsisted between us is dissolved. We owe him no longer obedience. We see in him no more than in different person, we can regard him only as Louis Capet.

What kind of office must that be in a government which requires for its execution neither experience nor ability, that may be abandoned to the desperate chance of birth, that may be filled by an idiot, a madman, a tyrant, with equal effect as by the good, the virtuous, and the wise? An office of this nature is a mere nothing; it is a place of show, not of use. Let France, then, having reached the age of reason no longer be deluded by the sound of words, and let her deliberately examine, if a King, however insignificant and contemptible in himself, may not at the same time be extremely dangerous.

TOM PAINE. Manifesto, following the flight to Varennes

IN THE CHAMP DE MARS

A number of people assembled in the *Champ de Mars*, to hear the inflammatory speeches of certain violent Republicans; some of whom, *it is pretended*, are Prussians and English. Their numbers gradually increased and at noon four commissioners arrived from the Jacobins, bringing with them a petition which they invited the mob to sign, in order that it should be presented to the National Assembly.

Two men, one of them an invalid with a wooden leg and the other a young hair-dresser, having imprudently concealed themselves under the boards which form the ascent to the altar of liberty, with an intention, *as it was said*, to peep at the ladies' legs, through holes which they had bored for that purpose, were discovered, and immediately dragged out of their lurking place.

They were accused of having intended to set fire to the altar of liberty; and it was pretended that on them some tow and matches had been found.

Others said that they had a design to blow up the *Champ de Mars*.

In one moment their heads were off.   *The Times*, London

The crowd had assembled to sign a petition for the King's dethronement. Fearing disorder, Bailly, Mayor of Paris, ordered it to disperse. In the resentful confusion, a shot was fired at the National Guard, whose commander, Lafayette, ordered it to fire on a particular group. In this, the 'Massacre of the Champ de Mars', some fifty were killed. This subsequently proved fatal for Bailly, and finally discredited Lafayette with the extremists.

THE CHIEF CLERK

What joy for these gentlemen to be in a position to order about their chief clerk – the King of France.   JACQUES NECKER

He should be condemned to live.   DEPUTY FAUCHET, on King Louis XVI

THE BRIDLE

'Tis said that Kings with Wild Ambition fir'd,
To Pow'r despotic always have aspir'd
Like untam'd Coursers whose indignant Soul
Spurns at Restraint and scorns all weak Control.
Hence British Senators with patriot Skill,
Have strove to check and Curb the Monarch's Will,
But Gallic Statesmen take a wiser Course
And make the Bridle stronger than the Horse.

GOUVERNEUR MORRIS

THREAT

From here I can see the windows of a palace within which counter-revolution is at work, where there is being planned details to thrust us back into the horrors of servitude. . . . Let each one of those dwelling therein realise that our Constitution allows inviolability to the King alone. Let them know that the law will stretch out without the slightest discrimination to all the guilty, and there is not one single head which, once convicted, can escape its sword.

PIERRE-VICTURNIEN VERGNIAUD, to the Legislative Assembly

There must be a war, so that we may be at last revenged for all the outrages committed in this country.

QUEEN MARIE ANTOINETTE, to Comte de Mercy-Argenteau

FORCE?

Force can be used only by the support of foreign armies, and this entails nothing less than reliance on war. Can a monarch really permit himself to introduce war into his own country; Would not the medicine prove worse than the sickness; I am aware that kings have always gloried in employing force to regain their possessions; I am also aware that it is held a weakness to be nervous of disaster in such circumstances as these. But I admit that such a reproach affects me less than the wretchedness of the people, and my heart recoils in contemplating the horrors which I should cause.

KING LOUIS XVI, to his émigré brothers, Comte de Provence
(later King Louis XVIII) and Comte d'Artois (later King Charles X)

PARISIAN SOCIETY

Never was Parisian society as a whole so brilliant and so serious-minded as between 1788 and 1791. Those who lived through those years are forced to confess that never in one single place was centred so much life and wit.   MADAME DE STAËL. *Du caractère de M. Necker.*
Considération sur les principaux événements
de la Révolution française, 1861 edition.

THE SALON OF 1791

No traditional salon with academicians comfortably hung, independents allowed to exhibit two morning hours of a single day and in the open, sun or rain, of Place Dauphine. Dr Angevilliers, derided by artists as the Elephant, had emigrated: this new Salon is widely representative, the non-elect, even the non-French, admitted on equal terms with sacrosanct Academicians, Jacques-Louis David exults; freedom has come to art but he will guide it; will inspire the Revolution with his Brutus and Horaces; will commemorate Jeu de Paume, death of Marat and other big moments; will design her triumphal arches and her feasts of Reason. He will sit on her Councils – he will also become Court Painter to Emperor Napoleon.

BEATRIX CARY DAVENPORT, 1939

One of David's most spectacular effects was the Feast of the Supreme Being, 1794.

Here in Paris I have made myself important. They ask my advice on affairs of great significance. On all sides they beg me to dine with them. I have everything save a place to live in. I implore your aid. Send me six louis or some bedding.   CAMILLE DESMOULINS, to his father

I am intimately acquainted with Mankind and am very familiar with the ignoble elements underlying its motives.   JOSEPH FOUCHÉ

THE CITIZEN AND
CITIZENESS ROLAND

A few days back, some half-dozen Paris artisans made a deputation to the home of that old humbug Roland. By mischance their arrival coincided with the Rolands' dinner time. 'What do you want?' asked the Swiss servant, barring the door. 'We want to address the virtuous Roland.' 'No one virtuous here,' replied the doorkeeper, very fat and close-cropped, though reaching out to allow them in. The worthy fellows tramp down a passage to the ante-room of the virtuous Roland. They are held up by the horde of flunkeys filling the approaches. Twenty cooks, laden with the choicest fricassees, exclaim, 'Careful there, careful! Make way!' These are the *entrées* for the virtuous Roland. Others carry the virtuous Roland's hors-d'oeuvre; others still, the virtuous Roland's roasts; yet more, the virtuous Roland's side-dishes. 'What do you want?' demands the virtuous Roland's *valet de chambre*. 'Why, we wish to address the virtuous Roland.' The valet departs with this news to the virtuous Roland, who emerges, his expression sulky, his mouth bulging, napkin on his arm. 'The Public must indeed be in danger for me to be compelled to desert my dinner in this way!' He leads them to his study, through the dining room, attended by more than thirty courtiers. At the top of the table, on the virtuous Roland's right, sat Bassatier; on the left, Robespierre's pet spy, little you-know-who, his papier-mâché face and hollow eyes glancing lewdly at the virtuous Roland's Madam. One of the deputation tries to go through the unlit pantry and, gracious, upsets the virtuous Roland's dessert. Informed of this loss, the virtuous Roland's wife tears her false hair in fury.

JACQUES RENÉ HÉBERT. Le Père Duchesne

THE SERIOUSNESS OF YOUTH

Sentiment! What is it? It is the life-force of existence, society, love, friendship. It joins son to mother, citizen to country, and dominates Natural Man. Loose living, sensuality, coarsen its delicacy but man regains it during adversity. It is the consoling element which death alone can destroy.

Have I not yet explained sufficiently? Then ascend some peak of Mont Blanc, watch the slow sunrise bearing consolation and hope to the ploughman's hut. Let its first gleam penetrate your soul, and never forget your sensations. Descend to the sea, until the day-star sinks majestically in to the depths of the Infinite. Melancholy will overcome you – surrender to it. The Melancholy of Nature is invincible.

Have you ever stood under the Saint-Rémy Monument contemplating its grandeur? Casting your imagination back to antiquity, the finger traced by proud Rome two thousand years ago places you in sight of Romulus, Scipio, Fabius. Then step back into your present being, to see far-off mountains gloomed by black cloud above the huge Tarascon plain, beneath which lie a hundred thousand Cimbri. On one side the Rhône, swifter than an arrow, the township not far off, sheep at pasture. Probably you dream – the dream of sentiment.

Abandon yourself to the landscape, hide in the shepherd's hovel, and sleep the night through on skins, the fire smouldering at your feet. A situation to awe you! You can hear midnight, nearby animals move out to grass, bleatings mingle with the herdsman's cry. Now, here, retreat into your innermost being and, while tasting its most exquisite joys, brood on the primal sources of entrails, to die with the Republic, to avoid the sight of Rome lost, liberty abandoned. I find pride in mankind. Such fortitude elevates me. I collapse beneath Cato's statue. Such reverence is the pride, the dignity, of sentiment.

Those Corsican slaves sold in Roman markets after defeat by Ciceraus, displayed only passivity. They steeled themselves against cruelty, made themselves immune to violence. Here is the true nature of Man. Has he not Reason – and Sentiment? Violence may assault him, tyrants ravage him. Very well then, let him perish rather than give the slightest assistance to the executioner.

NAPOLEON BONAPARTE, from *Discours sur l'Académie de Lyon*

ROASTING LIVE CATS

M. de Troudaine Ment[d.] as having heard from young Montmorin that the King is by Nature cruel and base. An Instance of his Cruelty among others was that he used to spit and roast live Cats. In riding with my friend I tell her that I could not believe such Things. She tells me that when young he was guilty of such Things. That he is very brutal and nasty, which she attributes principally to a bad Education. His brutality once led him so far while Dauphin as to beat his wife, for which he was exiled four Days by his Grandfather Louis XV. Untill very lately he used always to . . . in his Hand as being More convenient. It is no Wonder that such a Beast should be dethroned.

GOUVERNEUR MORRIS. *Diary*

THE QUEEN

It is out of the question for you to appear here at this moment; it would imperil our safety and if I tell you this you can believe me because I do so much want to see you. It seems that the Constitution-alists are assembling against the Republicans and Jacobins; having

contrived to gain support from a large group of the Guard, especially
those hired, who are to be enrolled into proper regiments very
shortly. They make a good show and are eager to settle accounts with
the Jacobins. These have performed all the dreadful and wicked
deeds but at present only rogues and street bandits support them; I
say, 'at present', because this country is changing from day to day,
one can recognise nothing at all.

But do understand my position and the part I must perform all
day long; sometimes I cannot even hear my own voice and have to
strain to understand that it really is I myself who is talking; but what is
to be done? All this must be endured. Believe me, we should be
undergoing worse if I had not quickly accepted our new situation. At
least like this we are winning a vital breathing space. How glad I
would be if a time would come when I should be powerful enough to
show these scoundrels that I am not their plaything.

How is your health? I am ready to wager that you neglect yourself; a mistake.   QUEEN MARIE ANTOINETTE, to Count Axel von Fersen

THE LANDLORD'S DAUGHTER

Eléonore had coarse features, vulgar appearance, thick lips. There
occurred, all the same, the inevitable. On this lower middle-class girl
Robespierre inspired irrefutable fascination. His public station, his
increasing celebrity, the idolising by a particular circle of friends,
provoked in her sensations akin to love. Did she genuinely love him?
Certainly, once he was dead, but, until then, it is questionable, without any supporting evidence. It is credible that she felt no more than
the proud ambition to believe herself chosen by he whose name alone
set all France a-tremble: something of the pleasure of the tamer
alongside a wild animal. And he? I myself disbelieve that he loved
her, for what stopped him offering marriage? However, there is only
mystery about this strange man, this silent phenomenon, who kept
secret his dreams and feelings. . . . Still, it remains true that she was
then assumed to be Robespierre's affianced, some said his mistress,
neither of these suppositions having any credible proofs. As 'Madame
Robespierre' she was laughed at by her fellow art-students in the
painting lessons she regularly attended throughout the Terror. Twice
a week, the new ten-day week, she would be noticed crossing the

almost empty Tuileries gardens, making for the lectures of Regnault, the famous painter, arch-rival of the equally famous David.

G. Lenôtre, 1894

Maurice Duplay, a cabinet maker of Rue Saint-Honoré who was Robespierre's landlord during his last three years, had four daughters, one of whom, Elizabeth, married the Jacobin, Philippe Lebas, who died with Robespierre. Their son, Philippe, always an unfailing republican, became tutor to Louis Napoleon, who was very fond of him, and, as prisoner, President, Emperor, never wholly forgot the older man's idealistic persuasions. The Emperor, never entirely insincerely, sometimes referred to himself as a socialist.

Eléonore never married, dying in 1832, two years after Lafayette had proclaimed as King of the French, Louis-Philippe, son of the regicide Égalité, duc d'Orléans.

GIRONDIN POLICY

The power of reason and fact has convinced me that a people which, after a thousand years of slavery has won its liberty, needs war. It needs war to consolidate its freedom. It needs war to purge the wickedness of tyranny. It needs war to exorcise those who might poison liberty.

Jacques-Pierre Brissot

I want to address you about the émigrés. Are you aware that they are said to have collected at Coblenz? A host of citizens must advance with all speed to attack them. Have they assembled on the Rhine? You must garrison your frontiers with two army corps. Are neighbouring countries sheltering them? You must steel yourselves to attack them too. Or have you heard the opposite, that they are in the heart of the Germanies? If so, you can disarm. Or are they preparing a new offensive? Your fury surges back. Are they misleading you with specious guarantees? You can once more disarm. So then – your real leaders are these émigrés and their advisers and their regard for you: they manipulate your troops and treasures; they decide whether or not you fight; they fix your destiny! I leave you to decide whether such a humiliating part suits a great nation.

Pierre-Victurnien Vergniaud, to the Diplomatic Committee

Though forced into war, the French Nation will fight with no wish for any annexations.

ANTOINE-NICOLAS DE CONDORCET, to the National Legislative Assembly

The French People renounce any war of conquest and will never use force against the liberty of any people.

Decree of the Constituent Assembly

Kings alone injure the peoples of the earth. The spirit of liberty is going to envelop the entire world. But it is fitting for citizens who have themselves been freed to come and help the rest of us. The French will thus show themselves better than the ancient Romans, who wanted liberty only for themselves.

VOLUNTEER GABRIEL NOEL. *Letters*, 1792

The principles of patriotism, freedom and the Republic are not only written but unalterably dyed on my heart, and will remain for as long as the Supreme Being, ruler of all of us, allows one remaining breath in me.   VOLUNTEER JOLICLERLE, 7th Battalion, Var Regiment. *Letters*, 1793

REVOLUTIONARY MARRIAGE

Pursued by Lafayette and his henchmen, Jean-Paul Marat was forced into flight. He was concealed by demoiselle Simone Evrard, who, studying the journals of this patriot, had felt in her heart the loftiest esteem. Marat, in deep gratitude towards his saviour, devined her emotions and promised her marriage. He despised formal marriage as a worn-out ritual, yet, not wanting to upset the modesty of Citizeness Evrard, one day summoned her to her window. Clasping the beloved's hand in his own, both of them bowed before the Supreme Being while he exclaimed, 'Here, in the vast temple of Nature, do I take as witness to the fidelity I now swear to you, the Creator who hears our words.'   *Journal of the Mountain*

JACOBIN POLICY

I also desire war, but a war solely for the national interest. Let us start by destroying our enemies at home, and only then march out against the foreign enemies, should any remain.   MAXIMILIEN ROBESPIERRE

Court and factions doubtless have reasons for their war policy. What should ours be? 'The honour of France' do I hear? Good God, the French nation besmirched by this gang of émigrés, as absurd as they are feeble, that it can be robbed of its all, before all the world, – by those branded with crime and treachery! Ah, the disgrace is in being deceived by the ruthless machinations of the foes of Liberty, Magnanimity, Wisdom, Well-being, Virtue, – in these is our honour. What you wish to restore is superstition, the crutch of tyranny; the 'Honour' of the heroes of the aristocrats, the 'Honour' of Crime! This 'Honour' is a strange hybrid compounded, I think, by some marriage of vice and virtue impossible to imagine; but it is allied with that same vice to destroy its own mother; it is allowed free range even in the home of Liberty. Disregard this 'Honour' or despatch it beyond the Rhine, where it can seek asylum in the heart or mind of the princes and fine gentlemen of Coblenz.

MAXIMILIEN ROBESPIERRE, to the Jacobin Club

The decoration of the hall did not cost much. At first the members were content to imitate the London Society of the Friends of the Revolution, by stationing before the tribune the English, American and French national flags. They then voted the instalment of busts of Dr Price and Benjamin Franklin, adding one of Mirabeau. One member demanded the same distinction for Jean-Jacques Rousseau; another ordained a bust to Algernon Sidney – then very much in vogue; yet a third demanded one to the Abbé Mably; all this was decreed. They then debated where the busts should be placed. Which hero of Liberty and Philosophy should command the place of honour? Should Rousseau reside on Mirabeau's right? Or must Mirabeau surrender his place to Rousseau? A question left unanswered.

In the hall's centre was exhibited a Bastille fragment, scarcely surprising; the patriot Palloy, who would have taken rights in selling off the old fortress one bit after another, would have grabbed his chance of disposing of them all. Various curiosities were also on show: pikes given by the men of July 14th, a *lettre de cachet* signed 'Louis', countersigned Baron de Breteuil, and much else.

G. LENÔTRE, 1894

How, when you have dedicated France to belief in individual freedom can you harbour within you an institution which is an excuse for all sorts of creeping inquisition established by unruly faction throughout our country?

What government can defend itself against tyranny from these political clubs? You have destroyed the power lent by the People, yet above you is erected an expression of collective power monstrous beyond belief. All France is now absolutely divided between decent citizens, moderates, who remain outside the struggle, mute and shocked, while others, the violent, terrorise the nation and stoke up a dreadful volcano which disgorges lava which can overwhelm all of us.   ABBÉ RAYNAL, letter to the Legislative Assembly

Far be it for me to wish to guide the harshness with which this man, still one of our great men, must be judged, not, I say, by this Assembly but by the voice of public opinion. I myself can readily excuse him because of what he has already reminded us, his very great age. I can even excuse those who have applauded his letter, because this itself will affect the People in ways quite different from what he perhaps intended.   MAXIMILIEN ROBESPIERRE, on Abbé Raynal

THE JACOBIN CLUB, PARIS

The Society of Friends of the Constitution, which owed its popular name to the Jacobin [Dominican] Monastery in which it met, was becoming increasingly important in French politics. By the end of 1790 it had spread 150 daughter clubs throughout France. In Paris membership was 1000, at first it was reserved for Assembly deputies, who still made up one-third of the whole, recruited from all professions. In the great library, which the Dominicans had leased to the club when its original quarters became too small, such writers as Laharpe, André Chénier, and Chamfort jostled with financiers like Chavière and speculators like Abbé d'Espagnoc and rising politicians like Danton and Tallien; amongst the members celebrities like Talma, the great actor, and David, renowned painter, rub up against printers and watchmakers; there were doctors like Mirabeau's friend Cabarnis and journalists like Fréron and Desmoulins. The club met between Assembly sessions; its President, a monthly office, had to be a Deputy. The vast low hall, its wall still adorned with bookshelves, paintings, frescoes was often filled with some 500 people, who could contemplate above them the calm figure of Thomas Aquinas, the

Fountain of Knowledge, beneath him, or the famous Jacobin motto, inside a Crown – Freedom or Death. ANTONINA VALLENTIN, 1948

THE CORDELIERS' CLUB, PARIS

Some three hundred people, of all ages, men and women together, filled the place; and so slovenly and dirty were their garments that they could have been mistaken for a concourse of beggars. On the wall behind the President a copy of the Declaration of the Rights of Man was pinned, topped by two crossed daggers. Plaster busts of Brutus and William Tell on either side seemed placed there significantly, sentinels of the Declaration. Opposite, to the rear of the tribune, pendant-wise, were busts of Mirabeau and Helvétius with Jean-Jacques Rousseau between them. Thick rusty chains festooned above the throne made a sort of crown.

ROUSSEL D'EPINAL. *Le Château des Tuileries*

THE REVOLUTIONS

Within the space of a few years we have seen two Revolutions, those of America and France. In the former, the contest was long, and the conflict severe; in the latter, the nation acted with such a consolidated impulse, that having no foreign enemy to contend with, the revolution was complete in its power the moment it appeared. From both those instances it is evident that the greatest forces that can be brought into the field of revolutions, are reason and common interests. Where these can have the opportunity of acting, opposition dies with fear, or crumbles away by conviction. It is a great standing which they have now universally obtained; and we may hereafter hope to see revolutions, or changes in governments, produced with the same quiet operation by which any measure, determinable by reason and discussion, is accomplished.

TOM PAINE. *The Rights of Man*, Part Two
(See A. J. Ayer, 1988)

For too long it has been left to the Public Prosecutor to summon the vengeance of the People against criminals: may criminals henceforth go in fear of as many accusers as there are virtuous citizens! It will be impossible to escape the vengeance of authority when there is no longer only one person exercising it, but the entire Nation, which never sleeps. Citizens, whenever you have anything to denounce, come to me.   CAMILLE DESMOULINS

WOMEN

The moment has arrived for women to reject their shameful quiescence in which ignorance, pride, and masculine tyranny have so long fettered them. Let us return to antiquity when our Gallic and proud Teutonic mothers addressed the assemblies and bore arms alongside their men.   THEROIGNE DE MERICOURT, to the Jacobin Club

Theroigne died in an asylum in 1817, probably mentally disturbed from having been beaten up by women in 1793. Insanity saved her from the guillotine.

(For a useful survey of women's position in the Revolution, see Claire Tomalin, Chapter 13.)

A SELF-PORTRAIT

At fourteen, as now, I was some five feet tall, having reached full growth. I had a trim leg, very well-shaped foot, very wide hips, deep and superbly modelled bust, straight shoulders, demeanour firm and gracious, a step brisk and light. My face was not really exceptional save for its real freshness and much sweetness. My mouth is somewhat large; you could notice a thousand people who are prettier but no child with a more tender and seductive smile. My eyes, open, candid, bright, gentle, are crowned by brows brown like the hair above, but more beseeching than those of most others and always provoking interest. My complexion is more striking than clear, its colours radiant; my skin soft, my arm rounded, my hand not small but attractive from long, slender fingers, suggesting cleverness and preserving grace. My teeth were white and regular, and I had the embonpoint of perfect health. Such are the gifts bestowed on me by Nature.   MANON ROLAND. *Memoirs*, written in prison

THE HÔTEL BRITANNIQUE, PARIS – HOME OF MANON AND JEAN-MARIE ROLAND DE LA PLATIÈRE

I inhabited a spacious apartment in a pleasant area. We arranged that the Deputies who habitually met for discussion should visit my place four times a week, between the last session of the Assembly and the first at the Jacobin Club. Installed on a window seat, at a small table stacked with books, things to be examined, small bits of needlework, I worked or wrote letters, the discussion going on around me. I preferred to be writing, because that distanced me from the talk, permitting me to listen perhaps more intently. I can always do several things at once, and letter-writing lets me keep up a correspondence while overhearing matters totally different. I seem to myself to be divided into three: I cut my attention in turn, as if physically, and use them both as if I made the third. I remember one day, when the men, heated by argument, were getting very loud, and Clavière, seeing me writing away so briskly, joked that only a female brain was capable of it, and was astounded when I asked with a smile 'What then would you have to say if I were to repeat to you every detail of your discusssions?'

Save for the compliments expected when these gentlemen arrived and left, I always maintained strict silence, though I often had to, so to speak, pin my lips together to prevent myself intruding. If anyone addressed me, it would be after the main gathering had dispersed and the serious talk was over. I must end by saying that a jug of water and a bowl of sugar formed the only refreshment that I deemed suitable for those present at discussions. . . .

Robespierre's behaviour at these conferences at my house was singular. He said little, often sniggered, emitted a few sarcasms, avoided giving an opinion; nevertheless, the next day, after a discussion, which had some bearing on any present business, he was careful to stand up in the Assembly and employ for his own advantage material he had picked up from his friends at my table.

MANON ROLAND. *Letters*

Within herself, Madame Roland was convinced that the Revolution would produce no good at all except from herself.

ALPHONSE AULARD. *La Révolution française*, 1891

WINDMILLS IN THEIR PATH

My other brother departed some days back to swell the forces of the knights of derring-do. Possibly they will encounter a few windmills in their path. I cannot credit, like our famous, so-called aristocrats, that they will cross the frontiers in triumph and unopposed, particularly as the nation is very able to defend itself. I admit that the soldiers are an unruly lot, but this notion of Liberty stimulates them into a striking resemblance of courage; despair too might do much the same. For myself, I am by no means at peace with myself. What fate awaits us all? A dreadful dictatorship if the people are again fettered. We will fall between Scylla and Charybdis.

CHARLOTTE CORDAY, from Rouen, to Mlle Levaillant

We must never rest until all Europe is in flames. There must be no slackening of our efforts. We must seize the offensive. We must publish Manifestoes in French and in Spanish. We must inflame every mind either to rebel or to accept revolution. If once we extend our frontier to the Rhine, if once free peoples exist on either side of the Pyrenees, then our liberty will be established for good.

JACQUES-PIERRE BRISSOT

A civil war could be a great school of public virtue. Peace will set us back. We can be regenerated only by bloodshed.   MANON ROLAND

WAR DECLARED ON AUSTRIA

Gentlemen, you have just heard the result of the negotiations in which I have been engaged with the Court of Vienna. The conclusions of the report have been unanimously approved by my Council. I have adopted them myself. They conform with the desire several times expressed by the National Assembly and with the feelings sent me by a great number of citizens in different parts of the realm. All would prefer war than to witness any more the insults to the dignity of the French people. Having done my best to maintain peace, as I was in duty bound to do, I have now come, as the constitution enjoins me, to propose war to the National Assembly.   KING LOUIS XVI

On entering the Assembly he looked right and left with that sort of vacant curiosity not unusual with those so short-sighted that their eyes seem useless. He proposed war in the same tone that he might have used in proposing the most trivial decree imaginable.

MADAME DE STAËL, on King Louis XVI. *Mémoires*, 1818

Victory does nothing but arm ambition, reawaken pride and hollow out with its own glistening hands the tomb of the Republic. . . . Loosen the reins of the Revolution for one instant and you will find military dictatorship taking power, and the leader of factions overthrowing the representatives they have abused.

MAXIMILIEN ROBESPIERRE

France renounces the notion of conquest.

National Constituent Assembly, 1790

We threaten foreign rulers with invasion, not with fire and sword but with Liberty. . . . Wherever the French armies arrive, all taxes, tithes, privileges of rank will be abolished and all existing authority be revoked.   The Legislative Assembly, 1791

The Republic must dictate laws to Europe.

MERLIN DE THIONVILLE, to the Convention, 1794

THE FIRST VICTIM

The thief, Nicholas-Jacques Pelletier, was the first Frenchman condemned to the guillotine.

The people were by no means satisfied. They had seen nothing. It was all over too swiftly. They dispersed disappointed.

Chronique de Paris

THE ANNIVERSARY OF
THE TENNIS COURT OATH, 20 JUNE

The late attempt of the Jacobins to intimidate His Most Christian Majesty has failed entirely and has served only to impress more strongly on the minds of those who wish for order and good government an abhorrence of their principles and practices. The majesty of the throne was sullied, but it gave the King a happy opportunity of displaying an extraordinary degree of calmness and courage, which may be of infinite service. The circumstance of his having applied the hand of a grenadier to his heart, saying 'feel here if there are any signs of fear' is perfectly true. . . .

The King, finding the mob determined to force the door of the ante-chamber of his apartment, ordered his attendants to withdraw, and placed himself in a recess of one of the windows, where, attended by a few grenadiers, he suffered the mob to approach him, accepted from them a red cap with tricolor ribands, which he wore the whole time that they remained in the palace, and upon their expressing a wish that he should drink to the health of the nation, His Majesty condescended to comply with their request, and drank the remains of some wine in a cup, out of which a grenadier had previously drunk. During this time the Queen and the Dauphin with their attendants were in the council chamber, guarded by a table from the too near approach of the mob. It is singular considering that the populace was in every part of the royal apartment except the King's private bedchamber, that no other mischief should have been done except taking away the locks, and breaking the panels of the doors.

The admission of the mob is entirely to be attributed to the infamous conduct of the municipal officers: the commander of the National Guard had in his pocket an order from the administrators of the department to oppose force by force, but the orders of the Municipality [Commune] were wanting.

LORD GOWER, British Ambassador. *Despatches*

INVASION OF THE TUILERIES

Sir, listen to us. It is your business to listen to us. You are a traitor. You have always deceived us and are still doing so. But beware. The cup is brimming over and the people are weary of acting as your bauble.   LOUIS LEGENDRE, Paris butcher, to King Louis XVI

I still live, but only by a miracle. The 20th was appalling. It is no longer against me that they hurl their fury, but against my husband's very life, and they do not disguise it.

QUEEN MARIE ANTOINETTE, to Count Axel von Fersen

I can see that M. de Lafayette wishes to save us, but who will save us
from M. de Lafayette?   QUEEN MARIE ANTOINETTE

If the insurgents murder me it will be a blessing, a rescue from a most
wretched existence.   QUEEN MARIE ANTOINETTE, to Mme Campan,
                                             refusing an offer of body-armour

> Madame is mounting to her tower,
> Who knows when she'll descend?   Street song

A YOUNG MAN

This June 20th, I was walking aimlessly in the Tuileries Gardens
amidst the uproar of the armed mob crashing into the Palace, when I
met M. Perronet, engineer of roads and bridges. We were both
deploring such an insult to the royal dignity, when we were interrupted by a young man, whom I would have distrusted save for his
reception by M. Perronet. He looked soldierly: his eyes were
piercing, his complexion pale; he had a common accent and a foreign
name. He spoke freely about the chaos before us, and remarked that
if he were king, such scenes would not have been tolerated. I paid
scant attention to this then: but later events stirred up my memory,
for the speaker was Bonaparte.   MAÎTRE LAVAUX. *Mémoires*

ANOTHER YOUNG MAN

Monarchy does not lie in kingship, it means crime. The Republic does
not reside in a senate, it means Virtue.   LOUIS ANTOINE DE SAINT-JUST

FROM ROUEN

You ask me about events at Verson. Every wickedness you can imagine. About fifty people were beaten and their heads shaved. Apparently the women were by and large the most unpopular with the
assailants. Three died a little later. The remainder are still weak.
Among them were Abbé Adam's mother and the Curé's sister; the
Mayor was also arrested. A peasant was asked by the commune

whether he was a patriot. 'Certainly, gentlemen, I am that. Who doesn't know that I was the very first to seize the priests' goods, and you'll understand that an honest man wouldn't do that!' I doubt whether a professional wit would have replied better than this wretched hobbledehoy. Even the judges could scarcely repress their grins.   CHARLOTTE CORDAY, to Mlle Levaillant

AT THE OPERA

After the 20th of June, the people who wished well to the King and Queen, were desirous that her Majesty should sometimes appear in public, accompanied by the Dauphin, a most interesting beautiful child, and her charming daughter, Madame Royale. In consequence of this she went to the Comédie Italienne with her children, Madame Elizabeth, the King's sister, and Madame Tourzel[le], governess to the royal children. This was the very last time on which her Majesty appeared in public. I was there in my own box, nearly opposite the Queen's; and as she was so much more interesting than the play, I never took my eyes off her and her family. The opera which was given was *Les Evénements Imprévus*, and Madame Dugazon played the *soubrette*. Her Majesty, from her first entering the house, seemed distressed. She was overcome even by the applause, and I saw her several times wipe the tears from her eyes.

The little Dauphin, who sat on her knee the whole night, seemed anxious to know the cause of his unfortunate mother's tears. She seemed to soothe him, and the audience appeared well disposed, and to feel for the cruel situation of their beautiful queen. In one of the acts a duet is sung by the *soubrette* and the *valet*, where Madame Dugazon says: '*Ah! comme j'aime ma maîtresse.*' As she looked particularly at the Queen at the moment she said this, some Jacobins, who had come into the playhouse, leapt upon the stage yelling 'no more mistresses', and if the actors had not hid Madame Dugazon, they would have murdered her. They hurried the poor Queen and family out of the house, and it was all the Guards could do to get them safe into their carriages.   LADY GRACE ELLIOT, mistress of the Prince of Wales, from her account of revolutionary Paris, written for King George III

WAR-TIME PARIS

Paris, 1792, had changed since 1789–90; here was no longer the pristine Revolution, but a drunken populace lurching towards its fate, across many an abyss and along dubious paths. People no longer looked excited, inquisitive, enthusiastic, but menacing. In the streets, faces were scared or fierce, their owners keeping close to the wall to avoid notice, or roaming for prey; frightened eyes averted from you, or grim eyes stared directly into yours to dig out your secrets.

Variety in dress was abandoned: the old regime had far receded; men all dressed alike, according to the new regimen, an attire which for the moment was merely the last garment of future victims. Already the social freedoms shown at France's rebirth, the freedoms of 1789, unfettered and capricious, those of a society now dissolving though not yet anarchical, were being levelled on orders of the People: a popular despotism could be scented, no doubt creative, filled with promise, yet far more powerful than the old, rotting monarchical despotism; for, as the sovereign People is everywhere, when it becomes a tyrant, he is likewise – the inescapable presence of a universal Tiberius.

Mingling with Parisians was a foreign crowd of southern cut-throats, vanguard of the Marseillais whom Danton was recruiting for August 10 and the September Massacres, recognisable by their tattered clothes, bronzed skins, expressions of cowardice and criminality, but crime under an alien sun.

FRANÇOIS-RENÉ DE CHATEAUBRIAND. *Mémoires*, 1842

This war is a crusade of individual freedom. JACQUES-PIERRE BRISSOT

SECRET LETTERS

I am ever disturbed because of your position. Your bravery will be much praised and the King's steadfast behaviour also. It is essential to maintain this, and above all else, to remain in Paris. This is absolutely essential. Thus it will be simple to reach you, and this the Duke of Brunswick is planning to accomplish. Before his actual entry he will publish a powerful Manifesto from the Allied Powers making all France, Paris especially, responsible for the lives of the Royal Family.

COUNT AXEL VON FERSEN, to Queen Marie Antoinette

I have had your last letter written in secret ink, and somebody has already managed to uncover the words; for the second time. Thus we have to proceed differently, I am certain you will see the importance of this. With the approach of Bastille Day we anticipate dreadful disaster, released by all Paris, led by the Jacobins. They preach regicide, evil plots abound.   QUEEN MARIE ANTOINETTE, to Count Axel von Fersen

During this week the National Assembly will move to Blois and depose the King. All changes daily, but they are always set to destroy the King and his family.

At the Bar of the National Assembly, people petition that, if he is not deposed, they will kill him. The Assembly applauds. . . . We are in direct peril, just one day's delay could bring some unpredictable catastrophe, the [Brunswick] Manifesto must be issued, we await it with the greatest impatience . . . the gang of assassins increases all the time.   QUEEN MARIE ANTOINETTE, to Count Axel von Fersen

I am trying to get money for you in England and perhaps also from the King of Sweden.

Once the Allied armies have entered France, I will apply for more, from the King of Prussia and the Duke of Brunswick; Baron de Breteuil will do likewise. Adding to my own troubles, my two dogs are gone, both poisoned one morning, dying simultaneously. This much distresses me because I was so attached to them.

When the Duke of Brunswick reaches Paris he must reside in the Palace, in preference to anywhere else. . . .

COUNT AXEL VON FERSEN, to Queen Marie Antoinette

THE BRUNSWICK MANIFESTO

Their Majesties the Emperor and the King of Prussia having given me command of the armies assembled on the French frontier I have thought it well to inform the French population.

[We undertake] to end the domestic anarchy of France, to halt attacks on altar and throne, to re-establish legitimate authority, to restore to the King the freedom and security of which he has been robbed, and to allow him the means to wield his rightful and lawful powers.

Assured as they are that the healthy portion of the French people loathes the excesses of a faction enslaving them, and that most people are impatiently awaiting relief that will allow them to openly proclaim themselves against the hateful plans of their tyrants, their Majesties the Emperor and the King of Prussia call upon them to immediately return to the call of reason, justice, order, peace. . . .

Their aforesaid Majesties declare, moreover, on their word and honour as Emperor and King, that if the Tuileries Palace be insulted or invaded, that if the least injury, be inflicted on their Majesties the King, Queen, and the Royal Family, and if measures are not at once taken for their safety, preservation, and security, they, their Imperial and Royal Majesties, will wreak exemplary and unforgettable vengeance by yielding the town of Paris to military execution and utter subversion, and the guilty rebels to deserved death. . . .

From our headquarters at Coblenz, July 28
CHARLES WILLIAM FERDINAND, DUKE OF BRUNSWICK, Luxembourg

ARRIVAL OF THE MARCHERS FROM MARSEILLES

A collection of foreign vagrants, scum of all nations, Genoese, Corsicans, Greeks. Their chief leaders were a fellow from the Indies, and a Pole, one Lazowski.   DEPUTY BLANC-GRILLI from Marseilles

On July 30, a month before the September Massacres, that these fearful confederates spat out by Marseilles reached Paris. I think it impossible to conceive anything more fearsome than these five hundred madmen, mostly drunk, in red caps, arms bare, followed by the lowest of the low from Faubourgs Saint-Antoine and Saint-Marceau fraternising in one pothouse after another with gangs as dreadful as their own. They went on like this in a sort of braggardly fanfare, down the main streets where the orgy promised them by Santerre was preceded by diabolical dances.   DEPUTY THIÉBAULT
(See S. Loomis)

August 4. Fine, warm. Visited Baron de Breteuil. The Duke of Brunswick tells him that the army left Coblenz on the 30th; is due at Trier on August 5th, and will stay there for bread and fodder. They are expected at the French frontier, 15th or 16th.

August 7. The Paris Commune has demanded the King's deposition; very alarming.

August 10. Reassuring news from Paris, it is no longer believed that the King will be deposed.   COUNT AXEL VON FERSEN. *Journal*

THE TENTH OF AUGUST, TRIUMPH OF 'THE PEOPLE'

The mob, master of the Palace's Grand Staircase, now overwhelms the interior. Swiftly it floods all rooms and despatches all Swiss Guards still in them. Corridors, roofs, offices, private exits, to the smallest cupboard and wardrobe are searched, and any unfortunates hiding there are butchered without pity. Others are thrown alive from high windows, vainly beseeching mercy, and are transfixed by pikes thrust from terrace and courtyard.

Unpublished description, in Paris Foreign Office archive

On the Tuileries garden terrace, quiet folk drawn thither by curiosity, to see whether the palace still stood, wandered slowly about, silenced by glum astonishment, in a terrace ashine with smashed bottles. Weep they did not, they seemed petrified, struck mute. Everywhere they stepped back, horrified by stench and sight of oozing corpses, throats cut, entrails hanging out, anger still screwing up their faces. The more stoical visitors pointed at the massed flies, agog for blood, drawn by the heat to the open wounds on corpses, the eyes torn from their sockets.

Under the terrace, by the river, was the body of one of the Hungarian military once admired riding behind the Queen's coach. Stripped naked, he was receiving cynical jokes from a crowd of repulsive old women. In the Carousel, the spectacle of corpses stacked as if in a timber-yard, rivetted the curious, crowding from even the most distant suburbs. Realising that the fighting was over, they wished to gloat and, once patriotic feelings had calmed, they were satisfied with mere curiosity. Above all sounds came a loud and dirge-like hooting from the chapel's grand organ. A young Savoyard at the top of the organ-loft was trumpeting the *Dies irae* – like the Destroying Angel announcing the last Judgment.

LOUIS-SÉBASTIEN MERCIER. *Le nouveau Paris*

A wretched under-cook, lacking time to save himself, was forced by these tigers into a boiler and kept there, savaged by the raging heat of furnaces. Then, swarming to the tables, each grabbed the nearest food. One stole a spit loaded with quails, another a turbot, a third a Rhine carp shaped like himself. The wine cellars were beyond belief. One walked over a mass of smashed bottles and flagons, on which, pell-mell, stretched the conquerors, overwhelmed by drink, and the lost corpses, while men and women, maddened with stupefying delight gathered in swarms by the Queen's staircase, dancing in gutters of blood and wine. One killer played a violin above the bodies, and plunderers, pockets filled with gold, hung up rivals from the balustrade.

G. LENÔTRE, 1894

THE MASSACRE OF THE SWISS GUARD AT THE TUILERIES, 1792

Some Swiss, being chased hid in a neighbouring stable, and I did so myself. They were swiftly cut to pieces almost beside me. Hearing the cries of these pitiful victims, M. le Dreux, the householder, ran up, and I took the chance of making for his door, and, though unknown to them, I was invited by him and his wife to remain until danger had gone. On me were letters and news sheets addressed to the Prince Royal and a passport to the Tuileries on which my name and employment were written: these would certainly have betrayed me, but I had just time to throw them away before an armed gang broke in, to discover whether any Swiss were hiding there. At M. le Dreux's suggestion, I feigned work on some drawings on a large table. Having searched in vain, this crew, hands stained with blood, ceased, and had the nerve to describe the murders they had performed. In this refuge I stayed until four p.m., unable to avoid seeing the horrors done in the Place Louis Quinze. For the men, some were going on slaughtering, others beheading the corpses; for the women, utterly shameless, they were indulging in the grossest mutilations of the dead, tearing off bits of flesh and triumphantly bearing them away.

JEAN-BAPTISTE CANT HANET CLÉRY, *valet de chambre*
to King Louis XVI. *Journal*, 1798

If Louis XVI had shown himself on horseback, he would have won.

NAPOLEON BONAPARTE

KING LOUIS AND HIS FAMILY SEEK PROTECTION FROM THE NATIONAL ASSEMBLY

When we were under the tree opposite the café on the Feuillants' terrace, we walked through the leaves that had dropped overnight and been swept up in heaps by the gardener. We sank in them up to our knees. 'What a lot of leaves,' the King remarked, 'they've started to fall very early this year.' In some newspaper Manuel had written that the King would not survive the fall of leaves. A colleague informed me that the Dauphin amused himself by kicking up the leaves onto the legs of the person preceding him.

PIERRE LOUIS ROEDERER. *A Chronicle of Fifteen Days*, 1832

Pierre Louis, a member of the Paris Commune, refused to vote for the King's execution, and was himself executed in 1793.

For the moment the King and his family are safe. Yesterday, none would have imagined it, now there is hope. The King has been stripped of all authority for the time being. They have all found protection in the National Assembly. . . .

No words can describe yesterday's horrors. All Paris heard shots discharged at the Palace without realising that the Royal Family was within the National Assembly. Seven hundred Swiss Guards are thought torn to bits by the mob and six hundred were killed by Swiss rifle shot, among them two hundred of the Marseillese.

Simultaneous with the attack on the Tuileries, some unfortunates were having their heads cut off outside the Feuillants Club: hearing gunshots, the mob rushed there. Nineteen were beheaded, that is really to say mutilated, their heads cut off only after they had been beaten to death. We do not yet know their names, probably they were all upper-class. Last night, all Swiss officers remaining in Courbeoie were transferred to Saint-Germain. All Swiss left in Paris are dead. Because of rumours that a few survivors were hiding in the Palace cellars, these are now being flooded. After 7 p.m. it seemed that a popular feast was being held, there was singing everywhere and taverns were packed.

E. BERGSTEDT, Swedish Chargé d'Affaires, to Count Axel von Fersen

Madame Broquin is still selling her celebrated pomade for dyeing hair, red or white into chestnut or black, on a single application. The price starts at nine francs per small jar.

Advertisement in *Le Moniteur*, August 15

TOTAL ECLIPSE

My dear Friend,

You have been acquainted with the atrocious events which have taken place in Paris, when the Jacobin faction on the tenth of August overthrew the Constitution, enslaved both the Assembly and the King, the one by terror, the other by destitution and confinement, and gave a signal for pillage and massacre.

I could have found a high station in the new order of things, without even having meddled with the plot. But my feelings did not admit of such an idea. I raised an opposition to Jacobin tyranny; but you know the weakness of our honest folk. I was abandoned; the army surrendered to deeds befitting political clubs. Nothing was left for me but to exile myself from France. We have been stopped on our road and detained by an Austrian detachment, absolutely contrary to international rights. . . .

You will greatly oblige me, my dear Sir, by making for Brussels on immediate receipt of this, and insisting on seeing me. I am an American citizen, an American officer, no more in the French Service. That is your right, and I do not doubt of your urgent and immediate arrival. God's blessing on you.

MARQUIS DE LAFAYETTE, to William Short, secretary to Thomas Jefferson

WAR CRISIS

Longwy has fallen, but Longwy is not France. . . . The moment has come to proclaim to the People that they must hurl themselves upon the foe *en masse*. In shipwreck, the crew jettisons all that imperils it. Likewise, all that might imperil the Nation must be cast off, and whatever can be at all useful be offered to the local committees, with compensation promised.   GEORGES-JACQUES DANTON, to the Assembly

The tocsin that will sound is not the warning of alarm; it is the call to charge against the enemies of the Nation. Gentlemen, to overwhelm them we must have Audacity, more Audacity, always Audacity – and France is saved.   GEORGES-JACQUES DANTON

CITIZEN MATTHIEU, Officer of the Temple Prison: 'You are un-
    aware, Monsieur, of what is happening outside. The country is in
    the greatest peril, the enemy armies have crossed into Cham-
    pagne and the King of Prussia is marching on Châlons. You your-
    self will bear the onus for all the mischief that may now happen.
    We realise that we ourselves, our wives and children, are going to
    die, but the People will be avenged. The very first to die will be
    yourself. However, there is some time left and you may . . .'
KING LOUIS XVI: 'I have done everything possible for the People, I
    reproach myself with nothing.'

ROBESPIERRE, THE INCORRUPTIBLE

The right of property, like all other rights, is bounded by the obligation of respecting the rights of others. It cannot be permitted to
prejudice the safety, the liberty, the life or property of our fellows.
Any commerce which transgresses this principle is illicit and
immoral. . . .

    It is the duty of society to provide for the subsistence of every
citizen, whether by providing them with work or by guaranteeing
the means of existence to those who cannot work. . . .

    It is much more important to make poverty honourable than to
condemn riches. . . .

    Equality of wealth is an idle dream.

Robespierre, in the theatre, enjoyed the declamatory tragedies dealing with the tribunate, tyranny, the people, resounding crime and
virtue.   ALPHONSE DE LAMARTINE, 1847

The National Convention decrees death for anyone who proposes an
Agrarian Law, or any other law to undermine Property – landed,
mercantile or industrial.   1793

I have but one fault to find in Robespierre; it is that he is too
kindhearted.   CITIZEN REWBELL, a Jacobin, later to be a Director

The people are never wrong.

The people are sublime.

The people are just, good, and magnanimous.

It is better to spare a hundred guilty than that one innocent should be condemned.

The man is a scoundrel. He deserves to die. But . . . to kill a fellow creature!   As a young lawyer, prosecuting a man on a capital charge

He had, in common with the whole of that French professional class from which he sprang, a pronounced habit of order, a regularity of demeanour, and a very remarkable capacity for prolonged mental work; but this last so tended to expend itself upon imaginaries and perpetual deductions that he lost the sustenance which it afforded in countless other cases to the more practical minds of the Revolution; nor did it produce in him that reaction towards common things which was so marked in Carnot, and which had at the end begun to appear in St Just. . . .

He pushed to some excess an amiable vice whereby the care of the person was made the special social duty of the old regime, and is still preserved in exaggerated reverence by the social class of which he formed a member. Moderate as was his expenditure at every period of his life, he found the means for a careful wardrobe, and devoted a regular portion of his time for its maintenance. In the variety of colours which the age permitted, he chose such as were best suited to his type and presence, and partly from a desire to avoid exaggeration, partly from taste, he preferred the sober colours of the contemporary fashion of his rank, a warm brown or olive green for the colour of his coat. Later he ventured upon the brighter colours of '93, and especially upon a favourite light blue, which the accident of two dates has rendered famous. In the careful elegance of his silk stockings, in the buckles which, even after the change of fashion in 1792, he continued to wear upon his shoes, in his white stock and small lace wristbands, he displayed at every point the general taste for his society, but that heightened by a far more scrupulous attention than his neighbours could show. It is evident that with such a taste he would observe to a detail the convention of the age of his barbering.

His brown hair, carefully brushed back and standing fully outwards, was powdered with exact and daily regularity, and it is related of him that in all the vigils and alarms of the last few years, even when those street battles joined up whole days and made men forget sleeping and waking, he was never seen unshaven till the awful watch that ended his life.   HILAIRE BELLOC, 1901

At the Salon in the autumn of 1791, alongside the *Horaces* and the sketch of the *Serment du Jeu de Paume* by Jacques-Louis David, and the *Paesiello* by Mme Vigée-Lebrun, was displayed a series of portraits of members of the National Assembly, by Mme Labille-Guyard. We see Bishop Talleyrand, holding papers inscribed: 'Religious toleration: national education'; then the handsome Barnave, Beauharnais and the two brothers Lameth. Above all, we see Maximilien Robespierre in a small cloak and a jabot of snow-white organdie. Instead of his name under the portrait was 'The Incorruptible'. That title summarised all that bore him to the summit; by itself, it had already won half the battle.   FRIEDRICH SIEBURG, 1936

This man's sadness resembled a dark pool from which his soul refused to surface. All to be seen in him was stiffness, mistrust, a timidity almost limitless. He would quiver all over when a fellow citizen, in the contemporary artificial heartiness, slapped him amiably on the back – a gesture, by the way, requiring considerable courage. The habit of fraternal embracing, a tribute to ideals of simplicity – literary, philosophical or political – was torture to him. At Jacobin sessions it sometimes occurred that he was obliged to undergo a ritual of reconciliation with some opponent, ending with a formal embrace. With an expression of disgust – 'the face of a cat that has tasted vinegar' (Danton) – and blushing deeply, he would offer his cheek, and for the remainder of the evening was like a bear with a sore head. The patriotic *tu*, part even of official language, was never easy for him, and usually he contrived the neutral *vous* amongst a general group.

His punctilious politeness made some woman compare him to an *ancien régime* dancing master. Spontaneity, informality, seemed to drench him with such fear that it is tempting to relate all his mannered stiffness to a necessity to unyieldingly cling to regulations and fixed habits in terror of being swept away by a torrent of surprises and violence. In short, he was so shy that he never dared behave naturally; much of his revolutionary behaviour, especially what they called his inhumanity, is explicable from lack of inner and outer confidence.

He lost this fear at least when living with the Duplays. In that atmosphere of timid respect and unobtrusive consideration, his life lost some of its terrors. Every humiliation and disturbance inflicted on him by reality were then exorcised before they could touch him. He inhabited, as it were, an asylum: all knives and fragments of glass, which might injure his ideas, all nails and hooks on which they might get strangled, were assiduously removed, leaving no vent through which stern reality might penetrate. FRIEDRICH SIEBURG, 1936

It is the most sacred duty of a people whose rights have been violated, to rebel. MAXIMILIEN ROBESPIERRE

DRESS

Why should a person who behaves only as an ordinary citizen desire to appear superior to others? Why should anyone wish to deceive the people?

A free nation should venerate only two things, the Law and Virtue. If the distinctive robe of a magistrate commands respect it is because it represents the Law. That is why he wears it only when he is pleading or acting in court. What would you make of a mayor who paced fields or market place in his official robes? Or of a judge foolish enough as to leave bed at dawn flaunting the plumed hat provided by the law for his position on the bench? We have seen one of the former noblemen inflated by the breeze of vanity so that he could never bear to leave off his Blue Riband. His mania for it was such that he wore it even while taking a bath. Well, priestly garb outside a church or clerical activities, if maybe less absurd, is also incongruous.

La Feuille Villageoise

THE DECLARATION OF UNITY

Their Majesties, the Emperor and the King of Prussia, having heard the wishes and representations of Monsieur [Comte de Provence] and the Comte d'Artois, declare jointly that they consider the situation in which the King of France is placed as an object of common interest to all European sovereigns.

They hope that this interest will not fail to be recognised by the Powers whose aid is invoked, and that in consequence they will not refuse to employ, conjointly with their said Majesties, the most efficacious means, having regard to the forces at their disposal, to place the King of France in a position to strengthen in perfect freedom the bases of monarchical government, according equally with the rights of sovereigns and with the well-being of the French nobility.

Then, and in that case, their said Majesties, the Emperor and the King of Prussia, are resolved to act promptly and in unison, with the necessary force, to achieve the common end proposed.

While waiting they will give their troops the requisite orders so that they will be in all readiness for action.

FROM ENGLAND

. . . the ancient dawn calls us
to awake from slumbers of five thousand years. I awake but
my soul is in dreams;
From my window I see the old mountains of France, like aged
men, fading away.   WILLIAM BLAKE. *The French Revolution*

SEPTEMBER DAYS

According to reports, Paris still remains quiet, I mean no serious massacres, but daily arrests. On the 4th a gang of brigands paraded the capital led by a disloyal Commune official. They halted all women, tearing off their earrings with their ears too. Several of these infamous bullies were arrested, nine hanged where they stood. . . .

Assassins cut off the nose and ears of the Duke de Brissac, leaving him like this for an entire day before despatching him. One of his legs they posted to Madame Dubarry. The Princesse de Lamballe was most fearfully tortured for four hours. My pen jibs at giving details. They tore off her breasts with their teeth and then did all possible, for two whole hours, to force her back to consciousness, to make her death the more agonising.   COUNT AXEL VON FERSEN, to the Duke of
Södermanland, Regent of Sweden, following the death of King Gustav III

There is a story of one killer grimacing before the Queen from behind moustaches made of the pubic hairs of Princesse de Lamballe.

In the glare of two torches I saw the dread tribunal in whose hands lay my life or death. The president, in grey, was leaning upright against a table strewn with papers, an inkhorn, pipes, several bottles. Ten figures, some seated, some standing, surrounded this table, two in vests and aprons; others slept, prone on benches. Two men in bloodsoaked shirts, bearing sabres, guarded the prison entrance; an old turnkey held the bolts. Watched by the president, three men grasped a prisoner, seemingly aged about sixty.

I was stationed in a corridor; my warders crossed their swords over my chest, warning me that at my least intimation of escape they would run me through. I saw a couple of National Guards offer the president a petition from the Croix-Rouge Section, on behalf of the prisoner before him. He announced that such petitions were unavailing to traitors.

The prisoner cried out, 'It's frightful: your so-called trial is nothing but murder!' The President retorted, 'I've washed my hands of it. Remove M. de Maillé.' At this Maillé was pushed into the street where, through the door, I saw him slaughtered. I believe I also saw the president was reluctant to condemn him, but, several of the executioners had tramped into the prison, causing much disturbance.

JOURGNIAC DE SAINT-MÉARD, military officer. *Mémoire*

Like everybody else, I was shaking with terror lest royalists be permitted to escape from prisons and arrive to murder me for having no holy pictures to show them. That was how the massacres of September 2, 1792, occurred. While shuddering with horror, we regarded the deeds as more or less justified; while it was actually happening, we went about our business as we would on any other day.

MARIE-VICTOIRE MONNARD, aged thirteen, apprentice
sempstress, quoted by Boustanquai

SEPTEMBER MASSACRES

There, in Faubourg Saint-Honoré, were six large carts which I thought were ordinary cattle carts. But people on the streets looked at them in terror and as they passed, I saw they were crammed with men and women only just butchered, and whose limbs still remained fairly flexible, not yet having had time to stiffen. Thus legs, arms, heads nodded and dangled from either side. . . .

Blood spots dropped from the cart, staining the road to the Pont Marie where the bodies of these unfortunates, massacred in prison, were lined up by more or less drunken scoundrels. I can see them yet and particularly recall one very lean man, very pallid with sharp, pointed nose. This beast crossed to some pal. 'See that rotten old priest on the pile there?' He went over to hoist the priest onto his feet, but the body, still warm, could not remain upright: the drunk held the body upright, slapping the face and shouting: 'I had trouble enough doing in the old dog and not before time, for in his pockets were money notes, all of them forged!'   MARIE-VICTOIRE MONNARD

My intention was to step aside from the other prisoners so that, being seen standing by myself, those nearest the table might overlook me and I might escape at the first opportunity. Already the row of prisoners was much dwindled. The killers had despatched successively the Abbé Gervais, secretary to the Archbishopric, the Grand Vicar of Strasbourg, that poor priest of the Hôtel Dieu, the President of the Higher Council of Corsica, and forty more. It was probably almost 2 a.m. though I was no longer aware of the clock. Seemingly, I was increasingly impervious to the incessant killings, and could think only of myself, though seeing all my companions slaughtered, lit by the many torches illuminating this grisly sight. A deathly chill enveloped me, my feet froze. My blood had all gone to my head; my cheeks burned and, squinting down, I fancied them actually on fire. Often I rubbed my right hand on my head and while seeking some plan to save myself, I automatically scratched so powerfully that I tore out the very roots of my hair. . . .

Nevertheless, I confess, in shame, that despite my imminent danger, my last moments apparently so close, I was not wholly concentrating on God, or resigned to death. Indeed, the very opposite. I did not cease scheming my escape from the terrifying massacre. Those blows from sabres, jabs from pikes, petrified me but without inspiring the piety which should inform our last hour. Certainly I did at intervals recite the *Pater*, the *Ave Maria* and the Act of Contrition, but without the deep feeling which death inspires. When my danger ravaged me, I could only repeat, 'What can I do to dodge the question about taking the oath to the Revolutionary Church?'

Sometimes the massacres were halted for the killers to hear the

exhortations from other Sections, reporting on the massacres in their own prisons.   ABBÉ DE SALAMON, one of the three survivors of
sixty-three priests and others imprisoned in the Abbaye. *Mémoire, c.*1800

My worthy friends, the Commune has sent me to tell you that you are actually dishonouring this beautiful day. They are informed that, having wreaked justifiable penalties on them, you have been robbing these aristocratic curs. Now, leave alone all jewels, money and objects they may have about them, to pay for the superb deeds of justice you are performing. The Commune will reimburse you, as you have been promised. Live up to the nobility, grandeur, magnanimity of your callings. May everything on this Day of Splendour be to the very great credit of the People, whose sovereignty you bear.

JACQUES-NICOLAS BILLAUD-VARENNE, to the killers

We have had one week of uncheck'd Murders here in which some thousands have perish'd in this City. It began with between two and three hundred of the Clergy who had been shut up because they would not take the Oath prescrib'd by Law and which they said was contrary to their Conscience. Thence these Executors of speedy Justice went to the Abbaye [prison] where the persons were confin'd who were at Court on the Tenth [August]. These were dispatch'd also, and afterwards they visited the other prisons. All those who were confin'd, either on the accusation or Suspicion of Crimes, were destroy'd. Madame de Lamballe was I believe the only woman kill'd and she was beheaded and emboweled, the Head and entrails paraded on Pikes thro the Street, and the body dragg'd after them. They continu'd I am told in the neighbourhood of the Temple [prison] until the Queen look'd out at this horrid Spectacle. Yesterday the Prisoners from Orleans were put to death at Versailles. The destruction began here about five in the afternoon on Sunday the second Instant. A Guard had been sent a few days since to make the Duke de La Rochefoucault prisoner. He was on his way to Paris under their Escourt with his wife and Mother when he was taken out of his Carriage and killed. The Ladies were taken back to La Roche Guyonne where they are now in a State of Arrestation.

GOUVERNEUR MORRIS, to Thomas Jefferson

The two Brutuses were truly *sans-culottes*: the elder embraced his son while condemning him to death; the younger wept on the breast of his father, as the father plunged in his dagger.   *Révolutions de Paris*

In the different prisons the mob formed a tribunal consisting of twelve persons; after examining the jailor's book, and asking different questions, the judges placed their hands upon the head of the prisoner, and said, 'Do you think that in our consciences we can release this gentleman?' – This word *release* was his condemnation. When they answered *yes*, the accused person, apparently set at liberty, was immediately dashed upon the pikes of the surrounding people. If they were judged innocent, they were released amidst the shouts of *Vive La Nation*!

(Read this ye ENGLISHMEN, with attention, and ardently pray that your happy Constitution may never be outraged by the despotic tyranny of Equalization.)   *The Times*, London

The subject utmost within us was to consider what posture we should adopt when dragged to the slaughter mart, so as to die with least pain. Occasionally we requested some of our companions to go to the turret window to watch the attitude of those being killed. They returned, saying that those who attempted to shield themselves suffered longest, because the blows of the knives were thus weakened before reaching the head; that some victims indeed lost hands and arms before falling; and that those who put their hands behind their backs obviously endured less pain.

JOURGNIAC DE SAINT-MÉARD, from the Abbaye Prison

I say that no throne was ever shattered without some worthy citizen being wounded by the fragments.

GEORGES-JACQUES DANTON, Minister of Justice

Is this the work of a furious and deluded mob? How is it that the Citizens of this populous metropolis remain passive spectators of so dreadful an outrage? Is it possible that this is the accomplishment of a plan concerted two or three weeks ago, that those arbitrary arrests were ordered with this view, that rumours of treasons and intended insurrections and massacres were spread about to exasperate the people and that, taking advantage of the rumours of bad news from the frontiers, orders have been issued for firing the cannon and sounding the tocsin to increase the alarm and terrify the people into acquiescence; while a band of selected ruffians was hired to massacre those whom hatred, revenge or fear had destined to destruction, but whom law and justice could not destroy? It is now past twelve at midnight and the bloody work still goes on! Almighty God!

DR JOHN MOORE. *Journal*

Everyone in Paris allowed this to happen. All Paris is for me under a curse, and I no longer have any hopes that liberty may be established amongst cowards, nerveless witnesses to dastardly acts that fifty brave people might have halted . . . Danton is the hidden hand behind the mob of killers.

MANON ROLAND. *Letters*

Are you aware of the organiser of those September Massacres about which you jabber so noisily and irresponsibly? It was I myself. I wanted the young men of Paris to reach Champagne bespattered with the blood that would guarantee us their fidelity; I wanted to throw a river of blood between them and the émigrés.

GEORGES-JACQUES DANTON, to the Duc de Chartres, son of Égalité Orléans (later Louis-Philippe, King of the French)

If you knew the dreadful details! Women brutally raped before being mauled to bits by these tigers! You are well aware of my passion for the Revolution; well, I am now ashamed of it; it is dishonoured by these dregs of Mankind, I now find it hideous.

MANON ROLAND, on the murders at Salpetrière prison. *Letters*

The People obeyed my voice. They saved France by making themselves Dictator, for the purpose of killing traitors.

JEAN-PAUL MARAT, to the Convention

ABSOLUTION

To this temptation of murder now another idea was joined: barbarous, childish, the one which one so often finds in the first youth of nations, in the high antiquity – the idea of a great and radical moral purge, the hope of making the world sane by an absolute extermination of evil.

The Commune, in that belief an organ of popular feelings, declared that it would not arrest aristocrats only, but also criminals, gamblers, the men and women of shady lives. The massacre itself, a fact not often observed, was of a greater general ferocity in the Châtelet, the district where the thieves were to be found, than in the districts of *L'Abbaye* and *Force* where lived the aristocrats. The absolute idea of a moral purge gave to many of them a terrible serenity of conscience, a terrifying scruple not to spare anything. A man came a few days after to confess himself to Marat, to confess that he succumbed to the weakness of sparing one aristocrat; he had tears in his eyes because of that. The Friend of the People talked to him with kindness and he gave him absolution – nevertheless the man in question could not forgive himself, couldn't be consoled.

JULES MICHELET. *Histoire de la Révolution française*, 1893–9

Norman Hampson quotes a further dialogue between Danton and Chartres, on the Massacres:
'You make me shudder, Monsieur Danton.'
    'Shudder as much as you like, but learn not to keep on shuddering in public.'   LOUIS-PHILIPPE, DUC DE CHARTRES. *Mémoires*, Paris, 1973

A PROCLAMATION

The Paris Commune hastens to inform its brothers in the Departments that many ferocious conspirators detained in its prisons have been executed by the People – acts of justice which seemed essential in order to terrorise the traitors hidden in its midst when it was preparing to march on the enemy. The entire Nation will certainly hurry to imitate this measure so vital to Public Safety, and the entire People of France will cry out like the People of Paris: We will march against the Enemy, but we refuse to leave bandits at our back to murder our wives and children.   JEAN-PAUL MARAT

Stanley Loomis comments, 1965:
This dispatch, a cold-blooded incitement to violence in the provinces, admits, in terms that could not be clearer, the concurrence of the Commune in those atrocities that conventionally have been attributed to 'a popular effervescence'. Its cynical reference to 'ferocious conspirators' evokes a picture of those women and girls of Salpetrière, the 170 derelicts and the 33 fourteen-year-olds of Bicêtre, of the defenceless priests of the Abbaye and the Carmes. . . .

AN ENGLISH INTELLECTUAL,
ON THE SEPTEMBER MASSACRES

Let me beg you not to mix with the shallow herd who throw an odium on immutable principles, because some of the mere instruments of the revolution were too sharp. – Children of any growth will do mischief when they meddle with edged tools. It is to be lamented that as *yet* the billows of public opinion are only to be moved forward by the strong wind, the squally gusts of passion.

MARY WOLLSTONECRAFT, to William Roscoe

(See Claire Tomalin, 1974)

AN ATTACK ON MARAT
AND ROBESPIERRE,
AFTER THE SEPTEMBER MASSACRES

These men of blood . . . wished to gorge their cruel eyes with the sight of 28,000 corpses sacrificed to their fury. I accuse you of having scattered and persecuted the Legislative Assembly, of having paraded yourself, Robespierre, as an idol, of having sought supreme power; and in this charge your behaviour will speak louder than words.

JEAN BAPTISTE LOUVET DE COUVRAI

The September Massacres were the act of men raised to defend their land after the disaster of Verdun. If people must lament them, let them lament the patriots massacred by Tyranny. I am always suspicious of that delicacy of feeling which is excited exclusively by the fate of enemies of the State.   MAXIMILIEN ROBESPIERRE

LONDON

His Majesty has learned with the deepest sorrow how far the excesses in Paris have gone. The unwavering feelings which His Majesty has for the persons of the King and Queen, his concern for their welfare, his desire for peace and the prosperity of the Royal couple to whom he is linked by bonds of friendship, make him doubly aware of the deplorable consequences.

As His Majesty the King of France appears to be deprived of his powers for the time being, your credentials are no longer valid. For that reason and also because of the neutrality observed so far, His Majesty considers it right that you leave Paris. It is therefore His Majesty's wish that you obtain the necessary papers and return to England without delay.   WILLIAM PITT, Prime Minister of Great Britain, to Lord Gower, British Ambassador to France

THE WAR

With the Prussians reaching as far as Champagne, one might have thought that panic might have inflamed many Parisians. No such thing! Theatres and restaurants, all of them jammed tight, showed only peaceful reports. All the boastful threats of our enemies, all their murderous hopes were absolutely ignored. People fancied their city invulnerable, notions of defending it were scoffed at.

LOUIS-SÉBASTIEN MERCIER. *Le Nouveau Paris*

The Champs-Elysées were crowded with all manner of people sauntering along. Many small booths sold refreshments, accompanied by noisy music and singing. Little theatricals and various puppetries were to be seen and at intervals people were dancing. 'Are these quite as merry as they appear?' asked my companion, a Frenchman. 'Oh yes, absolutely.' 'But do you imagine that they've forgotten the Duke of Brunswick?' 'I promise you that whatever else they're thinking about, it's not Brunswick.'   DR JOHN MOORE. *Journal*

Sept 10. Letter from Baron de Breteuil from Verdun, dated 8th. He arrived there on the evening of the 6th, saw the King of Prussia next day, highly appreciative of him and the Duke of Brunswick, both evincing deep sympathy for King Louis. Immense desire to reach Paris, where the Baron will establish a new government.

Sept 16. Robespierre is victorious, striving for a dictatorship, the National Assembly remains servile. Let us hope that this will happen. Robespierre has displayed less cruelty, has referred to respect due to the royal authority, and has abdicated the chair of the Revolutionary Tribunal; to cut it short, he has less crimes on his conscience and could easily make amends for those he has done when a different regime emerges; nevertheless, we must wait to see whether this is what he wants.

Sept 18. The Duc d'Orléans has changed his name to Egalité, and his Palais Royal to Palais de la Révolution. Terrible slaughter at Lyons and Besançon, all relatives of émigrés murdered.

COUNT AXEL VON FERSEN. Journal

THE DUKE OF BRUNSWICK
AND THE ALLIES REACH VALMY

The Army is in the most deplorable condition. If we retreat, I fear it will disband itself, and if we advance, as it does seem to wish, we will certainly get beaten.

GENERAL CHARLES FRANÇOIS DUMOURIEZ, commanding the French army

This Day we have an Account that the Enemy have been repulsed in an Attack upon Thionville. I think it is but a trifling Affair, much exagerated. There are Accounts also of an Action between the Army of Dumouriez and the Duke of Brunswick. No Details, but I conjecture that it is only a Feint to draw the French to their left in order to turn their Right. The Weather is very cool.

Nothing new except what I do not believe, that the Army of Dumouriez has repulsed the Enemy with considerable Execution. The Weather very pleasant.

This Day Accounts arrive from the Army to shew that Dumouriez has been defeated or Something very like it. The Weather cool for the season but pleasant.

By the official Reports of the Day Paris is in a State of imminent Danger from the internal Movements. The Factions grow daily more inveterate. The Weather is very cool.

Every Thing still wears an Appearance of Confusion. No Authority any where. The Weather is pleasant.

Nothing new this Day except that the Convention has met and declar'd they will have no King in France. The Weather is foul.

GOUVERNEUR MORRIS. Diary

THE BATTLE OF VALMY

The snoring, whistling and chattering voices of the bullets.

JOHANN WOLFGANG VON GOETHE

Cannon balls make a strange noise, something between the humming of a top, the splash of water and the cry of a bird.

JOHANN WOLFGANG VON GOETHE

From this place and from this day forth begins a new era in the history of the world and you gentlemen can all say you witnessed its birth.

JOHANN WOLFGANG VON GOETHE

The enemy had disappointed our hopes. Dumouriez and Kellerman had proved themselves generals not despicable. They had selected fine positions; they commanded all that remained of the old French line troops; volunteers helped by their numbers, and could give real assistance when attached to seasoned regulars; their light cavalry was excellent and quite fresh. Their army lacked nothing, and for us – we lacked everything. They were well fortified in their positions, before and behind, and their guns at least equalled our own. This is what prevented us striking a decisive blow.

Secretary to Frederick William, King of Prussia

After Valmy, every Frenchman who held sword or musket, regarded himself as champion of a cause fated to triumph.

ARTHUR CHUQUET. *Valmy*

You will see how those little cocks will lift themselves on their spurs. They have suffered their baptism of fire. We have lost more than a battle. September 20th has changed the direction of history. It is the most important day of the Century.

COLONEL MASSENBACH, one of the defeated

At midnight, a courier from Lord Elgin [British Ambassador, Brussels] informed us that on October 1st, the Prussian and Austrian armies had beat retreat first to Grandpré, thence to Verdun. An officer, he discloses that the Allied armies are exhausted and sick, short of everything because of the non-arrival of convoys. They are scared of encirclement. The French fought with valour, throwing up ever-increasing artillery. Shot at, they ignored it and kept on firing. . . . The courier complains of the laxness of the Duke of Brunswick, maintaining that he could have assailed Dumouriez on the 23rd, and captured him, a view shared in England. Public opinion holds that his Grace of Brunswick is notably inclined to seek terms.

COUNT AXEL VON FERSEN. *Journal*

THE REPUBLIC

On the 21st September at 4 pm, a certain Lubin, a Commune official, accompanied by horsemen and a huge crowd, appeared before the Temple Tower with a proclamation. Trumpets sounded, then utter silence. Lubin's voice was stentorian. The Royal Family within could clearly hear the announcement that Royalty had been abolished, the Republic established. Hébert, famous for his journal *Père Duchesne*, and Destournelles, later Minister of Public Contributions, were at that moment supervising the Royal Family, seated near the door, and staring hard at the King, grinning maliciously. He saw them, but continued reading his book, not allowing his features to betray the least emotion. The Queen was quite as resolute: no word or gesture came from them to increase the men's evil pleasure. The trumpets sounded again when the proclamation ended, and I crossed to a window. All eyes below were at once massed upon me, I was mistaken for my royal lord and abuse was hurled up at me in torrents. The horsemen threatened me with their swords and, to stop the uproar, I was forced to retreat. JEAN-BAPTISTE CANT HANET CLÉRY, *valet de chambre* to King Louis XVI. *Journal*, 1798

DANTON

Danton was Minister of Justice during the crucial months of the overthrow of the Monarchy, war and the September Massacres and effective leader of government and defence. Alphonse Aulard wrote of Danton's famous remarks: 'Probably he said them. One hopes he did so. Historically they are uncertain. They may be more true than authentic.'

Some of the most celebrated are:

The Kings of Europe threaten us. We hurl before them the head of a King.

All this talk is meaningless. I see only the enemy.

It often happens, especially during revolution, that one has to applaud deeds that one would neither have wished, nor dared to do, oneself.

I shall be Danton to the very end. Tomorrow, I'll sleep in glory.

A titanic revolutionary force, believing nothing blameworthy providing it was useful and holding that people were entitled to act according to the ranges of their audacity. Fiery, crushed with debts, and desires, dissolute, utterly addicted to his passions and his followers, he was formidable when setting himself a goal, but lost interest on gaining it. Impressive demagogue, he mingled in himself utterly contrasting vices and virtues. Though he accepted money from the Court, he never seemed tarnished. A thorough killer he was not personally ruthless. Revolution he interpreted as a sport in which whoever won had the choice of sparing or taking his victim's life. He regarded party needs as above the law, even above morality itself.

FRANÇOIS AUGUSTE MARIE MIGNET. *La Révolution française*, 1924

Danton, who saw straight, who understood, and who, when the victories began, found leisure to pity, is a type whose extremes are the romance, whose moderation is the groundwork of history. We have to deal in him with an enthusiast who is also a statesman, in whom the mind has sufficient power to know itself even in its violence, and to return deliberately within its usual boundaries after never so fantastic an excursion. With Hébert again we know the type. Those are not rare in whom passions purely personal dominate all abstract conceptions, and whose natures desire the horrible in literature during times of peace, and satisfy their desire by action during their moments of power.   HILAIRE BELLOC, 1899

Danton was huge-hearted. This tremendous orator, instinctive yet calculating, was rooted in popular affection by a temperament powerful and sensual, wholly made for sexuality, controlled by flesh and blood. Supremely, absolutely, totally, Danton was masculine. Beneath that mask, ferocious, furious, one could feel generosity beat. The tragic name, Danton, however muddied and distorted it may be, either by himself or faction, will yet linger within the affectionate memories and regrets of France.   JULES MICHELET, 1823

A strange figure, Danton! Somebody – perhaps Louis Blanc – has compared him with an etching by Rembrandt (full of lights and shadows), and Robespierre with one by Dürer (all on the same plane). He was a man of violent passions, a lover of life. He has been called 'the people's Mirabeau' and resembled Mirabeau in many particulars. There is something primitive and elemental about him, something of a natural force. Although a lawyer, he was comparatively uneducated and was never known to set pen to paper except to sign his name. The violence of his impulses may be judged by the fact that when his wife died while he was in Belgium, he had, on his return, her body dug up so that he might look on her face again. Yet, six weeks later, we find him marrying a sixteen year old girl and professing belief in Catholicism in order to do so.   RALPH KORNGOLD, 1937

Danton in fact collected dozens of the best books of his day, could read in English and Italian, loved Shakespeare and read deeply in the Encyclopaedia.

He was brave and resolute, fond of pleasures, of power and distinction, with vehement passions, with lax principles, but with many kind and manly feelings. He was capable of great crimes, but capable too of friendship and compassion.   LORD MACAULAY, 1843

The only member of the Government I saw, whose brutality revolted me, was Danton. There was something inexpressibly savage and ferocious in his looks, and in his stentorian voice. His coarse shaggy hair gave him the appearance of a wild beast. To add to the fierceness of his repulsive countenance, he was deeply marked with the small-pox, and his eyes were unusually small, and sparkling in surrounding darkness, like the famous carbuncle. David, who looked upon him as a demi-God, attempted several times to delineate this horrid countenance, but in vain; exclaiming: 'Il serait plus facile de peindre l'éruption d'un volcan, que les traits de ce grand homme.'

   This monster gave me but little consolation regarding my brother; and, having cast a hasty glance on my petition, he vociferated: 'You may thank your stars, *petit malheureux*, that you and all your family have not been sacrificed to public indignation, to avenge the wrongs inflicted on us by your perfidious country.'

   J. G. MILLINGEN (aged 12 in 1794). *Recollections of Republican France*, 1848

Satiated like this, the pack of starveling bullies and the incessant intrigues, all the doings of Sections and Clubs exist at his whim. In him, the disposition of a butcher and the sympathies of a human being, the shouts of a Club Cicero with the clarity of a politician; his own bombast does not fool him, and he knows to a sou what to pay his own bandits. Demagogue and bandit, gang leaders both.   HIPPOLYTE TAINE. *Origines de la France contemporaine*, Paris, 1876

Contemporary evidence is virtually unanimous in presenting Danton as a full-blooded man who enjoyed his pleasures, a good friend who was not too fastidious about the company he kept, and the coiner of phrases that were to drive his biographers into asterisks. This is all very well as far as it goes, which is not very far: he could still have been either a generous and open-hearted *bon viveur* or a cynical crook. Most of the *bon mots* attributed to him are apocryphal, however closely they correspond to what he is actually known to have said. If the biographer takes all this sort of evidence at its face value he can easily construct an 'Identikit' picture which is plausible enough and may well be reasonably accurate. The Danton of legend is hard to resist, especially since he imposed himself on contemporaries as well as posterity. To present him in these terms, however, is merely to endorse a tradition when one ought to be investigating its authenticity. As soon as one tries to do anything of the kind, to eliminate conjecture and start from a basis of verified fact, the whole structure disintegrates. Reduced to 'Danton was a man who – probably – said . . .' we find ourselves back at the starting-point, since we are seldom sure of what he did say and whether or not he meant it.

Danton's actions, paradoxically enough, provide a somewhat surer foothold, despite the fact that he has been labelled as everything from a republican Joan of Arc to a royalist gangster. Unlike many of his colleagues, he saw the Revolution in practical rather than ideal terms. He could speak the language of total revolution and perhaps even carry himself away by his own rhetoric, but he never shared the millenarian views of those intent on creating a new republican man such as the world had never seen. For him, the Revolution was about improving the conditions of men as they were. This still leaves plenty of scope for differences of opinion. Danton was not the kind of man to forget his own interests and his main concern may have been to provide himself and his friends with the means of gratifying their rather expensive tastes. Perhaps he also aspired to create a society in which more would be done for those who could not do very much for themselves. In either case he had both feet firmly planted in the world as he saw it, in which real people actually wanted material things. He saw the Revolution as the means to a political and social end, and not as some kind of transcendental god whose priests could aspire to nothing more than martyrdom. Sooner or later it would come to an end and he intended to be on the winning side.

NORMAN HAMPSON, 1978

Delicious grub, splendid liquor, women of one's dreams – that's what power wins when you grab it.   GEORGES-JACQUES DANTON

Totally lacking in honour, principles, morality, he enjoyed democracy only for its thrills . . . his real worship was for violence, nothing but violence. His genius was solely in his disdain of honesty and he rated himself above all others, because he himself had trampled down all scruples. For him, all was a means for his own ends. He was a statesman of materialism. . . .

A man like this naturally has the deepest uninterest in either tyranny or liberty. His contempt for the masses must make him prefer the former. The Court well knew that his conscience was up for sale, and he threatened the Court so that it would wish to purchase his support; he opened his mouth only so that others would stuff it with gold. His most revolutionary moments merely chalked up the price of his favours. Selling himself every day, by next morning he was again up for sale. Around him clustered those seeking wealth and security. However, while those others had only the vulgarities of crime, Danton's crimes reached a degree of heroism and his intellect approached genius.   ALPHONSE DE LAMARTINE. *Histoire des Girondins*, 1847

In the best-balanced of recent studies of Danton that I know, and to which I am indebted, Norman Hampson (1978) refers to a private letter of Lamartine, in which he reveals:

I accuse Danton without proof, out of the honest need to find a criminal in order to personify the horror that crime inspires.

Danton was a man, Robespierre was an idea.

ALPHONSE DE LAMARTINE

The Revolution is a battle. Shall it not be followed like all battles by a division of spoils amongst the victors?   GEORGES-JACQUES DANTON

A man who might easily become attached to good principles.

ANTOINE-NICOLAS DE CONDORCET

He was a dishonest politician, believing in nothing, ever ready to despair of the triumph of the Republic, a ruthless schemer whose behaviour in secret was quite the reverse of his public assertions, common and dissolute, attempting to transform war-weariness to whatever suited his own low ambition and to string together a shameful peace at whatever cost, the easy-going leader of all the contemporary defeatists.   ALBERT MATHIEZ. *La Révolution et les Étrangers*, 1918

When down on his luck a man seeks happiness somewhere else. When he sees the rich gratifying their tastes, satisfying every passion, while his own needs he must pare down to skinflint necessities, he believes, and is consoled by this, that joys in the hereafter will be granted in exact proportions to his mortal sufferings. Allow him his mistake. Don't prate to him of morality and philosophy until he has been persuaded to higher truths and can assess religious dogma at true value. Until that time comes, it is treason to wish to wrest from the people its beliefs and notions.   GEORGES-JACQUES DANTON

THE REVOLUTIONARY CALENDAR

Vendémiaire	Vintage month	September 22– October 21
Brumaire	Misty month	October 22– November 20
Frimaire	Frosty month	November 21–December 20
Nivôse	Snowy month	December 21–January 19
Pluviôse	Rainy month	January 20–February 18
Ventôse	Windy month	February 19–March 20
Germinal	Month of buds	March 21–April 19
Floréal	Month of flowers	April 20–May 19
Prairial	Meadow month	May 20–June 18
Messidor	Harvest month	June 19–July 18
Thermidor	Month of sun	July 19–August 17
Fructidor	Month of fruits	August 18–September 16

A ten-day week superseded the seven-day Christian week. Five complementary days, with six in leap year, completed the year. 1792 became Year I of the Republic.

REFUGEES

The late recent horrors in France have at least been attended with one good consequence, for they have turned the tide of general opinions here very suddenly. French principles and French men are daily becoming more unpopular and I think it not impossible that in a short time the imprudence of some of these levellers will work so much on the temper of our people as to make England neither a pleasant nor a secure residence for them.

JAMES BLAND BURGES, Under-Secretary for Foreign Affairs, to Lord Auckland, British Ambassador at The Hague

The levity and gaiety of the French in the midst of the calamities and the disgrace of their own country and in despite of the ruin of their own individual interests are beyond belief.

LORD AUCKLAND, to James Bland Burges

Even [Vicomte de] Noailles has taken refuge in England, the last country in which he ought to have shown his face. Lafayette and he, Noailles, were treated in England with a generosity and frankness that no foreigners ever before or since experienced, and yet they went, warm with our civilities, in the most treacherous manner, as if they had come here merely as spies, to attack us in America; the town swarms with these ex-members of the Assemblée Nationale.

ANTHONY STORER, to Lord Auckland

The poor French have had upon the whole a very good reception, such as does credit to the country. . . . The subscription in this country for the French refugees does us some credit but the backwardness of men in administration is passing strange, not one of them, except Lord Hawkesbury, has contributed.   LORD SHEFFIELD

There is no Frenchman in London who does not give thanks to the generous hospitality with which he has been received and always treated here. The obligations which a regenerated France has contracted to Great Britain during its long and painful distress are of a nature never to be forgotten. France may indeed once more become the rival of England in many spheres, but an eternal gratitude will never in any future century allow the return of a jealous hatred in a French heart.   CHARLES-PHILIPPE, COMTE D'ARTOIS (later King Charles X)

(See Margery Weiner)

FOUCHÉ

When elected [to the Convention] he is aged thirty-two. He is scarcely handsome. He is lean enough as to almost appear spectral. His face is narrow, angular, and bony; exceptionally unpleasant. His nose is sharp; his lips thin and usually tight: beneath heavy lids his eyes are fish-like and of greyish-green, like bottle glass. Everything in his face, in the man, seems devitalized: he resembles a figure in gas-light, faded, ashen. His eyes lack sparkle, his movements are slack, his voice has no edge. His scanty hair hangs in rats'-tails; his brows are reddish, scarcely discernible; his cheeks, grey. There seems not enough colour to suggest health. Despite toughness and supreme powers of work, one might imagine him imprisoned in endless fatigue, convalescing from exacting sickness.   STEFAN ZWEIG, 1929

M. Fouché's contempt for his fellow men is understandable; he has examined himself so minutely.   CHARLES MAURICE DE TALLEYRAND

A MADRIGAL

Romans, so proud of your gleaming birthright,
Observe from what chance Mighty Empire can flower,
Dido's charms themselves had insufficient power
To hold back her stubborn lover from seeking flight.

But if the very Dido of your realm the pride
Had herself been Queen of Carthage,
To be her slave, he would have rapturously his gods denied –
Love redeeming lands which hath hitherto been savage.

    NAPOLEON BONAPARTE, to the opera singer, Madame Saint-Hubert,
    the 'Dido' in Piccinni's opera of that name

RESIDENCE IN FRANCE

It was a beautiful and silent day
That overspread the countenance of earth,
Then fading with unusual quietness,
When from the Loire I parted, and through scene

Of vineyard, orchard, meadow-ground and tilth,
Calm waters, gleams of sun, and breathless trees
Towards the fierce Metropolis turn'd my steps
Their homeward way to England. From his Throne
The King had fallen; the congregated Host,
Dire cloud upon the front of which was written
The tender mercies of the dismal wind
That bore it, on the Plains of Liberty
Had burst innocuously; say more, the swarm
That came elate and jocund, like a Band
Of Eastern Hunters, to enfold in ring
Narrowing itself by moments and reduce
To the last punctual spot of their despair
A race of victims, so they seem'd, *themselves*
Had shrunk from sight of their own task, and fled
In terror; desolation and dismay
Remained for them whose fancies had grown rank
With evil expectations, confidence
And perfect triumph to the better cause.
The State, as if to stamp the final seal
On her security, and to the world
Show what she was, a high and fearless soul,
Or rather in a spirit of thanks to those
Who had stirr'd up her slackening faculties
To a new transition, had assumed with joy
The body and the venerable name
Of a Republic: lamentable crimes
'Tis true had gone before this hour, the work
Of massacre, in which the senseless sword
Was pray'd to as a judge; but these were past,
Earth free from them for ever, as was thought,
Ephemeral monsters, to be seen but once;
Things that could only show themselves and die.

This was the time in which inflam'd with hope,
To Paris I returned. Again I rang'd
More eagerly than I had done before
Through the wide City, and in progress pass'd
The Prison where the unhappy Monarch lay,
Associate with his Children and his Wife

In bondage; and the Palace lately storm'd
With roar of cannon, and a numerous host.
I crossed (a black and empty area then)
The Square of the Carousel, a few weeks back
Heap'd up with dead and dying, upon these
And other sights looking as doth a man
Upon a volume whose contents he knows
Are memorable, but from him lock'd up,
Being written in a tongue he cannot read,
So that he questions the mute leaves with pain
And half upbraids their silence. But that night
When on my bed I lay, I was most mov'd
And felt most deeply in what world I was;
My room was high and lonely, near the roof
Of a large Mansion or Hotel, a spot
That would have pleased me in more quiet times,
Nor was it wholly without pleasure then.
With unextinguish'd taper I kept watch,
Reading at intervals; the fear gone by
Press'd on me almost like a fear to come;
I thought of those September Massacres,
Divided from me by a little month,
And felt and touch'd them, a substantial dread;
The rest was conjured up from tragic fictions,
And mournful Calendars of true history,
Remembrances and dim admonishments.
'The horse is taught his manage, and the wind
Of heaven wheels round and treads in his own steps,
Year follows year, the tide returns again,
Day follows day, all things have second birth;
The earthquake is not satisfied at once.'
And in such way I wrought upon myself,
Until I seem'd to hear a voice that cried,
To the whole City, 'Sleep no more.' To this
I could not gather full security,
But at the best it seem'd a place of fear
Unfit for the repose which night requires,
Defenceless as a wood where tigers roam.

                                    WILLIAM WORDSWORTH. *The Prelude*

'THE DIRTY BEAST'

Towards the end of 1792, a time when Marat was in the midst of his campaign to destroy the Girondins, the actor Talma gave a reception to General Dumouriez, the hero of Valmy and the strongest remaining support of the Girondins' fast-collapsing hold on power. While the guests were enjoying refreshments to the acompaniment of music from the harp and the piano, a great clatter was heard on the stairs and Marat burst into the room. He was dressed in a *carmagnole*, his sockless feet were sheathed in dirty boots, a red bandana was bound around his head and bits of greasy hair caked with dirt stuck out here and there along its fringes. His twitching grin made the women's blood run cold. He was accompanied by several rough-mannered members of the General Security Committee.

'Citizen', he bawled at Dumouriez, 'a group of those who love liberty went to the War Office this evening to communicate certain dispatches that concerned you. They went to your house and didn't find you there either. We are dumbfounded to find you in a house like this surrounded by a flock of whores and counter-revolutionaries.'

Dumouriez answered, 'May I not rest from the fatigues of war in the midst of the arts and my friends without having them outraged by your indecent epithets?'

Marat spat on the floor and shook his fist at the shocked assembly. 'This house,' he cried, 'is the house of counter-revolution!' He turned on his heel and left, but not before he had uttered a great many threats of the most terrifying kind. After his departure one of the guests went about the room with scent in order to purify the air after this strange visit from 'the dirty beast'.   STANLEY LOOMIS, 1965

Dumouriez's subsequent desertion to the Austrians after his defeat at Neerwinden and his failure to rouse his troops for a march on Paris to overthrow the extremists, was fatal to his Girondin patrons. A Maratist faction in the War Office diverted arms and clothing intended for his troops to 'patriots at home', Marat's followers. Dumouriez's desertion and war reverses led to Danton's demand for a Revolutionary Tribunal, and the formation of a Committee of Public Safety, with unprecedented powers.

I represent the fury of the People.   JEAN-PAUL MARAT

SUPPORTERS OF MARAT AND THE REVOLUTIONARY COMMUNE AGITATE IN THE PUBLIC GALLERIES OF THE CONVENTION

Their ringleaders appeared to have scoured all the most fearful quarters of Paris and Europe for the most hideous and polluted. With dreadful faces, coarsened, black or coppery, eyes half-buried in their sockets, they uttered with loathsome breath the most obscene insults and the screeches of jungle beasts. The leaders were suited to their battalions: men whose terrifying features testified to crime and degradation, women whose shameless expressions showed the lowest excesses. When this mob, using feet, hands, voices, let loose their disgusting uproar, they seemed to be a convocation from hell.

FRANÇOIS BUZOT

THE ROYALIST EMIGRÉS AT THIONVILLE

Usually an army is formed of soldiers more or less similar in age, build, strength. Ours was quite different, an improvised gathering of men in their prime, veterans, children just out of the nest, all chattering away in Norman, Breton, Picard, Auvergnat, Gascon, Provençal and Languedocian. Fathers served with sons, fathers-in-law with sons-in-law, uncles with nephews, brothers with brothers, cousins with cousins. This peculiar array, outwardly ludicrous, yet possessed something honourable and moving by being stirred by sincere beliefs. It was an image of the old monarchy and gave a final glimpse of a dying world. I saw old noblemen, stern of visage, grey-headed, clad in ripped coats, pulling themselves forward with a stick, a son lending them an arm to lean on. I saw wounded youths stretched under a tree while a curé in frock-coat and stole knelt over them, despatching them to St Louis, whose heirs they had struggled to defend. All this impoverished lot, without a farthing from the Royal Princes, fought at its own expense, while in Paris the Assembly finished robbing it and thrust our wives and mothers into prison cells.

Near our wretched and obscure camp was a second; brilliant, opulent. At its centre was seen only chefs, valets, aides-de-camp.

There was no symbol more significant than this of Court and province, the monarchy that perished at Versailles, the monarchy that perished on moors once roamed by du Guesclin. We came to absolutely hate those aides-de-camp; when beyond Thionville we clamoured, 'Aides-de-Camp, to the front line!' like revolutionary 'patriots' shouting 'Officers to the front line!'

FRANÇOIS-RENÉ DE CHATEAUBRIAND. *Mémoires*, 1842

AT COBLENZ

We are utterly lacking in food and half of us have had none at all today. We are all so impoverished and all is so dreadfully managed that we find it impossible to get even the essentials. Weariness prevails entirely. Our existence is far harsher than that of the common soldier as we have no certainty about our commissariat and manoeuvres. Last night we slept under no cover at all, our stomachs empty. Before wrapping ourselves in our cloaks, we cried three times, in full throat, 'Long Live the King!'   MARQUIS DE FALAISEAU, to his wife

Less than 10 per cent of the nobility actually emigrated.

A ROYAL ERROR

The day when the Royal Family were imprisoned in the Temple seemed a Parisien Fête; crowds assembled round the buildings, yelling *Vive La Nation*! Lanterns on the outer walls illuminated the barbarous spectacle. Thinking that it was the Temple *palace* now selected for his lodging, the King requested to inspect the apartments. While the jailer found cruel sport in allowing him to continue this mistake so as to enjoy his coming discomfiture all the better, His Majesty was happy in distributing, as he thought, the various lodgings. Before long, the interior of the Temple had filled with a gathering of officials, in the midst of whom the King displayed the calm accompanying a quiet conscience.

An officer, breaking the dismal silence he had maintained during our walk, now said, 'Your employer is used to gilded halls. Well, he'll now see how we deal with murderers of the people! Come along.' . . .

An alcove, bare of hangings and curtains, held a small bed with an old mattress, full of bugs. We tried hard to make the room and the bed as clean as we could. The King arrived, showing neither surprise nor anger. The walls however had pictures on them, mostly more or less indecent; these he removed himself, remarking 'I do not wish my daughter to see such things.' Then His Majesty went to bed and slept peacefully.   M. HUË, Usher to the King's Chamber. *Memoirs*

DIALOGUE IN
THE TEMPLE PRISON

DEPUTY MANUEL, former solicitor to the Commune: 'How are you faring? Have you all you need?'

KING LOUIS XVI: 'I am content with what I am given.'

MANUEL: 'Doubtless you know of the triumphs of our armies, the capture of Spires, Nice and the conquest of Savoy?'

KING LOUIS: 'I heard one of these gentlemen [Commune officials] refer to it recently, from the *Journal du Soir*.'

MANUEL: 'What, you don't get the Journals, now so full of important matters?'

KING LOUIS: 'I am sent none of them.'

MANUEL: 'Indeed? Citizens, you must let Monsieur have the Journals; it is right that he should learn of our victories. Now, Monsieur, you know that the People have abolished kingship and established the Republic?'

KING LOUIS: 'This I do know, and I pray God that the French may become as happy as I have ever wanted to make them.'

MANUEL: 'You also know that the Convention has abolished all orders of chivalry: you ought to have been instructed to put away all your decorations denoting them. Now that you are back amongst the rest of the citizens you must expect the treatment they are given: save for this, ask for whatever you need, it will be at once got for you.'

KING LOUIS: 'I thank you. There is nothing I need.'

At this, His Majesty again took up his book: and Manuel, who had been trying to extract mortification or provoke impatience, was irritated at seeing only stoicism and unshakeable calm.

JEAN-BAPTISTE CANT HANET CLÉRY, *valet de chambre*
to King Louis XVI. *Journal*, 1798

THE KING DENOUNCED
IN THE CONVENTION

I demand that the Convention declares him now, at this instant, a traitor to the French Nation, a criminal to the human race. I demand that he provides a true example to the world in that very place where the selfless martyrs of liberty died on August 10. I demand that this memorable event be consecrated by a memorial which shall foster in the heart of the people an awareness of their rights and a horror of tyrants and, in the souls of tyrants, a healthy fear of the people's justice.   MAXIMILIEN ROBESPIERRE

For myself, I see no compromise. This man should reign, or he should die.   LOUIS ANTOINE DE SAINT-JUST

GUILTY BEFORE NATURE

Someone of fine temper could declare, in some other period, that a King ought to be accused, not for the wickedness of his rule but for that of being king, as that is a usurpation totally unjustified by mortal provenance. Whatsoever illusions, whatsoever customs, that fashion Monarchy's disguises, it remains a crime everlasting, against which every single person has the right to level and take up arms. Monarchy is an outrage unjustified even by popular myopia; whatever such community sustains monarchy must hold itself guilty before Nature herself; from Nature we all gather the secret quest to destroy such tyranny, wherever we perceive it.

No man can reign innocently. The madness of personal rule is axiomatic. Each King is both rebel and usurper. Do Kings themselves behave in any other way towards pretenders? Was not the very memory of Cromwell brought to the bar? And Cromwell was undeniably no more a usurper than Charles I, for when a people is weak enough to prostrate itself to tyranny, power is the light of whoever next arises, and is no more sanctified and 'legitimate' for the first than for the second. Here are the principles which a great Republic should remember when placing a King before the seat of justice.

                                    LOUIS ANTOINE DE SAINT-JUST, to the Convention

AN AMERICAN MEMORANDUM

Let these United States be the guard and the asylum of Louis Capet. There, in the future, remote from the miseries and crimes of royalty, he may learn, from the constant presence of public prosperity, that the true system of government consists, not in monarchs, but in fair, equal, and honorable representation. In recalling this circumstance, and submitting this proposal, I consider myself a citizen of both countries. I submit it as an American who feels the debt of gratitude he owes to every Frenchman. I submit it as a man who, albeit an adversary of Kings, forgets not that they are subject to human frailties. I support my proposal as a citizen of the French Republic, because it appears to be the best and most politic measure that can be adopted. As far as my experience in public life extends, I have ever observed that the great mass of people are always just, both in their intentions and their object; but the true method of attaining such purpose does not always appear at once. The English nation had groaned under the Stuart despotism. Hence Charles I was executed; but Charles II was restored to all the powers his father had lost. Forty years later the same family tried to re-establish their oppression; the nation banished the whole race from its territories. The remedy was effectual; the Stuart family sank into obscurity, merged itself in the masses, and is now extinct.   TOM PAINE

Paine overlooks the fact that James II, though expelled, was succeeded by his daughter Mary, and son-in-law William, as joint rulers; who were themselves succeeded by his younger daughter, Anne Stuart.

A SUMMONS FOR THE KING

The Mayor did not arrive until one o'clock. With him were Chaumette, Solicitor to the Commune, Coulombeau, Secretary of the Rolls, several Commune officials, and Santerre, Commandant of the National Guard, with his aides. The Mayor informed the King that he was to lead him to the Convention, in accordance with its decree, which the Commune representative would now read aloud. The gist was that 'Louis Capet' should be brought to the bar of the National Convention. 'Capet', the King replied, 'is not my name, it belonged to one of my ancestors.' He added, 'I could have wished,

monsieur, that the Commissioners had left me my son for the two
hours in which I have sat waiting for you, but such behaviour is at one
with all that I have been granted these last four months. I am prepared
to follow you, not in order to obey the Convention but because my
enemies hold the power.'

I handed His Majesty his overcoat and hat and he followed the
Mayor. A large number of Guards awaited him at the Temple gate.

JEAN-BAPTISTE CANT HANET CLÉRY, valet de chambre
to King Louis XVI. Journal, 1798

On leaving the Riding School after his pre-trial examination, the ex-
king was taken to the conference room at the Tuileries. As five
o'clock was approaching, the Mayor inquired whether he wanted
refreshment. He replied in the negative but, almost immediately,
noting a grenadier take a crust from his pocket and giving me half,
Louis stepped towards me and asked for a piece. I stepped back. 'Just
demand whatever you want, Monsieur.' Capet replied that he would
like a morsel of bread. 'Willingly, take this and break it. A spartan
breakfast! Had I a root, you could have had half.' Descending with us
to the courtyard, he then re-entered his coach, eating only the crust
of bread. Not knowing how to deal with the rest, he mentioned it to
the deputy, who flicked it out of the window. 'Ah,' he continued, 'it
is wrong to throw away bread in that way, particularly when it is
scarce.' 'And how do you know that?' I demanded. 'Because what I
had appears somewhat mouldy.' After a pause, I said 'My grandma
always told me, "Little boy, one should never lose even a crumb: you
would not be able to make for yourself even as much as that."'
'Monsieur Chaumette,' Louis Capet replied, 'your grandmother
seems to have been a lady of excellent sense.'

PIERRE GASPARD CHAUMETTE, Public Prosecutor
of the Paris Commune. Mémoire

Paris, December 11th, 1792
Citizen President,

I do not yet know whether the Convention will permit Louis XVI
to be defended by Counsel, or not. If it is permitted, and if he is
allowed to choose his Counsel, I request that he be informed that, if
he deems me fit for this purpose, I am prepared to accept. I am
not asking you to inform the Convention of my offer, for I scarcely
imagine myself important enough to deserve their notice, but in the
past I was twice appointed Member of Council of my former master,

in a day when this was a generally recognised ambition; I consider it my duty to propose myself as his Counsel, now that such a position is a dangerous one, to most eyes. If I knew any likely means of letting him know my intention, I should not take the liberty of applying to yourself. I imagine your own office affords you, above all, the opportunity of passing him this information.

I remain, with respect etc,

L. DE MALESHERBES

PRISON READING

Immediately after dinner, the King usually went to the library of the Archives of the Knights of Malta, who once resided in the Tower. The books still filled the shelves, and His Majesty would select some of them. Once when I was with him, he pointed to those of Rousseau and Voltaire, and, in a low voice, said, 'These two have ruined France'. Hoping to recover his fluency in Latin and being able, during his imprisonment, to give the Dauphin elementary lessons in that tongue, he translated the Odes of Horace and selections of Cicero.

M. HUË, Usher to the King's Chamber. *Memoirs*

AN ENGLISHWOMAN HAS SEEN KING LOUIS XVI DRIVEN TO HIS TRIAL ALONG THE RUE DU TEMPLE, SOUNDLESS AND GUARDED

I have been alone ever since; and, though my mind is calm, I cannot dismiss the lively images that have filled my imagination all the day – Nay, do not smile, but pity me; for, once or twice, lifting my eyes from the paper, I have seen eyes glare through a glass-door opposite my chair, and bloody hands shook at me. Not the distant sound of a footstep can I hear. – My apartments are remote from those of the servants, the only persons who sleep with me in an immense hotel. . . . I wish I had even kept the cat with me! – I want to see something alive; death in so many frightful shapes has taken hold of my fancy. – I am going to bed – and for the first time in my life, I cannot put out the candle.

MARY WOLLSTONECRAFT, to Joseph Johnson
(See Claire Tomalin, 1974; Rupert Christiansen, 1988)

THE TRIAL OF THE KING

I come now to the Trial of the King, and the Circumstances connected therewith. To a Person less intimately connected than you are with the History of human Affairs, it would seem strange that the mildest Monarch who ever fill'd the french Throne, one who is precipitated from it precisely because he would not adopt the harsh Measures of his Predecessors, a Man whom none can charge with a Criminal or cruel Act should be prosecuted as one of the most nefarious Tyrants that ever disgraced the Annals of human nature. That he, Louis the sixteenth, should be prosecuted even to the Death. Yet such is the Fact. I think it highly probable that he may suffer, and that for the following causes. The Majority of the Assembly found it necessary to raise against this unhappy Prince, the national Odium, in order to justify the dethroning him (which after what he had suffer'd appeared to be necessary even to their safety) and to induce the ready Adoption of a republican Form of Government. Being in Possession of his Papers, and those of his servants, it was easy (if they would permit themselves to extract, to comment, to suppress, and to multilate) it was *very* easy to create such opinions as they might think proper. The Rage which has been excited was terrible, and altho it begins to subside, the Convention are still in great Streights; fearing to acquit, fearing to condemn, and yet urg'd to destroy their Captive Monarch. The Violent Party are clamourous against him for Reasons which I will presently state. The Monarchic and Aristocratic Parties wish his Death, in the Belief that such a catastrophe would shock the national Feelings, awaken their hereditary Attachments, and turn into the Channels of loyalty the impetuous Tide of Opinion. Thus he has become the common Object of Hatred to all Parties, because he has never been the decided Patron of any one. If he is saved it will be by the Justice of his Cause, which will have some little Effort, and by the Pity which is universally felt (tho none dare express it openly) for the very harsh Treatment which he has endur'd. I come now to the Motives of the violent Party. You will see that Louvet (whose Pamphlet with many others I send you) has charg'd on this Party the Design to restore Royalty in the Person of the Duke of Orleans. This Man's Character and Conduct give but too much Room to suspect him of criminal Intentions. In general I doubt the public Virtue of a Profligate, and cannot help suspecting Appearances put on by such Persons. . . .

Shortly after the tenth of August, I had Information on which you may rely, that the Plan of Danton was to obtain the Resignation of the King, and get himself appointed Chief of a Council of Regency (composed of his Creatures) during the Minority of the Dauphin. This Idea has never, I believe, been wholly abandon'd.

GOUVERNEUR MORRIS, to Thomas Jefferson

One day men will be astonished that the eighteenth century was less progressive than the age of Caesar, when the Tyrant was killed in the Senate House with no formalities save twenty-three dagger thrusts, and by no law save that of the liberty of Rome.

LOUIS ANTOINE DE SAINT-JUST, to the Convention

I felt my own republican Virtue faltering when faced by guilt humbled by the Sovereign Law. Loathing of tyranny and love of mankind equally derive from the human heart, that of the just patriot. But, fellow-Citizens, the final proof of their zeal that the people's delegates owe to the Nation is to sacrifice those spontaneous urgings of natural feeling to the security of a great people and of victimised Humanity. Citizens, the sympathies that sacrifice innocence to crime are in fact cruel; forgiveness that surrenders to tyranny is the mark of the barbarian.   MAXIMILIEN ROBESPIERRE, to the Convention

THE LAST OF THE KING

No trial should be held here. Louis is not a prisoner at the bar. You are not judges but statesmen; the People's representatives can be no more. You have no sentence to make on him, either for or against, but a decree to pass vital for the Welfare of the State. Louis denounced the French People as rebels. He called in foreign tyrants, his colleagues, to punish them. Victory, and the People, decide that he himself is the rebel. He cannot be judged, he is already condemned, otherwise the Republic has no point.

If Louis can be tried, he can be acquitted, declared innocent. What am I saying? – he is presumed innocent until declared guilty. But if he is absolved, what happens to the Revolution? If he is really innocent, then all the defenders of Liberty are Malefactors and the royalists are friends of violated purity. If that is the case, his present imprisonment is criminal, and the Fédérés, the people of Paris, all French patriots, are the guilty.

The People do not pass judgments like a law court. They do not pronounce sentence, they hurl thunderbolts. They do not condemn kings, they hustle them into the void.

I once demanded the abolition of the death penalty, in the Constituent Assembly, but you, who never imagined yourselves imploring mercy for so many unfortunates whose crimes were less their own than of their chosen government, how in logic do you implore it on this occasion on behalf of the prime Misdoer?

Yes, in general, the death penalty is a crime, and can thus be defended only when the safety of the individual or of the body politic makes it absolutely essential. Public safety is not endangered by common crime, for it can always defend itself in other ways, and stop the criminal becoming a danger. But a dethroned king, surviving in the midst of a revolution – not prison, nor exile can make his life a question of indifference to the State. Louis must perish, because the Fatherland must live.

In a Republic a dethroned king has but two uses: to disturb the peace of the State and endanger its freedom, or to strengthen both. Now, what choice does right thinking demand, a choice needful to consolidate a Republic only now coming into existence? The correct choice is that which will engrave contempt for kings irrevocably on the souls of every citizen, and stun all royalists.

MAXIMILIEN ROBESPIERRE, to the Convention

Let us cut the Pig's throat! Divide him into as many pieces as there are Departments, so as to despatch a bit of him to each! Let the head stay here in Paris, hanging from the ceiling of this hall of ours!

DEPUTY LOUIS LEGENDRE, at the Cordeliers' Club

It would be unwise to issue an appeal to the People, for Virtue has always been in a minority in this world.   MAXIMILIEN ROBESPIERRE

An appeal to the People might result in the restoration of the Monarchy.   LOUIS ANTOINE DE SAINT-JUST

My people, what have I done to you?
Virtue I loved, justice was my breath,
Your happiness was my only aim,
And now you drag me to my death,
And now you drag me to my death.

Paris street-song, about King Louis XVI

You, who uphold the warring nation against the flood of despotism and intrigue; you, whom I know only as I know God – by your miracles. It is to you, citizen, that I address myself.

LOUIS ANTOINE DE SAINT-JUST, to Robespierre

The back of the hall was converted to boxes like a theatre, and here ladies in most delightful costume ate ices and oranges, and imbibed liqueurs. Deputies would go and greet whoever they wished to, then resume their seats. The ushers did the job of those women who escort you to your box at the Opera. Throughout they could be seen opening the reserved sections of the galleries and with gestures of gallantry showing in the mistresses of the Duc d'Orléans, strewn with tricolour ribbons. Though all signs of assent or protest were prohibited, nevertheless, from where deputies of the Mountain, the extremists sat, the Jacobin Amazons would bawl long, noisy laughter when not screaming for the death penalty. The top galleries, open to the general public, were always crowded with foreigners and people of all sorts, swigging wine and brandy as if in some vulgar, smoky tavern. In every nearby café, bets were being wagered on the verdict.

LOUIS-SÉBASTIEN MERCIER. *Nouveau Tableau de Paris*, on the trial of King Louis XVI

THE KING'S FATE

Were it possible that a majority should decide imprisonment for him, I would propose that the bust of Brutus be veiled. My vote is for death.   LOUIS-MARIE-STANISLAS FRÉRON

My vote is for the imprisonment of the tyrant while the war lasts, in that place where the victims of his tyranny languished, and that, when peace is won, he should be banished.   LOUIS PIERRE MANUEL

I am a Republican and have no hesitations about the choice of punishment for Louis the Last. You should fill tyrants with terror – I vote for the penalty of death.   GEORGES-JACQUES DANTON

On behalf of Mankind, my vote is for the death of Louis.

'ANACHARSIS' CLOOTZ

You have recognised the tyrant's crimes. Your duty is to punish them. Nothing whatever should allow you to hesitate over the punishment for the greatest criminal in all history. I vote for death.

MAXIMILIEN ROBESPIERRE

I vote for the provisional imprisonment of Louis, and for his expulsion when the war ends.

TOM PAINE

The Tree of Liberty pines unless refreshed by royal blood. My vote is for death.

BERTRAND BARÈRE DE VIEUZAC

It would have been desirable that the punishment for Louis should have been declared by the entire nation. It would have been the best way of influencing on our behalf the feelings of our neighbours and of overcoming the designs of the European tyrants, who wish Louis to be punished, in order to better quicken anger and hate against the National Convention. But, the Assembly having deemed it fitting to reject a Plebiscite, I now believe that the only way to escape the perils that threaten us, is to pronounce the death-sentence on Louis, postponing its execution until the People have sanctioned the Constitution which we will be offering them.

JACQUES-PIERRE BRISSOT

I owe to my honour, I owe to my family, not to admit a sentence which declares me guilty of a crime with which I cannot associate myself. Thus, I appeal to the Nation against the sentence inflicted by its Representatives; and I commit, by these words, and trusting to the loyalty of my Defenders, to publish this appeal to the National Convention, in all ways they can, and to request that it may be inserted in the minutes of their sittings.

KING LOUIS XVI

At last we have landed on the Isle of Liberty, and we have burned the boats that brought us.

DEPUTY PIERRE JOSEPH CAMBON

Uniquely dedicated to the performance of my duty and convinced that any who have conspired or are likely to conspire against the Sovereignty of the People deserve the utmost penalty, I cast my vote for Death.

PHILIPPE EGALITÉ, DUC D'ORLÉANS, cousin of
King Louis XVI, to the Convention

He was himself guillotined in 1793 'for conspiracy'.

Addressing you perhaps for the last time, I declare that in no way does my conscience reproach me, and that my supporters have told you only the truth. I have never feared any public inquiry into my own behaviour, but my heart suffers to find that the tribunal accuses me of wishing to shed the blood of my people: and, above all else, that the unhappiness of August the Tenth was my personal responsibility. I admit that my many instances of the love for my people which I have always showed, and my habitual manner of behaviour, did appear to me obvious proof that I had little fear of putting myself in danger, so as to spare their lives, and that these instances, this behaviour, should safeguard me for ever from any such accusation.   KING LOUIS XVI

Terrible news, torturing me, my tears stream down unceasingly. The King was condemned to death. . . . I cannot imagine how to survive all this, the desolate queen and her poor children, I have no strength to think of it. Providence cannot exist if the scoundrels are allowed to endlessly maltreat these good people. Why was I unable to rescue her, with my life, no greater happiness could I have sought. Oh, my friend, my wretchedness is agonising.

COUNT AXEL VON FERSEN, to Baron Taube

Faces made more sombre by the faint lights followed each other into the Tribune. In measured, sepulchred tones only one word was audible. *Death.* Face succeeded face. Each voice sounded a different note. Some deputies calculated whether they had sufficient time to dine before casting their vote. Some fell asleep and had to be roused to render their verdict. What I saw that night I cannot really describe. A novelist himself would be unable to get within distance of it.

LOUIS-SÉBASTIEN MERCIER. *Nouveau Tableau de Paris*

On Thursday January 17, M. de Malesherbes arrived about 9 am. I hastened to meet him. 'All is over,' he told me, 'the King is condemned.' At the sight of him, the King stood up to greet him. The former Minister knelt before him; stifled by tears, for a while he could say nothing. The King then raised him, and embraced him. M. de Malesherbes at last informed him of the decree sentencing him to death. The King betrayed neither surprise nor agitation, seeming concerned only with the sorrow of the venerable man, trying indeed to comfort him.

M. de Malesherbes told His Majesty all he could of the voting. Informers, personal relatives and enemies, laymen, clergy, absent Deputies, had cast their votes irrespective of legal forms, though, those favouring death, as politically necessary or from a pretence of genuinely believing the King guilty, still amounted to a majority, but a majority of five only. Several had wanted a suspended death sentence. On this, a second vote was decided, on the assumption that those wishing to postpone regicide, added to the votes against death, would become the majority. But at the Assembly entrances, murderers, of the Duc d'Orléans faction and of the Paris Deputies, terrorised with shouts and threatened with daggers any who were reluctant to support them; so, whether from paralysis or unconcern, Paris either did not dare or did not wish to make the slightest effort to rescue its King.

JEAN-BAPTISTE CANT HANET CLÉRY, *valet de chambre* to King Louis XVI. *Journal*

The King said to me, 'You have heard of the sentence they have given me?'

'Ah! Sire, let us hope for suspension, M. de Malesherbes has some confidence in that.'

'I myself look for no such hope, but I am very greatly distressed that M. d'Orléans, my own relative, should have voted for my death. Read this list of the voters.'

'The public, Sire, is showing much dissent. Dumouriez has arrived in Paris. People believe that he is well disposed to you and that he represents the army's hostility to Your Majesty's trial. Everyone is shocked by the wickedness of M. d'Orléans. They say too that the foreign ambassadors will all go together to the Assembly, on your behalf. Indeed, it is confidently maintained that the Deputies fear a street rising.'

'If that happens, I will be very distressed, for it would only mean more victims. I myself have no fear of death, but I cannot imagine without a shudder the cruel fate which I must bequeath to my family – the queen and our unhappy children. Also those loyal servants, always true to me, and those old men whose only support lay on small pensions I could give them – who will help and look after them? I see the people surrendered to anarchy, becoming victims of every faction; then one crime after another, France riven by endless quarrels. Oh God – is this my reward for my sacrifices? Have I not attempted all I could, to win the happiness of France?'

He happened to pick up an old *Mercure de France*, and there saw a riddle which he invited me to solve, though in this I failed. 'What, you can't do it, Cléry, and yet the word is most appropriate to myself.

Sacrifice!' He then asked me to go to the library for Hume's History of England, the volume containing the death of Charles I, which he read the next days. I then realised that during his time at the Temple His Majesty had read two hundred and fifty books.

At 8.30, the door opened. The Queen came first, holding the Dauphin's hand, followed by Madame Royale and Madame Elizabeth. All threw themselves into the King's embrace. A melancholy stillness ensued for a little, interrupted only by sighs and tears. The Queen made a movement towards the King's room. 'No,' he said, 'let us go into this room, I can only see you there.' They entered, and I closed the glass door. The King seated himself, the Queen on his left, Madame Elizabeth on his right. Madame Royale more or less opposite, the little Dauphin immediately before him. All leant on the King, often pressing him to themselves. This sad sight lasted an hour and three quarters, throughout which I could hear nothing, though I managed to observe that whenever the King paused, the ladies' agitation increased, lasting until he resumed. Their gestures showed plainly that he was telling them that he had been condemned to die.

I undressed the King and as I was about to roll his hair, he said, 'No, it is not worth the trouble.' Afterwards when he was in bed and I was drawing the curtains, 'Cléry. Call me at five.'

JEAN-BAPTISTE CANT.HANET CLÉRY, *valet de chambre* to King Louis XVI. *Journal*

I was then told to get ready to go with the King, so as to undress him on the scaffold. At this I was terrified but, collecting myself, I was braced to do this last service to my Master, who felt disgust at being served thus by the executioner, when another Commune official entered and told me that I was to remain behind, adding, 'The common executioner is quite good enough for him.'

Since five, all the troops in the capital had been standing to arms. Now the beat of drums, clash of arms, thud of horses, noise of cannon, sounding throughout Paris, echoed through the Tower.

At eight-thirty the clamour redoubled, the doors clattered open and Santerre, with seven or eight Commune officials, entered, leading ten soldiers, who at once formed a double line. At this, the King emerged from his closet. 'You are come for me?' he addressed Santerre.

'Yes.'

'One moment.' The King went back, but at once returned with his Confessor. His Majesty was clutching his Will and said to Jacques

Roux, from the Commune, a renegade priest, 'I beg you to give this
to the Queen, to my wife.'

Roux thrust it aside. 'That's no business of mine. I'm only here to
take you to the knife.'

At the head of the stairs, the King encountered Mathey, Warden
of the Tower.

'M. Mathey, the day before yesterday I spoke to you somewhat
hastily. I pray you, do not bear me a grudge.' Mathey said nothing,
and even affected to turn away before the King had finished.

JEAN-BAPTISTE CANT HANET CLÉRY, *valet de chambre* to King Louis XVI. *Journal*

FROM THE WILL OF KING LOUIS XVI

I entreat all whom I may have offended inadvertently (for I do not
remember ever having given deliberate offence), or to whom I may
have given some bad example or scandal by my behaviour, to forgive
the evil I may have done them. I entreat all charitable people to join
their prayers with my own, that God may grant me pardon for my
sins. For my part I wholeheartedly forgive those now my enemies,
without my having given them just cause for being so, together with
those who, through false or misconceived zeal, have rendered me
much evil.

I recommend my children to my wife. I have never doubted her
tenderness as a mother. I particularly recommend her to raise them as
good Christians, promote their minds to virtue, make them regard
worldly pomps, if they are condemned to experience them, as a perilous and transitory heritage, and to deflect their thoughts to the only
solid and lasting glory, that of eternity. I entreat my sister to continue
her love for my children, and to be their mother should they tragi-
cally be deprived of their own.

I entreat my wife to forgive me all the evils now inflicted upon
her because of me, and whatever troubles I may have caused her
throughout our marriage; as she may be absolutely certain that I
secrete nothing against her, should she imagine anything with which
to reproach herself.

I recommend to my son, should he suffer the misfortune of himself becoming King, to consider that he ought to wholly dedicate
himself to the happiness of his fellow citizens, forget all hatred and
grievance, particularly whatever is connected to the misfortunes and

injuries which have fallen upon myself; that he cannot enhance the contentment of a nation save by ruling under the law, yet, by the same token, a king is powerless to enforce that law unless he has the requisite power, otherwise, being circumscribed in his actions and winning no respect, he does more harm than good.

I recognise that there are certain individuals, once in my service, who have not behaved to me according to their duty and have shown me only ingratitude, but I forgive them. In times of confusion and feverish minds we cannot always be sure of controlling ourselves, and I beg my son, if the chance ever comes, to consider only their misfortunes.

I also most freely forgive my former jailers for the ills and restraints they thought proper to inflict on me. There were also those of tender and compassionate spirit; may they enjoy that peace of the heart that should reward such natures.

While you weep for those close to us, you must remember how useful their deaths will be for the kingdom. Console yourself with this reflexion, and consider that your son is, after myself, the Royalist heir and hope.   COMTE DE PROVENCE (later King Louis XVIII), to
                                          Comte d'Artois (later King Charles X)

REGICIDE

The tyrant's crimes have been visible to everyone, and have filled all hearts with anger. Unless the sword of law strikes off his head, the bandits and murderers will continue to stalk, heads erect, and society will be threatened with direst anarchy.

JOSEPH FOUCHÉ, to the voters at Nantes

Monarchy is not a crime, it is THE Crime.

LOUIS ANTOINE DE SAINT-JUST

It is for you to vote, before the statue of Brutus, before your country, before the whole world. It is by judging the last king of the French that the National Convention will enter the fields of Fame. . . .   LOUIS ANTOINE DE SAINT-JUST

EXECUTION

The Late King of this Country has been publically executed. He died in a manner becoming his Dignity. Mounting the Scaffold he Express'd anew his Forgiveness of those who persecuted him and a Prayer that his deluded people might be benefited by his Death. On the Scaffold he attempted to speak but the commanding Officer, Santerre, ordered the Drums to beat. The King made two unavailing Efforts but with the same Bad Success. The Executioners threw him down and were in Such haste as to let fall the Axe before his Neck was properly plac'd so that he was Mangled.

GOUVERNEUR MORRIS, to Thomas Jefferson

> Fame, let thy trumpet sound
> Tell all the world around
>   How Capet fell
> And when great George's poll
> Shall in the basket roll
> Let mercy then control
>   The Guillotine

JOEL BARLOW, London, to the tune of the National Anthem
(See Claire Tomalin, 1974)

A CURIOSITY

On the 21st April, 1770, Louis XVI was married at Vienna, by the sending of the ring.

On the 21st June, in the same year, took place the fatal festivities of his marriage.

On the 21st January, 1781, was the *fête* at the Hôtel de Ville, for the birth of the Dauphin.

On the 21st June, 1791, took place the flight to Varennes.

On the 21st January, 1793, he died on the scaffold.

S. BARING-GOULD, 1892

CONFLICT

Posterity will condemn those members of the Constituent Assembly, who allured by the metaphor of fake philosophy, madly burst asunder the bonds of popular subordination; tore down the pillars of monarchy and religion, and left Louis defenceless, forsaken and abandoned to those hordes of Monsters, who, under the different appellation of legislative assemblies, Clubs and Sections, have inflicted on their miserable victim a thousand agonising deaths and apprehensions before they delivered him up to the axe of the executioner.   *The Times*, London, January 25

England, to whom the loss of Antwerp meant far more than the death of Louis XVI, financed the operations [of Russia and Austria], and, while acting as banker, denounced the killing of the King as the most odious and atrocious crime in history; forgetting, for the moment, the doing to death of Mary Queen of Scots by Elizabeth, and the murder of Charles I. These suspicious and unenthusiastic avengers trailed in their wake the discontented French nobles, who soon began to realise that it was not for love of them that the allies were on the move to meet civil war in the Departments, treason and grotesque lack of discipline on the frontiers, and the menace of conquest. France had three men of a military temperament, and these three men saved her – Danton, Carnot, Saint-Just.   J. B. MORTON, 1939

We have often discovered in the past that the French temperament is this, that it requires peril, to extract its total energy. . . .

Paris, saddled with a bad reputation, is, I tell you, again called upon to give France the spirit which last year blazed into all our victories. We promised the army in Belgium 30,000 men, on February 1. Not one man has reached their ranks. I demand that commissioners be appointed to assemble the reinforcements in the 48 Sections of Paris.   GEORGES-JACQUES DANTON, to the Convention

Revolutions are not made by half-measures. I am convinced that you who sit in this place are fated to transform the regimes of all Europe. You cannot rest until Europe is free. Her liberty will guarantee your own. In this world there are three kinds of wickedness. The first is Monarchy; the second is Obedience to Monarchy; the third is to cease fighting while there remains anywhere a single master, a single slave.   LOUIS ANTOINE DE SAINT-JUST, to the Convention

A SIGHT OF MARAT

Marat has carried his calumnies to such length that even the party
which he wishes to support seems to be ashamed of him, and he is
shunned and apparently detested by everyone else. When he enters
the hall of the Assembly he is avoided on all sides, and when he seats
himself those near him generally rise and change their places. He
stood a considerable time yesterday near the tribune, watching an
opportunity to speak. I saw him at one time address himself to Louvet
and in doing so he attempted to lay his hand on Louvet's shoulder.
Louvet instantly started back with looks of aversion, as one would do
from the touch of a noxious reptile, exclaiming, 'Ne me touchez pas'.

DR JOHN MOORE. *Memoir*

WAR DECLARED AGAINST ENGLAND

In France, the Men who for their desperate ends
Had pluck'd up mercy by the roots were glad
Of this new enemy. Tyrants, strong before
In devilish pleas, were ten times stronger now,
And thus beset with Foes on every side
The goaded land waxed mad; the crimes of few
Spread into Madness of the Many, blasts
From hell came sanctified like airs from heaven;
The sternness of the Just, the faith of those
Who doubted not that Providence had times
Of anger and of vengeance, – theirs who throned
The human Understanding paramount
And made of that their God, the hopes of those
Who were content to barter short-lived pangs
For a paradise of ages, the blind rage
Of insolent tempers, the light vanity
Of intermeddlers, steady purposes
Of the suspicious, slips of the indiscreet,
And all the accidents of life were press'd
Into one service, busy with one work;
The Senate was heart-stricken, not a voice
Uplifted, none to oppose or mitigate;

Domestic carnage now filled all the year
With Feast-Days; the old Man from the chimney-nook,
The Maiden from the bosom of her love,
The Mother from the cradle of her babe,
The Warrior from the Field, all perish'd, all,
Friends, enemies, of all parties, ages, ranks,
Head after head, and never heads enough
For those that bade them fall: they found their Joy,
They made it, ever thirsty as a Child,
If light desires of innocent little ones
May with such heinous appetites be match'd,
Having a toy, a wind-mill, though the air
Do of itself blow fresh, and make the vane
Spin in his eyesight, he is not content
But with the plaything at arm's length he sets
His front against the blast, and runs amain,
To make it whirl the faster.

WILLIAM WORDSWORTH. *The Prelude*

A JACOBIN COCTEAU

People say I am a luxury lover. Actually, my love of every art is very deep. Beauty delights me as much as virtue. I paint, I draw, I compose music, I carve, I engrave, I write poetry, I have written seventeen comedies in five years, my apartment is decorated by my own hand – here is the luxury they speak of.

FABRE D'ÉGLANTINE, Paris Deputy to the Convention

A secretary to Danton when Minister of Justice and executed with him. He is remembered for his association with the Revolutionary Calendar.

Between the offering and receiving of snuff there lies a comedy.

FABRE D'ÉGLANTINE

THE CONCIERGERIE PRISON

I believe that, in that period, none of the Paris thoroughfares presented a sight of such gracefully attired women as the Conciergerie Courtyard at noon. Enclosed by iron, they yet resembled a flowerbed in full blossom. Probably, France is the only country, and French the only women able to hold out such strange mixtures and with no effort at all showing the most attractive and seductive against the most repulsive, the most awful, imaginable. I loved to watch these ladies at noon, while preferring their earlier converse, and, in the evening, to partake in talk more personal, myself without any risk of upsetting anyone's pleasure. In the evening, you see, we all turned everything to our advantage – deepening shadows, gaolers' fatigue, many prisoners' absence, others' tact, and, at that peaceful moment which heralds night, we often gave blessings on whatever artist designed the railings. Yet those beings capable of such inexplicable transports carried upon them their death warrants.

I half-glimpsed an occurrence yet more singular. A woman of about forty, but still fresh, with attractive features and trim waist, was sentenced to death in the first ten days of Frimaire [November], with her lover, a military officer from the North, a youth who seemed to unite enlightenment with grace. They returned together from the Tribunal around 6 pm, and had to separate for the night. The woman was experienced in sexual wiles and procured permission to rejoin her lover. That last night they devoted to their passion, once more drinking its goblet dry, wresting themselves from their embrace only at the final moment, at the steps of the fatal tumbril.

COMTE BEUGNOT
(See C. A. Bauban. *Les Prisons de Paris sous la Révolution*, Paris, 1870.)

THE PROCESS

In the centre of the hall, under a statue of justice, holding scales in one hand, and a sword in the other, with the book of laws by her side, sat Dumas, the president, with the other judges. Under them were seated the public accuser, Fouquier-Tinville, and his scribes. Three coloured ostrich plumes waved over their turned up hats, *à la Henri IV* and they wore a tri-coloured scarf. To the right were benches on which the accused were placed in several rows, and gendarmes, with carbines and fixed bayonets by their sides. To the left was the jury.

Never can I forget the mournful appearance of these funereal processions to the place of execution. The March was opened by a detachment of mounted gendarmes – the carts followed; they were the same carts as those that are used in Paris for carrying wood;

four boards were placed across them for seats, and on each board sat two and sometimes three victims; their hands were tied behind their backs, and constant jolting of the cart made them nod their heads up and down, to the great amusement of the spectators. On the front of the cart stood Sanson, the executioner, or one of his sons or assistants. . . .

In the middle of the Place de la Révolution was erected a guillotine, in front of a colossal statue of Liberty, represented seated on a rock, a Phrygian cap on her head, a spear in her hand, the other reposing on a shield. On one side of the scaffold were drawn out a sufficient number of carts, with large baskets painted red, to receive the heads and bodies of the victims. Those bearing the condemned moving on slowly to the foot of the guillotine; the culprits were led out in turn, and, if necessary, supported by two of the executioner's valets, as they were formerly called, but now denominated *élèves de l'Exécuteur des hautes oeuvres de la justice*; but their assistance was rarely required. Most of these unfortunates ascended the scaffold with a determined step – many of them looked up firmly on the menacing instrument of death, beholding for the last time the rays of the glorious sun, beaming on the polished axe; and I have seen some young men actually dance a few steps before they went up to be strapped on the perpendicular plane, which was then tilted to a horizontal plane in a moment, and ran on the grooves until the neck was secured and closed in by a moving board, when the head passed through what was called, in derision, *la lunette républicaine*; the weighty knife was then dropped with a heavy fall; and, with incredible dexterity and rapidity, two executioners tossed the body into the basket, while another threw the head after it.

J. G. MILLINGEN. *Recollections of Republican France*, 1848

Wicked men have the courage deriving from envy and hatred, while the good only have their innocence and timidity derived from virtue.

ANDRÉ CHÉNIER. *The Altars of Fear*

INVASION OF THE REPUBLIC

TO ARMS, CITIZENS, TO ARMS.
If you hesitate, ALL IS LOST! ! !

A considerable part of the Republic is being invaded; Aix-La-

Chapelle, Liège, Brussels may even now be captured; the army's heavy guns, baggage, monies, have had to be hurriedly withdrawn towards Valenciennes, the only town which can briefly obstruct the enemy's advance. All that is unable to follow will be hurled into the Meuse. General Dumouriez is winning victories in Holland, but unless considerable levies of recruits go to his help, he and the best of the French armies may be lost without recall.

People of Paris! Consider the size of the peril. Will you allow the enemy to once more devastate this land of liberty, to desolate with fire your towns, your homes?

People of Paris! It is particularly against yourselves that this monstrous war is aimed. They wish to slaughter your wives and children, reduce Paris to ashes. Remember that the insolent Brunswick has promised to leave not one stone standing.

People of Paris! Once more, rescue the Republic, again set an example; rise, arm yourselves, march and those slave hordes will again flee before you. One last effort is needed, it must be a terrible, a decisive blow. The fate of the world depends on this campaign. Kings must be filled with terror, must be destroyed. Men of July 14, October 5, Men of August 10, rise.

Your brothers and children, hunted by the foe, perhaps even encircled, implore your help; your brothers and children, massacred on the plains of Champagne and beneath the smoking ruins of Lille, your comrades killed at Jemappe – Rise and avenge their death.

Let all our arms in the Sections be taken up. Citizens! Go to them and promise to save the country – save it! Woe to whoever hesitates. Let thousands march out of Paris. This is the moment of a deadly duel between the People and the Kings, Slavery and Liberty.

JEAN NICOLAS PACHE, Mayor of Paris

Later, as Minister of War, he seems to have withheld supplies, reinforcements and orders from the armies, in order to discredit his own Girondin government, on behalf of the Jacobins.

REBELLION IN LA VENDÉE

Wednesday, 13 March, about 5 pm, a large body of men armed with guns, hooks, forks, scythes and other weapons, all with white cockades and adorned with small, square cloth medallions embroidered with such varied shapes as crosses, small hearts stuck with pikes and other emblems of this sort, turned up in the township of Saint-Pierre. All these nondescripts yelled 'Long live the King and our good Priests! We want our King, our Priests, and the old ways.' And they wanted to murder all Patriots, especially we too, who were ignoring the lot of them. All of them, a horribly large number, charged the Patriots who had gathered to oppose them, many they killed, many others they took captive and all the rest they dispersed.

Two Bretons

GIRONDINS

The moment has arrived for terror to penetrate that palace from which it has issued so often. Let all within it tremble; there is no one of them who is inviolable.

PIERRE-VICTURNIEN VERGNIAUD, to the Assembly

What need is there for us to produce evidence? Conspiracy never offers evidence for its own existence.

JACQUES-PIERRE BRISSOT, denouncing the Royalists

Any nation is allowed to thrust out of itself those who try to injure it.

PIERRE-VICTURNIEN VERGNIAUD

If you bring about this Revolutionary Tribunal, you will be establishing an Inquisition a thousand times worse than that of Spain.

PIERRE-VICTURNIEN VERGNIAUD

Their real fault was their social doctrine – Liberty without Equality . . . a bizarre mingling of lofty patriotism and ambition, magnanimity and intrigue, fantasy and prudence.

LOUIS BLANC. Histoire de la Révolution française, Paris, 1864–6

(For considerations of whether the Girondins were an organised, unified Party with distinct territorial affiliations and plans to limit the powers of Paris in favour of 'Federalism' – a grave crime in Jacobin eyes, during a period of civil and external wars, rebellions and food shortages – see M. J. Sydenham.)

Constitutions founded on balance of power assume or create two political parties, and a primary need of the French Republic is to dispense with party altogether.   ANTOINE-NICOLAS DE CONDORCET

I tell all of you, in the name of all France, that if these everlasting revolts end in damaging the Assembly elected by the People, Paris will be destroyed, and people will vainly try to discover its traces on the banks of the Seine.   MAXIMIN ISNARD

A FUTURE DUKE

My original entry into government was on the Committee of Public Instruction, where I associated with Condorcet and, because of him, with Vergniaud. An event later connected with one of my most vital crises I should now mention. By strange chance I had known Maximilien Robespierre when I was Professor of Philosophy at Arras and had indeed given him some financial help to assist him in establishing himself in Paris, when he was elected deputy in the National Assembly. When we came across each other in the Convention, to begin with we often met but our differences of opinion and perhaps still more, of character, quickly divided us.

Once, after dinner at my house, Robespierre started to violently abuse the Girondins, particularly Vergniaud, who was actually a fellow guest. I much liked him, great orator, and a man of unpretentious style. I crossed to him and then addressed Robespierre. 'This violence of yours may well get you popular enthusiasm but will never get you esteem and confidence.' Offended, Robespierre departed, and the future showed the distance that this malicious man bore his hostility to me.   JOSEPH FOUCHÉ, DUC D'OTRANTO. *Mémoires*, 1824

DUMOURIEZ, THE GIRONDIN FAVOURITE, DESERTS HIS ARMY

My friends, Treachery is upon us! To arms! To arms! Here is the dire hour when the Motherland's battalions must conquer or suffer slavery beneath the toppled pillars of the nation. Frenchmen, never has your liberty been more endangered; the monstrous stab in the back of our enemies is now at its most dire, and, in a final blow, their fellow-conspirator Dumouriez is marching on Paris. . . .

However, my brothers, my friends, there are other dangers; I have to prove to you something yet more lamentable; your worst foes are amongst yourselves; they rule your attacks and counter-attacks, they organise your defences! Yes, my brothers, my friends, it is in the Convention that parricides scratch at your hearts! Yes, counter-revolution lurks in the government and the Convention; it is planted in the midst of your security and your hopes that the criminal members hold the strings of the conspiracy which they have concocted with the gang of tyrants now advancing to butcher us. . . .

JEAN-PAUL MARAT. *Adresse des Amis de la Liberté*

KING LOUIS XVII

Every day we heard him and Simon singing the Carmagnole, the Marseillaise and many other horrid songs. Simon made him wear a red bonnet and a Carmagnole jacket and forced him to sing at the windows so as to be heard by the guard and to blaspheme God and curse his family and the aristocrats. My mother, fortunately, did not hear all these horrors, as she had been removed.

MADAME ROYALE, daughter of King Louis XVI
and Marie Antoinette, on her brother

Antoine Simon, a shoemaker, had been appointed gaoler to the young boy, who seems to have died of tuberculosis in the Temple Prison in 1795.

ACQUITTAL

In the Tuileries Gardens he heard the distant roar of many voices, that tremendous sound of men all shouting together, so familiar in the great early days of the Revolution but which its enemies pretended would never be heard again. He hastened his steps as the roar grew louder and louder, reached the Rue Honoré and found it thronged with a crowd of men and women shouting: 'Vive la République! Vive La Liberté!' The walls of the gardens, the windows, the balconies, the roofs were packed with spectators waving their hats and hand-kerchiefs. Preceded by a sapper who was clearing a way for the procession, and surrounded by municipal officers, National Guards, gunners, gendarmes, hussars, there was advancing slowly, borne about the heads of the citizens, a man with a morose complexion, his forehead encircled with a crown of oak leaves, his body enveloped in an old green indoor coat with an ermine collar. The women were throwing him flowers. As he was carried along he darted all around him the piercing look of his jaundiced eyes, as if, in that enthusiastic multitude, he was still seeking enemies of the people to denounce, traitors to punish. As he went by, Gamelin took off his hat, and joining his voice to a hundred thousand others, shouted:

'Vive Marat!'

Like the personification of Fate itself, the conquering hero entered the Hall of the Convention. Whilst the crowd slowly dispersed, Gamelin sat on a stone post in the Rue Honoré, pressing his hand over his heart to contain its wild beating. What he had just seen had filled him with an emotion unearthly in its blazing enthusiasm.

He venerated, he worshipped Marat who, sick, feverish and devoured by ulcers, was exhausting the last remnants of his strength in the service of the Republic, and who, in his poor house, open to all, always welcomed Gamelin with open arms, always spoke to him afire with enthusiasm about public affairs, sometimes questioned him about the plans of scoundrels. So now Gamelin was rejoicing that the enemies of 'The Friend of the People', in plotting his downfall had achieved his instant of triumph; he blessed the Revolutionary Tribunal which, in acquitting the Friend of the People, had given back to the Convention the most vehement, the most uncompromising of its legislators. In his mind he saw again that head burning with fever, garlanded with the civic crown, those features alive with intransigent pride and pitiless love, that powerful face, worn and ravaged, that clenched mouth, that broad chest, the agony-racked strength of this man who from up on his living chariot of triumph had seemed to be saying to his fellow-citizens: 'Follow my example! Be you all patriots to the death!'

ANATOLE FRANCE. *Les Dieux ont soif*, 1912 (translated by Frederick Davies, 1979)

Incited by Marat and the Commune, a street mob invaded the Convention in May 1793, and illegally forced out the Girondin leaders, first to house arrest, then to proscription and death.

Make one accusation against one; then, ignoring time and circumstance, they will contrive by crafty ambiguities to accuse the rest of us for the same crime. ROGER DUCOS

There has been a great conspiracy to destroy the Republic, a giant plot to conquer and enslave the French People. The Convention

Let us pull down these deluded people, traitors to their own responsibilities. The People's cry for vengeance and the safety of the State demand that this conspiracy be extinguished with the lives of the conspirators.   JACQUES-NICOLAS BILLAUD-VARENNE

Nature, embrace me! God of Justice, accept me! I am only thirty-nine.   MANON ROLAND, concluding her memoirs in the Conciergerie Prison, November 8, 1793

O Brutus, you so bravely, so vainly, rid the people of corruption. We have made mistakes, as you did. These pure men whose ardour sought freedom, for which they prepared themselves in calm study and austere solitude, believed, like you, that to overthrow despotism would be to start the rule of justice and peace; but actually it only heralded the surge of passions most repellent, vices most hideous.

MANON ROLAND. *Mémoires*

A PRAYER FOR THE TIMES

Our Father who art in Heaven, from where you so marvellously protect the French Republic and the *Sans-Culottes*, your most passionate defenders, blessed be thy name, made holy amongst us, as ever it has been; may your unbreaking will, by which men live free, equal and happy, be done on Earth as it is in Heaven. Give us this day our daily bread, despite the hopeless efforts of Pitt, Coburg and all Tyrants, banded together to enforce famine upon us. Forgive us our sins, in maintaining so long the Despots from whom we have purged France, as we give the Enslaved Nations, when they copy our past behaviour. Keep them from suffering any longer the chains which bind them and which they are so vigorously attempting to break; but may they free themselves, like us, from Nobles, Priests, Kings. Amen.

Annales historiques de la Révolution française, Paris, 1924

It is essential that every justified denunciation should entitle the informer to public respect. Each unfounded denunciation, if made from patriotic motives, should not expose the informer to any penalty.   JEAN-PAUL MARAT. *L'Ami du Peuple*

THE CONSTITUTION OF JUNE '93

The Constitution is about to be offered for ratification by the Sovereign People. Does it outlaw speculation? No. Have you decreed death for hoarders? No. Have you restricted freedom of trade? No. Well, we must inform you that you have yet to go to the limits of securing happiness for the People. Liberty is no more than a hollow mirage if one class freely can force another into starvation and continue unpunished. Equality is a vain mockery when the rich, through monopoly, can hold powers of literal life and death over their fellows. The Republic is equally illusionary when daily the counter-revolution juggles with the price of food which three-quarters of our people are unable to secure without torment.

JACQUES ROUX, to the Convention

On paper, the 1793 Constitution was nevertheless the most democratic yet envisaged, surpassing the achievements of Britain, America and Switzerland, but the exigencies of the time prevented its being actually enforced. Military defeats, invasion, rebellion, civil war, inflation, Marat's murder, food shortages, concentrated power not in the Convention, Paris Sections, Communes, but in the Committee of Public Safety, until July 1794.

Similarly, the Russian Constitution of 1936 was superbly democratic and wholly ignored.

AN ADDRESS TO THE PEOPLE OF FRANCE

How long, oh unhappy Frenchmen, are you going to endure this distress and disunity? Too long have conspirators and criminals put personal ambition above the common good. Why, wretched victims of these agitations, do you cast out your hearts and ravage yourselves to erect this tyranny on the ruins of France in all its desolation? Oh, my native land! your trials are breaking my heart; all I can sacrifice to you is my life, and I give thanks to Providence that I remain free to rid myself of it as I like.

CHARLOTTE CORDAY

DR JEAN-PAUL MARAT,
THE FRIEND OF THE PEOPLE

From the very start I was bitten by a passionate desire for glory which changed course at different stages of my life but has never for a single instant abandoned me. At five, I wished to be a schoolmaster, at fifteen a university professor, at eighteen a writer and at twenty a creative genius. At present my ambition is to martyr myself for my country.   *Autobiography, Collected Works*, Paris, 1869

Liberty must be established by violence and the moment has come for the temporary suspension of the despotism of liberty in order to destroy the despotism of kings.

Citizen Marat,
    I have arrived from Caen. Your patriotism should arouse your curiosity about the plots in being there. I will wait for your answer.

Marat,
    I wrote to you earlier in the day. Did you receive my note? Could I hope for a brief interview with you, for the business is most interesting. My own great sorrow makes me entitled to your protection.
                                                    CHARLOTTE CORDAY

Received with justifiable suspicion, she swiftly knifed him in his bath.

On the night of Marat's death, the Jacobin Club sent to Maure and myself the news. I discovered him in an attitude I found significant for my purpose: he had a wooden billet near him, on which were ink and paper; and his hand, but just emerged from the bath, wrote his last considerations for the People's safety. Yesterday, the surgeon who embalmed him, sent to ask how it should be publicly exposed in the Cordeliers' church. None of his body could be left naked, for he suffered from a leprosy and his blood was wholly inflamed, but I thought it interesting to depict him in the original attitude in which I found him, writing for the happiness of the People.
                    JACQUES-LOUIS DAVID, on his painting, *Marat assassiné*

The body of Marat in eight hours after his death was so putrified and discoloured, that to expose it to the public they were obliged to paint it white, and to colour red his lips and the wound he had received, which was entirely mortified from the state of his health before his death; he was besides exceedingly ravaged and emaciated by his indefatigable attention to the service of his party.   *The Times*, London

Though slaves reviled you as a bloodsucker, you did no more than wish to rid the world of those who had made it too full. 'Great men'! Their blood alone you wished to spill, and you were lavish with it, so that the lives of the real people should be spared. With so many against you, how could you ever manage to survive? You pointed out to us the traitors, a traitor cut you down.

MARQUIS DE SADE, address in the Place de Piques

The difference between his talents and his ambitions was disproportionate.   HIPPOLYTE TAINE. *La Révolution française*, 1876

Marat was the only one, we may say, of the revolutionary leaders who had a real understanding of events and the power to grasp them as a whole, in their intricate bearings on one another.

PETER KROPOTKIN. *The Great French Revolution*, 1909

MARAT'S FUNERAL

Marat's funeral, which had taken place the day before Charlotte Corday's trial, provided a suitable overture for the real drama. The funeral, an almost incredible ceremony, had been organized and designed by the wretched David, one of the more violent Extremists, a man who in Danton's contemptuous phrase, 'had the soul of a lackey', but who also happened to be one of the great artists of the century. In a few years his genius was to be fawningly laid before the satin slippers of the Emperor Napoleon, and posterity was to be made the richer, thanks to David's magnificent canvases of imperial grandeur. In 1793, however, his services were at the disposal of less exalted masters and he was appointed director of the obsequies of his friend and hero, Marat.

Marat's body – neither surgery nor cosmetics could conceal the fact that his face in death was uglier than it had been in life – was extended on a sort of couch raised on steps and drawn by twelve men. Around the funeral car, young girls dressed in white, carried wands and branches of cypress in their hands; the whole of the Convention followed. Next came the Municipal Authorities and then 'the

People', disposing themselves beneath the banners of their Sections. Revolutionary hymns and patriotic airs were chanted and, surrounded by all the paraphernalia – urns of incense, symbolic pyramids, cardboard trees and mountains – that were the indispensable properties of Republican ceremony during the Revolution, Marat's body was carried to its temporary tomb in the garden of the Cordeliers' Club. The crowd that attended these elaborate obsequies seems to have been close to delirium. Many people fell to their knees and through their sobs began to chant the blasphemous prayer, 'Oh heart of Jesus! Oh sacred heart of Marat'.   STANLEY LOOMIS, 1965

A REQUEST FROM THE ABBAYE PRISON

Because I have but a few remaining moments to live, might I hope, citizens, for your permission to have my portrait painted? I would enjoy bequesting this as a memento to my friends. Indeed, just as we cherish the picture of the virtuous, curiosity can impel us towards representations of great criminals, which makes it possible to keep alive the memory of their evils. If you are good enough to incline to this petition, I would beg you to send me tomorrow a miniaturist. I would also repeat my request for permission to sleep unattended. Believe, I beg you, in my sincere gratitude.

CHARLOTTE CORDAY, to the Committee of General Security

She was a woman who simply renounced her sex; when nature reminded her of it she felt only irritated disgust; romantic love and other tendernesses no longer affect a woman who hankers after knowledge, wit, scholarship, philosophy, and seeks personal fame. Decent men dislike such females and they retort by claiming contempt for men. They end by seeing this contempt as a mark of true character, and their bitterness they conceive as energy. Their tastes and daily habits swiftly degenerate to folly and licence, which they call philosophic behaviour.   *Répertoire du Tribunal Révolutionnaire*

AN ENCOUNTER

I went into my chamber to write and sign a certificate for them [two Englishmen], which I intended to take to the guard house to obtain their release. Just as I had finished it, a man came into my room, dressed in the Parisian uniform of a Captain, and with a good address. He told me that two young men, Englishmen, were arrested and detained in the guard house, and that the Section had sent him to ask me if I knew them, in which case they would be liberated. This matter soon being settled between us, he talked to me about the Revolution, and something about (my) 'Rights of Man', which he had read in English; and at parting, offered me, in a polite and civil manner, his services. And who do you think the man was who offered me his services? It was no other than the public executioner, Sanson, who guillotined the King, and all who were guillotined in Paris, and who lived in the same street with me.   TOM PAINE, to Thomas Jefferson (?)

J. M. Thompson (1938) prefaces this:
The office of public executioner had been hereditary in the Sanson family for over a century. C. H. Sanson, who held the office from 1778 (he had done the work for his father since 1758) to 1795, was the fourth of his family to do so since 1684. He was assisted by his two brothers, and his elder son, till the latter's death (August 27, 1792); and he was succeeded by his younger son, a captain of artillery (1795), and his grandson (1840).

CONTRASTS

Robespierre's elegance was world-renowned. He loved daring colours and his innumerable waistcoats were exceptionally audacious. His cravats were invariably snow-white, changed at the least wrinkle. Though lace-cuffs were becoming increasingly out-moded, he wore them almost daily, and his gesture of shaking them back from his hands was often his only lapse from immobility while speaking. He preferred to carry his hat in the old style so as not to disturb his hair which, each morning, was curled into two side rolls and powdered snow-white, the short pigtail being secured by a black satin ribbon. . . .

The methodical shabbiness of many revolutionaries who dressed up to resemble genuine *sans-culottes*, was not only suspect to him but instinctively unpleasant. Many, though possessed of a carriage and horse, and beautiful silver in crowded cupboards, paraded like tramps, with handkerchiefs about their heads and long trousers striped with patriots' red white and blue; they brandished huge knotted sticks, hoping to be acknowledged as loyal egalitarians. Others blew their noses on their hands or urinated on church doors, to erase all memories of once making fortunes as court purveyors or ducal confessors. . . .

Most people let their hair grow down over their foreheads, with long tufts, 'dog's ears', across their cheeks. The future Count Thibaudeau, respectable Deputy certainly no self-dramatiser, so far violated his sense of decorum as to walk around in a studiously arranged *sans-culotte* outfit of loose trousers and open shirt. The wealthy Granet, soon to reach better days, dressed in soiled rags with a strip of torn sackcloth about his dishevelled head, displaying himself as one with the People. A cockade in the hat was insufficient; it was sensible to sport a tricolor rosette on the lapel. This could well be the width of a plate and form the start of a ribbon as much as eight inches wide, hanging down modestly or fluttering proudly in the wind. Especially favoured was a bright poster on your door, showing, framed by a sapper and a *sans-culotte* pikeman, crowned with a Phrygian cap, the inscription: 'Unity, Indivisibility of the Republic; Liberty, Equality, Fraternity – or Death'. . . .

In honour of Roman virtue the Rue Notre Dame des Champs was named 'the Street of Lucretia Avenged' – giving a difficult problem for fathers to explain to their children on Sunday walks. . . .

In official correspondence the designations *town, village, place, hamlet*, were abolished, because they outraged the notion of equality, and instead the universal *commune* was applied to all places, whatever the size of their population. . . .

Insignificance, silence and dissimulation were the most important conditions of survival. Condorcet would never have been recognised, but for carrying his small, leather-bound edition of Horace. A toss of the head, a delicate wrist, the indefinable atmosphere of good education and independent style, could alike betray one as an enemy of the Revolution.   FRIEDRICH SIEBURG, 1936

A French child was named 'Civilis Victoire Jemappes Dumouriez': another 'Phytogneatropé' ('Warrior bearing'). Unorthodox nomenclature was not limited to Revolutionary France. Seventeenth-century English Puritans decorated their children with such names as Mephibostheth, Lamentation, Humiliation, Sorry-for-Sin, Praise God, The Lord is Near, Misericordia Adulterina, In the Gall of the Bitterness in which He Died, Were it not for Jesus We'd All

Be Damned – or adopted them for themselves. Revolutionary Russia indulged in such names as Ideal, Industrialisation, Tractor, Five Year Plan. An American child was given the name 'Welcome Lafayette'. Mikhail Gorbachev was born in a village renamed 'Liberty'.

THE CLUBS

In considering these famous and often confusing institutions of the Revolution – the Jacobin Club, the Cordeliers' Club, the Commune, etc – one must be careful always to remember that the character informing each institution was in a constant condition of change. Resembling the shell of a hermit crab, these institutions were occupied by one interest at one time and by another at the next. The Jacobin spirit during the Terror was diametrically opposed to what it had been during the early days of the Revolution, when the Vicomte de Noailles and the Duc de Biron had been among the men who occupied the President's chair. The Cordeliers' Club, founded by Danton, was one day to become the bitterest of Danton's enemies. The Commune, which in the beginning had been at the command of Bailly and Lafayette, was taken possession of by Danton, by Marat, and finally by Robespierre.   STANLEY LOOMIS, 1965

Modern French political nomenclature can still mislead. The Radicals, for instance, are far from what their name suggests in English.

AT THE JACOBIN CLUB

Robespierre slowly advanced. He was one of the few who at this time still wore the attire fashionable before the Revolution. His hair was dressed and powdered in the former style. He looked like an *ancien régime* tailor more than anything else. He wore glasses which were probably used to hide the twitchings of his pallid face. His speech was slow and deliberate, his sentences so long that whenever he stopped to raise his glasses it seemed that he had no more to say, but after staring slowly and intently over the audience in all parts of the room he would replace the glasses and add some more embellishments to his sentences, already insufferably long.   M. FIEVÉE

I never see the name Marat or Robespierre under a poster without saying to myself – A pity these fellows are so clever, and so out of contact with those they are supposed to rule. They are exactly like the former court and aristocracy. They seem to imagine that people's souls are entirely different from their own and are unable to think things out as well as they do. I can almost hear their words: 'The common herd are ignorant of literature, geography, history, or mathematics; they are incapable of dancing, playing cards, or addressing a lady, as we can; they cannot reason.' But none who actually lives among the people would argue this. The people possess as much pride, vanity, self-respect as any aristocrat. In their limited field, they at times reason more seriously than their enlightened fellow-citizens; and during revolution have usually shown themselves as more sensible than the educated. . . .

A bottle of wine, a glass of beer, a joke, a handshake – that is what the *sans-culottes* enjoy.   M. DUTARD

THE COUNTRY IS IN DANGER

From this moment until that when the enemy shall be expelled from the territory of the French Republic, all French people shall be in permanent requisition for the service of the armies. The young men will go out to fight. The married men will forge the arms and transport the supplies. The women will make tents and clothes and act as nurses in the hospitals. The children will make lint from rags. The old men will be conveyed to public places to arouse the courage of the Warriors, to preach hatred of kings and love of the republic.

The Committee of Public Safety

THE TERROR

Jean Baptiste Henry, 18, journeyman tailor, convicted of having sawn down a tree of liberty, executed 6 September 1793.

Henriette Françoise de Marboeuf, 55, widow of ex-Marquis de Marboeuf, convicted of having desired the arrival of the Austrians and Prussians and of storing food for them, condemned and executed the same day.

Marie Angélique Plaisant, sempstress at Douai, convicted for having announced herself an aristocrat and that she 'did not give a brass farthing' for the nation, condemned at Paris and executed the same day.

General List of the Condemned

I acknowledge as a patriot only the man who, if necessary, would denounce his father, mother and sister, and drink a glass of their blood on the scaffold.   DEPUTY JAVOGUES

The cemeteries, not the prisons, must be filled.

JEAN-BAPTISTE CARRIER

THE QUEEN'S TRIAL

Today a great example is upheld to the universe and will doubtless not be ignored by all peoples within it. Nature and Reason, long violated, are at last satisfied. Equality triumphs. A woman once surrounded with all the brilliant splendour that royal pride and slavish servility could concoct, now occupies in the National Tribunal the place given two days back to another woman, an equality assuring her impartial justice. Citizen jurors, this matter is not one of those in which a single deed, a single crime, is submitted to your conscience and intelligence. You have to judge the accused's entire political career since she came to sit beside the last King of the French. But, chiefly, you must consider the stratagems which she never once ceased to deploy, for the destruction of our nascent liberty, either at home, by her intimate connections with unworthy ministers, traitorous generals and disloyal deputies, or abroad, by conniving with that monstrous alliance of European tyrants which Europe will ridicule for impotence, and by her letters to former émigré French Princes and their trusty agents.

NICOLAS-FRANÇOIS HERMAN, President of the Revolutionary Tribunal

It was by her scheming and intriguing, continuously fatal to France, that the first French retreat from Belgium was engineered. It was the Widow Capet who despatched to the alien governments the plans of campaign worked out in council, so that by such double-treachery the enemy was always forewarned of the Republic's military movements, from which it is clear that the Widow Capet is the cause of the defeats severally suffered by the French armies.

Finally, the Widow Capet, in all ways immoral, a new Agrippina, so perverted, an old hand in all crimes, forgetting both her role as mother and the bonds established by Nature, has not drawn back from enjoying with her son, Louis-Charles Capet – as he has confessed – indecencies whose very notion and name arouse a shiver of horror.   ANTOINE FOUQUIER-TINVILLE, Public Prosecutor

There is reason to believe that this criminal intercourse was not governed by pleasure but by the calculated expectation of enervating the child whom the family still liked to consider as fated to sit on a throne and whom they wished to be thereby certain of dominating. As a result of these forced exertions he developed a hernia, requiring a bandage. Now that the child has been taken from the mother, he has become healthy and strong.   JACQUES RENÉ HÉBERT

A JURYMAN: 'Citizen President, would you have the goodness to observe to the accused that she has not replied concerning the matter mentioned by Citizen Hébert, concerning the doings between herself and her son.'

Ex-QUEEN MARIE ANTOINETTE: 'If I do not answer, it is because Nature recoils from such an accusation against a mother, . . . I appeal to every mother here.'

Although no proof exists against this unfortunate Princess, how can one hope for anything with scoundrels who invent the proofs which they lack and who condemn on no more than vague assertions and suspicions. No, let us hope for nothing at all. We must be resigned to God's Will. Her fate is assured. We must prepare ourselves for it and summon enough strength to endure this terrible stroke. I have long been trying to steel myself for it, and feel that I shall actually receive the news of it calmly. God alone can save her; let us beg His mercy and submit ourselves to his decrees.   COUNT AXEL VON FERSEN

CONDEMNATION

The Tribunal, according to the unanimous declaration of the jury, which complied with the indictment of the Public Prosecutor, and according to the laws dictated by him, condemns the said Marie Antoinette, called Lorraine d'Autriche, widow of Louis Capet, to the pain of death: declares in accordance with the law of 10 March last; that her possessions, if she has any within French territory, are taken and confiscated on behalf of the Republic and orders that, at the request of the Public Prosecutor, the present judgment shall be carried out in the Place de la Révolution and printed and exhibited throughout the Republic. NICOLAS-FRANÇOIS HERMAN

A LETTER

It is to you, my sister, that I write for the last time. I have just been condemned, not to a shameful death, for it is shameful only for criminals, but to rejoin your brother. Like him innocent, I hope to display the same firmness as he did in his last moments. I am calm, as one is when one's conscience holds no reproach. I regret deeply having to abandon my poor children. You know that I lived only for them and for you, my good and kind sister. In what a situation do I leave you, who from your affection sacrificed everything to be with us. I learned from the pleadings at the trial that my daughter was separated from you.* Alas! poor child, I dare not write to her, she would not receive it. I do not know even if this will reach you. Receive my blessing on them both. I hope that one day, when they are older, they will be able to join you again and profit to the full from your tender care and that they both remember what I have always tried to instil in them: that the principles and the execution of their duty should be the chief foundation of their life, that their affection and mutual trust will make it happy. Let my daughter remember that in view of her age she should always help her brother with the advice that her greater experience and her affection may suggest, and let them both remember that in whatever situation they may find themselves they will never be truly happy unless united. Let them learn from our example how much consolation our affection brought us in the midst of our unhappiness and how happiness is doubled when one can share it with a friend – and where can one find a more loving and truer friend than in one's own family? Let my son never forget his father's last words, which I distinctly repeat to him, never to try to avenge our death. I have to mention something which pains my heart. I know how much

---

* Madame Elizabeth and Madame Royale were questioned *separately* in the apartment occupied by the Simons and the little King. Hence the Queen's misapprehension on hearing the report of the interrogations.

distress this child must have given you. Forgive him, my dear sister, remember his age and how easy it is to make a child say anything you want, even something he does not understand. The day will come, I hope, when he will be all the more conscious of the worth of your goodness and tenderness towards them both. I now have only to confide in you my last thoughts. I would have liked to write them at the beginning of the trial, but apart from the fact that I was not allowed to write, everything went so quickly that I really would not have had the time.

I die in the Catholic, Apostolic and Roman religion, in the religion of my father, in which I was brought up and which I have always professed, having no expectation of spiritual consolation, and not even knowing if there still exist any priests of that religion here, and in any case the place where I am would expose them to too much danger if they should enter. I sincerely beg pardon of God for all the faults I have committed during my life. I hope that in His goodness He will receive my last wishes, and those I have long since made, that He may receive my soul in His mercy and goodness. I ask pardon of all those I know, and of you my sister in particular, for all the distress I may, without wishing it, have caused them. I forgive all my enemies the harm they have done me. I say farewell here to my aunts and to all my brothers and sisters. I had friends. The idea of being separated for ever from them and their troubles forms one of my greatest regrets in dying. Let them know, at least, that up to my last moment I was thinking of them.

Farewell, my good and loving sister. May this letter reach you! Think of me always, I embrace you with all my heart, together with those poor, dear children. My God! what agony it is to leave them for ever! Farewell! Farewell! I shall henceforth pay attention to nothing but my spiritual duties. As I am not free, they will perhaps bring me a (conformist) priest, but I protest here that I shall not say a word to him and that I shall treat him as a complete stranger.

EX-QUEEN MARIE ANTOINETTE, awaiting execution

MARIE ANTOINETTE'S LAST WORDS

Sir, I beg your pardon. I did not do it on purpose.

To the Executioner, having stumbled on his foot

THE BILL

The widow Capet, for the Coffin . . . . 6 livres
For the grave and grave diggers . . . . 15 livres 35 s.

MEN OF GENIUS

They were men of enlarged views and great literary attainments; but they seem to have been deficient in that vigour and daring activity which circumstances made necessary. Men of genius are rarely either prompt in action or consistent in general conduct: their early habits have been those of contemplative indolence; and the daydreams with which they have been accustomed to amuse their solitude, adapt them for splendid speculations, not temperate and practical counsels. Brissot, the leader of the Gironde party, is entitled to the character of a virtuous man and an eloquent speaker; and his excellences equally with his faults rendered him unfit for the helm in the stormy hour of Revolution. Robespierre, who displaced him, possessed a glowing ardour that still remembered the *end*, and a cool ferocity that never either overlooked or scrupled the means.

S. T. COLERIDGE. *Canciones ad Populum*, 1795

A group of this sort can scarcely be said to have had any specific policy. The men concerned, however, may be regarded as representing in some respects a great many *arrivistes*, drawn together even before 1789 by their profound dissatisfaction with the society in which they lived. In their letters, in Brissot's *Patriote Française* and at Madame Roland's first receptions, they had expressed their discontent with the existing order and anticipated the opening of a new era. When their opportunity occurred in 1791–2 they showed themselves avid and irresponsible in their pursuit of power and place, even to the extent of encouraging incipient insurrection in order to gain political advantage. Then, when leadership had been won, they proved irresolute in everything but the endeavour to retain it, vacillating at all critical times and showing determination only in their efforts to crush Robespierre, the man who impugned their integrity and challenged their authority.

M. J. SYDENHAM, 1961

THE END OF THE GIRONDINS

Accordingly, at ten o'clock on the night of the 30th of October, the twenty-two, summoned back once more, receive this information, that the Jury feeling themselves convinced have cut short, have brought in their verdict; that the Accused are found guilty, and the sentence on one and all of them is Death with confiscation of goods.

Loud natural clamour rises among the poor Girondins; tumult; which can only be repressed by the gendarmes. Valazé stabs himself; falls down dead on the spot. The rest, amid loud clamour and confusion, are driven back to their Conciergerie; Lasource exclaiming, 'I will die on the day when the People have lost their reason; ye will die when they recover it.' No help! Yielding to violence, the Doomed uplift the Hymn of the Marseillaise; return singing to their dungeon.

Riouffe, who was their prison-mate in these last days, has lovingly recorded what death they made. To our notions, it is not an edifying death. Gay satirical *Pot-pourri* by Ducos; rhymed Scenes of Tragedy, wherein Barère and Robespierre discourse with Satan; death's eve spent in 'singing' and 'sallies of gaiety', with 'discourses on the happiness of peoples': these things, and the like of these, we have to accept for what they are worth. It is the manner in which the Girondins make *their* Last Supper. Valazé, with bloody breast, sleeps cold in death; hears not their singing. Vergniaud has his dose of poison; but it is not enough for his friends, it is enough only for himself; wherefore he flings it from him; presides at this Last Supper of the Girondins with wild coruscations of eloquence, with song and mirth. Poor human will struggles to assert itself; if not in this way, then in that.

But on the morrow morning all Paris is out; such a crowd as no man has seen. The Death-carts, Valazé's cold corpse stretched among the yet living twenty-one, roll along. Bareheaded, hands bound; in their shirt-sleeves, coat flung loosely round the neck: so fare the eloquent of France; bemurmured, beshouted. To the shouts of *Vive la République*, some of them keep answering with counter-shouts of *Vive la République*. Others, as Brissot, sit sunk in silence. At the foot of the scaffold they again strike up, with appropriate variations, the Hymn of the Marseillaise. Such an act of music; conceive it well! The yet living chant there; the chorus so rapidly wearing weak! Sanson's axe is rapid; one head per minute, or little less. The chorus is worn out; farewell for everyone ye Girondins. Te Deum – Fauchet has become silent; Valazé's dead head is lopped: the sickle of the Guillotine has reaped the poor Girondins all away. 'The eloquent, the young, the beautiful and brave!' exclaims Riouffe. O death, what feast is toward in thy ghostly Halls?   THOMAS CARLYLE, 1837

Thus fell the Girondins, by Insurrection; and became extinct as a Party: not without a sigh from most Historians. The men were men of parts, of Philosophic Culture, decent behaviour; not condemnable in that they were Pedants and had not better parts; not condemnable, but most unfortunate. They wanted a Republic of the Virtues, wherein themselves should be head; and they could only get a Republic of the Strengths, wherein others than they were head.

For the rest, Barère shall make a report of it. The night concludes with a 'civic promenade by torchlight': surely the true reign of Fraternity is now not far?   THOMAS CARLYLE, 1837

The Revolution, like Saturn, is devouring its own children.

PIERRE-VICTURNIEN VERGNIAUD

It is of the utmost importance that there should not emerge in the Republic a single man . . . assembling in his hands total power; who, when he has it, will employ it in the destruction of any who refuse to march under his banner.   MAXIMILIEN ROBESPIERRE

VOICES

'Wonderful news, Danton!'
    'What is it?'
    'The Girondins were condemned and have all been executed.'
    'You call that wonderful news? It's the reverse.'
    'But, all in all, they were factionalists.'
    'Factionalists! Aren't we all? We deserve the scaffold as much as they do. And we'll get it, first one, then the other. Those Paris fellows will guillotine the entire Republic.'

GEORGES-JACQUES DANTON AND A NEIGHBOUR. *At Arcis Sur l'Aube*

THE JACOBIN
DICTATORSHIP

THE ARCHANGEL OF DEATH

From what unknown abyss rose this genius? From what maternal depths did this creature strive towards the light? Robespierre was timeless, sterile, neither young nor old. But beside him was that mysterious being who was simultaneously the day and the night, the soldier and magistrate Saint-Just, who, at twenty-seven, still beside him, was to climb the scaffold. The World's amazement at this youth will not fade; never will it manage to decide between a verdict between cautious admiration for his greatness and horror of his cruelty. Saint-Just was not of the common world, but none can assert whether he had ascended from the regions of Death as a warning to the frailty of mortal pleasures and ambitions, or whether he was a messenger from that kingdom of Light where bodies are incorporeal, tears unknown, and the Book of Wisdom is forever open in the brilliance of infinite day.

His beauty was unearthly: the eyes, large and profoundly blue reflected the firmament of a mysterious universe. The fair, curled hair dropped over his crested forehead, almost to his brows, whose delicate arches continued the curve of his nose. The mouth was well-cut, of almost unnatural purity, as though from an artist's blade. From where the almost toxic charm of these features? Perhaps from an ability to evoke both gentleness and ice-cold terror. Should one feel tempted to touch those golden tresses so thick on the boyish head, one also sought flight to the furthest horizon to escape the enigmatic ruthlessness of his expression. Had mother's lips ever met those perfect ones? How did that face appear, in sleep: cheeks flushed, mouth open? Did he indeed ever sleep? Was he alive, was he dead? His carriage veered on rigidity: with measured tread he mounted the tribune in the Convention, hands folded behind him, without a single movement. His chin lay motionless on his huge stock, always meticulously starched. Golden earrings alone moved, gently swinging about his high collar.

In boyhood, studying art, he had liked to draw the head of Antinous, Hadrian's lovely youth. He himself had been a spoilt child, greatly worrying his mother, finally decamping with the family silver. The anxious parent had him traced by the police and incarcerated in a mental hospital [actually, a privately managed prison], where he wrote *Organt*, an epic in twenty cantos, both fantastic and frivolous in Voltaire's manner, prefaced: '*J'ai vingt ans. J'ai mal fait, je pourrai faire mieux.*'

His earliest letter to Robespierre, August 1790, began: 'You who uphold the tottering land against the flood of tyranny and intrigue, you whom I know only as I know God – through your miracles . . .' Written on behalf of the local economic concerns, it concluded: 'I have never met you, but you are a great man. You represent, not only the province, but mankind and all the Republic.'

FRIEDRICH SIEBURG, 1936

SAINT-JUST

The free man prefers poverty to humiliation.

There is silence round a throne.

What a government it is, which plants the Tree of Liberty on the scaffold, and places the scythe of Death in the hands of the Law!

All must live an independent life.

The Republic will never bear arms to conquer or oppress another nation, will make no peace with any foe yet remaining on French soil, save to win the peace and happiness of all lands. The French People vote the Liberty of the World.

Only the laconic can govern.

The conscience of the people is the City.

Whoever confesses disbelief in friendship or who has no friends of his own, shall be banished.

Force of circumstances is leading to unforeseen results. Profits are being won by many hostile to the Republic.

Necessity is making working citizens dependent on their enemies. Do you think that a state can exist if its social organs are opposed to its form of government? Those who make a revolution half-heartedly only dig their own graves. The Revolution is making us acknowledge the principle that whoever shows himself unpatriotic can own nothing in it. Do not allow a single unhappy or poor person to exist; at this cost alone can a real Revolution, a real Republic, exist.

The property of patriots is sacred, but that of those who conspire against the State is forfeit to the unprivileged. Those are the Lords of the Earth.

The only way to establish a Republic is to utterly destroy all opposition.

Republican children must be strictly trained to speak laconically, which suits the nature of the French language.

The War of Liberty must be waged with fury.

Vanity breeds the spirit of Faction. Factions are exploited by governments adjacent to a free nation to assail its prosperity. In the entire social order, factions are the poison most deadly. By power of lying, they imperil the lives of the virtuous, and when they control the State, one can foretell the outcome.

Happy is the country where punishment is a free pardon.

When savages are cruel, they take the first step towards civilisation.

The ship of Revolution can reach safe haven only from a sea reddened by torrents of blood.

Exaltation derives from unbending resolution to protect the rights of the People and of the Convention. It derives from disdain for riches and from habits bold and simple. Exaltation is not wrath, it is virtue.

Saint-Just's unfinished Republican Institutions *included:*

Each man over 21 must name his friends aloud in the temple; if he renounces a friend, he must publicly explain why, in the temple.

If anyone, when intoxicated, behaves or talks illegally, he shall be exiled.

Murderers shall wear black until their death, and shall be executed if found wearing anything else.

Whoever has always lived virtuously shall, after 60, wear a white scarf.

Citizens should gather in temples to examine the private life of officials, and of all under 21.

Each citizen shall annually declare in the temple how he has made use of his possessions.

A soldier must never return to his home if he has deserted in battle or lost his weapon or committed indiscipline or complained of hardships. A father who embraces a son guilty of cowardice forfeits his scarf of seniority.

Censors must never speak in public. In modesty and severe austerity consists their virtue. They are inflexible. They summon officials to justify their conduct. They denounce all governmental abuses and injustice, extenuating or pardoning nothing.

A DECREE OF THE PARIS COMMUNE

No Certificate of Citizenship shall be issued to:

1) Those who, at public meetings, obstruct progress by malicious speeches, disorderly shouts, threats.

2) Those who, more prudently, talk in mysterious words about the set-backs of the Republic, lamenting the fate of the people.

3) Those who have played no positive role in the Revolution but, in excuse, emphasise their cash contributions, service in the National Guard, through a substitute or elseways.

4) Those who, while in no ways hostile to the Revolution, have lifted no finger on behalf of it.

5) Those who ignore meetings of their Sections on the excuse that they do not know how to speak, or that they are hindered by business matters.

6) Those who talk contemptuously of the lawful authorities, emblems of the law, the popular Societies and defenders of Liberty.   PIERRE GASPARD CHAUMETTE

A POET'S VIEW OF THE JACOBINS

A few hundred idlers gathered in a garden or theatre, or a few gangsters plundering shops, are with brazen effrontery called 'the People', and the most arrogant tyrants have never accepted from their greediest courtiers such foul and nauseating incense as the obsequious toadying with which these several thousand purloiners of national sovereignty are daily intoxicated by the scribblers and demagogues of this Club, who are thrusting France into chaos. As outward patriotism is the only virtue required, a few, dirtied by shameful careers, hurry to display their patriotism by florid rhetoric, hoping to bury their past and secure their future by mere declamation, and, by inflaming the crowd and redeeming their shame by candid insolence. . . .

Called *usury* and *monopoly*, industry and trade are depicted as crimes . . . the most hateful suspicions and most headlong slanders are called *freedom of opinion*. If you demand proof of an accusation, you are denounced as a suspect, an enemy of the people. Women attend the Jacobin Club to applaud the outbursts of sanguinary lunacy. They presume to confer *certificates of correct thinking*. All members and supporters of this brotherhood are virtuous, all others are hypocrites. Mere admission to it, like the baptism of Constantine, washes away all crimes, bloodshed, murder. The Popular Societies, linked together, surround France with an electric chain, simultaneously agitating in all corners, uttering the same cries, dancing the same steps. Their unceasing rowdiness has reduced the Government to terrified torpor. . . .

Usurping the authority of the State itself, they surge into the law courts and interrupt trials, force commune officials to appear before them for orders. In various places they have dared to forcibly push into Citizens' homes, search them, then formally pronounce condemnation or release. Every revolt against legal authority is protected by them.   ANDRÉ CHÉNIER. *Journal de Paris*

EXERCISE IN
THE MADELONNETTES PRISON

Those darkened passages, pallid men, lurching shadows, marsh-lights twisting this way and that, forming lines, casting indistinct reflections onto flowery dressing-gowns, white quilted surcoats, nightcaps, onto faces that the promise of an empire could not induce to laugh, and made more comic still by the lights from below, held in unseen hands, and which seemed to daub with lustre all significant features and enlarge only the staring eyes; all that disorder of dark and light, movement and stillness, jabber and silence, could have been prepared for some expert painter. The chief jailer's wife periodically visited us and was wont to declare that, once we started to move, we were worthy subjects for Rembrandt himself. I consider she was going a bit far here, and little Vaubertrand's laugh more than once forced me to consider that we more resembled Callot's grotesques, especially when worthy M. d'Allerary, holding up his candlestick, managed to scorch the chin or jabot of M. the *ci-devant* Lieutenant-General de Crosne, who never managed to learn how to start with left foot forward.

M. FLEURY, of the Théatre Français
(See Olivier Blanc, 1987)

Olivier Blanc is instructive on the different ways and conditions of the Paris prisons. Almost all included muddle. He gives as an example the confusion between Citizeness Mayet and Madame de Maillé. The former was, mistakenly, summoned before the Tribunal and executed. The latter was finally released, after the convulsions of the 8th Thermidor.

FROM SAINTE-PÉLAGIE PRISON

I know not, *ma petite*, if I will be allowed ever to see you or write to you again. Remember your mother. These few words hold all the best that I can give you. You have witnessed my happiness in doing my work and helping the distressed. There is no other way of life. You have seen me calm in misfortune and as a prisoner, because my conscience is clear and because I retain the recollections and joy granted by good deeds. These are the only means to suffer misfortune and the turn of Fortune's wheel.

It may be, and I trust that this will be so, that you will not inherit these wretchednesses of my own: but others remain against which you will find equally necessary to protect yourself. A life strictly and busily performed is the best defence to such dangers, and not only necessity but wisdom imposes on you the responsibility of serious work.

Deserve well your parents; they bequeath you a good example, and if you can turn it to account you will not have lived pointlessly. Farewell, my beloved child, whom I have nourished at my breast and whom I would desire to stamp with all my sentiments. One day you will be able to judge the effort I am now making not to fall into weeping by my memories of you. I embrace you.

MANON ROLAND, to her daughter Eudora

THE LAW OF SUSPECTS
AT LIMOGES

There was found tried before us, in accordance with the indictment, Gabriel David, who was interrogated as follows:

Did you write 'Shit on the Nation' on your leave pass? He replied 'No'; that he did not know how the shocking words got there and did not know whose was the sacrilegious hand which had written them; that he was taken by surprise when the commissioner for war had read them to him, that he swore once again that he was not the author and as evidence of his innocence pointed to the fact that if his leave pass had contained anything counter-revolutionary he would have consigned it to the flames rather than have shown it to the commissioner for war.

Archives départementales, Haute-Vienne
(See D. G. Wright, 1974)

Citizen David was sentenced to imprisonment.

The Terror is less a particular principle than the outcome of the application of the principle of democracy to the most urgent needs of the nation.

MAXIMILIEN ROBESPIERRE

From Strasbourg, following military collapse and demoralisation:
We are here. We swear, in the name of the Army, that the foe is going to be overcome. If there exist among you traitors, or any indifferent to the People, we bring a sword to strike them down. Soldiers, we are

here to redress your wrongs and find you generals to lead you to victory. We are absolutely resolved to discover, to reward, to promote genuine merit, and to hunt down crime without fear or favour. Take courage, then, heroic Army of the Rhine, henceforward you are going to be happy and to advance in triumph, hand in hand with Liberty herself. All generals, all other officers and all Government agents are hereby ordered to satisfy within three days all just complaints of you, the soldiers. After that, we ourselves are going to listen to such complaints, and make examples of justice and severity as never before seen by a French army.

SAINT-JUST and LE BAS, Citizen Representatives on Mission
from the National Convention, Paris

There followed requisitions, dismissals, reorganisation, imprisonment or execution of thieves, bureaucrats, embezzlers, traitors, speculators, spies and incompetents, and an eventually successful counter-attack against the Austrians and Prussians.

The spirit of oppression and ambition for power are common to soldiers of all countries. MAXIMILIEN ROBESPIERRE

The civilian Representatives on Mission were employed by the Committees and Convention to supervise the provinces and armies, forerunning twentieth-century commissars.

They must be fathers and friends to the soldiers; must sleep under canvas and witness all military exercises. They must not be too intimate with generals, so that ordinary troops shall the more trust their justice and impartiality. The soldiers should always find them prepared to listen to them, day or night. They should eat alone. They must remember that it is they who are responsible for the public security and that the final defeat of Kings is more important than brief spells of comfort. LOUIS ANTOINE DE SAINT-JUST

10,000 of our soldiers lack shoes. You will at once confiscate the shoes of all aristocrats in Strasbourg and, by 10 am tomorrow, 10,000 pairs must be on their way to our headquarters.

All overcoats of the citizens of Strasbourg are hereby commandeered. Tomorrow evening, they must be given to the commissariat of the Republic. SAINT-JUST and LE BAS, to the Strasbourg Commune

A HUSBAND, FROM THE ARMY
OF THE RHINE, AT SAVERNE, ALSACE

Elizabeth, my dear,

I am seizing the chance of a moment's leisure to speak to her who is dearer to me than my very life. How endlessly have I not yearned to be back with you once more! How sorrowful I am that my return to Paris has been delayed! The countryside round here is superb. Nowhere have I seen nature so beautiful, so majestic; a range of lofty mountains, on the brow of which, on a mighty rock, is an ancient, ruined fortress. As we gazed about us, joy flooded us both. This was our very first day of any rest at all. For myself, however, there was a gap. How much would I have given to be beside you, sharing my delight – yet you are a hundred leagues distant! To comprehend this too often desolates my soul, and without question I require all the devotion which true patriotism can induce, to help me tolerate the thought of your own burdens. There is scarcely an instant, even when I am engrossed in the gravest duties, when you are not in my thoughts. But, as it is, we must accept necessity. The worst is behind us. Soon my hard sacrifice will be rewarded. Just a few days, and I hope to be back with my Elizabeth for a long time. Also, I hope that the bliss of our reunion will be redoubled by news of a lasting victory in the field. Saint-Just and myself are giving all possible orders to ensure just this as swiftly as we can. We never stop work, we supervise everything to the last button. One general or other sees us turn up at his HQ, when least expected, to demand a report on his behaviour. Our advance on Landau is under way. There is not the slightest doubt of its relief, and then our mission will be over. We have all possible reasons for haste. Saint-Just is almost as urgent as myself to see Paris again. I have promised that you will give him one of your delicious dinners. I am so very pleased that you are well-disposed to him. He is a really good chap. Each day my love and admiration for him is greater. The Republic has no defender more ardent or intelligent. We have complete understanding, utter harmony of outlook. Also, what makes me feel for him still more is his frequent mention of you, and his constant efforts to restore my spirits. I really think he values our friendship very high, and sometimes he utters most kind words to me. Adieu now, my dear love, I am now going to scrawl a few lines to Henriette. I imagine you are still the firmest friends. What a splendid trio we shall be – until our little group is increased!

PHILIPPE LE BAS, to his wife

His sister Henriette and Saint-Just were for a time in love with each other, but the affair mysteriously collapsed. Le Bas' last words here may refer to his hopes of their marriage or, of course, to his wife's pregnancy. She gave birth next year to a boy, also Philippe (future tutor to Louis Napoleon) who, revering his father's high-minded and self-sacrificing loyalty to Robespierre at Thermidor, remained a steadfast Jacobin sympathiser. His mother died in 1859, a contemporary of Gladstone, Lincoln and Bernard Shaw.

J. B. Morton, a sympathetic, sometimes romantic, biographer of Saint-Just, comments:

This letter provides us with one of our very rare glimpses of Saint-Just in private, when the discipline which he imposed upon himself was laid aside for a moment. For my part, I think the chief interest of the letter is that it gives us Saint-Just as he was seen by his closest friend. It is inconceivable that those who still think of him as a monster can have read what Le Bas says of him – Le Bas of whom nobody can say a bad word; a man of the highest principles and of a character that made him respected and loved wherever he went.

HENRIETTE

J. B. Morton adds:

The two Commissaries were on the point of leaving Paris again when Elizabeth, who could not endure another separation, implored her husband to take her with him. He hesitated, knowing that Commissaries were not encouraged to take their wives with them, and realising that the situation would be an embarrassing one for Saint-Just. Elizabeth pointed out that of course Henriette could not be left behind, and Le Bas, probably without much hope of success, smiled at the little plot, and asked his friend what he thought of the idea. Saint-Just allowed himself to be persuaded but insisted on their discreet behaviour. They would be left at Saverne, must remain there, must not interfere in any way with the work to be done, and must be ready to start on the following morning, on pain of being left behind. They accepted the conditions, and the four young people set off together from Saint-Just's house in the rue Gaillon. Mme Le Bas was then twenty-one years of age. She lived to the age of eighty-seven, but never forgot that strange journey in the coach, along vile roads in the wintry weather, with Henriette huddling close to her for warmth, and the two men singing and jesting, and doing all in their power to make the fatiguing journey tolerable. Sometimes Saint-Just read a passage from Molière, whose plays he carried with him, or from his favourite, Rabelais. Sometimes the two men sang Italian airs. Once there was a great deal of mockery and laughter when Elizabeth, the Parisian, seeing the fields covered with snow, exclaimed, 'Heavens! What a calamity! There'll be no corn this summer!' When they climbed into the Vosges, and the carriage clattered and bumped over rocky ground beside precipices, Elizabeth became afraid, and cried out that they would be dashed to death. Le Bas comforted her and reassured her. The short hours, which had been such an agony for her, were, we may be sure, rather exciting than terrifying for the eighteen-year-old Henriette. There is no record of what she and Saint-Just said to each other, but their unfulfilled love was to have so few moments of happiness, that they both probably remembered those days in the months to come.

Morton suggests that estrangement from Henriette and, therefore, also from Le Bas, helped Saint-Just, still only twenty-six, towards personal disillusion and loss of ardour, which might explain something of his silence at the very end.

There is something terrible in the sacred love of one's country; a love that is so exclusive that it sacrifices everything, pitilessly, fearlessly, with favours to none, to the public good.

LOUIS ANTOINE DE SAINT-JUST

CHALIER, LOVER OF THE PEOPLE, EX-PRIEST

For him the Revolution was now what Christianity had been earlier, the truth, the whole truth, and nothing but the truth; and he had embraced it with a fervour self-sacrificing and superstitious. Disciple of Jean-Jacques Rousseau, he felt that the Perfect State would be built by forcing reason and equality upon all; and his ardent love of humanity emerged in a faith in universal breakdown ushering in a reborn and deathless society. . . . Marat, bloodthirsty pamphleteer, he venerated as god, or anyway oracle, and took from him the tone of his own utterances, sometimes mystical, even childish, but which stirred Lyons workers to the depths. Instinctively they sensed him overflowing with humanity; while, elsewhere, the town conservatives believed his unspotted enthusiasm, towering love of the people, made him more dangerous than the loudest Jacobin agitator. So he was simultaneously the object of love and hatred. His opponents, therefore, grabbed this neurotic and rather ludicrous zealot and thrust him into prison. Accusations were fortified by a forged letter and, to warn other radicals and to challenge the Convention, he was condemned to death.

Shocked, the Convention sent successive delegates to Lyons, hoping to save Chalier. It was useless. Threats were hurled against the town-council, but this had crossed its Rubicon. Earlier, receiving a guillotine, they had only reluctantly accepted this implement of Terror and had left it to rust somewhere or other; but now, clearly, was the moment to terrorise the Terrorists by using this professedly humanitarian tool upon a revolutionary. . . . The blunt knife descended three times without penetrating the neck. Horrified, the populace watched their hero, bound, and blood-boltered, writhing under this dreadful torture until finally the executioner beheaded him with the more gentle sword. But wretched Chalier's head, treated so pitifully, was swiftly to be a symbol of survival for the revolution and a Gorgon's Head for its opponents.

The Convention was alarmed by reports of this crime. Was a French town so bold as to defy the national will? Those daring challengers must be drowned in their own blood.   STEFAN ZWEIG, 1929

THE CONVENTION

1) In accordance with the proposal of the Committee of Public Safety, the National Convention shall appoint an Extraordinary Commission to immediately enforce the military punishment of counter-revolutionaries at Lyons.

2) All people at Lyons shall be disarmed. Their weapons shall be immediately distributed to the defenders of the Republic. Some shall be given to the patriots of Lyons oppressed by the rich and by counter-revolutionaries.

3) The town of Lyons shall be destroyed. All houses of the rich shall be razed. There shall remain only the homes of the poor, of massa-

cred or proscribed patriots, the buildings reserved for industry, and monuments dedicated to mankind and popular education.

4) The name of Lyons shall be wiped off the list of towns of the Republic. Henceforth, the collection of dwellings remaining extant shall be called Ville Affranchie.

5) There shall be erected above the ruins of Lyons a pillar announcing to posterity the crime and punishment of the royalists of that city, inscribed, 'Lyons made war on liberty. Lyons no longer exists.'

The virtual destruction of the second city of France could not be carried out literally, but wholesale vandalism and massacre ensued, supervised first by Georges Couthon, then by Collot d'Herbois and Joseph Fouché. Couthon, at least, seems to have recognised the absurdity of the order and made showy but ineffective compliance. The other two were far more brutal, exacting and murderous.

LYONS

Nantes, Brest, Orange, Arras, Marseilles, Lyons, where Girondin support was strong, revolted against Paris, and were savagely suppressed by Jacobin Representatives on Mission, despatched by the Committee of Public Safety.

Least of all cities can Lyons escape. . . .

The Lyons Jacobins were hidden in cellars; the Girondin municipality waxed pale, in famine, treason and red fire. Précy drew his sword, and some Fifteen Hundred with him; sprang to saddle, to cut their way to Switzerland. Lyons, on the 9th of October, surrenders at discretion; it is become a devoted Town. Abbé Lamourette, now Bishop Lamourette, whilom legislator . . . is seized here; is sent to Paris to be guillotined: 'he made the sign of the cross', they say when Tinville intimated his death-sentence to him; and died as an eloquent constitutional bishop. But woe now to all Bishops, Priests, Aristocrats and Federalists that are in Lyons! The *Manes* of Chalier are to be appeased; the Republic, maddened to the Sybilline pitch, has bared her right arm. Behold! Representative Fouché, it is Fouché of Nantes, a name to become well-known; he with a Patriot company goes duly, in wondrous procession, to raise the corpse of Chalier. An Ass, housed in Priest's cloak, with a mitre on its head, and trailing the Mass-Books, some say the very Bible, at its tail, paces through Lyons streets; escorted by multitudinous Patriotism, by clangour as of the Pit; towards the grave of Martyr Chalier. The body is dug up and burnt: the ashes are collected in an Urn; to be worshipped by Paris Patriotism. The Holy Books were part of the funeral pile; their ashes are scattered in the wind. Amid cries of 'Vengeance! Vengeance!' – which, writes Fouché, shall be satisfied.

Lyons in fact is a Town to be abolished; not Lyons henceforth but 'Commune Affranchie, Township Freed'; the very name of it shall perish. It is to be razed, this once great city, if Jacobinism prophecy right; and a Pillar to be erected on the ruins, with this Inscription, Lyons rebelled against the Republic; Lyons is no more. Fouché, Couthon, Collot, Convention Representatives succeed one another: there is work for the hangman; work for the hammerman, not in building. The very Houses of Aristocrats, we say, are doomed. Paralytic Couthon, borne in a chair, taps on the wall, with emblematic mallet, saying, 'La Loi te frappe, the Law strikes thee'; masons, with wedge and crowbar, begin demolition. . . . Had Lyons been of soft stuff, it had all vanished in those weeks. . . .

Neither have the Lyons Girondins all one neck, that you could despatch it at one swoop. Revolutionary Tribunal here, and Military Commission, guillotining, fusillading, do what they can: the kennels of the Place des Terreaux run red; mangled corpses roll down the Rhône. Collot d'Herbois, they say, was once hissed on the Lyons stage: but with what sibilation, of world-catcall or hoarse Tartarean Trumpet, will ye hiss him now, in his new character of Convention Representative, – not to be repeated? Two hundred and nine men are marched forth over the river, to be shot in mass, by musket and cannon, in the Promenade of the Brotteaux. It is the second of such scenes; the first was of some seventy. The corpses of the first were flung into the Rhône, but the Rhône stranded some; so these now, of the second lot, are to be buried on land. Their long one grave is dug; they stand ranked, by the loose mould-ridge; the younger of them singing the Marseillaise. Jacobin National Guards give fire; but have again to give fire, and again; and to take the bayonet and the spade, for though the doomed all fall, they do not all die; – and it becomes a butchery too horrible for speech. So that the very Nationals, as they fire, turn away their faces. Collot, snatching the musket from one such National, and levelling it with unmoved countenance, says, 'It is thus that a Republican ought to fire.'

This is the second Fusillade and happily the last: it is found too hideous; even inconvenient. There were two hundred and nine marched out; one escaped at the end of the bridge; yet behold, when you count the corpses, they are two hundred and *ten*. Read us this riddle, O Collot? After long guessing, it is called to mind that two individuals, here in the Brotteaux ground, did attempt to leave the rank, protesting with agony that they were not condemned men, that they were Police Commissaries: which two we repulsed, and disbelieved, and shot with the rest! Such is the vengeance of an enraged Republic. Surely this, according to Barère's phrase, is Justice 'under rough forms, *sous des formes acerbes*'. But the Republic, as Fouché says, 'must march to liberty over corpses'. . . . . Terror hovers far and wide: 'The Guillotine goes not ill.'   THOMAS CARLYLE, 1837

Collot d'Herbois had been an unimpressive actor and playwright. Generations later, Heinrich Himmler reassured the SS that the road to greatness lies over corpses.

PROTO-MARXISM AT LYONS

All is allowed to those labouring for the Revolution; the sole peril for the Republican is to lag behind Republican Law: he who outstrips it, gets ahead of it: he who apparently overshoots the goal, often has failed to reach it. While anyone yet remains in the world unhappy, there are still some steps to take in the race-course of Liberty.

The Revolution is made for the People; and it is easy to grasp that when we speak of the People, we do not mean that class, privileged by opulence, which usurped all pleasures of life, all the goods of the common weal. The People is all French citizens: the People is, supremely, the huge class of the poor; that class which yields the country its men, the frontiers their defenders; the class whose toil nourishes society. The Revolution would be monstrous, politically and morally, if its sole aim were to ensure the happiness of a few hundreds, and consolidate the wretchedness of twenty-four millions. It would be to ludicrously insult humanity to continue talking everlastingly about Equality if, in regard to Happiness, there were still to exist vast reaches between one man and another.

Make no mistake: to be a true republican, every citizen must feel and act within himself a revolution equivalent to that which has changed the face of France. Nothing, absolutely nothing, links a tyrant's slave to the citizen of a free state; the style and customs of the latter, his ethics, sentiments, deeds, must be wholly new. You were oppressed; you must overwhelm your oppressors. You were slaves of superstition; now, your only deity must be Freedom. Anyone to whom such fervour is alien, anyone who recognises other pleasures and cares than the happiness of the People; anyone who allows himself to receive the cold speculations of self-interest; anyone who calculates the profit he may get from a parcel of land, a position, a talent, and can, even for an instant, divide an idea from that of the common good; anyone whose blood fails to boil at the very mention of tyranny, slavery, or gross riches; anyone who has tears to shed for the enemies of the People, who fails to keep all his feelings for the victims of tyranny and for the martyrs of liberty – all of that ilk, who dare call themselves republicans, are contradicting Nature and their own hearts. Let them flee from the soil of liberty, for they will soon be recognised for what they are, and will water it with their impure blood. The Republic needs only free men, it has resolved to exterminate all the others, and take as its children only those who know how to live, fight, and die for it alone.

Take all that is beyond what a citizen essentially needs, for more than this is an obvious and gratuitous violation of the People's rights.

We shall be stern in using to the utmost the powers delegated to us, and shall punish as treachery, whatever, in other circumstances, you could have called laziness, weakness, or negligence. The time for half-measures and backsliding is totally finished. Help us strike hard blows, for, if you do not, your own backs will receive them. Liberty or Death! Think it over, then choose.   JOSEPH FOUCHÉ. From *Instruction*

Fouché, whose career so fascinated Balzac, was to become Napoleon's Police Chief, then a minister of Louis XVIII. Made Duke of Otranto by Napoleon, he acquired, and kept, a huge fortune.

A POSTER

The People's Representatives will remain inexorable in fulfilling the mission entrusted to them. The People have given them thunderbolts of vengeance and will not put them aside until all their enemies are extinguished. They will be sufficiently brave and vigorous to advance through holocausts of plotters and tramp over ruins to establish the happiness of the Nation and the regeneration of the World.

JOSEPH FOUCHÉ

AN ACT OF MERCY AT LYONS

We shot down two hundred in a single moment, and are informed that it was a crime! How is anyone incapable of seeing that it is an example of sensibility? When twenty culprits are guillotined, the last to be executed dies twenty times, but these two hundred conspirators died together.   COLLOT D'HERBOIS, to the Jacobin Club, Paris

The sentences passed by this tribunal may scare criminals, but they reassure and comfort the People. Let none imagine that we have reprieved any offender. Not once has this happened.

JOSEPH FOUCHÉ, to the Convention

SLEEP

At Mousseaux Cemetery, a huge ditch, always open, and adorned along the margins with bands of quicklime, gathered a gruesome medley of bodies and heads. It was a sewer of blood. Over the gate was inscribed: SLEEP. It seemed as if the executioners had wished to soothe their nerves with a persuasion that their victims would never again open their eyes. ALPHONSE DE LAMARTINE. *Histoire des Girondins*, 1847

To those who act according to the spirit of the Republic, all is permitted.

COLLOT D'HERBOIS and JOSEPH FOUCHÉ, Representatives on Mission

THE REVOLUTION COWS LOIRE, NEVERS AND MOULINS REGIONS

Citizen Fouché has worked the miracles of which I have been speaking. Old age has been honoured: infirmity aided: misfortune respected: fanaticism extirpated: federalism wiped out: iron production stepped up: suspects arrested: exemplary crimes punished: swindlers prosecuted and imprisoned – there you have a list of the labours of Fouché as Representative of the People.

PIERRE GASPARD CHAUMETTE, to the Convention

TERROR AT LYONS

We are carrying out our mission with vigour necessary for fully responsible republicans. We shall be absolutely inflexible: and will not descend from the height granted us by the People in order to accede to the wretched pleas of those who are, in whatever degree, guilty. We have totally isolated ourselves, for we are in haste, and would allow no favouritism; we should not see, we do not see, anything but the Republic itself, anything but your orders, which tell us to make an unforgettable example, to give a most particular lesson; we shall be deaf to all but the cry of the People, who demand that the death of patriots shall be quickly and terribly avenged, so that humanity will not be forced to mourn fresh emissions. Convinced that the only innocent ones are those oppressed or shackled by murderers of the People, we arm ourselves against repentant tears, and nothing shall weaken our severity. It is our obligation to promise you, Citizen Colleagues, that mercy is perilous feebleness, likely to excite criminal hopes precisely when they deserve extermination. It has been urged towards someone, and the rest of his type, to neutralise your own justice. The demolitions are proceeding too slowly, and republican impatience demands haste. Only the explosion of mines and ready maw of fire can fulfil the omnipotence of the People. Its will cannot be frustrated like that of tyrants, and should have the force of a thunderbolt.

COLLOT D'HERBOIS and JOSEPH FOUCHÉ, to the Convention

Perhaps two thousand perished in December 1793, in large groups, by pistol,

cannon, sword, and guillotine. The last to be guillotined, under mysterious
orders from Fouché alone, were the Lyons executioners.

A NOVELIST LOOKS BACK
ON 1794

Jean Blaise went on with an air of superior complacency.

'You live in a dream; I see life as it is. Believe me, my friend, the
Revolution's become a bore: it's lasted too long. Five years of rapture, five years of brotherly love, of massacres, of endless speeches,
of the Marseillaise, of bells ringing to man the barricades, of aristocrats hanging from lamp-posts, of heads stuck on pikes, of women
with cannons between their legs, of little girls and old men in white
robes on flower-bedecked chariots, the prisoners, the guillotine,
semi-starvation, proclamations, cockades, plumes, swords, car-
magnoles, it's all gone on too long! Nobody knows any more what
it's all about! We've seen too much, we've seen too many of these
great patriots raised up for us to worship only for them to be hurled
from your Tarpeian Rock – Necker, Mirabeau, La Fayette, Bailly,
Pétion, Manuel and all the rest of them. How do we know you're not
preparing the same fate for your new heroes?'

At that time, little thatched cottages, built by shrewd architects to
flatter the rustically inclined tastes of city people, were to be found in
all the pseudo-English gardens and along all the fashionable country
walks. The owner of this particular thatched cottage, La Belle
Lilloise, had made it into a café, and to enhance its rustic charm had
had it built on top of the artistically imitated remains of a ruined castle. And, as if a thatched cottage on a ruined castle were not enough to
attract sensitive-natured customers, he had erected a tomb beside it
beneath a weeping willow: a column surmounted by a funeral urn
bearing the inscription: 'Cleonice to her faithful Azor.' Cottages,
ruins, tombs: on the brink of its own extinction, the aristocracy had
erected in its ancestral parks these symbols of poverty, decadence and
death. And now the patriotic citizens took their pleasures – drinking,
dancing, making love – in sham thatched cottages, in the shade of
sham ruins, and amongst tombs; citizens and aristocrats, all were loving disciples of Rousseau and of Nature, all throbbed to the same
pulse of philosophic sensitivity. . . .

ANATOLE FRANCE. *Les Dieux ont soif*, 1912
(Translated by Frederick Davies, 1979)

THE FEAST OF REASON

A grand Festival dedicated to *Reason* and *Truth* was yesterday celebrated in the *ci-devant* Cathedral of Paris. In the middle of this church
was erected a mount, and on it a very plain temple, the *façade* of which
bore the following inscription:– *A la Philosophie.* Before the gate of
this temple were placed the busts of the most celebrated philosophers. The Torch of Truth was in the summit of the Mount upon the
Altar of Reason, spreading light. The convention and all the constituted Authorities assisted at the ceremony.

Two rows of young girls, dressed in white, each wearing a crown
of oak leaves, crossed before the Altar of Reason, at the sound of
Republican music; each of the girls inclined before the torch, and
ascended the summit of the mountain. Liberty then came out of the
Temple of Philosophy towards a throne made of grass, to receive the
homage of the Republicans of both sexes, who sung a hymn in her
praise, extending their arms at the same time towards her. Liberty
descended afterwards to return to the Temple, and on re-entering it,
she turned about, casting a look of benevolence on her friends. –
When she got in, every one expressed with enthusiasm the sensations
which the goddess excited in them by songs of joy, and they swore
never to cease to be faithful to her.   *The Times*, London
(For the role of such festivals, easily mocked, but seen as a serious part
of an attempt to transform society, see Mona Ozouf, *Festivals and
the French Revolution*, Harvard University Press, 1988.)

The maddened population were capering before the sanctuary and
bawling out the Carmagnole, men without breeches, women with
bare necks and breasts. Their frenzied girations made them resemble
whirlwinds, outriders of hurricanes, ravaging and sweeping away all
before them. There, in the glooms of the sanctuary they slaked all
those wicked lusts fermenting in them throughout the day.

LOUIS-SÉBASTIEN MERCIER. *Nouveau Tableau de Paris*

Little cubs, every one of them.   JEAN-BAPTISTE CARRIER

*Carrier ordered the killing of five hundred children at Nantes, during his mis-
sion of pacification at the behest of the Paris Commune and with the conni-
vance of the Committee of Public Safety. One might query whether this was
fulfilled to the letter.*

REVOLUTIONARY GODDESSES: MR SCROPE ENQUIRES

'I am happy, Ma'am,' he said, 'to have met with you again; for I have wished for some time to hold a little discourse with you, relative to the rites practised abroad, as to that Goddess of Reason, that, as I am credibly informed, has been set up by Mr Robert-spierre. Now I should wish to enquire, what good they expect to accrue by proclaiming, one day, that there is no religion, and then, the next day, making a new one by the figure of a woman. It is hardly to be supposed that such a sort of fickleness can serve to make a government respectable. And as to so many females being called Goddesses of Reason, – for I am assured there are some score of them, – one doesn't very well see what that means; the ladies in general, – I speak without offence, as it's out of their line, – not being particularly famous for their reason; at least not here; and I should suppose they can hardly be much more so in that light nation. The Pagans, it is true, though from what mode of thinking we are now at a loss to discover, thought proper to have Reason represented by a female; and that, perhaps, may be the cause of the French adopting the same notion, on account of their ancient character for politeness; though I cannot much commend their sagacity, taken in a political point of view, in putting the female head, which is very well in its proper sphere upon coping, if I may use such an expression, with the male. FANNY BURNEY. *The Wanderer*, 1814

TWO WOMEN IN PARIS

Dame whilom Countess Dubarry, unfortunate female, had returned from London; they snatched her, not only as the ex-harlot of a whilom Majesty, and therefore suspect; but as having 'furnished the Emigrants with money'. Contemporaneously with whom, there comes the wife of Beauharnais, soon to be the widow: she that is Joséphine Tascher Beauharnais: that shall be Joséphine Empress Bonaparte, for a black Divineress of the Tropics prophesied long since that she should be a queen and more. THOMAS CARLYLE, 1837

Madame du Barry died on the guillotine, terrified and without dignity, pleading for 'one minute more'.

A MIRACLE

Today a miracle has occurred in Paris. A man died in his bed.

CAMILLE DESMOULINS. *Le Vieux Cordelier*

THE RIGHTS OF WOMEN

The first voices for women's rights were heard during the American Revolution. When the Continental Congress convened in 1776, Abigail Adams wrote her husband, John, that women were determined to rise if the representatives of the nation should neglect their interests. She also demanded that women be admitted to the schools of higher learning. Her words, however, were given little heed.

The situation in revolutionary France was much the same. When the National Assembly met in 1789, it was showered with petitions demanding the recognition of women's rights. If Liberty, Fraternity, and Equality were to be guiding stars of public and private life, they asked, how was it possible to exclude one half of humanity from the enjoyment of its rights? Some of the members of the National Assembly, Talleyrand for instance, frankly admitted to the contradiction, but the majority were not willing to take any definite stand. Not even in the realm of education were men and women placed on an equal footing.

On the other hand, women in great numbers participated in the drama of the Revolution. Women entered the political clubs; feminine associations for the debate of political issues made their appearance. *Femmes républicaines et révolutionnaires* in Paris counted six thousand members. Madame Roland influenced the policies, and Olympe de Gouges became the most eloquent defender of women's rights, publishing in 1791 her *Déclaration des droits de la Femme*. 'Women are born free and men's equal . . . if women have the right to ascend the scaffold, they must have the right to ascend the Tribune.' One of these privileges was granted her: the right to end her life on the guillotine. The Convention adopted an antifeminist attitude and dissolved all political women's clubs in 1793.

Certain isolated individuals, like Condorcet, had asked for complete equality of the sexes. Women, he said, should be enfranchised and should not be excluded from public office. In 1789 he published an article demanding that the Bill of Rights be extended to women.

The natural rights of mankind, he asserted, called for no less. But Condorcet remained a lonely pioneer in a country whose political outlook was soon to be determined by Napoleon.

GERHARD MASUR, 1963

What, to you, can it matter, that my valueless preference should be acknowledged from the spur of passion, or the dictates of reason? – And yet, to the receiver as well as to the offerer, a sacrifice brings honour or disgrace, according to its motives. Listen, therefore, for both our sakes, to mine: though they may lead you to a subject which you have long since, in common with every man that breathes, wished exploded, the Rights of woman: Rights, however, which all your sex, with all its arbitrary assumption of superiority, can never disprove, for they are the Rights of human nature; to which the two sexes equally and unalienably belong. But I must leave to abler casuists, and the slow, all-arranging ascendence of truth, to raise our oppressed half of the human species, to the equality and dignity for which equal Nature, that gives us Birth and Death alike, designs us. I must spend my remaining moments in egotism; for all that I have time to attempt is my personal vindication.

FANNY BURNEY. *The Wanderer* (a novel set in England and France, 1794), 1814

Our sessions are public, the galleries open to every citizen, male and female, but I observe a large number of women seated down here in the Convention itself. I therefore put the motion, in the name of Equality, that from this day, no female citizen, save those admitted in a deputation, may sit in the Convention.

DEPUTY ROGER DUCOS, to the Convention, 1792

THE ANCESTOR OF
MODERN FEMINISM

Olympe de Gouges was the author of Declaration des Droits de la Femme.

The blood of the condemned, even of the guilty, contaminates revolution for all time.

Her offer to the Convention to act as the King's defence council
caused a scandal.   OLIVIER BLANC, 1987

I perish, dear son, victim of my adoration for Fatherland and People.
Plausibly disguised as lovers of the Republic, the Republic's haters
have, without qualms, dragged me to the scaffold.

Following five months' imprisonment, I was transferred to an
asylum where I was free as in my own house, where escape was easy,
as my foes and killers realised perfectly well, but, convinced that all
the malice in the world, while trapping me, would fail to stir me one
jot against the Revolution, I demanded fair trial. Could I have
thought that unmuzzled tigers would act as judges against the law
itself, even against the People, who will soon condemn them for
having killed me.

I was handed my accusation three days before the date fixed for
my execution; as soon as this was officially signed I had legal right to
see defence counsel and anyone else I felt could help me. None were
allowed to see me. I was kept as if ordered to solitary confinement,
forbidden to speak even to the jailer. Legally, too, I was permitted to
select my jurymen and was handed their names at midnight; then, at
7 am, I was taken before the Tribunal, weakened and ill, and a novice
in public speaking. . . .

I requested my defence counsel, the one I had selected, to be
informed that no defence counsel had arrived, or else my one had
refused my case. When I demanded a replacement, they retorted that
I was intelligent enough to see to myself.

Yes indeed, I dare say I had intelligence enough to defend my
innocence, perfectly obvious to the onlookers, though I cannot deny
that trained assistance could have added to my case by underlining all
that I had done for the people. Twenty times my words proving my
innocence and their falsehood drove the blood from my killers' faces.
They condemned me, to forestall popular recognition that their treatment of me was unique in its depravity.

Farewell, my son. When you receive this, I will be dead . . . I die,
my son, my dear son, innocent. All laws have been violated, for the
most virtuous woman of her time. . . .

Leave your wife's watch as well as the receipt for her jewellery at
the pawnbroker's, the jar and the keys to the trunk that I sent to
Tours.   To her son, General Degouges, serving on the Rhine

(All this entry I owe to Olivier Blanc's *Last Letters: Prisons and Prison-*

ers of the French Revolution 1793–4. Those further interested should consult his *Olympe de Gouges*, Paris, 1981.)

Civil and political liberty is no concern of women and should thus be denied them. . . .

A woman is acceptable only by right of her father's or husband's domain. She needs no knowledge of anything beyond that, save what they may think advisable to inform her.   *Révolutions de Paris*

VOTING

Since not the Convention only, that pale shadow of the Executive, but also almost all public offices were elective, the populace was endlessly voting. Nevertheless it was slowly surrendering almost entirely the exercise of its rights. In Paris as early as August 1790, out of a total of 81,200 voters more than 67,000 did not record their votes, and this abstention increased still further during the Reign of Terror, so that eventually the Jacobins were left almost alone to appoint 83 bishops, 400 criminal judges, 3,700 civil judges, 8,000 J.P.s with 20,000 assessors, 42,000 local tax-collectors, 46,000 priests and countless secretaries, controllers, police officials and officers. To exclude any chance of mistakes, the mother-society in Paris was always dispatching black-lists, Marat's invention, naming those who, in the eyes of 'Patriots', were unfit for office.   FRIEDRICH SIEBURG, 1936

A MESSAGE FROM THE
PARIS COMMUNE

Afraid that ordinary trade might be unable to supply sufficient food for this enormous city, birthplace of the Republic, the National Convention and the Committee of Public Safety have taken measures vital to provide Paris with its chief needs. Why then these assemblies at butchers' doors, and other shops? None aware of his real interests would wish to be the tool of wickedness, for malice alone instigates such meetings, now becoming a scandal. Aristocrats grin cheerfully at the doings of traitors, and spies sent by tyrants now allied against our liberty and who insinuate themselves into such meetings, encouraging them and striving to excite the hopes of enemies whom we have overthrown, by kindling amongst us a dangerous and mistaken defiance of the law. You will recognise these treason mongers amongst those at the centre of these daily gatherings; far from joining them, you must obey the law and perform your duty. Denounce them. Do this without protest; it will be your triumph over the aristocrats, over intrigue, over corruption; continue to be worthy of the title of republicans by showing invincible steadfastness and calm.

THE GOAL

Briefly, we desire to fulfil Nature's needs, the destiny of mankind, the promises of philosophy, absolve Providence from the long rule of crime and despotism. Let France, once so shining among enslaved Nations, overshadowing the glory of all the free peoples known to history, become the model for all nations, the terror of tyrants, the consolation for the oppressed, the star of the whole world, and let we ourselves, in signing our deeds with our very blood, at least witness the sunrise of universal happiness. That is our ambition, our goal.

What species of rule can bring such glories about? Only a democracy or republic – the two words are identical, despite being muddled in everyday language – because an aristocracy is no nearer being republican than is a monarchy. Democracy is not a state in which the whole people, in endless gatherings, themselves make the laws of society; even less is it a state in which the merest fraction of the people, by decisions isolated, hurried, contradictory, decide the destiny of the All. Such a regime has never existed, and if it did, would only restore the people to tyranny.

Democracy is a state in which the Sovereign People, led by laws of its own making, does for itself all that it is best fitted to do, and leaves it to its delegates to perform what it cannot do.

Now, what is the basic principle of popular or democratic rule, I mean the fundamental motive which sustains and impels it? It is virtue. I refer to the public Virtue which accomplished so many marvellous things in Greece and Rome, and which should create even more wondrous things in our Republican France – that Virtue which is nothing more than love of the Nation and its laws.

However, as the essence of the Republic or of democracy is Equality, it follows that patriotism as a matter of course ardently cherishes Equality.

We must overcome the enemies of the Republic, at home and abroad, or die with them. Now, in this situation, your first principle of policy should be to guide the People by reason, and the People's enemies by terror.

If the governing element of peacetime democratic rule is Virtue, amid Revolution it is simultaneously Virtue and Terror. Virtue without which Terror is fatal; Terror, without which Virtue is helpless. Terror is only justice, prompt, severe, inflexible. It is therefore an emanation of Virtue, less a special principle than a result of the general principle of democracy applied to the most urgent of our national needs.

They have said that terror was the governing principle of despotism. Does this government of ours, then, resemble a despotism? Yes, the despotism of the sword glittering in the grasp of the heroes of Liberty as against the sword which adorns the lackeys of Tyranny. Let the tyrant rule his brutalised people by terror; being a tyrant, he is right to do this. Crush Liberty's enemies by terror, and you too will be right, as founders of the Republic. The Revolutionary Government is the Despotism of Liberty against Tyranny. Is force designed only for the protection of crime?   MAXIMILIEN ROBESPIERRE, to the Convention

THE INCORRUPTIBLE PRONOUNCES

The Revolutionary Government owes its opponents nothing but Death.

This Revolution of ours forces me to understand absolutely the axiom that History is fiction.

Child and citizen both belong to the Nation.
  Communal education is essential.
  At school. Children will wear linen throughout the year, and subsist on roots, fruit, vegetables, milk foods, bread and water.

Social protection is allowed only to docile citizens; in the Republic, the only citizens that can exist are republicans.

Virtue is simple, modest, humble, often ignorant, sometimes boorish; the natural inheritance of the poor, the patrimony of the masses. Vice

is surrounded by opulence, armed with every lust to attract the sensu-
alist and trap the weak.

Whoever hates vice, hates humanity.   GEORGES-JACQUES DANTON

Robespierre, pillar of the Republic, protector of Patriots, incorruptible genius, enlightened Man of the Mountain, who sees all, foresees
all, unravels all, who cannot be deceived or seduced.

Two workmen of Saint Calais, to Maximilien Robespierre

*Such adulation is part of the entire history of politics. Compare the above to
Khrushchev, 1936:* 'By rebelling against Comrade Stalin, they rebelled
against all the best that mankind possesses. For Stalin is Hope, he is
Expectation; he is the Beacon that guides all progressive Humanity.'

AGAINST INDULGENCE

Citizens, how can any of you delude yourselves of showing cruelty?
Your Revolutionary Tribunal has despatched three hundred scoundrels in a year. Has not the Spanish Inquisition far exceeded that, and,
heavens, for what reason! Have English judges butchered no one in
that period? And what can we say of Bender, who gives Belgian
infants to the flames? And the Kings of Europe, who whines about
pity to them? O, do not relapse into sentimentality! To regard the
compassion demanded by a minority, you would imagine that this lot
controls our fate and are the high priests of liberty! Since last May,
our story is one about the fearful extremes that compassion assures.
Then, Dumouriez had deserted the regions we had won; patriots
were being slaughtered in Frankfurt; Custine had fled from Mainz,
Palatinate, the shores of the Rhine; Calvados had rebelled; the Ven-
dée was triumphant; Lyons, Bordeaux, Marseilles, Toulon, were
fighting the people of France; Condé, Valenciennes, Le Guesnoy had
surrendered; our armies were being thrust back in the Pyrenées and
around Mont Blanc. All were showing treachery to you and men
appeared to be in charge of government and armed forces for the purposes of destruction, then pillage of the ruins. The navy was crushed
by bribery, arsenals and ships were burnt, the currency inflation was
rife, our banks and factories given over to aliens. Yet, above all this,
was a certain fear of the concentrated authority vital to save the

Republic. Right wing conspirators had, by an unsuspected trick, hunted in advance the weapons with which you were to resist and punish them. Now, at this moment, there remain those anxious to do the same. LOUIS ANTOINE DE SAINT-JUST, to the Convention

Seven out of every ten persons guillotined or shot during the French Terror were workers, peasants, and members of the lower middle class . . . of the approximately 17,000 victims, ie, those sentenced after 'trial', not counting those shot out of hand or those among the 500,000 political prisoners who succumbed to horrible prison conditions, 31½ per cent were workers, 28 per cent peasants, and 10¼ per cent belonged to the lower middle class.

SIDNEY HOOK, 1945, citing official statistics examined by Donald Greer

HAPPINESS

In his journal, *Le Vieux Cordelier*, Camille Desmoulins pleaded for a regime of Happiness, against Robespierre's regime of Virtue. He wrote that he was a republican, because a Republic would increase human happiness, and also because trade, industry, civilisation in general, prospered more brilliantly in an Athens or Venice than in any monarchy. 'I believe that Liberty is not a matter of equality of poverty. I consider the highest praise for the Convention would be "I found the nation naked, and I left it clothed." Once the divine Socrates encountered Alcibiades, who looked thoughtful and sad because, it seemed, he was upset by some letters from Aspasia. "What is the matter," demanded the most serious of all Masters, "have you lost your shield in a battle? Have you lost out in camp or on the race course? Have you been outmatched in song or play at the leader's table?" This little tale perfectly illustrates the Athenian style. What delightful Republicans.'

LOUIS ADOLPHE THIERS. *Histoire de la révolution française*, 1823–7
(in partial association with Félix Bodin)

All this terrorist legislation was due to the triumvirate: Robespierre, Saint-Just, Couthon. The last was the gentlest, the quietest inquisitor in world history. He had a family which he loved to extreme, and playing with his little son was his greatest pleasure. He had tenderness for animals as well; a visitor could find him feeding a white rabbit, and a tiny greyhound often slept on his knees. But he had a formidable handicap, complete paralysis of both legs from the waist down, and he had to use a self-propelled wheel-chair. A gendarme carried him in his arms into the Convention, up to the tribune, or to his desk at the Committee of Public Safety. Almost always he suffered dreadful headaches and an almost continuous, and painful, hiccup. Nevertheless, he was amiable, polite, always soft-spoken. The Triumvirate assuredly constituted the three best-mannered individuals in all the Convention.   FRIEDRICH SIEBURG, 1936

A SECRET REPORT

Many patriots are complaining that the Egalité palace still harbours aristocrats and counter-revolutionaries, that this brothel is patronised by no one else. These personages are particularly visible at Roberts's Restaurant: they assume the guise of *sans-culottes* but are really only counter-revolutionaries who try to provoke patriots.

These people are also seen at the Café Valois: the café no longer carries this forbidden title, because a patriot had it taken down, but nothing has replaced it, despite an order to re-name it Café Marat. Patriots believe that counter-revolutionaries are merely waiting to restore the former name.

It is amazing that more investigations are not made into this cesspool. Also, it should no longer be called Egalité, considering the great varieties of crime committed there.

A group of worthy republicans were saying that there should be a maximum limit on all capital, though without the Agrarian Law: rather that people should be forbidden to increase their fortunes beyond what would give them reasonable comfort. That a rich citizen should marry a pauper, while a rich girl should be able to do likewise, and that poverty should no longer be a reason for marital dispute. It's only fair, they say, that the fortunate should help the rest.

The butchers have no meat at fourteen or even fifteen sous, only at twenty-five to twenty-seven. People demand where, at such cost, they can get meat at any time.

Numerous citizens are astonished at the very large groups of volunteers wandering the streets, and in the gardens of the former Tuileries, arm in arm with prostitutes. They say that if this isn't attended to, when the call comes to rejoin their regiments, these youths won't be able to play their part because they'll have picked up all possible infections and that they'll reach the garrison only to be removed to hospital.

LATOUR-LAMONTAGNE, local Commissioner-Observer for the Paris Department, Purveyor to the Ministry of the Interior, the Committee of General Security and the Committee of Public Safety (See Richard T. Bienvenu)

MEMORANDA

The spirit of Freedom originated in the Popular Societies, where it grew and reached its present stature. The Societies are the vigilant sentinels guarding the outposts of opinion and have sounded the alarm in all perils and treasons. In their sanctuaries, patriots have discovered and sharpened the weapons of victory. The Republic expects free services from the Popular Societies. The Revolutionary Government organised in its different organs, will develop full power and, despite all resistance, will advance against all enemies of the People. The Convention summons you to shoulder the common cares and joint efforts essential to firmly establish the Republican building. You will be our strongest support.   The Committee of Public Safety, Paris

We propose to burn the academic libraries, because Theology is only fanaticism, History is lies, Philosophy dreams and Science is unnecessary.   The Commune of Marseilles

PARIS, A DRAMATIST'S VISION OF TERROR

DANTON [*to* Camille Desmoulins]: Oh, stop your bloody solemnity. I'll never understand why people don't stop on the pavement and bellow with laughter in each other's mugs. They should laugh till the windows crack and laugh the dead from their graves, and smash the sky in two with laughter. Laughter should make a worldwide earthquake.

[*Exit. Enter two Citizens*]

FIRST CITIZEN: I assure you an amazing discovery. Every bit of technology will alter its whole physiognomy. Humanity advances, Monsieur, with giant strides to its loftier destiny.

SECOND CITIZEN: Have you seen that new play, on that poster? There's a Babylonian ziggurat, and a cluster of clouds, and two flights of steps and a real vista – all of it, Monsieur, wafted high, high in the air, easy as you please. Each step makes me feel giddy. O strange intelligence behind it all! But, pardon!

FIRST CITIZEN: What's wrong?

SECOND CITIZEN: Oh, nothing. Nothing at all. Only this puddle. Could I have your hand? A thousand thanks, Monsieur. I can scarcely move, you know. There's danger, perhaps.

FIRST CITIZEN: But surely you're not scared?

SECOND CITIZEN: Well, Monsieur, you must understand that the Earth's surface is very thin – very thin – very thin indeed. A wafer. I continually imagine that I might fall through, all the way, if I step into a hole like that puddle. We must all tread very carefully – very carefully indeed. We could break through entirely! But you ought to go to that play. Take my advice, Monsieur, and give it your blessing.   GEORG BÜCHNER. *Danton's Death*, 1835

VIRTUE

I'll tell you what this Virtue you go on about really is. It's what I get up to with my wife every night.

GEORGES-JACQUES DANTON, to Robespierre

Danton mocks the word Virtue as if it were a joke. How can a man with so little notion of morality ever be a champion of freedom?

MAXIMILIEN ROBESPIERRE, *Notebook*

Robespierre simply can't fuck, and money scares the hide off him.

GEORGES-JACQUES DANTON

Champagne is poison to freedom.   MAXIMILIEN ROBESPIERRE

The people of Europe have made astonishing progress in what are known as the arts and sciences, while they seem ignorant of the first elements of public morality.   MAXIMILIEN ROBESPIERRE

On such a day I demanded the institution of the Revolutionary Tribunal. I ask pardon of God and Man.   GEORGES-JACQUES DANTON

I see that in Revolution, power falls into the hands of rogues.

GEORGES-JACQUES DANTON

In a gathering at the Place de la Révolution, certain citizens were discussing the Tribunal's procedure at the Hébertists' trial. One heard, 'They were scarcely permitted to defend themselves. The President addressed them cruelly, constantly lecturing them to reply only Yes or No. No "phrases" permitted.' Another citizen added, 'The people, though indignant with the conspirators, are agitated by "the Tribunal behaving in a manner inhuman and unjust".' At this, the speaker was interrupted by several *sans-culottes* protesting. One called out: 'I've never before heard any complaints against the Tribunal and it's odd that people have waited so long to make any. He who finds the Tribunal so severe now – would he perhaps show delight if the entire Convention and Jacobin Club were to replace Hébert, and his fellow conspirators?' This retort won noisy applause and the fellow deserving the rebuke hastily decamped.

LATOUR-LAMONTAGNE, local Commissioner-Observer for the Paris
Department, Purveyor to the Ministry of the Interior, the Committee
of General Security and the Committee of Public Safety
(See Richard T. Bienvenu)

EXTRAORDINARY ARREST

I said to Danton, 'We should immediately return to the Convention; take the floor, you can rely on us, but we should not delay, for you are probably to be arrested tonight.'

'They wouldn't dare,' he retorted disdainfully, then invited me to go with him and help eat a pullet. This I declined. Brune was with us, Danton's inseparable friend and adjutant, and I told him to keep a careful eye on Danton, because when he should have attacked he had merely threatened.

Suddenly, at nine am, 11th Germinal, I heard of Danton's arrest. I hurried to his home in the Passage du Commerce, where I had dined two nights ago where the news was confirmed. He had been dragged from sleep and thrown into the Luxembourg, in close confinement. I hastened to the Convention, around 11. Members were on their way, mostly quite unaware of this extraordinary arrest – extraordinary even then when such things were daily routine yet increasingly unexpected. A number had indeed heard rumours, which they discounted, and questioned me about my own information. While I was talking, the members of the Committee of Public Safety entered, Saint-Just the last. Immediately he climbed the tribune and read out the strangest, most monstrous indictment conceivable. Impassive, sententious, he recited this incredible thesis, holding his papers in one quite still hand while the other moved in one monotonous gesture, monotonous, inescapable, up and down, like the very blade of the guillotine. . . .

Saint-Just's reading of this report, though thirty years ago, still overwhelms me with amazement, and chokes me as much as when I actually heard it.

PAUL JEAN FRANÇOIS NICOLAS DE BARRAS. *Mémoires*, Paris, 1895

DANTON IN GERMAN DRAMA

Georg Büchner imagines him in prison, March, 1794:

Will that clock sound forever? Every tick shoves these walls nearer, nearer . . . the room transforming to a coffin! When I was a kid I read some such story, it made my hair stand up! Just a kid! Yes! Strange, all that fuss they made over me, stuffing my belly, sheltering me from cold! Now it's a job for the grave digger! I feel myself stink! O my body, honoured sir, permit me to pinch my nose and imagine you as a young filly all sweat and stench from a dance – and shower you with compliments. We've shared good days, you and I. Tomorrow you'll be a broken fiddle, all your tunes lost. A drained bottle, not a dreg left. But I'm not drunk, I'll go to bed like a log. Fortunate fellows who can still get drunk! Tomorrow, Monsieur Body, you'll be tattered breeches slung into a cupboard for moths to gobble, stale too. Stale. Ugh! What in hell does all this add up to? It's wretched to die, true enough. Death's an imitation birth. In death we're childless, just born-naked, helpless. They swaddle us in shrouds. Is that any use? In our graves we may moan, as in our cradles. Camille! Are you asleep? A dream dancing behind his eyelids. I'll not sweep away the golden dews of dreamland! Julie, thanks. I'll not depart alone. I'd have preferred another sort of finish, all the same . . . something gentle . . . a fading star, a flake of music expiring . . . sunlight dying on a calm sea. Stars are scattered across the night like quivering tears, the eyes that shed them must have known some mighty grief.   *Danton's Death*, 1835

DANTON IN GERMAN THOUGHT

Can it be maintained that modern France in her supreme crisis, which simultaneously provoked a European crisis, decided to support not Rousseau but Voltaire? We can at least assert that her verdict was for Danton, not Robespierre. France *is* Danton: sceptical and humanitarian, amorous and witty, harmonious and undisciplined, patriotic and easy-going; – in short, human to a degree of suicide, and confused when faced with a dogmatism like Robespierre's, borne along to such inhuman limits.   FRIEDRICH SIEBURG, 1936

THE POOR FISHERMAN

There's not one of them who knows even the first principle of government. If I left my balls to that capon Robespierre and my legs to Couthon the Committee of Public Safety might last a bit longer. But, as it is . . . Robespierre is bound to follow, I will drag him down.

I am leaving everything at sixes and sevens: one would be better at being a poor fisherman than meddle with the art of governing men.

Gentlemen, I had hoped to have soon freed you from all this, but here I am myself, and we can't see where it's going to end.

                                             Entering the Luxembourg Prison

DANTON ON TRIAL

My name is Danton, a name tolerably well known in the Revolution: my abode will soon be Annihilation; but I shall live in the Pantheon of History. . . .

    Let the men of the Committee come as witnesses and accusers, I will cover them with ignominy. . . .

    Danton lying concealed on August 10th! Where are those who had to force Danton to show himself that day? Where are those high-gifted souls from whom he stole the energy? Let them show their faces, these my accusers! I have all the clarity of self-possession when I demand them. I will tear off the masks of three shallow scoundrels . . . who fawn upon Robespierre and lead him to destruction. Let them produce themselves here; I will plunge them into the void out of which they ought never to have emerged. . . .

I demand an uninterrupted hearing. . . .

You are murderers! Murderers! Look at them! They have hounded us to our deaths! . . . but the people will rend my enemies within three months.

I have served long enough, and my life is a burden to me, but I will defend myself by telling you what I have done. It was I who made the pikes rise without warning on June 20th and prevented the King reaching Saint Cloud. The day after the massacre of the Champ de Mars a warrant was out for my arrest. Men were sent to kill me at Arcis, but my people came and defended me. I had to flee to London, and I returned, as you all know, the instant Garran was elected. Do you not remember me at the Jacobins, and how I demanded the Republic? It was I who knew that the Court was eager for war. It was I, amongst others, who denounced the policy for war. . . .

It was I who prepared August 10th. You say I departed to Arcis. I admit it, and am proud of it. I went there to spend three days, to bid my mother farewell, and tidy up my affairs, because I would soon be in danger. I hardly slept that night. It was I who had Mandat killed, for giving orders to fire on the people. . . .

You have told me that my defence has been too violent, you have recalled to me the great names of the Revolution, and have told me that Marat when he appeared before the Tribunal might have been a model for me. Well, in regard to those names, once my friends, I will tell you this: Marat had a nature fiery and unstable; Robespierre I had known as a man, above all, tenacious; but I – I have served in my own way, and I would embrace my worst enemy for the sake of the country and yield her my body if she needs the sacrifice.

That a man should be violent is, I know, wrong in him, unless it is for the public good, and such a violence has often been in me. If I exceeded on this occasion, it was because I find myself accused with such intolerable injustice.

But as for you, Saint-Just, you will have to answer to posterity.

No documents have been produced. No witnesses have been called. We are to be condemned without being heard.

GEORGES-JACQUES DANTON

BEFORE SENTENCE

The natural defenders and inevitable friends of accused patriots are the patriotic jurymen. Conspirators shall be allowed no defenders.

This is not actually a trial, it is a decree. We are not jurymen, we are statesmen. The two together make an impossible situation. One must go. Would you really kill Robespierre? Of course not. Well, by admitting that, you have condemned Danton.

JURYMAN TOPINO-LEBRUN, to Juryman Souberbeille, at Danton's trial

I am unconcerned whether the accused are guilty of the charges made against them. What really matters is that they are aristocrats, priests, in short, not virtuous Republicans. Here is the means of eliminating them.
JURYMAN PRIEUR

To have Danton's defence halted, Saint-Just lies to the Convention and secures permission to stop the trial and a verdict of guilty is extracted:
The Public Prosecutor of the Revolutionary Tribunal has sent to tell you that the prisoners are in open rebellion and have interrupted the hearing, saying they will prevent it from continuing until the Convention has taken measures. You have barely escaped from the greatest danger that has yet threatened our liberty, and this rebellion in the very seat of justice, of men in terror of the law, reveals their thinking. Their despair and fury are plain proof of the hypocrisy they displayed in keeping up appearances before you. Innocent men do not rebel. Dillon, who ordered his troops to march on Paris, has informed us that Desmoulins' wife received money to assist the conspiracy. We are grateful to you for having placed us in the difficult and perilous position you see us in.

Danton, Desmoulins, Fabre d'Églantine and Hérault de Séchelles were unanimously found guilty.

'PURE' REPUBLICANISM

All they asked me. Had I ever conspired against the Republic? What a mockery! Is it possible that the purest republicanism can be so insulted? I foresee the fate awaiting me. Adieu, my Lucile, my darling Lolotte, my own wolf: say adieu to my father. . . .

I was born to write verses, to defend the unfortunate, to make you happy, to create with your mother and my father and a few people of our persuasion a new Tahiti. I had dreamed of a republic which all would have adored. I could never realise that men were so cruel and so unjust. . . .

I see the shores of life receding before me. I still see Lucile. My arms embrace you yet, and I hold you with my shackled hands, while my head as it falls will rest its dying eyes upon you. I am going to die.

CAMILLE DESMOULINS, to his wife, from the Luxembourg Prison

We've got them at last!

JACQUES-LOUIS DAVID, after the condemnation of Danton and Desmoulins

Danton was a man whose lack of resentment, and liking for low company, passed too easily into a criminal indulgence, whose talk of national unity too often diverted attention from the irregularities of his friends, whose want of political principles and statesmanship made him too easy a prey for cleverer men; and who was deservedly caught in the toils he spread for others. Not a great man, not a good man, certainly no hero; but a man with great, good, and heroic moments.

J. M. THOMPSON, 1929

> When Danton, Desmoulins, and d'Églantine
> Were ferried over to the world unseen,
> Charon, that equitable citizen,
> Handed their change to these distinguished men.
> 'Pray keep the change', they cried; 'We pay the fare
> For Couthon, and St-Just, and Robespierre.'
>
> P. A. LECOMTE (translated by Hilaire Belloc)

Dupré told Desmoulins of a girl in the rue Saint-Honoré, who said to her friends, 'I want to be guillotined; I don't see why I shouldn't be talked about as well as another.' For a long time the authorities refused to make a martyr of her. When everything else failed, she opened her window, and shouted at the top of her voice, *Vive le roi, Vive le roi!* This time the police could not refuse to arrest her. At her trial she denied indignantly that she had been drunk. 'I was as sober as I am now,' she said and started shouting again, *Vive le roi!* 'Goodbye, my dear friends,' she said, on the way to the scaffold; and just before the blade fell she turned her head towards the crowd, and remarked, 'Goodbye, rabble, goodbye!'

J. M. THOMPSON, 1943

It is not enough for you to have murdered your best friend. You must have his wife's blood as well. Your monster, Fouquier-Tinville, has just ordered Lucile to be carried off to the scaffold. In less than two hours she will be dead. . . .

If Camille's blood has not sent you mad, if you can still remember the happy evenings you once spent at our fireside holding our little Horace [Robespierre's godson], spare an innocent victim. If not, then hurry and take us all, Horace, myself and my other daughter, Adèle. Hasten, and tear us apart with your talons that still drip with Camille's blood. Hasten, hasten, so that we can all rest in the same grave.   MADAME DUPLESSIS, Lucile Desmoulins' mother, to Robespierre

I shall await the belated help of Time, which must avenge betrayed humanity and oppressed peoples.   MAXIMILIEN ROBESPIERRE

I'm leaving this world, where nothing now remains for me, I am far less the object of pity than you are.
          LUCILE DESMOULINS, to the Public Prosecutor, Fouquier-Tinville

ROBESPIERRE REMARKS

All is legal to Virtue, in order to conquer Vice.

There are times in all revolutions when the mere fact of being alive is a crime.

Jacobinism . . . by its very nature is incorruptible.

A single will is necessary.

Robespierre did not remove conscience from the revolutionary vocabulary, but relied on it too much. His political conscience insisted on the removal of Danton, and forbade him saving his old schoolfellow, Desmoulins.

The Incorruptible was very difficult to satisfy. To be ostentatiously revolutionary was to be a secret aristocrat; to go on as usual revealed indifference and therefore a hidden hostility to the great cause. To demand bloodshed was to be secretly plotting with Lafayette to render the Convention and its committees unpopular by encouraging excess; to advise moderation was to secrete some personal fear of Terror. To suggest a donation to the military was to distract from civilian mishaps; to oppose the presumptuous petition of a regiment was proof of English bribery to discontent the army. . . . To offer praise to Robespierre was mere flattery, to blame him for anything was proof of unpatriotic conspiracy.   FRIEDRICH SIEBURG, 1936

I regard you, Citizen Robespierre, as the Messiah promised us by the Supreme Being to reform everything.   A veteran soldier

SAINT-JUST REMARKS

Great men do not die in their beds. Tear out my heart and eat it. Then you will be what otherwise you will never be: Great!

Humanity drops anchor in the future.

Power belongs to the impassive.

It is your task to build a city whose denizens treat each other as friends, guests and brothers. It is your task to re-establish public confidence, and to make it understood that revolutionary government means not war or conquest, but the passage from misery to happiness, from corruption to honesty and from bad principles to good.

Fanaticism is the work of European priestcraft.

When all men are free, they will be equal, and, when equal, just.

The art of government has produced nothing but monsters.

I think I may say that most political mistakes come from regarding legislation as a difficult science.

We make too many laws and too few examples.

Be inflexible: indulgence is to be feared because it threatens the country.

Some people have an appalling idea of happiness and confuse it with pleasure.

A man is guilty of crime against the Republic when he shows compassion for prisoners. He is guilty because he lacks desire for Virtue. He is guilty for being opposed to the Terror.

In a Republic, which can only be founded upon Virtue, any pity shown towards crime is proof of treason.

The words we have spoken will never be lost upon Earth.

A dialogue about Saint-Just:
'He carries his head like the Holy Sacrament.'
'He'll soon be carrying it like St Denis.'

According to tradition, St Denis carried off his own head after beheading by Roman pagans.

SAINT-JUST'S EDUCATIONAL SYSTEM

At sixteen the child would reach emancipation. He would be forbidden to see his parents before his actual majority, at twenty-one – the Republic indeed distrusted the family – and before that he would be allowed to choose a profession and discard his linen smock, adopting instead 'The Costume of the Arts'. This favour, however, would not be granted until the passing of a solemn endurance test. He must 'swim across a river watched by all the people', at the Festival of Youth.   JEAN ROBIQUET, 1938

MORE WARNINGS

Any nation anxious for its liberty must beware the very virtues of those in the highest authority. . . .

The cunning Pericles used popular attributes to disguise the fetters he was forging for Athens. He long made people believe that he never appeared on the rostrum without reminding himself that he was addressing a free people. And this very Pericles, having managed to win absolute power, became the most bloody tyrant.

JACQUES-NICOLAS BILLAUD-VARENNE

Woe to the Republic when the merits or even the virtues of a single man become indispensable.　　　LAZARE CARNOT

You are absurd dictators.

LAZARE CARNOT, to Saint-Just, about 'the Triumvirate' of
Robespierre, Saint-Just and Couthon

One might conclude that the Convention no longer existed, or at least no longer mattered to anyone, and that the armies were only fighting for one single individual to whom justice was no longer owed.　　　BERTRAND BARÈRE DE VIEUZAC

A VIRTUOUS CITIZEN

One day, a man with shaven neck and bound wrists, one Gossin, pursued the tumbrils, shouting: 'Take me too. I have been condemned!' The tumbrils stopped, a silence petrified the crowd. The very condemned appeared to forget their personal tragedies and stared curiously at him who was so wildly crying for his own extinction. The executioner, pulling out the list, demanded his name. 'François Gossin.' Failing to find the name, the executioner then shoved him off. 'You madman, go to the devil, you're not on the list!' But the bound man refused to be repulsed, moaning, his eyes deranged: 'Yes, yes, I really was condemned, take me too!' 'Fuck off, to hell with you.' The executioner, losing all patience, was about to order the tumbrils forward, when a judge appeared and explained that the list was indeed incomplete and that Gossin had in truth been condemned. Gossin then clambered excitedly onto the last tumbril but the procession had scarcely resumed when the unfortunate creature regained his common sense, realising what he had done. 'Oh! my wife and children!' he cried, horrified as the tumbrils rattled mercilessly over the bridge to the Right Bank.　　　FRIEDRICH SIEBURG, 1936

FROM A POLICE SPY

Yesterday a woman lost consciousness at the sight of the condemned in the tumbril, and fell. A crowd gathered, displaying anger. Aristocrats shrewdly exploiting everything, take advantage of such an incident to craftily emphasise to people the very numerous executions and, if they can, provoke pity for their own enemies and hatred for those actually preparing their own victory. 'One can no longer venture out of doors,' declare these aristos, 'without meeting the guillotine or those being taken to it. Children are learning cruelty, and one fears that the pregnant may bear infants marked on the neck, or lifeless as statues, from a sight of those dismal spectacles.' People usually accept these words, apparently words of good faith and compassion, with grave reflective expressions, and the result may be their acquiring notions and feelings quite contrary to what is desirable.

P. CARRON, *Paris pendant La Terreur. Rapport des agents secrets du Ministre de l'Interieur*, Paris, 1910–49
(See Olivier Blanc, 1987)

ROBESPIERRE ATTACKS FOUCHÉ

Inform us, then, inform us who told you to announce to the People that God does not exist, you, so dedicated to that belief! What good will it do you to persuade Mankind that some blind power directs its fate and in equal measure rewards crime and virtue; to persuade it that the soul is naught but a gentle breeze extinguished at the portals of the tomb?

Wretched sophist, what right have you to seize from innocence the sceptre of Reason in order to entrust it to the hands of Crime; to spread a funeral pall over Nature, reducing misfortune to despair, filling Crime with delight, saddening Virtue, degrading Humanity.

A villain, covered with self-contempt, disgusting to others, is actually convinced that the finest gift of Nature is annihilation!

From the speech to the Convention proposing the existence of
the Supreme Being and the immortality of the soul

THE SUPREME BEING

Nature is the veritable priest of the Supreme Being; the Universe is his temple; Virtue his cult, and the happiness of a great people gathering in his sight to link all the loved elements of universal fraternity and offer him the homage of hearts pure and receptive, all these constitute His festivals.   MAXIMILIEN ROBESPIERRE

The French People recognises the existence of a Supreme Being and the immortality of the soul.   Decree of the Convention

The particular intelligence of every individual, led astray by passions, is frequently mere sophistry, a plea for those same passions, and mortal authority can be disproved by mortal vanity. All that can create or replace the precious instinct which compensates for the inadequacy of such authority, is religious sentiment, which stamps on men's minds the notion of divine sanction lying behind moral precepts.   MAXIMILIEN ROBESPIERRE

THE FESTIVAL OF
THE SUPREME BEING

Elsewhere in Europe, a labourer is a beast fostered only for upper class pleasures; but in France the upper classes seek to transform themselves into labourers and workers and cannot even gain this honour. The other Europeans cannot imagine that life is possible without kings or nobles; we ourselves cannot imagine existing alongside them. The other Europeans shed blood to fetter mankind, and we shed blood to smash those fetters. Yea, this delightful realm, our home, which Nature caresses, is fashioned to be the domain of Liberty and Happiness; this people, proud, sensitive, is verily created for Glory and Virtue.

O my country! If Fate had caused me to be born in a land foreign and remote, I would have continually implored Providence for your prosperity; I would have dropped tender tears over the epic of your strivings and virtues; my soul would have observed with all attention, every convulsion of your glorious Revolution; I would have envied the fate of your citizens and their leaders. I am a Frenchman, one of your representatives. O people sublime! Accept my whole being as a sacrifice; happy is he who is born amongst you. Happier still is whoever can die for the sake of your own happiness.

MAXIMILIEN ROBESPIERRE, inaugural speech in the Convention

At the Champ-de-Mars, where once had stood the Altar of the Fatherland, there had been heaped up a great symbolical mountain, shaded
by a tree of liberty. The deputies, headed by Robespierre, ascended
the mountain, around which ranged themselves in solid phalanx what
in the literature of the day are referred to as 'adolescents', each with a
sword at his thigh. On either side were grouped thousands of musi-
cians and choristers. A vast multitude was all around.

Clouds of incense ascended. A trumpeter, perched upon a column, blew a starting signal, and there rose towards heaven the hymn
Chénier had written for the occasion and Grossec had set to music. A
hundred thousand voices took up the chant, trumpets blared, the bells
of the city started clamouring, cannon boomed, the boys drew their
swords and raised them aloft, girls flung handfuls of flowers into the
air. At the summit of it all stood the little lawyer from Arras, and
closed his eyes, and perhaps thought what he had said at the Convention after the frustrated attempt upon his life: 'I have lived enough.'

It was while the procession was returning to the Tuileries that
Robespierre's ear caught most of the venomous remarks made by his
colleagues. After the exaltation he had felt they filled him with an
evil foreboding. When he returned home that evening he felt greatly
depressed, and when the Duplays spoke to him enthusiastically about
the feast in which they had taken part, he said enigmatically: 'I'll not
be with you long any more', and retired to his room.

RALPH KORNGOLD, 1937

A voice from the crowd: 'The little wretch. He's not satisfied by
    being leader. He wants to be God Almighty as well.'
Another voice: 'There are still those who can act Brutus.'

THE REVOLUTIONARY
TRIBUNAL

The Tribunal was reorganised. The two sections became four, and
more judges were appointed. The jury too was reorganised: twenty-
nine kept their places, the remainder were freshly nominated by the
Committee of Public Safety. To this reform, Robespierre gave his
personal consideration. He began by weeding out 'the feeble', those
disturbed by legal pedantries or by their conscience. Then, from the

best of the Jacobins, he gathered his most passionate adherents. His landlord, Duplay, was first on the list of the trustworthy, then his own secretary, Didier, then Saint-Just's secretary, Villers. With these were Nicolas, Cravier, Pigeot, Masson, Fillon and Fauvety, all unconditional disciples of the Incorruptible or more or less intimate at the Duplay household. Some had been jurymen already, with shining results. Trinchard, and the two painters, Châtelet and Piceur, were absolutely reliable, and of course Leroy, who could be considered the perfect juryman for this particular Tribunal, being deaf. The President, Dumas, Vice-President, Coffinhal, and the judge, Garnier-Launay, were Robespierre's devoted creatures. Briefly, the Law of 22nd Prairial can be seen as his completely personal tool, being worked out by him to the least detail. It enabled his dictatorship and was the only political action of his career about which even zealous youths such as Buonarroti had serious misgivings of his good faith.

Couthon declared, 'It is less a question of punishing than exterminating.'   FRIEDRICH SIEBURG, 1936

REPRESENTATIVES ON
MISSION, AT COUSOIRE

Soldiers,
    We hereby remind you of that stern discipline which alone can bring you victory and save you from many casualties. Abuses of discipline have been seen amongst you which we are resolved to eliminate. Those who incite the infantry to break ranks before battle, during battle, or during a retreat, will at once be arrested and shot. Each sector will supply a patrol, to find and arrest deserters. Any attempt to escape will invite gunshot. Soldiers, we hand you out justice, we will punish whoever denies you justice, we will share your toils, but whoever refuses to play his part will receive immediate death. Now show contempt to the enemy facing you. He is employed by a lunatic tyrant with but one throne, a toy at the mercy of victory, and the prospect of victory will urge you forward.   SAINT-JUST   LE BAS

June 25–6 saw the French victory over the Austrians at Fleurus, in which Saint-Just had an active part, and the French reoccupation of Belgium. This to some extent balanced Lord Howe's defeat of the French Navy on the 'Glorious First of June'.

FROM THE CARMES PRISON

It seems from the sort of examination undergone today by quite a number of prisoners that I have been vilely slandered by several 'patriots', aristocrats themselves under this roof. Convinced that this diabolical alliance will pursue me to the Revolutionary Tribunal, it is hopeless for me to expect another sight of you, my friend, or a last embrace for my beloved children.

I will not discourse on my sorrows; my tender love for them and the fraternal ties between you and me will assure you of my feelings at this time of death. I also grieve at departing the land I love and for which I would have sacrificed a thousand lives. Not only will I be prevented from serving her, but she will see me dragged from her clutches and imagine that I am unworthy of her. This horrible thought is no obstacle to my request that you will preserve my true nature, work for my rehabilitation, prove that a life wholly dedicated to patriotic service and the victory of Liberty and Equality must, in the popular gaze, withstand the disgusting slanderers, each one of them from a most dubious caste. Your work must await the future, for in this, the revolutionary gale, a great people struggling against its fetters must protect itself with justified suspicions, and nerve itself not to overlook the guilty, just as it condemns the innocent.

I shall die steadfast, though this permits me sensations of the most loving affection to the end, reinforced by the courage of an independent spirit, an unsullied conscience, an honest soul fervently clamouring on behalf of the Republic.

Farewell, my friend, find refuge in my children, in teaching them, and, above all, by showing them that republican virtue demands forgetfulness of my execution, and the recollections of my services to the nation, and my claims on its gratitude. . . .

GENERAL ALEXANDRE BEAUHARNAIS, to his wife, Joséphine
Tascher de la Pagerie (later first wife of Napoleon Bonaparte
and Empress of the French), herself also in prison

Anyone who in future is found guilty of complaining about the Revolution, who lives without any employment and who is neither over sixty nor ill, will be deported to Guiana. Committee of Public Safety

AN ENGLISH GIRL IN FICTION
RHAPSODISES THE REVOLUTION

The grand effect, she continued, of beholding so many millions of men, let loose from all ties, divine or human, gave such play to my fancy, such a range to my thoughts, and brought forth such new, unexpected, and untried combinations to my reason, that I frequently felt as if just created, and ushered into the world – not, perhaps, as wise as another Minerva, but equally formed to view and to judge all around me, without the gradations of infancy, childhood, and youth, that hitherto have prepared for maturity. Every thing now is upon a new scale, and man appears to be worthy of his faculties; which, during all these past ages, he has set aside, as if he could do just as well without them; holding it to be his bounden duty, to be trampled to the dust, by old rules and forms, because all his papas and uncles were trampled so before him. However, I should not have troubled myself, probably, with any of these abstruse notions, had they not offered me a new road for life, when the old one was worn out. To find that all was novelty and regeneration throughout the finest country in the universe, soon infected me with the system-forming spirit; and it was then that I conceived the plan I am now going to execute.

FANNY BURNEY. *The Wanderer*, 1814

A DEEP POLITICIAN
IN ENGLAND

'I find Ma'am, you are lately come from abroad,' said Mr Scrope, a gentleman self-dubbed a deep politician, and who, in the most sententious manner, uttered the most trivial observations: 'I have no very high notion, I own, of the morals of those foreigners at this period. A man's wife and daughters belong to any man who has a taste for them, as I am informed. Nothing is very strict. Mr Robert-spierre, as I am told, is not very exact in his dealings.'

FANNY BURNEY. *The Wanderer*, 1814

FEAR IN PARIS

Near the Jardin des Plantes a big crowd was discussing Robespierre's illness. People seem so affected by this that they say that his death would ruin everything. One woman remarked, 'Only he roots out criminal conspiracies. God alone can preserve this incorruptible patriot.' I observed that while *sans-culottes* discussed Robespierre's illness, better-dressed individuals kept quiet, but their expressions revealed satisfaction.

Police report

THE YOUNG CAPTIVE

Spared by the scythe, ripens the growing ear,
The grape-vine of the wine-press knows no fear,
    But takes what life can give;
And I, who am like them both young and fair,
Although the present moment has its care
    I too desire to live.

Though Stoics with dry eyes embrace their death
I weep and hope; and to the North Wind's breath
    I bow, and raise my head.
Some days are bitter, others sweet no less
And even honey has its bitterness
    And seas their tempests dread.

By prison walls in vain am I oppressed;
Illusion nurtures hope within my breast,
    Her wings remain to me.
Freed from the fowler's nets, the captive bird
More joyously far in the skies is heard
    Singing of liberty.

Is it for me to die? My quiet rest
And quiet waking never are distressed
    By terror of my fate;
But the oppressed, with laughter in their eyes
Seeing me greet the dawn, themselves arise
    With joy re-animate.

Far from its end my path. I cannot stay,
For of the shady elms that flank my way
        I have but passed these few.
The feast of life hardly have I commenced,
One instant only have my warm lips sensed
        The cup that was my due.

I, who would live my harvest to behold
And like the sun see green leaves turn to gold,
        Ask that my days be long.
Pride of the garden, I have seen the fires
Of morning only, and my heart desires
        Its noon and evensong.

Death, thou canst wait for me. Get thee from here.
Go, and console those hearts which shame and fear
        And cold despair devour.
Pallas has still her verdant bowers for me,
Love, its embrace; the Muses, melody –
        It is not yet my hour.

                    ANDRÉ CHÉNIER, in prison, before execution

A LAST POEM,
SAINT-LAZARE PRISON

Perhaps within these pallisades of terror
Death's messenger, infernal recruiting officer,
Escorted by monstrous troopers,
Making these long, blackened passages echo my name
Perhaps, without warning, they will force
Me to leave my poem still on my lips and,
Strapping me up, they will force me out,
A crowd of my desolate fellow prisoners collecting
About me, all of them my friends before the
Dreadful call, but now turning their heads.

                                        ANDRÉ CHÉNIER

We will set a torch to all libraries; we need no more than the History
of the Revolution and of the laws.   BERTRAND BARÈRE DE VIEUZAC

PRISON

Prison life was by no means intolerable for those who had plenty of
money. Coittant who was confined in the Port Libre prison along
with the poet Vigée and twenty-seven former tax farmers, recalled
that at the end of the corridor on the first floor there was a large hall,
known as the salon, where six tables of six places each were laid for
dinner every evening for the richer prisoners.

To pass the time Coittant edited a daily prison newspaper
announcing the names of new arrivals and rumours of arrests elsewhere. The men prisoners composed odes of gallantry to the women,
declaring that it was pointless for the warders to have taken away
dangerous weapons such as scissors and pen-knives from Lisa and
Chloë while leaving them their enchanting smiles and great big eyes.
Others organized tables for whist, piquet or chess.

The more affluent sent home for wines that they had put by in
their cellars. Frequently their jailers were drunk with wine provided
by the prisoners and quite incapable of verifying whether their
charges were still in captivity.

It happened that towards the end of the Terror two women
named Biron were imprisoned in the Conciergerie. One day
Fouquier gave orders to fetch 'the Biron woman' for trial. He was
told that there were two women of the same name and was asked
which of them he had intended to call. 'Take them both', he said –
and they were guillotined the same afternoon. . . . André Chénier, the
poet, was confused with his brother Sauveur. But indeed without
photographs or fingerprints or indeed warders capable of reading,
some lapses in identification were inevitable.

There were so many people in prison that only a few could be
dealt with. Each morning the jailor called out the list of those whose
cases had come to the top of the folder and who were to be trans-
ported to the Conciergerie for trial and almost certain death. Those
who were lucky not to be drawn in this lottery of blood surrendered
themselves once more to the only pleasures they were capable of
enjoying.

Many of the condemned reacted with indifference, light-heartedness or even bravado. Colonel Vaujour, told that he would be executed at two in the afternoon, was heard to remark, 'What a pity. That's when I usually eat. However, I'll have my meal earlier today', and he was still eating when they came to fetch him.

The Princesse de Monaco put extra rouge on her cheeks to make sure that the crowd should detect no sign of weakness in her on her way to the scaffold. When the Maréchal de Mouchy was called to take his place in the tumbril, he recalled, 'When I was fifteen I went into battle for my King. At eighty I go to the scaffold for my God. I am not unfortunate.'   JOHN FISHER, 1966

TOM PAINE

The book of Ecclesiastes, or the Preacher, is also ascribed to Solomon, and that with much reason, if not with truth. It is written as the solitary reflection of a worn-out debauchee, such as Solomon was, who, looking back on scenes he can no longer enjoy, cries out, *All is vanity!* A great deal of the metaphor and of the sentiment is obscure, most probably by translation; but enough is left to show they were strongly pointed in the original. From what is transmitted to us of the character of Solomon, he was witty, ostentatious, dissolute, and at last melancholy; he lived fast, and died, tired of the world at the age of fifty-eight years.

Seven hundred wives, and three hundred concubines, are worse than one; and however it may carry with it the appearance of heightened enjoyment, it defeats all the felicity of affection by leaving it no point to fix upon; divided love is never happy. This was the case with Solomon; and if he could not, with all his pretensions to wisdom, discover it beforehand, he merited, unpitied, the mortification he afterwards endured. In this point of view his preaching is unnecessary, because, to know the consequences, it is only necessary to know the case. Seven hundred wives and three hundred concubines would have stood in place of the whole book. It was needless after this to say that all was vanity and vexation of spirit, for it is impossible to derive happiness from the company of those whom we deprive of happiness.

The Age of Reason

CHARACTER OF TOM PAINE

Among the persons whom I was in the habit of receiving, and of whom I have already described the most remarkable, Paine deserves to be mentioned. Declared a French citizen, as one of those celebrated foreigners, whom the nation was naturally desirous of adopting, he was known by writings which had been useful in the American revolution, and which might have contributed to produce one in England. I shall not, however, take upon me to pronounce absolute judgment upon his character, because he understood French without speaking it, and because that being nearly my case in regard to English, I was less able to converse with him than to listen to his conversation with those whose political skill was greater than my own.

The boldness of his conceptions, the originality of his style, and the striking truths which he throws with defiance into the midst of those whom they offend, have necessarily attracted great attention; but I think him better fitted to sow the seeds of popular commotion than to lay the foundation or prepare the form of a government. Paine throws light upon a revolution better than he concurs in the making of a constitution. He takes up, and establishes, those great principles of which the exposition strikes every eye, gains the applause of a pub, or excites the enthusiasm of a tavern.

MANON ROLAND. *Mémoires*

CONSPIRACY

Fouché had undeniably and consistently been a revolutionary zealot, constant in support of the Terror, but was scarcely in sympathy with Robespierre, or, more exactly, had become a rival, or had offended him by being the more extremist. His delicate position with Robespierre prevented him presenting himself as a candid, clear-cut personality, capable of open attack. Robespierre had told him that his face was a revelation of crime. Not only did Fouché make no reply but he accepted the insult as natural. Expelled from the Jacobin Club (under pressure from Robespierre), he could not return and no longer risked attending the Convention. Nevertheless, he engaged in very active business, with delight in intrigue and base deeds. I myself employed him, despatching him all over Paris to tell our friends whatever we knew that Robespierre, Saint-Just, and Couthon were planning. Fouché's personal terror of the Triumvirs only magnified for him the extent of their plottings. All that he sincerely dreaded was artfully exaggerated by him when attempting to rouse those whom he sought to provoke to action. Rising at dawn, he scurried about until darkness calling on deputies of every persuasion, telling each that either he or Robespierre would die on the morrow. To mourners of Danton, imperilled by those who had done away with him, Fouché habitually said, 'We may, if we care to, take revenge tomorrow, and then only save ourselves.' Such was the terror exercised by Robespierre that a deputy who thought the dictator was staring at him at the instant when he touched his forehead reflectfully, swiftly ceased, thinking, 'He will imagine that I am thinking of something!'

To inspire new courage into those so scared, many different incitements were required, so that all could recognise their own vital interests. Thus, by gathering together all feelings hostile to Robespierre, by adroit intrigues, Fouché was certainly a real catalyst for the varied elements essential to make the decisive attack on the tyrants of the Convention.

PAUL JEAN FRANÇOIS NICOLAS DE BARRAS. *Mémoires*, Paris, 1895

My reason, not my heart, is beginning to doubt this Republic of Virtue which I have set myself to establish.   MAXIMILIEN ROBESPIERRE

Men do not desire Virtue, they would prefer merely to live.

MAXIMILIEN ROBESPIERRE

FOUCHÉ

This remarkable genius which inspired in Napoleon something closely akin to terror, did not manifest itself all at once in Fouché. An obscure member of the National Convention, one of the most exceptional men of his day and one of the most misconstrued, he was moulded in the storms that were then raging. Under the Directory, he rose to that height from which men of discernment, thanks to their knowledge of the past, are able to foresee the future; then, all in a moment, like a second-rate actor who becomes first-rate when enlightened by a sudden gleam, he manifested his ability during the swift revolution of the Eighteenth Brumaire. Pallid of visage, trained in monastic dissimulation, aware of the secrets of the men of the Mountain to whose group he had belonged, and of those of the royalists whose group he was ultimately to join, he had been slowly and silently studying the personalities, the things, and the interests on the political stage; he divined Bonaparte's secrets, and gave the Corsican useful advice and valuable information. At this time neither his former colleagues nor his new ones had any inkling of the scope of his genius, which was purely ministerial, essentially governmental, accurate in all its forecasts, and incredibly shrewd.

HONORÉ DE BALZAC. *Une ténébreuse affaire*, 1841

Fouché is one of the persons who have so many aspects, and so much depth beneath each aspect, that they are inscrutable in the moment of action and only become comprehensible long after the event.

HONORÉ DE BALZAC

Fouché was Minister of Police for the first time from 1799 till 1802, and was reappointed in 1804. Napoleon was inclined in principle to instil fear in any opposition by exemplary, large-scale executions. Fouché, on the other hand, preferred to nip hostile movements in the bud, to warn those tempted, and to bribe those detected into working for him. This relatively humane attitude was a novelty in France, and has not often been copied in the police-states of our day.

H. D. ZIMAN, 1972

Joseph Fouché, one of the most powerful men of his day, and one of the most remarkable men of all time, was little loved by his contemporaries and has received even less justice from posterity. Napoleon in St Helena; Robespierre at the Jacobin Club; Carnot, Barras, and Talleyrand in their memoirs, the French historians, no matter whether royalist, republican, or Bonapartist – one and all spit venom as soon as his name comes up for discussion. . . . No term of abuse is spared him. . . .

In general, however, we find that this man who during one of the most salient periods in history was a leader of every party in turn and was unique in surviving the destruction of them all, this man who in duels upon the psychological plane was able to get the better of a Napoleon and a Robespierre, is tacitly relegated to the back rows among the supers instead of being given his proper place in the centre of the stage. . . .

Only one imaginative writer has seen this unique figure in its true proportions – Balzac, whose own greatness made it easy for him to recognise greatness in another.   STEFAN ZWEIG, 1929

ANDRÉ CHÉNIER

Chénier's work took some time to impose itself in France because of his untimely death, his father's death a few months afterwards, and the moral weakness and physical ill-health of his brother Marie-Joseph, who died at the age of forty-seven. When his work appeared for the first time, twenty-five years after his death, rapidly going into new editions over a period of fifty years, it was his legend and personality, as much as his verse, which imposed itself on the Romantics. He became for them, a symbol of the Poet as Hero – to use Carlyle's words – rather than one whose work was to be closely studied and imitated. He and his friends Alfieri and Niemcewicz were in the forefront of that great tide which, with Chateaubriand, Byron, Lamartine, Hugo, and so many others, brought poetry and action together.   FRANCIS SCARFE, 1965

THERMIDOR, TWO PRISONERS

The Tumbrils move on. But in this set of Tumbrils there are two other things notable: one notable person: and one want of a notable person. The notable person is Lieutenant-General Loiserolles, a nobleman by birth, and by nature; laying down his life here for his son. In the prison of Saint-Lazare, the night before last, hurrying to the Gate to hear the Death-list read, he caught the name of his son. This son was asleep at the moment. 'I am Loiserolles', cried the old man: at Tinville's bar, an error in the Christian name is little; small objection was made. The want of the notable person, again, is that of Deputy Paine. [Tom] Paine has sat in the Luxembourg since January; and seemed forgotten; but Fouquier had picked him at last. The Turnkey, list in hand, is marking with chalk the outer door of tomorrow's *Fournée*. Paine's door happened to be open, turned back on the wall; the Turnkey marked it on the side next to him, and hurried on: another Turnkey came, and shut it, no chalk mark now visible, the *Fournée* went without Paine.

THOMAS CARLYLE. *The French Revolution*, 1837

This story of Paine escaping death is queried by his latest biographer, A. J. Ayer, 1988. Rather a pity!

AFTERNOON 8TH THERMIDOR, IN THE CONVENTION

I recognise only two parties: virtuous citizens, bad citizens. Patriotism I hold not a party matter but a movement of the heart, consisting not in insolence, not in any impulsiveness regardless of principles, common sense, morality; far less involving devotion to factions. My spirit, scorched by knowledge of so many treasons, makes me increasingly convinced of the necessity, permanent necessity, of invoking Integrity and all other generous feelings to succour the Republic – but, above all else, Integrity. I feel that wherever an honest man exists, wherever he inhabits, we must extend our hands to him in friendship and embrace him. I also believe in certain disastrous liabilities of the Revolution, quite distinct from criminal designs – that is, the loathsome effect of intrigue, and, supremely, the sinister potency of slander. I see the world filled with dupes and scoundrels, but the latter, though an inconspicuous minority, create all the evils.

While our enemies pretend to extend to a weak individual, exposed to the abominable hatred of all the factions, an importance inflated and absurd, what aim have they save to divide us all, to degrade you by denying your actual existence, like the irreligious scoundrel who denies the existence of the Supreme Being whom he nevertheless dreads. However, this word *Dictatorship* can act like magic; it sears liberty, cheapens government, uproots the Republic, degrades all our revolutionary institutions by ascribing them to a single individual; it makes republican justice hateful, a weapon of personal ambition; it directs to a single target all the resentments, and all the daggers, of fanaticism and aristocracy.

They name me, Tyrant! Oh, were I actually so, they would

grovel before me. I need only stuff them with gold and permit them all manner of crime, and they would abase themselves in sheer gratitude. Were I tyrant, the monarchs we have overthrown, instead of denouncing me as they do – how tender is their concern for our Liberty! – would offer me their guilt-laden support and we would soon be in treaty. But is it really myself at whom they stare? Why, what are these tormented sovereigns really expecting but help from a faction they protect, a faction actually selling them our national glory and liberty! How does humanity acquire tyranny, save by help of treacherous bandits? Yes, criminals assist tyranny. But where are their enemies hastening? To death, to immortality! Who is the tyrant defending me, which is my faction! Name both! The answer is you yourselves. To you, you alone, I belong. Which is the faction that from the start of the Revolution has toppled all others and distressed so many traitors? You! the people! our beliefs!

Let but the reins of government loosen for a mere second in your grasp and you will find them seized by a military despotism, and the leaders of rival factions overthrow the crushed representatives of the Nation. An age of civil war and tribulation will ravage our Land and we will die for failing to exploit a particular moment marked in human history for the founding of a Temple of Liberty.

What can be objected against whoever decides to speak out, speak the truth, and agrees to die for it? Let us then state openly that a conspiracy has been formed against public Liberty, that its strength depends upon a criminal alliance, plotting within the convention itself, with accomplices in the Committee of General Security, on which they have the upper hand; that haters of the Republic have set off this Committee against the Committee of Public Safety, thus forming a rival government, in coalition with members of the latter, seeking to ruin patriots and France itself. How can we cure this evil? To punish traitors, reconstitute and purge the Committee of General Security, totally subordinate it to the Committee of Public Safety, likewise purged, then establish governmental unity under the supreme power of the Convention and thus overcome all factions by the force of the National Will and on their ruins build the authority of Justice and Liberty. These are the necessary principles. If they cannot be restored by anyone, without him being abused for ambitiousness, then I must realise that such principles are themselves criminal, that Tyranny controls us, but not that I should hold my tongue, for what is reprehensible to anyone supported by Reason and ready to surrender his life for his country? I am made to fight crime, not to preside over it.

MAXIMILIEN ROBESPIERRE, from his last completed speech to the Convention

I have read in history how the defenders of Liberty have succumbed under the weight of slander, but their oppressors have followed them into the grave. Both the good and the evil vanish from this earth, though under different circumstances.   MAXIMILIEN ROBESPIERRE

I will let others paint you flattering pictures; instead, I will unveil some home truths. . . .

Of all revolutions, the French is the first founded on the rights of man and the principles of justice. Nevertheless, conspirators have crept into the movement and are seeking to topple the defenders of liberty by calling them tyrants. I am about to disclose abuses pointing towards national collapse, and which only your honesty can overcome. And if I simultaneously say some words about the persecution I have suffered, you will not reproach me. . . .

I am arraigned, unofficially, by innuendo, of holding sole responsibility for all the good, all the bad. My colleagues are scrupulously informed of what I have said and, chiefly, what I have not said. Any suspicion that anyone else has helped towards unpleasantness is carefully overlooked; I am held to have done everything, demanded everything, for you all know I am called dictator. . . . I confess an immense fatigue. . . . For over six weeks the nature and power of slander and my inability to do good and prevent evil has forced me to entirely surrender my duties on the Committee of Public Safety. . . .

Frenchmen, do not tolerate the humiliation of your souls by enemies and the weakening of your virtue by their cold doctrine! No, Chaumette! No, Fouché! Death's not an eternal sleep. Citizens! Efface from your tombstones that motto which hides nature with mourning-crêpe, discourages persecuted innocence, and insults death, then engrave instead this: Death is the beginning of immortality. Some time ago I promised to leave the oppressors of the people a powerful testament. I now spell it out with the detachment fitting the situation I am now in. I bequeath them the terrible truth – Death.

MAXIMILIEN ROBESPIERRE

Before my name is dishonoured, France shall hear my voice. It is time that all here should recognise the whole truth. One man has paralysed the Will of the National Convention. That man is Robespierre.

DEPUTY PIERRE JOSEPH CAMBON

The mask must be torn away, no matter whose the face it conceals. Better my corpse should serve some ambitious man as his throne than that I, by holding my tongue, should become the accomplice of his crimes. DEPUTY BILLAUD-VARENNE

Robespierre has prepared a list of victims, and I'm told I am on it.

DEPUTY ETIENNE PANIS

I will publish the list when I judge the time is proper.

MAXIMILIEN ROBESPIERRE

FOUCHÉ PERSISTS

Fouché will play a subordinate part softly: without moving an eyelash, he will coolly, smilingly, accept the grossest insults, the most shameful humiliations. No threat, no torrent of passion, will affect his fishiness. Both Robespierre and Napoleon beat as uselessly against this stone-like impassivity as water against a rock. Three generations of such passion ebb and flow about him while he remains obstinately immune, more dispassionate than any. In this chilliness is the gist of his genius. His body neither obstructs nor envelops him; one can call him outside all spiritual tumult. Blood, senses, soul, the violently astray particles of an energetic mortal have no being in the soul of a secret gambler whose entire passion is locked within the intelligence. Truly, this arid figure at his desk has a hankering for adventure, intrigue is his passion, but he can consummate that passion only intellectually, and nothing gives better cover for his sinister joy in confusion and intrigue than the barren activities of the obedient and candid bureaucrat he always claims to be. To sit in his office spinning the threads, barricaded behind papers and files, while, unseen, without warning, he launches mortal attacks – such are his manoeuvres. We must penetrate the historical underworld if, amid the glare of the Revolution and the legendary radiance of Napoleon, we can notice him at all. STEFAN ZWEIG, 1929

EVENING IN THE JACOBIN CLUB

Of all the decrees which have rescued the Republic, the most sublime, unique in eradicating corruption and saving the People from tyranny, is that establishing trust and virtue as the norm. If this were fully enforced, Liberty would be installed absolutely, and popular tribunes be rendered unnecessary, but some men, with no more than the mask of Virtue, greatly obstruct the enforcement of virtuous laws, desiring to use this mask as a way of gaining personal power.

MAXIMILIEN ROBESPIERRE

Robespierre was convinced that his programme of Virtue was winning popular acclaim; he failed to understand that the applause was really for the chances it promised for plundering the rich, enslaving the important and humiliating the aristocrats.

FRIEDRICH SIEBURG, 1936

The night is hot to suffocation, moonlight shines on the blade of the guillotine. When it falls tomorrow, will the sharp edge sever the necks of Tallien, Barras, and Fouché, or will Robespierre's head drop into the basket? None of the six hundred deputies retires to bed that night; both parties are arming for the final struggle. From the Convention, Robespierre has sped to the Jacobin Club where, trembling excitedly, he repeats the speech earlier rejected by the deputies. Thunderous applause acclaims it, as ever, but for the last time, and he, heavy with gloomy forebodings, is not deceived by the shouts and crush of the three thousand. He describes the speech as his 'Testament'. Meanwhile Saint-Just, his lieutenant, is at the Committee of Public Safety, where he desperately argues till dawn against Collot d'Herbois, Carnot, and the other conspirators, while, in Tuileries corridors, the net is being woven in which Robespierre will be entangled in the daylight. Twice and thrice the threads, like those born on a weaver's shuttle, pass from Right to Left, Mountain to Marsh, until finally, at grey morning, understanding is reached. Here, once more, Fouché rejoins them, for night is his element, and intrigue his rightful habitation. His face, made more than usually pallid by anxiety, is spectral in the dimness. He whispers, begs, promises, he scares and threatens one figure after another; he moves unceasingly until the past is finalised. At last, in the small hours, the several enemies come to common resolution to destroy him who is foe to them all – Robespierre. Fouché can enjoy well-earned rest. STEFAN ZWEIG, 1929

Fine weather for tomorrow.

MAXIMILIEN ROBESPIE.RE, to Eléonore Duplay

NINTH THERMIDOR

I belong to no faction. I will oppose them all. But factions can only be eliminated by institutions, bearing guarantees; institutions which will set limits to the executive, and once and for all compel human arrogance to submit to the yoke of the People's Liberty. Events have ordained that this tribune may perhaps be the Tarpeian Rock for whoever announces to you that the Government has closed its eyes to wisdom. . . .   LOUIS ANTOINE DE SAINT-JUST, to the Convention

At about this stage he was silenced by what appears to have been a planned demonstration, and made no effort to continue. The rest of his speech was preserved in manuscripts. Too long for full quotation, it includes:
I am about to tell you of certain men who, out of jealousy, have managed to increase their power and concentrate authority in themselves by suppressing or removing whatever obstructed their designs, by winning control of the Paris garrison, by usurping the Magistrature.

You have entrusted the Government to twelve men. For the last month, however, the Government has actually rested only with two or three. Such imprudence delivers you to a risk that men will acquire appetites for personal rule. Imagine the result of this innovation. Imagine Paris divested of central control, without law courts; the Revolutionary Tribunal destroyed, or delivered to the minions of these two or three, now a despotism. Your own authority would soon be crushed. One factor alone would remain to defy the despotism – the Jacobin Club, called by those persons the dictatorship of opinion. They would demand that you sacrifice the most influential Jacobins.

The leaders of this conspiracy are Billaud-Varenne and Collot d'Herbois. No reason exists for the two Committees to forfeit the People's trust. Only these are unworthy of this trust who yield to personal ambition disguised by a veneer of impartiality, and who have wished to appropriate the right to accuse members of this Convention. I believe it is your duty to justice and our country to examine my denunciation. Every Committee decree not signed by six members should be seen as an act of tyranny.

I accuse the conspirators of having exploited the Committee for their own ambitions. Sulla was an excellent general, great statesman and ruler. Nevertheless, he employed his gifts to further his own career.

I pronounce no verdict on those I have named. I want them to give justification for their actions, I want all of us to become wise.

To listen to Robespierre, it appears that he alone defends Liberty; he is giving it up for lost, he is going to abandon everything; a man of exceptional modesty, he uses a single everlasting refrain: 'I am the oppressed one, they won't allow me the rostrum.' He, it seems, is alone in having anything to say, for what he wants is always performed. He says 'this man, that man, plots against me, I who am the best friend of the Republic.' Therefore, he plots against the Republic? a novel view of things indeed!   DEPUTY VADIER, to the Convention

Tallien's eyes beamed bright, on the morrow, Ninth of Thermidor 'about nine o'clock', to see that the Convention had actually met. Paris is in rumour: but at least we are met, in Legal Convention here; we have not been snatched seriatim; treated with a *Pride's Purge* at the door. '*Allons*, brave men of the Plain, late Frogs of the Marsh,' cried Tallien, with a squeeze of the hand as he passed in; Saint-Just's sonorous organ being now audible from the Tribune, and the game of games begun.

Saint-Just is verily reading that Report of his; green Vengeance, in the shape of Robespierre, watching nigh. Behold, however, Saint-Just has read but few sentences, when interruption rises, rapid *crescendo*; when Tallien starts to his feet, and Billaud, and this man starts and that, – and Tallien, a second time, with his: 'Citizens, at the Jacobins last night I trembled for the Republic. I said to myself if the Convention dare not strike the Tyrant, then I myself dare; and with this I will do it, if need be,' said he, whisking out a clear-gleaming dagger, and brandishing it there: the Steel of Brutus, as we call it. Whereat we all bellow, and brandish, impetuous acclaim. 'Tyranny! Dictatorship! Triumvirate!' And the *Salut* Committee-men accuse, and all men accuse, and uproar, and impetuously acclaim. And Saint-Just is standing motionless, pale of face; Couthon ejaculating, 'Triumvir?' with a look at his paralytic legs. And Robespierre is struggling to speak, but President Thuriot is jingling the bell against him, but the Hall is sounding against him like an Eolus-Hall: and Robespierre is mounting the Tribune-steps and descending again; going and coming, like to choke with rage, terror, desperation: – and mutiny is the order of the day.

O President Thuriot, thou that wert Elector Thuriot, and from the Bastille Battlements sawest Saint-Antoine rising like the ocean-tide, and hast seen much since, sawest thou ever the like of this? Jingle of bell, which thou jinglest against Robespierre, is hardly audible amid the Bedlam-storm; and men rage for life. 'President of Assassins,' shrieks Robespierre, 'I demand speech of thee for the last time!' It cannot be had. 'To you, O virtuous men of the Plain,' cries he, finding audience one moment, 'I appeal to you!' The virtuous men of the Plain sit silent as stones. And Thuriot's bell jingles, and the Hall sounds like Eolus's Hall. Robespierre's frothing lips are grown 'blue'; his tongue dry, cleaving to the roof of his mouth. 'The blood of Danton chokes him,' cry they. 'Accusation! Decree of Accusation!' Thuriot swiftly puts that question.

Accusation passes; the incorruptible Maximilien is decreed Accused.

'I demand to share my Brother's fate, as I have striven to share his virtues,' cries Augustin, the younger Robespierre: Augustin also is decreed. And Couthon, and Saint-Just, and Lebas, they are all decreed; and packed forth, – not without difficulty, the Ushers almost trembling to obey.   THOMAS CARLYLE, 1837

I move that Robespierre be arrested.

DEPUTY LOUCHET, to the Convention

On the 9th, an attack on Robespierre was led by Tallien, himself almost within reach of the guillotine. Robespierre demanded the floor, for his reply, then called us murderers because the floor was allowed first to another deputy, though he had prior right. His brother supported him. The Convention, already angered, decreed his, Robespierre's, arrest. Things then went awry, in this manner. The Committees of Public Safety and General Security, ordered to enforce the arrests (the Robespierres, Couthon, Saint-Just, Le Bas), delivered the accused to officials who, failing to get them received at the Luxembourg Prison, escorted them to the Commune where Robespierre's friends and favourites had already gathered. They embraced, sounded the tocsin, the populace assembled, thirty cannon menaced the avenues off the Place de Grève. While these matters were occurring, by seven pm, when we reached the Convention, everyone was still unaware of the crisis. The rostrum was occupied by most petty affairs for about an hour when without warning it was announced that the Committee of General Security had been invaded and that Hanriot, commander of the National Guard, and seventeen officers, already detained there, had escaped. If they had at once marched on the Convention, just a hand's breadth away, we would have been crushed. Had Robespierre, instead of wasting time elaborating orders at the Hôtel de Ville, led eight or ten thousand men from the crowd packing the Place de Grève, and if, aided by Couthon, he had inflamed the mob by his eloquence, we would have lost the day, but Fate decreed otherwise. We did at last use our good sense and take steps to retaliate, instead of indulging in mutual declamations about dying where duty had placed us.

Robespierre was deserted by all, he is dead. For the Republic, it is grievous that this has to be rated as a major historical event. In a Republic, one man's death should make no great commotion.

JEAN DYZEZ, to M. Lafitte
(See Richard Bienvenu, 1968)

The worst misfortune mankind could have sustained.

ROBERT SOUTHEY

However his faults might have been, one can at least declare this on Robespierre's behalf; he did not include a majority of his personal friends amongst those he destroyed. Those whom he sacrificed he killed on behalf of a *system*, however misguided that might have been; by no means from petty, personal malice.

STENDHAL. *Rome, Naples et Florence en 1817*

A DEATH

Robespierre lay in an anteroom of the Convention Hall, while his Prison-escort was getting ready; the mangled jaw bound up rudely with bloody linen; a spectacle to men. He lies stretched on a table, a deal-box his pillow; the sheath of the pistol is still clenched convulsively in his hand. Men bully him, insult him; his eyes still indicate intelligence; he speaks no word. 'He had on the sky-blue coat he had got made for the Feast of the Etre Suprême' – O reader, can thy hard heart hold out against that? His trousers were nankeen;

the stockings had fallen down over the ankles. He spoke no word more in this world.

And so, at six in the morning, a victorious Convention adjourns. Report flies over Paris as on golden wings; penetrates the Prisons; irradiates the faces of those that were ready to perish; turnkeys and *moutons*, fallen from their high estate, look mute and blue. It is the 28th day of July, called 10th of Thermidor, year 1794.

Fouquier had but to identify; his Prisoners being already Out of Law. At four in the afternoon, never before were the streets of Paris seen so crowded. From the Palais de Justice to the Place de la Révolution, for *thither* again go the Tumbrils this time, it is one dense stirring mass; all windows crammed; the very roofs and ridge-tiles budding forth human curiosity, in strange gladness. The Death-tumbrils, with their motley Batch of Outlaws, some twenty-three or so, from Maximilien to Mayor Fleuriot and Simon the Cordwainer roll on. All eyes are on Robespierre's Tumbril, where he, his jaw bound in dirty linen, with his half-dead Brother, and half-dead Hanriot, lie shattered; their 'seventeen hours' of agony about to end. The Gendarmes point their swords at him, to show the people which is he. A woman springs on the Tumbril; clutching the side of it with one hand; waving the other Sibyl-like; and exclaims: 'The death of thee gladdens my very heart, *m'enivre de joie*.' Robespierre opened his eyes; '*Scélérat*, go down to Hell, with the curses of all wives and mothers!' – At the foot of the scaffold, they stretched him on the ground till his turn came. Lifted aloft, his eyes again opened; caught the bloody axe. Sanson wrenched the coat off him; wrenched the dirty linen from his jaw: the jaw fell powerless, there burst from him a cry; – hideous to hear and see. Sanson, thou canst not be too quick. Sanson's work done, there burst forth shout on shout of applause. Shout, which prolongs itself not only over Paris, but over France, but over Europe, and down to this Generation. Deservedly, and also undeservedly. O unhappiest Advocate of Arras, wert thou worse than other Advocates? Stricter man, according to his Formula, his Credo, and his Cant, of probities, benevolences, pleasures-of-virtue, and such like, lived not in that age. A man fitted, in some luckier settled age, to have become one of those incorruptible barren Pattern-Figures, and have had marble-tablets and funeral-sermons. His poor landlord, the cabinet-maker in the Rue Saint-Honoré, loved him; his brother died for him. May God be merciful to him and to us.

THOMAS CARLYLE, 1837

ASSESSMENT

The eventful man is a creature of events in that by a happy or un-happy conjunction of circumstances he finds himself in a position where action or abstention from action is decisive in a great issue. But he need not be aware of that issue and how his action or inaction affects it. The members of the Committe of Public Safety during the French Revolution were, as a group, eventful men. But only Robespierre and St-Just were event-making in that they realised above all others what was at stake after Louis XVI had been deposed. Napoleon believed that if Robespierre had remained in power, France would have settled down to orderly processes of republican government and made Napoleon's accession to power impossible. But Robespierre was the architect of his own downfall and, despite all the politically motivated efforts to rehabilitate him, of the downfall of Republican France. Together with St-Just, he is responsible for carrying the Terror *beyond* the interests of national defence and public safety.

Although Robespierre disapproved of the more barbaric excesses of indiscriminate executions and juridical frame-ups, it was his own policy that prepared the way for them. The Terror, to the point that Robespierre approved it, did not save France from the flames of counter revolution. It supplied fuel to those flames. By terrorizing tens of thousands of Frenchmen who were genuinely hostile to des-potism, it made easier Napoleon's usurpation. An incidental distinc-tion of Robespierre is that by charging his opponents, even when they were as far apart as Danton and Anacharsis Clootz, with being spies in English pay, he set a fashion that was to be followed in the Russian Revolution. It was bad enough that Robespierre proclaimed: 'The Republic owes its enemies nothing but death.' It was historically fatal when he began to regard the enemies of Robespierre as the enemies of the Republic. SIDNEY HOOK, 1945

The Committee of Public Safety had taught the militants to obey the government. On the Ninth of Thermidor Robespierre and his friends were destroyed partly because the *sans-culottes* had learned their les-sons well. RICHARD BIENVENU, 1968

THE MAN OF THE MOUNTAIN

Charlotte's brother, Maximilien, had as little to do with the upheaval of August 10 as he had with the massacres of September 2. He is about as suited to lead a political faction as he is to arrive on the moon. He is as self-absorbed as a philosopher; dry as a businessman; but gentle as a lamb and moody as Young's *Night Thoughts*. Obviously he lacks *our* sensibility; but I like to imagine that he hopes to benefit humanity, though more through justice than through love.

MADAME GULLIAN, to her son Marc-Antoine, after having given dinner
to Charlotte, Augustin and Maximilien Robespierre

If anybody asked me how Robespierre managed to win so much influence over public opinion, I would reply that it was by showing the most austere virtues, the most complete dedication and most unsullied principles.   JEAN-NICOLAS BILLAUD-VARENNE

He was so good.   MADAME ELIZABETH LEBAS, daughter of Maurice Duplay,
Robespierre's landlord

He had but one more thing to accomplish, to become supreme over the Revolution – but that required the loss of thirty more heads.

JOSEPH FOUCHÉ

Robespierre could never forgive friends the wrongs he inflicted on them, nor the kindness they gave him, nor the talents enjoyed by some of them but which he himself lacked.   FRANÇOIS BUZOT

Robespierre was Liberty's most strenuous champion, showing democracy in its purest form, at its noblest and loftiest. Never lived there a greater friend of justice and mankind.   ERNEST HAMEL

Of no one of whom so much is said is so little known.

J. W. CROKER

What did he do?

He held first a group, then a great political machine, then a sovereign assembly, and at last a nation, attentive. He became the title and front of the republic: the kings regarded him; he put some fear into the priests; the armies converged upon his tenement; the general run of European society stood aghast at his supposed enormities; the most generous, the most practical, and the most violent of the great Reformers alike insisted upon his bearing their standard.

The character of Robespierre is contained in these two connected facts; first, that he was a man of the old régime – divining nothing outside it, undisturbed by that germinating of the future which worked in and troubled the great minds around him, and threw an energy of travail into their splendid tragedy; secondly, that he had to an inhuman, or (if the word be preferred) to an heroic, degree the potentiality of intense conviction; for God had given him a kind of stone tabernacle within the soul where he could treasure absolute truths and this tabernacle remained impregnable.

HILAIRE BELLOC, 1901

During his ascendency I suffered prison, was almost guillotined, and saw many friends and relations dispatched to the scaffold. If I have so little hatred for his memory, this is due to my conviction that all the enormities enacted by his forerunners, his associates, betrayers and destroyers have been heaped on his reputation. His most obsequious flunkeys were his loudest killers, burdening him with the entire mass of blood enveloping the Terror, which he might have ended by disposing of them.

In beheading Robespierre, these curs finished off their own Jacobin revolution and the methods on which they relied so as to grab the succession; they lacked time to keep pace with the legend they were establishing. In human memory the defeated are always malodorous. At least I am prepared to grant M. de Robespierre the fine title of 'Incorruptible'. AIMÉE DE COIGNY, Duchesse de Fleury

Olivier Blanc describes her as 'very royalist . . . an active agent of the British secret service'.

Everywhere he saw conspiracies, treason, plots; he never forgave injuries to his self-esteem; he was prey to the most fleeting suspicions and was always convinced that he was being watched and persecuted.

PÉTION DE NEUVILLE

Don't forget Robespierre! There was a man without fault, noble to the core, true republican. Vanity ruined him, and tetchiness, unjustifiable suspicion of colleagues. A great misfortune.

BERTRAND BARÈRE DE VIEUZAC

Robespierre's political doctrine accorded exactly with his strongly unpolitical character. It was a policy of principles and those of others were his chief concern. In this incessant supervision and investigation of principles other than his own he exhausted his main talents. All in his political vision was correct, complete, undeniable; there was only one difficulty: human nature. Real human beings, of passion, impulse, habit, indeed their entire behaviour, upset his dogma. Thus he became an enemy of life. He had precisely worked out where his doctrine would lead, in political terms. All would prove right: a problem must work its way out, and if it ran into confusion, the blame must be fixed on man's evil will. So his favourite words were *conspiracy, cloak, disguise, unmasking, treason* and *criminality*. He used these so extravagantly that police and tribunal could scarcely use any others, and *conspiracy* on an official paper simply meant that the person concerned must perish . . . the veiled threat was his favourite weapon: 'He who trembles is guilty.' A hint from his mouth had an edge so cutting that at last it struck down himself.

FRIEDRICH SIEBURG, 1936

THE DYING ROBESPIERRE
IN POPULAR FICTION

You lay on a wooden table in the ante chamber of the Committee of Public Safety.

All night long, between those two open doors, rats had scurried, tempted into the lamplight by the smell of carrion that lay within its circle. All night, mocking at him, jeering at him, spitting at him; and whisking away, even now, out of reach. . . . And he lying there with the breath coming from his mouth in bloody bubbles that burst and ran in frothy slime down his chin. Then someone had raised his head, pushed a despatch-case under it, given him a handkerchief. He'd said 'Merci, Monsieur.'

'Monsieur.' That was curious, wasn't it? The old word, the old regime, for the first time, coming back through his own mouth, his shattered mouth.

After that they had left him alone, though not before they brought Saint-Just to him. They had brought him between two gendarmes, his hands bound behind his back. To hear Saint-Just accuse, complain, cry out? Saint-Just? He had stood there for a moment, looking down, calm, silent, expressionless, unirked by his bonds, the fathomless limpidity of his eyes untroubled by emotion. He had looked down, the carven beauty of his face ageless and inhuman; timeless, save for the little pendulums of his earrings, swinging. . . . Then he had turned and gone; aloof, remote, passionless.

Fear had come and gone with Saint-Just. . . . He wondered if he had ever seen Saint-Just before – if anybody had ever seen him. Saint-Just who had followed him like a shadow when he had the sun in his face, but whom he himself must follow, now that the sun was at his back. Looking with calm, incurious eyes, then turning and going back whence he had come. A shadow. The shadow that walks with a man every day of his life, invisible, unknown, and that only on the last day turns and looks him in the face out of the pitiless purity of his eyes.

Son of the absconding debtor; son of the king; son of the labourer. That was what you'd fought against in your tower of isolation. Blood of extermination; extermination of the sons of men, so that men themselves could be men in their own right. *The Rights of Man. I did that. However they may gloat over my blood or spit on the Declaration of the Rights of Man.*

I would have done more. I would have drowned the ancient evil in the blood of extermination. I would have freed mankind from the slavery of a man-made heredity, that chain growing heavier to bear with the added link of every generation. I would have. . . . But the People didn't want it. They only wanted to live. No, not the People. Rats. Rats who preferred the life of vermin to the death of men. Rats, without strength or virtue. . . . Pah! the loathsome touch of them, the unclean heat of their bodies, the foulness of their breath! Not the People. Rats, burrowing under the walls of fear, until they cracked and fell inwards upon you.

You lay on a wooden table. You had lived for thirty-six years. In as many minutes you would be dead.

You would be dead. You had done no more than the others – the Kings, the Captains, the Saints. You had done no more than scratch the surface of the rough block of humanity with a name, a date, a symbol. Ah, but you had, you had! You had carved on it something greater than that: carved deeply, indelibly, for all the ages to come:

I, Maximilien Robespierre – I, the Incorruptible – I did that. I made the Declaration of the Rights of Man.   Adapted from MARJORIE CORYN, 1944

SAINT-JUST: 1767–1794

Saint-Just: the name seems stolen from the Missal. . . .
He thought only the laconic fit to rule.
His chamois coat, the dandy's vast cravat
knotted with pretentious negligence:
he carried his head like the Holy Sacrament.
If such a man wants to enlighten the world,
he must move with the stone footstep of the sun –
faction follows the course of revolution,
as reptiles follow the course of a torrent.
'I'm twenty, I've done badly, I'll do better;'
he did, he reached the scaffold. *'Je sais où je vais.*
I am young and therefore close to nature.
Happiness is a new idea in Europe;
we've bronzed liberty with the guillotine.'   ROBERT LOWELL, 1970

THE FRENCH SPARTAN

If he had lived in the Greek Republican age, he would have been a
Spartan. His *Fragments* reveal that he would have chosen the institutions of Lycurgus. He would have lived like Agis or Cleomones. Had
he been a Roman, he would have led revolutions, in the style of
Marius, but would never have been a tyrant like Sulla. He loathed
aristocracy as much as he loved common folk. His way of displaying
his love was certainly unsuitable for his country, his era, his
contemporaries; without it, he would have survived. But at least he
stamped upon France and the 18th century a profound impression of
ability, character, republican sentiment. His style was laconic, his
character austere, his political principles puritan. What hope, therefore, for success? The signal distinction of his mind was audacity.
He was the first to declare that 'to dare' was the secret of the Revolution; and he did just that. It was he who declared, 'the only rest for a
revolutionary is in the grave,' and, at twenty-seven he rested in his
own. He had read greatly in Tacitus and Montesquieu, those two
geniuses who shortened everything because they perceived everything. From them he acquired his vivid, pithy and epigrammatic
style; his manner too possessed something of their strength,
incisiveness and profundity.   BERTRAND BARÈRE DE VIEUZAC

Together with Fouché, Tallien, Barras, and others less famous, Barère helped overthrow Saint-Just, Robespierre and Couthon, on 9th Thermidor 1794.

One day you could feel only kindness for him, the next day a compulsion to hate him.   AUGUSTINE LEJEUNE, Saint-Just's Police Secretary, 1812

The very thought of him still makes me shudder.

COMMISSIONARY BAUDOT, 1824

His soul lived in his mouth.   HILAIRE BELLOC, 1899

THERMIDOR IN POETRY

Without me and within, as I advanced,
All that I saw, or felt, or communed with
Was gentleness and peace. Upon a small
And rocky island near, a fragment stood
(Itself like a sea rock) of what had been
A Romish chapel, where in ancient times
Masses were said at the hour which suited those
Who crossed the sands with ebb of morning tide.
Not far from this still ruin all the plain
Was spotted with a variegated crowd
Of coaches, wains, and travellers, horse and foot,
Wading beneath the conduct of their guide
In loose procession through the shallow stream
Of inland water; the great sea meanwhile
Was at safe distance, far retired. I paused,
Unwilling to proceed, the scene appeared
So gay and cheerful, when a traveller
Chancing to pass, I carelessly inquired
If any news was stirring; he replied
In the familiar language of the day
That, *Robespierre was dead* – nor was a doubt,
On further question, left within my mind
But that the tidings were substantial truth;
That he and his supporters all were fallen.
Great was my glee of spirit, great my joy
In vengeance, and eternal Justice, thus

Made manifest. 'Come now, ye golden times,'
Said I, forth-breathing on these open sands
A hymn of triumph: 'as the morning comes
Out of the bosom of the night, come ye:
Thus far our trust is verified; behold!
They who with clumsy desperation brought
Rivers of Blood, and preached that nothing else
Could cleanse the Augean stable, by the might
Of their own helper have been swept away;
Their madness is declared and visible;
Elsewhere will safety now be sought, and earth
March firmly towards righteousness and peace.'
Then schemes I framed more calmly, when and how
The maddening factions might be tranquillised,
And, though through hardships manifold and long,
The mighty renovation would proceed.

WILLIAM WORDSWORTH. *The Prelude*

AFTER THERMIDOR

Immediately after 9th Thermidor, all hearts embraced the most joyful hopes. It was affecting to witness the zest of citizens searching for each other, exchanging their experiences, good or bad, of the Terror, congratulating, or comforting. Jacks in office no longer looked stern and threatening, only showed minor malice and shame. Some, through cowardice, or indeed sincerity, even took part in the general rejoicings. Among victims, calm happiness had replaced inhibition and wretchedness. It was a sort of resurrection of the dead. . . .

Paris regained her position of arbiter of fashion and taste. Two ladies, celebrated beauties, first Madame Tallien, then Madame Récamier, were the leaders. Then it was that the revolution in private life, begun in 1789, was completed. The cult of the classical, already influencing the arts through David and his followers, now invaded women's attire, the hair style of the sexes, and indeed domestic furniture. All this ousted the Gothic, feudal, and those grotesque hotchpotches concocted by court hirelings. If utility was at times sacrificed to purity of design and appearance, for furniture, both were combined in Ladies' dresses.

M. THIBADEAU. *Mémoires*
(See Richard Bienvenu)

The men of 9 Thermidor were devoid of conviction, in principles and beliefs. They paid attention to public opinion so that they could follow it, and whatever they did was dictated from outside themselves. So, when they saw that moderation was demanded, they conformed; Fréron even preached leniency with the same personal vigour with which he had enforced Terror. With figures like this, the pendulum had to swing back. Yet their past political associations and their own roles in the blood-drenched Terror temporarily arrested them on the counter-revolutionary descent which fairly soon would claim them. When, however, middle-class prejudices were obviously triumphant, when, and chiefly, the restoration of the former Girondin beliefs showed that in politics, success carries all before it, they made themselves leaders of the new times. In speeches, journals, actions were nothing but a lengthy sequence of accusations against their former acts and speeches. They condemned themselves when condemning one-time associates. They risked more, by forming youth squads which, pretending revenge for victims of the Terror, themselves proceeded to indulge in unforgivable excesses. Called Fréron's 'gilded youth', adorned with exquisite elegance which made people term them Dandies, these youths crowded streets and squares, dominating by sheer violence, abusing patriots, and, lastly, replacing by their atrocious revenges those of the sans-culottes with their pikes and clogs of whom they were in a manner the successors.

Besides this, reaction instituted corruption. After the ferocious alliances of the Mountain came the frivolity of Thermidoreans, but too connected with the characteristics of the French court and the disgusting practices which so blemished the Regency. The Jacobin Mountain had practised outward simplicity, frugality, austere incorruptibility; the counter-revolutionaries, quite opposite to this, displayed an ardour for showy attire, for shocking luxury and pleasure, quite the reverse of true republicanism. On all sides were seen sumptuous feasts, balls, private fêtes soon crowded with anti-revolutionaries. Intrigue reappeared everywhere, accompanied by women interfering in politics. Beauty was once more a corrupting agency and we saw Madame Tallien more or less officially co-opted on the Committee of Public Safety. Gradually the old aristocracy, which had pretended ruin from the revolutionary requisitions and taxes, now openly proclaiming splendour and lavishness; the men of Thermidor, and Girondin survivors, managed admission to the aristocratic St Germain salons, and under such roofs shed that republican simplicity which had earlier guaranteed their integrity. . . .

I have also to remember a really shameful detail of the orgiastic carnival that had usurped the rule of unbending republicans. Amid the balls that now seemed the chief concern of those once acclaimed for Virtue, one above all was exciting, incredible to posterity. In the St Germain area arose a dancing club, called 'The Victims' Ball'. To join it, you had to prove some relative had been a victim of the guillotine.

RENÉ LEVASSEUR. *Mémoires*
(See Richard Bienvenu)

A FINE HOUR

This is one of Liberty's finest hours, the heads of the conspirators have just fallen on the scaffold. The Republic is victorious, and the same thrust makes the thrones of all mortal tyrants shudder. The example will convince them, should any still doubt it, that the people of France will never submit to a master. Let us then go and unite ourselves to our fellow citizens, let us go out and share the universal happiness; the hour of a tyrant's death is a festival of Fraternity.

JEAN-LAMBERT TALLIEN, to the Convention

ONCE MORE LAFAYETTE

As when far off the warbled strains are heard
    That soar on Morning's wing the vales among;
      Within his cage the imprison'd Matin Bird
Swells the full chorus with generous song:

He bathes no pinion in the dewy light,
    No Father's joy, no Lover's bliss he shares,
      Yet still the rising radiance cheers his sight –
His fellows' Freedom soothes the Captive's cares!

Thou, Fayette! Who didst wake with startling voice
    Life's better sun from that long waking night,
      Thus in thy Country's triumphs shalt rejoice,
And mock with raptures high the Dungeon's might:

For lo! The Morning struggles into Day,
And Slavery's spectres shriek and vanish from the ray!

SAMUEL TAYLOR COLERIDGE, on a false report
of Lafayette's escape from an Austrian prison

THE BITER BIT

Despite the fact that my interrogation still awaits me, I must anticipate, dear friend, being soon sent for trial. In ordinary times, I could
rely on my innocence and would have no need to fear the approaching trial, but in our wretched position, and after all the slanders, the
dreadful insults and noisy assaults of every kind that have been flung
at me since my imprisonment, it would be useless to have any illusions about what will be done to me. Engulfed as I am in this terrible
abuse, hearing myself called wicked plotter, bloodthirsty tiger and
the like, without one scrap of evidence, is the mere preface to my
trial, a tactic used by those who hate Liberty, in order to be rid of me
with complete finality.

So I expect to be offered up to public opinion, inflamed against
me by every sort of machination, and given no real trial at all. I long
realised this, though said nothing so as not to upset you, by the injury
that all this may give you. Thus I shall meet my death for too much
zeal in serving my country, too much assiduity, and for performing
the government's orders – my hands, my heart, alike blameless. But,
dear friend, what will be your fate, and that of my unhappy children?
You will soon be thrown into direst poverty; that, at least, will be the
most significant proof that I have done my patriotic duty with genuine Republican purity; nevertheless, what is to happen to you all?
Such evil broodings attack and torture me night and day! Was it my
destiny to meet such an end? A dreadful idea! To perish as a conspira-
tor, I, who have ever fought such creatures! Is this to be my reward
for patriotic fervour? Through all these dire happenings only one ray
of satisfaction remains for me, the knowledge of your conviction that
I am innocent. Knowing this at least makes me hope that you will
never fail to reiterate to our children that their father died miserable
but innocent, and that you ever trusted and respected him. I implore
you, do not surrender to grief, but keep yourself well for yourself, for
your poor children. Forget any small differences between us, they
came only from my own quick temper, they meant nothing to my

true feelings, which have always been devoted to you. Alas! My dear friend, who could have imagined such an end for me, always a stranger to intrigue, never given over to an itch for wealth. . . .

ANTOINE FOUQUIER-TINVILLE, to his wife

THE GREAT PAINTER
AS TURNCOAT

Citizens, with the majestic and grand position you have adopted, with that ineffable power you have displayed so magnificently, will you still continue to tolerate a traitor, accomplice of Catiline, on your Committee of General Security? Will you tolerate David, usurper, artistic tyrant, as feeble as he is criminal, will you tolerate, I must repeat, that contemptible creature, who refused to show his face amongst us on that memorable night of the 9th, yet who continues to venture unpunished into regions where he dreamed of committing the crimes of his leader, Robespierre, the tyrant? The moment has arrived, citizens, when the shadows of the monster whom France has now vanquished, must be dispersed; that power, protector of Liberty, that heroism, national champion, must be maintained. David is not alone in selling himself to Robespierre: Cromwell's court remains alive: his ministers, their faces daubed with crime, will shortly be revealed. I myself swear, at this very moment, to hunt them down, to the death, but meanwhile I say no more than to move that David, traitor, be removed from the Committee and be at once replaced.

ETIENNE DUMONT, to the Convention

I am unaware of the accusations against me, but none can more vehemently accuse me than I do myself. The extent to which that cur deceived me is unimaginable. He betrayed me by hypocritical professions and, citizens, I assure you managed to do so only by such means. My candour has periodically earned your respect, so, citizens, I beg you to believe me when I declare that death is more tolerable than my present emotions. From now, I solemnly swear, and am convinced that, even in these wretched circumstances, I am fulfilling my oath and will no longer devote myself to men, but to principles alone. . . .

It was in no welcome to Robespierre that I approached Robespierre [at the Jacobin Club], it was to ascend the dais and request that the hour of the Festival of the 10th Thermidor be put forward. I did not embrace him, did not even touch him, for he was repulsive to all. Certainly, when Couthon addressed him about despatching his speech to the provincial communes, I remarked that this would agitate the entire Republic. At this, Robespierre cried out that he had nothing left, but to drink the hemlock. I did assure him that I would drink it with him. I am not alone in being deceived by him; many other citizens also considered him a man of Virtue.

JACQUES-LOUIS DAVID, to the Convention

THE FUTURE

Do we not recognise once more, the little bronze-complexioned Artillery-Officer of Toulon, home from the Italian Wars? Grim enough; of lean, almost cruel aspect: for he has been in trouble, in ill-health; also in ill-favour, as a man promoted, deservingly or not, by the Terrorists and Robespierre Junior. But does not Barras know him? Will not Barras speak a word for him? Yes, – if at any time it will serve Barras so to do. Somewhat forlorn of fortune, for the present, stands that Artillery-Officer; looks, with those deep earnest eyes of his, into a future as waste as the most. Taciturn; yet with the strangest utterances in him, if you awaken him, which smite home, like light or lightning: – on the whole, rather dangerous.   THOMAS CARLYLE, 1837

COUNTER-TERROR

The insurgents' guns are aiming at the city at the former Porte Saint-Antoine; the Grande Rue du Faubourg is packed with squads of citizens bearing pikes and a few old-style muskets; no armed pickets as yet in the rues Charonne, Nicholas, Montreuil, Traversière, etc.; yet the people seem resolute not to be disarmed. Women have gathered in every street and are making uproar. Bread is the physical cause of their revolt, but its soul is the Constitution of 1793, as they confess.

Police report

I OBEYED ORDERS

I have no reproach for myself. I have always obeyed the laws. I was never the creature of Robespierre and Saint-Just, quite the reverse. Four times I myself was almost arrested. I obeyed orders. I die for my country blameless, and I die satisfied. Posterity will recognise my innocence.

ANTOINE FOUQUIER-TINVILLE, ex-Public Prosecutor, last note before execution

HOPE?

They have murdered one Robespierre. This Robespierre they tell us was a cruel tyrant, and now that he is put out of the way, all will go well in France. Astraea will again return to that earth from which she has been an emigrant, and all nations will resort to her golden scales. It is very extraordinary, that the very instant the mode of Paris is known here, it becomes all the fashion in London. This is their jargon. It is the old *bon ton* of robbers, who cast their common crimes upon the wickedness of their departed associates. I care little about the memory of this same Robespierre. I am sure he was an execrable villain. I rejoiced at his punishment neither more nor less than I should at the execution of the present Directory, or any of its members. But who gave Robespierre the power of being a tyrant? And who were the instruments of his tyranny? The present virtuous Constitution-mongers. He was a tyrant, they were his satellites and his hangmen. Their sole merit is in the murder of their colleague. They have expiated their other murders by a new murder. It has always been the case among these banditti. They have always had the knife at each other's throats, after they had almost blunted it at the throats of every honest man. These people thought that, in the commerce of murder, he was likely to have the better of the bargain if any time was lost; they therefore took one of their short revolutionary methods, and massacred him in a manner so perfidious and cruel, as would shock all humanity, if the stroke was not struck by the present rulers on one of their own associates. But this last act of infidelity and murder is to expiate all the rest, and to qualify them for the amity of a humane and virtuous sovereign and civilized people. I have heard that a Tartar believes when he has killed a man, that all his estimable qualities pass with his clothes and arms to the murderer; but I have never heard that it was the opinion of any savage Scythian, that, if he kills a brother villain, he is, *ipso facto*, absolved of all his own offences. The Tartarian doctrine is the most terrible opinion. The murderers of Robespierre, besides what they are entitled to by being engaged in the same tontine of infamy, are his representatives, have inherited all his murderous qualities in addition to their own private stock. But it seems we are always to be of a party with the last and victorious assassins. I confess I am of a different mind, and am rather inclined, of the two, to think and speak less hardly of a dead ruffian, than to associate with the living. I could better bear the stench of the gibbeted murderer than the society of the bloody felons who yet annoy the world. Whilst they wait the recompense due to their ancient crimes, they merit new punishment by the new offences they commit. There is a period to the offences of Robespierre. They survive in his assassins. Better a living dog, says the old proverb, than a dead lion; not so here. Murderers and hogs never look well till they are hanged. From villainy no good can arise, but in the example of its fate. So I leave them their dead Robespierre, either to gibbet his memory, or to deify him in their Pantheon with their Marat and their Mirabeau. EDMUND BURKE

NEW RELIGION IN BRITTANY

I went upon Easter Sunday to the Cathedral (at Quimper), and found a numerous congregation there. The altar was lighted up by twelve large waxen tapers; the holy water was sprinkled upon the congregation; and the incense was burnt, with the accustomed ceremonies; but even here democratic spleen manifested itself in disturbing what it is no longer allowed to interdict. In the most solemn part of the service, the *Marseillois Hymn* was heard from the organ: that war-whoop, to whose sound the band of regicides who attacked their sovereign in his palace marched; and which, during the last three years, has been the watch-word of violence, rapine, and murder! How incongruous were its notes in the temple of the Prince of Peace! A blackguard-looking fellow close to me, whom I knew, by his uncombed hair, dirty linen, ragged attire, and contemptuous gestures, to be a *véritable sans-culotte*, joined his voice to the music, and echoed '*Aux armes, citoyens!*' Fear alone kept the people quiet; and of its influence in this country I have witnessed astonishing proofs, which demonstrate, beyond volumes of reasoning, the terror inspired by the revolutionary government.

MAJOR TRENCH, of the Marines (shipmate, on HMS *Alexander*,
of the famous William Bligh), prisoner of war in France, 1794–5.
Letters written in France to a Friend in London, 1796

A CHIMERA

Absolute equality is a chimera. If it existed, one would have to assume complete equality in intelligence, virtue, physical strength, education and fortune among all. . . . We must be governed by the best. . . . Now with very few exceptions, you will find such men only amongst property-owners. . . . You must therefore guarantee the rights of the rich.

FRANÇOIS ANTOINE BOISSY D'ANGLAS, introducing the Constitution of 1795

THE DIRECTORY

A better *organized* constitution has never yet been organized by human wisdom.   TOM PAINE

In all constituted communities, society consists only of those possessing property. The rest are merely Fourth Estate who ranged amongst those called 'supernumerary citizens' await the time when they themselves gain property.   *Gazette de France*

THE END OF THE CONVENTION

Some call for Barras to be made commandant; he conquered in Thermidor. Some, what is more to the purpose, bethink them of the Citizen Buonaparte, unemployed Artillery Officer, who took Toulon. A man of head, a man of action: Barras is named Commandant's Cloak; this young Artillery Officer is named Commandant. He was in the Gallery at the moment, and heard it; he withdrew, some half hour, to consider with himself: after a half hour of grim considering, to be or not to be, he answers *Yea*.

And now, a man of head being at the centre of it, the whole matter gets vital. Swift, to Camp of Sablons; to secure the Artillery, there are not twenty men guarding it! A swift Adjutant, Murat is the name of him, gallops; gets thither some minutes within time, for Lepelletier was also on march that way: the cannon are ours. And now beset this post, and beset that; rapid and firm: at the Wicket of the Louvre, in the Cul de Sac Dauphin, in Rue Saint-Honoré, from Pont Neuf all along the North Quays, southward to Pont *ci-devant* Royal, – rank round the Sanctuary of the Tuileries, a ring of steel discipline; let every gunner have his match burning, and all men stand to their arms!

Thus there is Permanent-session through night; and thus at sunrise of the morrow, there is seen sacred Insurrection once again: vessel of state labouring on the bar; and tumultuous sea all around her, beating *générale*, arming and sounding, – not ringing tocsin, for we have left no tocsin but our own in the Pavilion of Unity. It is an imminence of shipwreck, for the whole world to gaze at. Frightfully she labours, that poor ship, within cable-length of port; huge peril for her. However, she has a man at the helm. Insurgent messages, received, and not received; messenger admitted blindfolded; counsel and counter-counsel: the poor ship labours! – Vendémiaire 13th, year 4: curious enough, of all days, it is the fifth day of October, anniversary of that Menadmarch, six years ago; by sacred right of Insurrection we are got thus far.

Lepelletier has seized the Church of Saint-Roch; has seized the Pont Neuf, our piquet there retreating without fire. Stray shots fall from Lepelletier; rattle down the very Tuileries staircase. On the other hand, women advance dishevelled, shrieking, Peace: Lepelletier behind them waving his hat in sign that we shall fraternise. Steady! The Artillery Officer is steady as bronze; can be quick as lightning. He sends eight hundred muskets with ball-cartridges to the Convention itself; honourable Members shall act with these in case of extremity: whereat they look grave enough. Four of the afternoon is struck.

Lepelletier, making nothing by messengers, by fraternity or hat-waving, bursts out, along the Southern Quai Voltaire, along streets and passages, treble-quick, in huge veritable onslaught! Whereupon thou bronze Artillery Officer – ? 'Fire!' say the bronze lips. Roar and again roar, continual, volcano-like, goes his great gun, in the Cul de Sac Dauphin against the Church of Saint-Roch; go his great guns on the Pont Royal; go all his great guns; – blow to air some two hundred men, mainly about the Church of Saint-Roch! Lepelletier cannot

stand such horse-play; no Sectioner can stand it; the forty-thousand
yield on all sides, scour towards covert. 'Some hundred or so of them
gathered about the Théâtre de la République; but,' says he, 'a few
shells dislodged them. It was all finished at six.'

The ship is over the bar; free she bounds shoreward, – amid
shouting and vivats! Citizen Buonaparte is 'named General of the
Interior, by acclamation'; quelled Sections have to disarm such
humour as they may; sacred right of Insurrection is gone for ever!
The Sieyès Constitution can disembark itself, and begin marching.
The miraculous Convention Ship has got to land; – and is there, shall
we figuratively say, changed, as Epic Ships are wont, into a kind of
Sea Nymph, never to sail more; to roam the waste Azure, a Miracle in
History!   THOMAS CARLYLE, 1837

A FICTION WRITER

Clisson, from the start, was fated to be a soldier. Even in childhood
he was soaked in the careers of famous generals. He was a student of
military elementals while his fellow scholars merely chased whores.
When reaching military age he made each stage of his service
extraordinary by some glittering action. Still adolescent, he yet
gained supreme rank. His triumphs followed each other, he became
famous, hailed by the people as one of their champions.

Envy and slander, vile instincts gnawing at growing fame, undermine many useful men, stifle much genius. Talent, self-confidence,
bravery, determination, only increased Clisson's detractors, offending those who were in positions to help him. His greatness of spirit
was condemned as hauteur, his very resolution earned rebuke. Naus-
eated by his achievements, which magnified his foes without attract-
ing friends, he found himself compelled to retire into introspection.
For the first time he examined his career, his inclinations, his being.
He spent a month in the countryside around Lyons with an acquaintance. Always passionate for soldiering, he had been swept along by
the gales of history, overwhelmed by his desires. His soul, enslaved
by them, was still unaware of other interests, other values.

This introspection forced him to comprehend that life offered
more than war, that destructive impulses are insufficient. The arts of
human sympathy, helping humanity, creating happiness, are at least
their equal.

He wished to spend time assessing such thoughts, hoping to construct order from the intellectual muddle that had begun assailing him. Taking leave, he hastened to neighbouring Champvert, inviting himself to a friend's manor.

This region, encircling the town, was of the finest, uniting the best of human effort and natural beauty. He drew wonder from the ravishing sight of dawn and dusk, the track of the evening star which throws silver over copse and meadow. All gave his senses a freshness he had never envisaged: changes of light and landscape, bird song, murmurs of streams, despite being long familiar with all of them, though without sensitivity, without the least agitation. Poor fellow: so loaded with illusions, impulses, cares, your soul had been impervious to beauty, to Nature.

A natural sceptic, Clisson relapsed into melancholy, meditation became mere dreaminess. His future seemed a waste, without hope or fear. Such apathy, foreign to one of his exceptional stamp, might have caused a mood of sleep-walker's unconsciousness. Rising at dawn, he now trudged the countryside, always brooding over his novel thoughts, and often visiting the spa at Alles, a league distant, there to pass whole mornings watching passers-by, wandering through trees, perusing some serious book.

Then, one day, amongst these few who chanced to be in his vicinity, he saw a pair of pretty girls, clearly absorbed in their walk. They had arrived on their own, with the lively merriment of adolescents.

Amélie possessed a beautiful figure, eyes, skin, hair, and was seventeen. Eugénie, at sixteen, was less beautiful. Amélie's eyes appeared to say: 'You are in love with me, but not you alone. Plenty of others are under my sway. You must realise that flattery alone will gratify me. I delight in compliments, in inflated addresses.'

Eugénie disdained to stare at men. Her smile disclosed the loveliest teeth you could imagine. If a hand was offered, she accepted it shyly, withdrew it swiftly. It might be considered provocative to show so briefly the daintiest of hands, whose whiteness of skin markedly set off the blue veins.

Amélie resembled some French music, enjoyable because the chord sequences are easily followed and tuneful: most of us enjoy harmony. Eugénie was more like the nightingale's song, or a piece by Paesiello, accessible only to the sensitive, music whose melody gives rapture and passion to those who can profoundly appreciate it, ordinary as it may be to others.

Amélie conquered most youths: she was a general in the field of love. Eugénie attracted only the man of passion, whose love is not that of convention and caste gallantry, but that of the true ardour of the heart. Amélie stimulated by beauty. Eugénie was destined to arouse stormy passion in one heart alone, a passion worthy . . . of a hero. Amélie's splendid skin and eyes were equal to Clisson's present disposition. He managed a chance to speak, then escorted both girls back to their own manor, where he besought leave to visit them alone. He was utterly entranced by them, was never tired of recollecting the figure of Amélie, of repeating her words. He let himself linger over her alluring outlines, yet was also pursued by a memory equally vivid, that of silent and modest Eugénie. He discovered that she held mysterious power over him, even surpassing the smiles of gorgeous Amélie.

For their part, the pair were reacting in ways very dissimilar. . . .

NAPOLEON BONAPARTE. *Clisson et Eugénie*

Napoleon began a life of action because of his failure in literature.

JOHANN WOLFGANG VON GOETHE

France has now for its chief the most enterprising and fortunate man, either for project or daring execution, the world has known for many ages. Compared with him, there is not a man in the British government, or under its authority, has any chance with him. That he is ambitious, the world knows, and he always was so; but he knew where to stop.

TOM PAINE, 1804
(See A. J. Ayer)

BURKE REBUKES THE DIRECTORY

On this their gaudy day the new regicide Directory sent for their diplomatic rabble, as bad as themselves in principle, but infinitely worse in degradation. They called them out by a sort of roll of their nations, one after another, much in the manner in which they called wretches out of their prison to the guillotine. When these ambassadors of infamy appeared before them, the chief director, in the name of the rest, treated each of them with a short, affected, pedantic, insolent, theatric laconium: a sort of epigram of contempt. When they had thus insulted them in a style and language which never before was heard, and which no sovereign would for a moment endure from another, supposing any of them frantic enough to use it; to finish their outrage, they drummed and trumpeted the wretches out of their hall of audience.

Among the objects of this insolent buffoonery was a person supposed to represent the king of Prussia. To this worthy representative they did not so much condescend to mention his master; they did not seem to know that he had one; they addressed themselves solely to Prussia in the abstract, notwithstanding the infinite obligation they owed to their early protector for the first recognition and alliance, and for the part of his territory he gave into their hands for the first-fruits of his homage. None but dead monarchs are so much as mentioned by them, and those only to insult the living by an invidious comparison. They told the Prussians they ought to learn, after the example of Frederick the Great, a love of France. What a pity it is, that he, who loved France so well as to chastise it, was not now alive, by an unsparing use of the rod (which indeed he would have spared little) to give them another instance of his paternal affection. But the Directory were mistaken. These are not days in which monarchs value themselves upon the title of *great*: they are grown *philosophic*: they are satisfied to be good. . . .

The imperial ambassador was not in waiting, but they found for Austria a good Judean representation. With great judgment his highness the Grand Duke had sent the most atheistic coxcomb to be found in Florence to represent at the bar of impiety, the house of apostolic majesty, and the descendants of the pious, though high-minded Maria Theresa. He was sent to humble the whole race of Austria before those grim assassins, reeking with the blood of the daughter of Maria Theresa, whom they sent, half-dead in a dung-cart, to a cruel execution; and this true-born son of apostasy and infidelity, this renegade from the faith, and from all honour and all humanity, drove an Austrian coach over the stones which were yet wet with her blood; – with that blood which dropped every step from her tumbril, all the way she was drawn from the horrid prison, in which they had finished all the cruelty and horrors, not executed in the face of the sun!

EDMUND BURKE, 1796

TALLIEN

Nero wished the Roman people had but one neck.* The wish of the more exalted Tallien, when he sat in judgment, was that his sovereign had eighty-three heads, that he might send one to every one of the departments. Tallien will make an excellent figure at Guildhall at the next sheriff's feast. He may open the ball with my Lady Mayoress. But this will be after he has retired from the public table, and gone into the private room for the enjoyment of more social and unreserved conversation with the Ministers of State and the judges of the bench. There these ministers and magistrates will hear him entertain the worthy aldermen with an instructing and pleasing narrative of the manner in which he made the rich citizens of Bordeaux squeak, and gently led them by the public credit of the guillotine to disgorge their anti-revolutionary pelf.

All this will be the display, . . . when our regicide is on a visit of ceremony. At home nothing will equal the pomp and splendour of the *Hôtel de la République*. There another scene of gaudy grandeur will be opened. When his citizen excellency keeps the festival, which every citizen is ordered to observe, for the glorious execution of Louis the Sixteenth, and renews his oath of detestation of kings, a grand ball, of course, will be given on the occasion. Then what a hurly-burly; – what a crowding; – what a glare of a thousand flambeaux in the square; – what a clamour of a thousand footmen contending at the door; – what a rattling of a thousand coaches of duchesses, countesses, and Lady Marys, choking the way, and overturning each other, in a struggle who should be first to pay her court to the Citoyenne.   EDMUND BURKE

THE NEW ARRIVAL

Do you think I am conquering Italy to bring fame and fortune to advocates of the Directory like Carnot and Barras? And do you think I am doing it to establish a Republic? What an idea! It is an illusion that infatuates the French, but it will pass like all the rest. They need glory, they need to satisfy their vanity; as for liberty, however, they do not know its meaning.   NAPOLEON BONAPARTE, to Count Metzi

* *Burke may have libelled Nero and overlooked Caligula. London, in fact, was not rewarded with a sight of Tallien.*

The real conquests, the only unregretted ones, are those against ignorance. The worthiest and most significant occupation for nations is to enlarge the frontiers of human knowledge.

NAPOLEON BONAPARTE

THE SPIRIT OF LIBERTY

Religion, the feudal system, and monarchy have in turn governed Europe for twenty centuries, but from the peace you have just concluded dates the era of representative governments. You have succeeded in organising this great nation so that its territory is circumscribed by the bounds which Nature herself has set. You have done even more. The two most beautiful countries in Europe, once so famous for arts, sciences and the great men whose cradle they were, behold with joyful expectation the Spirit of Liberty rise from the graves of their ancestors.

GENERAL NAPOLEON BONAPARTE, to the Directors

Napoleon was referring to his own Treaty of Campo Formio, signalling Austrian defeat and her relinquishing of two Italian provinces to form two 'independent' Italian republics.

THE SUPPER PARTY

Several days before the one appointed for the coup, which, of course, he already knows, Fouché gives a supper party. Bonaparte and Réal are invited, and, glancing around as they settle down to eat, they realise that all the conspirators are around them, the entire cabal pledged to overthrow the Directory. The guests swap uneasy looks. Can the police be without, poised to arrest them all and strangle the plot at birth? Perhaps there are some who know sufficient history to remember the macabre banquet which Peter the Great gave in Old Moscow to the Strelitzy Guards Officers, at the end of which the guests' heads were offered him – dessert! But such candid atrocities are scarcely Fouché's way, and when tonight, amazing the plotters, the last arrival is seen to be President Gohier – in humour diabolically menacing – against whom the plot is concentrated, they listen to a staggering exchange. The newcomer asks the Police Chief for the latest news. Fouché looks unconcerned, eyes half-closed, as if barely aware of all his guests; 'Nothing new, always the same babble about plots. I know how much and how little to believe. If anything really serious is about, you will soon see the mark of it in the Place de la République.'

This deft reference to the guillotine freezes the conspirators. Is he mocking Gohier, or themselves? Probably Fouché himself cannot answer that, and is surrendering to his sole pleasure, the stimulant of deception, the luxury of danger that spices the alarming danger of playing the double game.   STEFAN ZWEIG, 1929

A MEETING

Generals, deputies, ministers of state, Talleyrand himself, pay their respects to the warlord, and of course the Minister of Police is soon calling. Driving to Rue Chantereine, he sends in his card to Bonaparte. But, as far as the General is concerned, this M. Fouché is small beer. . . . Let him wait a bit. Thus, Joseph Fouché, no less patiently sits through his weary hour, could doubtless expect another, another still, had not Réal, one of Bonaparte's associates in the approaching coup, noticed the man of power, he with whom all Paris desires audience, esconced so humiliatingly. Horrified at this unfortunate solecism, he hurries to the General and explains that to prolong Fouché's ordeal would be catastrophic. This man with a gesture could undermine the whole conspiracy. At this, Bonaparte strides to the waiting room, overwhelms him with apologies, escorts Fouché back to his study, and remains alone with him for two hours.

STEFAN ZWEIG, 1929

As Chief of Police, Fouché long ensured Napoleon's power, until his dismissal in 1810.

A MINISTER

The Minister of Police is one who minds his own business, before proceeding to mind that of others.

CHARLES MAURICE DE TALLEYRAND, on Joseph Fouché

BRUMAIRE, THE END OF THE DIRECTORY

The Minister of Police informs his fellow citizens that the Council met at Saint-Cloud to discuss the interests of the Republic, when General Bonaparte, who had appeared before the Council of Five Hundred to reveal the revolutionary conspiracy, narrowly missed becoming victim of assassination. However, the Genius of the Republic saved the General. All republicans can remain calm, for their wishes will now be fulfilled. The weak may remain calm, for they will be succoured by the strong. Those only need fear who encouraged disorder, tried to muddle public opinion, and stirred up breaches of the peace. All necessary measures have been taken to restrain persons in the last category.   JOSEPH FOUCHÉ

NAPOLEON BONAPARTE

What have you done with the France I left so prosperous in your hands? I left you peace, I find you at war. I left you victorious, I find only defeats. I left you the spoils of Italy and find only penal laws and wretchedness. What have you done with the hundred thousand Frenchmen, my friends, my comrades in glory? They have perished. All this I cannot endure.   To the Directors

Representatives of the people, you are in no ordinary situation, you are perched on a volcano. Yesterday when you summoned me to inform me of the order for your removal and charged me with carrying it out, I was content. I gathered my comrades immediately, we hurried to help you. But now, I am crushed by slander. People are talking of Caesar, Cromwell, Martial Law! Had I wanted to wipe out my country's freedom, I would not have bothered myself with your orders.

I swear before you that the nation has no defender more whole-hearted than I, but its safety depends on you, you alone! The Government no longer exists. Four Directors have submitted resignations, the fifth is under arrest for his personal security. The Council of Five Hundred is divided, nothing remains but the Council of Ancients. Let it adopt measures. It has only to speak. I am ready to obey its orders. Let us save Liberty! Let us save Equality!   To the Council of Ancients

THE AFTERMATH

A PRIME ENCHANTRESS

Oh! pleasant exercise of hope and joy!
For mighty were the auxiliars which then stood
Upon our side, we who were strong in love!
Bliss was it in that dawn to be alive,
But to be young was very heaven! – Oh! times
In which the meagre, stale, forbidding ways
Of custom, law, and statute, took at once
The attraction of a country in romance!
When Reason seemed the most to assert her rights,
When most intent on making of herself
A prime Enchantress – to assist the work
Which then was going forward in her name!
Not favoured spots alone, but the whole earth,
The beauty wore of promise, that which sets
(As at some moment might not be unfelt
Among the powers of paradise itself)
The budding rose above the rose full blown.

WILLIAM WORDSWORTH. *The Prelude*

A SUMMING UP

With respect to the French revolution, it was begun by good men and
on good principles, and I have always believed that it would have
gone on so, had not the provocative influence of foreign powers, of
which Pitt was the principal and vindictive agent, distracted it into
madness, and sown jealousies among the leaders.

The people of England have now two revolutions before them.
The one [American] as an example; the other as a warning. Their own
wisdom will direct them what to choose and what to avoid, and in
everything which regards their happiness, combined with the common good of mankind, I wish them honour and success.

TOM PAINE
(See A. J. Ayer)

EPITAPHS ON THE REVOLUTION

The Revolution could not tolerate a Church. Why? Because it was itself a church.   JULES MICHELET

Today there are few châteaux left. The decrees of Richelieu and the Revolution have seen to that. Yet when we find ourselves even now in our travels under the walls of Taillebourg or Tancarville, when in the depths of the Ardennes forest, in the Montsornet Gorge, we catch sight above our heads of the squinting oblique eye watching us pass, our heart contracts and we feel something of the sufferings of those who for so many centuries waited at the foot of the towers. To know it we do not even need to have read the old histories. The souls of our fathers still throb in us for pains that have been forgotten, almost as the man who has been wounded feels an ache in the hand he has lost.
                                                          JULES MICHELET

The Revolution was a fall of snow on blossoming trees.
                                                    ALBERT SCHWEITZER

Let this society perish, then, through the fury of its factions and the fierceness of its civil wars. Let the cities return to their original state of forests, let the forests become the dens of mankind, and then, after many centuries have passed, when their wickedness and perversity have vanished under the rust of barbarity, and they have again relapsed into the primitive, then once more they will be ready to be civilised.   JULES MICHELET

I blame no one for the evils of this Revolution, for at the start all desired it, all tried to assist it within his limits and talent; from the King to the most humble subject, all laboured for it, to a greater or less degree.   LOUIS-PHILIPPE, COMTE DE SÉGUR

What was the Revolution? Myself!   NAPOLEON BONAPARTE

A doctrine that started as a method of emancipating the middle class changed, after 1789, into a method of disciplining the working class.
                                                        HAROLD J. LASKI

NAPOLEON I

We hear nothing in derogation of women, we Westerners. We regard them as being almost equal to ourselves, a great error. Orientals are wiser and juster. They have pronounced females the natural property of males. And, in effect, Nature has made them our slaves. It is only because of masculine foolishness that they have dared claim equality. They abuse their rights in order to corrupt and dominate us.

Courage is like love, it feeds on hope.

I have always enjoyed analysis, and if I were to be seriously in love, I'd analyse my love bit by bit.

Man has been made from the earth, warmed by the sun, and bound together by an electric fluid.

In Religion, I see not the mystery of the Incarnation but the mystery of the social order. It links the idea of equality with Heaven, and this prevents the rich being massacred by the poor. . . . Unbelievers are not to be governed, they are to be shot.

I felt bound to organise the education of the future generation and in such a way that their political and moral opinions could be supervised.

My motto was the career open to talents, without distinctions of birth or fortune.

Money is stronger than Despotism.

Power is never ridiculous.

What was it that made the Revolution? It was Vanity. Liberty was only the pretext.

Do you know, Fontanos, what amazes me most in the world? The inability of force to maintain anything at all. There are only two powers in the world; the sword and the mind. In the long run the sword is always defeated by the mind.

War is a good sport, a beautiful occupation.

I am not a man like other men; the laws of morality and decorum could not be intended to apply to me.

Noisy festivals are a necessity. Blockheads love noise, and the masses are blockheads.

A lump of shit in silk stockings.   On Talleyrand

What a pity that so great a man should have been so badly brought up!
                        CHARLES MAURICE DE TALLEYRAND, on Napoleon I

I loved Napoleon; I had even become personally attached to him despite his faults; at the start of his career I had felt drawn to him by the irresistible magnetism displayed by every great genius: I was sincerely grateful for his many kindnesses. Why should I hide it? I had basked in his glory and in the rays it threw over all those who helped in his noble endeavour.   CHARLES MAURICE DE TALLEYRAND. *Mémoires*

EMPEROR NAPOLEON I: 'Tell me, Duc d'Otranto, isn't it true that you voted for the execution of Louis XVI?'
JOSEPH FOUCHÉ: 'That Sire, is perfectly true. It was the first service that I was able to render your Majesty.'

Treason! That is nothing more than a matter of timing.
                              CHARLES MAURICE DE TALLEYRAND

ANOTHER VOICE

Vernon, the butcher Cumberland, Wolfe, Hawke,
     Prince Ferdinand, Granby, Burgoyne, Keppel, Howe,
Evil and good, have had their tithe of talk,
     And filled their signposts then, like Wellesley now.
Each in their turn like Banquo's monarchs stalk,
     Followers of fame, 'nine farrow' of that sow:
France too had Buonaparte and Dumourier
Recorded in the *Moniteur* and *Courier.*

Barnave, Brissot, Condorcet, Mirabeau,
    Pétion, Clootz, Danton, Marat, La Fayette,
Were French, and famous people, as we know;
    And there were others, scarce forgotten yet,
Joubert, Hoche, Marceau, Lannes, Dessaix, Moreau,
    With many of the military set,
Exceedingly remarkable at times,
But not at all adapted to my rhymes.   Canto I

And I will war at least in words (and should
    My chance so happen – deeds) with all who war
With thought; and of thought's foes by far most rude,
    Tyrants and sycophants have been and are.
I know not who may conquer. If I could
    Have such a prescience, it should be no bar
To this my plain, sworn, downright detestation
Of every despotism in every nation.

It is not that I adulate the people.
    Without me, there are demagogues enough
And infidels to pull down every steeple
    And set up in their stead some proper stuff.
Whether they may sow scepticism to reap hell,
    As is the Christian dogma rather rough,
I do not know. I wish men to be free
As much from mobs as kings – from you as me.

The consequence is, being of no party,
    I shall offend all parties. Never mind.
My words at least are more sincere and hearty
    Than if I sought to sail before the wind.
He who has nought to gain can have small art. He
    Who neither wishes to be bound nor bind
May still expatiate freely, as will I,
Nor give my voice to slavery's jackal cry.   Canto IX
    GEORGE GORDON, LORD BYRON. *Don Juan*

THE URN OF BITTER PROPHECY

The world's great age begins anew,
    The golden years return,
The earth doth like a snake renew
    Her winter weeds outworn:
Heaven smiles, and faiths and empires gleam,
Like wrecks of a dissolving dream. . . .

Oh, write no more the tale of Troy,
    If earth Death's scroll must be!
Nor mix with Laian rage the joy
    Which dawns upon the free:
Although a subtler Sphinx renew
Riddles of death Thebes never knew. . . .

Oh, cease! must hate and death return?
    Cease! must men kill and die?
Cease! drain not to its dregs the urn
    Of bitter prophecy.
The world is weary of the past,
Oh, might it die or rest at last!

PERCY BYSSHE SHELLEY. *Hellas*

A LAST WORD

A DOCTOR: 'You, sir, are the Father of the French People.'
MARQUIS DE LAFAYETTE, dying: 'That is so – to the extent that they
    do nothing I tell them to.'   (See Peter Buckman, 1977)

Earlier James Fenimore Cooper had written in the Evening Post, *on
Lafayette in America:*

He owed us no allegiance, no duty, not one drop of blood. In possession of all that commonly renders life desirable, he abandoned his
pleasures to risk life itself in our behalf. . . . In the darkest period of
our distress, he joined us, not an adventurer in quest of preferment,
but one who had all to bestow and little to receive.

(See Stephen Railton, 1978)

THE SECRET PEOPLE

A war that we understood not came over the world and woke
    Americans,
Frenchmen, Irish; but we knew not the things they spoke.
They talked about rights and nature and peace and the people's
    reign:
And the squires, our masters, bade us fight; and never scorned us
    again.
Weak if we be for ever, none could condemn us then;
Men called us serfs and drudges; men knew that we were men.
In foam and flame at Trafalgar, on Albuera plains,
We lay in living ruins; firing and fearing not
The strange fierce face of Frenchmen who knew for what they
    fought . . .
And the man who seemed to be more than man we strained
    against and broke,
And we broke our own rights with him. And still we never
    spoke.
                                 G. K. CHESTERTON

A NINETEENTH-CENTURY
REVOLUTIONARY LOOKS BACK

His dressing-gown was red; his neck was long and scraggy; when
swallowing, his Adam's apple jerked up and down, very obviously.
This swallowing motion was frequent, because of his stimulating
reading matter. His hair bristled alarmingly above a huge forehead,
and he had a habit of tugging his goatee, index and middle finger wed
like scissors. He might almost be assumed to be the Devil, or an executioner. Both these would have found his papers amusing, for they
were death-warrants. Five hundred, on his desk, literary contraband,
having been filched from the archives of the bloodiest period in all
the blood-drenched record of the Hôtel de Ville, that evil period
with the powerful and unique title, the Terror.

What did he desire, what was his quest? These were printed
forms. The Terror engorged so many people that it had no time to
write out each warrant in full, before it was signed and sealed. The
text was prepared in advance for the hurried insertion of a name, and,

beneath each was the arrogant signature of the Terror's most terrifying exponent – A. Fouquier. Below, on the right, the same hand had inscribed 'Three tumbrils,' 'Four tumbrils,' 'Five tumbrils,' to fit each need. The Public Prosecutor was simultaneously the stage-manager and outrider of death.

Rochefort, in that red robe, examined the activities of this Fouquier-Tinville, Iron Mouthpiece of Terror, as possible hero of a novel. Beside the death-sentences, propped up against a heap of volumes, was opened the *Histoire des Girondins*, written by the famous poet Lamartine, so ingloriously defeated in his attempt for the Presidency of the Republic, against Louis Napoleon, the new Caesar.

The open page displayed Raffet's engraving of the Public Prosecutor; low forehead, arched eyebrows, nose straight but blunt, high cheekbones, very heavy jaw, a physiognomy almost perfectly matching the fellow's job. It was impossible not to reflect that he was rather too unsubtle a target. Was he, Rochefort, to employ his own fire to warm up a stew of this coarse and bestial creature, a murder-machine which had slaughtered two-thousand of his fellows – Girondists, Hébertists, Dantonists, the duc d'Orléans, Marie Antoinette, and finally Robespierre himself?

What did Rochefort in the red gown do with the red killer? Searching out human inadequacy he again fluttered those death-warrants. Each was signed: A. Fouquier. Not one carried the complete, the notorious surname, Fouquier-Tinville. There are so many Fouquiers, are there not, Citizen? That's the reason, Public Prosecutor, you omitted the Tinville, as a precautionary ruse, by writing the commonplace Fouquier alone, often illegibly. Fortunately, the deception did not prevent you becoming the two thousand and first to ride in a tumbril to the knife; but it may possibly rescue you from eternal curses, you, wretched being, who craved the cap of invisibility. . . .

Rochefort lifted the warrant he had found the most moving of all.

L'exécuteur des hautes oeuvres will proceed to the Place de la Révolution, there to transfer from life to death the individuals hereafter named: Danton, Camille Desmoulins, Hérault-Séchelles, Fabre d'Églantine, Chabot, Basire, Delaunay, d'Espagnac, Westermann.

A. Fouquier   Three Tumbrils

It was not Danton's fate which engrossed him: Danton, who, like himself, had had a knobby forehead; also, like himself, was savage and ugly; whom his schoolfellows had nicknamed Catiline, as he himself had been at the Lycée Saint-Louis. Danton had been a bull, trumpet-blast, athlete of rebellion, Goliath of ambition, intoxicated by power, a manipulator, despiser, catalyst, hammer of the unloved people, despot of liberty, tyrant with a fixed rate of bribery. Lamartine had written that the rest were vicious in a vulgar way, but Danton's vice was heroic. Rochefort disliked all vice, vulgar or heroic, and had no love for Danton. He loved the delicate Camille Desmoulins who never roared but wrote: great pamphleteer, great lover. He had composed the Lantern's speeches and loved his wife, Lucile. He was the great journalist who led the popular movement, and loved Lucile. For him the Lantern from which aristocrats were hanged was also the lamp which lightened the way. He was the example, Lucile his beloved, and her name was on the next group of death-warrants, the couple's love being thus completed. So beautiful had been their love that Rochefort had taken the name Lucile for his own little miracle of a daughter.

He reflected: 'Now I've my own Lucile. One day I will also have a newspaper to lighten the way, and which will likewise be the torch to start a real conflagration. I'll call it *La Lanterne.*'

ALFRED NEUMANN. *Kaiserreich*, Amsterdam

Henri Rochefort (1830–1913), a declassed nobleman, was a playwright and bitter, sardonic political journalist. His paper, La Lanterne, *with its scurrilous mockery of Napoleon III, helped undermine the Second Empire in its last years:*
'Monday August 10. Seventy-eight years ago today at this very hour the people were plundering the Tuileries. Today it is exactly the reverse.'

AN HOTEL

'Excuse me, Mademoiselle,' I said. 'Could you tell me if this house used to be called the Hôtel de la Providence?'

She looked puzzled. 'De la Providence? No. Hôtel des Victoires, Monsieur. You would like a room?' I tried again, more carefully.

'Mademoiselle,' I said, 'I am a schoolmaster' (I suppose I was searching for some convincing reason for my presence – I remember I had the idea that the girl might think me a little mad, and schoolmasters are generally considered to be sane), 'I am looking for the room of Mademoiselle Charlotte Corday, who . . .'

'One moment, Monsieur,' she cut in, 'I will see for you.' She turned to a desk by the wall opposite and ran her finger down the page of a large flat book lying on it. Now she understands, I thought, and is going to tell me the number of the room. I waited in suspense for her to say, 'Number Seven, Monsieur' – After a moment or two, during which she turned the pages back once or twice, running her finger down each, she said, still looking at the book, 'I am sorry, Monsieur, Mademoiselle Corday is not here – she must have left some time ago.'   JOHN ELLIOT

The Hôtel de la Providence, where Charlotte Corday spent her last three nights of freedom, was, Sir John discovered from Lenôtre's Paris Revolutionnaire *(1894), on the opposite side of the same street, rue des Augustins (now rue Hérold), though long demolished.*

THE PROFESSOR

The street [rue de L'École de Médecine] was quiet, few people entered or left it, and I stood in front of the large gateway to the school with the pavement to myself, looking up at these modern walls and windows and trying to recapture something of the tremendous drama which had once been played here. So rooted was I to the spot that a voice at my side made me jump.

'You are looking for someone, Monsieur?' I turned to find an elderly man, hatless, with grey hair *en brosse*, and a large portfolio under his one arm, looking at me with interest. No doubt he found it unusual to see someone loitering in this street at such an hour.

'Yes, Monsieur. Perhaps you can help me,' I answered. 'Do you know if Marat lived here at one time, and is there anything of interest to see concerning him?'

The man puckered his brows for a moment. 'Marat, did you say. Was he perhaps one of the professors who worked here?'

I could not resist a smile.

'A professor,' I said at last. 'Yes, perhaps he was.'   JOHN ELLIOT

398–400 RUE SAINT-HONORÉ

On the right is a ladies' hairdressing salon, on the left a *pâtisserie* with a bakery behind. Between the two is the entrance.

The first time, many years ago, that I ventured to penetrate the forbidding passage between the street and the little courtyard beyond, I felt apprehensive, uneasy. I did not know what to expect, what to look for, and seeing an old woman plying a broom on some steps as I emerged from the passage, I hesitated. As usual, curiosity got the better of me, and I asked the woman if she could tell me, where was the Maison Duplay?

'*La porte de Robespierre, Monsieur,*' she answered unemotionally, and with a wave of the broomstick towards the other end of the yard, added '*C'est là,*' and went on with her sweeping. Evidently I was no trespasser, and no curiosity either.

I look around. The court is narrow, running at right angles to the street outside. The first thing to catch the eye is a flight of three steps leading to the doorway on the left hand side, those which were being swept as I entered. The building to which this door gives entrance has today six storeys, of which only the ground and first floors hold an interest to us. This is the main part of the Duplay house, and in the building next to it, now joined as one, but then detached, Robespierre had his room on the first floor. Facing us, at right angles to the other, is a further building, and it is in the corner where the two meet that the door of Robespierre stands.

When I first saw it, it was painted a dark green, almost black; cobwebs hung unbroken over its two large panels and over the grille at the top. It looked what it was – old, neglected, but important, and from it exuded that strange oppressiveness which haunts the places of the past. It is small, it hides itself away in this corner, it belongs to a great epoch, yet it is marked by no plaque or monument. Only a few yards away the noise of modern Paris comes strangely through the passage, halts confused, and eddies weakly back from whence it came.

I stood for a long time in front of this door, thinking of its story, of what it had seen and heard in all its lengthening years. For this is the door which Maurice Duplay, the cabinet maker, had specially installed when Robespierre rose to greatness under his roof. It gave a separate guarded entrance to a new stairway which led up to his bedroom. It was fitted, in those days, with a massive lock, and bolts on the inner side. Behind it, I thought, lies history. Timidly I touched it, ran my finger along the bottom of the lower panel, felt the dust move with my finger, thought of Thermidor, and shivered.

It was some years later before I turned again into the dark passage, through into the courtyard and stood in front of it. This time no one was about, the place was silent. Nothing was changed, and I was no better informed about it than I had been. Bolder this time, I went up the stone steps, and tried the handle of the other door, the one nearest the street. Locked. . . .

It was more than a year later when I returned, this time with fortune at my side, for I was able to enter the old house at last.

As I walked along the now familiar passage I could sense the change, and the moment I came into the courtyard, there it was in front of me: nothing less than a smart Parisian bar! Where a plain wall had been there now appeared a front of polished wood and smooth plate glass. . . . In front of me was a washbasin, and behind the door of Robespierre was nothing more terrible than a roller-towel, damp and rather frayed at the edges.

Again, recently, I visited No. 398. A friend was with me, who had said he would like to see the courtyard of the Maison Duplay.

It was a Sunday, and at eleven o'clock in the morning there were few people in the rue St Honoré. As we entered the courtyard our footsteps rang out sharply. The door above the steps was locked firmly. It was very warm and close in the little yard, and above it the windows of the Duplays were shut and bolted.

We stood in front of Robespierre's door while I told my friend a little of its story, and as we talked a dog began to howl somewhere in the building. At first we paid no heed to it, until it grew and drowned our voices. We listened, looking up at Maison Duplay.

Soon the whole courtyard was filled with the sorrowful baying, and I remembered that on his last evening's walk with Eléonore, three days before he died, Robespierre had taken his dog Brount with him, of whom he was very fond, and who slept always in his room.

JOHN ELLIOT

After Robespierre's fall, Maurice Duplay was imprisoned, and ruined; Madame Duplay, in one tradition, hanged herself; Eléonore lived on, with her secret memories, in spinsterhood.

ROBESPIERRE AND MOZART
AS STAGE

Robespierre could live saying, 'The republic
of Virtue without *la terreur* is disaster',
saying, 'Loot the châteaux, spare Saint Antoine',
saying to Danton, 'I'll love you till I die',
Clean prisons! They learned the guillotine is painless –
La Révolution, her old Jacobin saying:
'The theater must remain and remain theater,
play for the traditional barren audience orgy,
play back the Revolution . . .' Ask the true voyeur
what blue movie is worth a seat at the keyhole. . . .
Even the prompted Louis Seize was living theater,
sternly but lovingly judged by critics, who knew
a Mozart's insolent slash at folk could never
cut the gold thread of the suffocating curtain.

ROBERT LOWELL, 1970

AFTERTHOUGHT

We have tried in this country to impose many things from above. Nothing ever comes from this. What we must do is involve the people in the processes of government, and the people will at once put everyone in his right place.   MIKHAIL GORBACHEV, June 31, 1988

SELECTED BIBLIOGRAPHY

To have numbered all the quotations in my Introduction would have disfigured the pages, and most are to be found in the following Bibliography.

ASCHERSON, NEAL (ed.): *The French Revolution: Extracts from* The Times *1789–1794*, London, 1975.

AULARD, A.: *Histoire politique de la Révolution française*, Paris, 1910. *La Révolution française*, Paris, 1891.

AYER, A. J.: *Thomas Paine*, London, 1988.

BARING-GOULD, S.: *Curious Myths of the Middle Ages*, London, 1892.

BELLOC, HILAIRE: *The Life of Danton*, London, 1899. *Robespierre*, London, 1901. *The Eye-Witness*, London, 1908. *Marie Antoinette*, London, 1909.

BIENVENU, RICHARD T. (ed.): *The Ninth of Thermidor*, Oxford, 1968.

BLANC, LOUIS: *Histoire de la Révolution française*, Paris, 1864–6.

BLANNING, T. C. W.: *The French Revolution: Aristocracy Versus Bourgeois*, 1987.

BOLITHO, WILLIAM: *Twelve Against the Gods*, London, 1929.

BOUSTANQUOI, E. O.: *Les Souvenirs d'une femme du peuple*, Senlis, 1920 (see Jean Robiquet).

BRAUDEL, FERNAND: *The Perspective of the World*, London, 1984.

BUCKMAN, PETER: *Lafayette*, London, 1977.

BURKE, EDMUND: *Reflections on the Revolution in France*, London, 1790. *An Appeal from the New to the Old Whigs*, London, 1791. *Letters on a Regicide Peace*, London, 1795–7.

CASTELOT, ANDRÉ: *Marie Antoinette*, Paris, 1956.

CHARAVAY, ETIENNE: *Lafayette*, Paris, 1898.

CHRISTIANSEN, RUPERT: *Romantic Affinities*, London, 1988.

COBB, RICHARD: *The People's Armies*, Yale, 1987. *The Daily Telegraph*, London, 1988.

COBBAN, ALFRED: *A History of Modern France, Vol. 1*, London, 1957.

COHN, NORMAN: *Warrant for Genocide*, London, 1967.

COLE, HUBERT: *Fouché*, London, 1972.

CORYN, MARJORIE: *Ridiculous Dictator*, London, 1944.

COWIE, LEONARD W.: *The French Revolution*, London, 1987.

CRONIN, VINCENT: *Louis and Antoinette*, London, 1974.

Napoleon, London, 1971.

CURTIS, E. N.: *Saint-Just: Colleague of Robespierre*, New York, 1935.

DARNTON, ROBERT: *Literary Low Life in Pre-revolutionary France*, London, 1976 (see Douglas Johnson).

DAWSON, CHRISTOPHER: *The Gods of Revolution*, London, 1972.

ELLIOT, JOHN: *The Way of the Tumbrils*, London, 1958.

LORD ELTON: *The Revolutionary Idea in France*, London, 1923.

FAY, BERNARD: *Louis XVI*, Paris, 1966.

FERSEN, AXEL VON: *Journals and Letters 1789–93*, Stockholm, 1878.

FISHER, JOHN: *The Elysian Fields*, London, 1966.

FRANCE, ANATOLE: *Les Dieux ont soif*, translated by Frederick Davies.

FULLER, J. F. C.: *The Decisive Battles of the Western World. 1792–1944*, London, 1954.

GODECHOT, JACQUES: *La Prise de la Bastille*, Paris, 1965.

GOUGH, HUGH: *The Newspaper Press in the French Revolution*, London, 1988.

GREEN, DAVID: *The Incidence of Terror during the French Revolution: a Statistical Interpretation*, Cambridge, 1935.

HAMPSON, NORMAN: *Danton*, London, 1978.

The Life and Opinions of Maximilien Robespierre, London, 1974.

HAYMAN, RONALD: *De Sade*, London, 1978.

HIBBERT, CHRISTOPHER: *The French Revolution*, London, 1980.

HOOK, SIDNEY: *The Hero in History*, London, 1945.

JOHNSON, DOUGLAS (ed.): *French Society and the Revolution*, Cambridge, 1976.

KORNGOLD, RALPH: *Robespierre: First Modern Dictator*, London, 1937.

LAFAYETTE, MARIE JOSEPH PAUL YVES ROCH GILBERT MOTIER DE: *Mémoires*, Paris, 1837–8.
LAMARTINE, ALPHONSE MARIE LOUIS DE: *Histoire des Girondins*, Paris, 1847.
LATEY, MAURICE: *Tyranny: A Study in the Abuse of Power*, London, 1969.
LENÔTRE, G.: *Paris Révolutionnaire*, Paris, 1894.
LOOMIS, STANLEY: *Paris in the Terror*, London, 1965.
LOWELL, ROBERT: *Notebook*, London, 1970.

MASUR, GERHARD: *Prophets of Yesterday*, London, 1963.
MATHIEZ, ALBERT: *La Révolution française*, Paris, 1935.
MICHELET, JULES: *Histoire de France*, Paris, 1833–67.
MORRIS, GOUVERNEUR: *A Diary of the French Revolution*, ed. Beatrix Cary Davenport, New York, 1939.
MORTON, J. B.: *Saint-Just*, London, 1939.

PALMERSTON, 2ND VISCOUNT: *Diary in France during July and August 1791*, Cambridge, 1885.

RAILTON, STEPHEN: *Fenimore Cooper*, Princeton, 1978.
ROBIQUET, JEAN: *La Vie ordinaire pendant la Révolution française*, Paris, 1938.
RUDÉ, GEORGE: *The Crowd in the French Revolution*, Oxford, 1959. *Robespierre*, London, 1975.

SCARFE, FRANCIS: *André Chénier*, Oxford, 1965.
SIEBURG, FRIEDRICH: *Robespierre*, Berlin, 1936.
SYDENHAM, M. J.: *The Girondins*, London, 1961.

THOMPSON, IAN: 'The Envied City', in *London Magazine*, April 1988.
THOMPSON, J. M. (ed.): *English Witnesses of the Revolution*, Oxford, 1938.
The French Revolution, Oxford, 1943.
Leaders of the French Revolution, Oxford, 1929.

TOCQUEVILLE, ALEXIS DE: *L'Ancien Régime et la Révolution*, Paris, 1855.

TOMALIN, CLAIRE: *Mary Wollstonecraft*, London, 1974.

VALLENTIN, ANTONINA: *Mirabeau: Voice of the Revolution*, London, 1948.

VANSITTART, PETER: *Pastimes of a Red Summer*, London, 1969.

WEINER, MARJORIE: *The French Exiles 1789–1815*, London, 1960.

WHITLOCK, BRAND: *Lafayette*, New York, 1929.

WRIGHT, D. G.: *Revolution and Terror in France 1789–1795*, London, 1986.

YOUNG, ARTHUR: *Travels in France 1787–89*, London, 1792.

ZIMAN, H. D.: 'Fouché', in the *Daily Telegraph*, 1972.

ZWEIG, STEFAN: *Joseph Fouché*, Vienna, 1929.

INDEX

Entries in capitals refer to authors or sources; the remainder
refer to subjects of comment in the text.